SOFTWARE EVOLUTION
AND MAINTENANCE

SOFTWARE EVOLUTION AND MAINTENANCE

A Practitioner's Approach

PRIYADARSHI TRIPATHY
KSHIRASAGAR NAIK

WILEY

Published by John Wiley & Sons, Inc., Hoboken, New Jersey.
Published simultaneously in Canada.

For general information on our other products and services please contact our Customer Care Department with the U.S. at 877-762-2974, outside the U.S. at 317-572-3993 or fax 317-572-4002.

Wiley also publishes its books in a variety of electronic formats. Some content that appears in print, however, may not be available in electronic format.

Library of Congress Cataloging-in-Publication Data

Tripathy, Priyadarshi, 1958–
    Software evolution and maintenance : a practitioner's approach / Priyadarshi Tripathy, Kshirasagar Naik.
       pages cm
    Includes index.
    ISBN 978-0-470-60341-3 (cloth)
    1. Software maintenance.   I. Naik, Kshirasagar, 1959–   II. Title.
    QA76.76.S64T75 2015
    005.1'6–dc23

                                                                            2014033541

10 9 8 7 6 5 4 3 2 1

To our parents
Kunjabihari and Surekha Tripathy
Sukru and Teva Naik

CONTENTS

Preface   xiii

List of Figures   xvii

List of Tables   xxi

1 Basic Concepts and Preliminaries   1

   1.1 Evolution Versus Maintenance, 1
      1.1.1 Software Evolution, 3
      1.1.2 Software Maintenance, 4
   1.2 Software Evolution Models and Processes, 6
   1.3 Reengineering, 9
   1.4 Legacy Systems, 11
   1.5 Impact Analysis, 12
   1.6 Refactoring, 13
   1.7 Program Comprehension, 14
   1.8 Software Reuse, 15
   1.9 Outline of the Book, 16
   References, 18
   Exercises, 23

2 Taxonomy of Software Maintenance and Evolution   25

   2.1 General Idea, 25
      2.1.1 Intention-Based Classification of Software Maintenance, 26
      2.1.2 Activity-Based Classification of Software Maintenance, 28
      2.1.3 Evidence-Based Classification of Software Maintenance, 28

2.2   Categories of Maintenance Concepts, 37
    2.2.1   Maintained Product, 37
    2.2.2   Maintenance Types, 40
    2.2.3   Maintenance Organization Processes, 41
    2.2.4   Peopleware, 43
2.3   Evolution of Software Systems, 44
    2.3.1   SPE Taxonomy, 46
    2.3.2   Laws of Software Evolution, 49
    2.3.3   Empirical Studies, 54
    2.3.4   Practical Implications of the Laws, 56
    2.3.5   Evolution of FOSS Systems, 58
2.4   Maintenance of Cots-Based Systems, 61
    2.4.1   Why Maintenance of CBS Is Difficult?, 62
    2.4.2   Maintenance Activities for CBSs, 65
    2.4.3   Design Properties of Component-Based Systems, 67
2.5   Summary, 70
Literature Review, 73
References, 75
Exercises, 80

3   Evolution and Maintenance Models   **83**

3.1   General Idea, 83
3.2   Reuse-Oriented Model, 84
3.3   The Staged Model for Closed Source Software, 87
3.4   The Staged Model for Free, Libre, Open
       Source Software, 90
3.5   Change Mini-Cycle Model, 91
3.6   IEEE/EIA Maintenance Process, 94
3.7   ISO/IEC 14764 Maintenance Process, 99
3.8   Software Configuration Management, 111
    3.8.1   Brief History, 112
    3.8.2   SCM Spectrum of Functionality, 113
    3.8.3   SCM Process, 117
3.9   CR Workflow, 119
3.10 Summary, 125
Literature Review, 126
References, 129
Exercises, 131

4   Reengineering   **133**

4.1   General Idea, 133
4.2   Reengineering Concepts, 135
4.3   A General Model for Software Reengineering, 137
    4.3.1   Types of Changes, 140

4.3.2   Software Reengineering Strategies, 141
4.3.3   Reengineering Variations, 143
4.4   Reengineering Process, 144
4.4.1   Reengineering Approaches, 144
4.4.2   Source Code Reengineering Reference Model, 146
4.4.3   Phase Reengineering Model, 150
4.5   Code Reverse Engineering, 153
4.6   Techniques Used for Reverse Engineering, 156
4.6.1   Lexical Analysis, 157
4.6.2   Syntactic Analysis, 157
4.6.3   Control Flow Analysis, 157
4.6.4   Data Flow Analysis, 158
4.6.5   Program Slicing, 158
4.6.6   Visualization, 160
4.6.7   Program Metrics, 162
4.7   Decompilation Versus Reverse Engineering, 164
4.8   Data Reverse Engineering, 165
4.8.1   Data Structure Extraction, 168
4.8.2   Data Structure Conceptualization, 169
4.9   Reverse Engineering Tools, 170
4.10 Summary, 174
Literature Review, 176
References, 178
Exercises, 185

5   **Legacy Information Systems**   **187**

5.1   General Idea, 187
5.2   Wrapping, 189
5.2.1   Types of Wrapping, 189
5.2.2   Levels of Encapsulation, 191
5.2.3   Constructing a Wrapper, 192
5.2.4   Adapting a Program for Wrapper, 194
5.2.5   Screen Scraping, 194
5.3   Migration, 195
5.4   Migration Planning, 196
5.5   Migration Methods, 202
5.5.1   Cold Turkey, 202
5.5.2   Database First, 203
5.5.3   Database Last, 204
5.5.4   Composite Database, 205
5.5.5   Chicken Little, 206
5.5.6   Butterfly, 208
5.5.7   Iterative, 212
5.6   Summary, 217

Literature Review, 218
References, 219
Exercises, 221

6 Impact Analysis   **223**

6.1   General Idea, 223
6.2   Impact Analysis Process, 225
        6.2.1   Identifying the SIS, 228
        6.2.2   Analysis of Traceability Graph, 229
        6.2.3   Identifying the Candidate Impact Set, 231
6.3   Dependency-Based Impact Analysis, 234
        6.3.1   Call Graph, 234
        6.3.2   Program Dependency Graph, 235
6.4   Ripple Effect, 238
        6.4.1   Computing Ripple Effect, 238
6.5   Change Propagation Model, 242
        6.5.1   Recall and Precision of Change Propagation Heuristics, 243
        6.5.2   Heuristics for Change Propagation, 245
        6.5.3   Empirical Studies, 246
6.6   Summary, 247
Literature Review, 248
References, 249
Exercises, 253

7 Refactoring   **255**

7.1   General Idea, 255
7.2   Activities in a Refactoring Process, 258
        7.2.1   Identify What to Refactor, 258
        7.2.2   Determine Which Refactorings Should be Applied, 259
        7.2.3   Ensure that Refactoring Preserves the Behavior of the
                   Software, 261
        7.2.4   Apply the Refactorings to the Chosen Entities, 262
        7.2.5   Evaluate the Impacts of the Refactorings on Quality, 263
        7.2.6   Maintain Consistency of Software Artifacts, 265
7.3   Formalisms for Refactoring, 265
        7.3.1   Assertions, 265
        7.3.2   Graph Transformation, 266
        7.3.3   Software Metrics, 267
7.4   More Examples of Refactorings, 271
7.5   Initial Work on Software Restructuring, 273
        7.5.1   Factors Influencing Software Structure, 273
        7.5.2   Classification of Restructuring Approaches, 275
        7.5.3   Restructuring Techniques, 276
7.6   Summary, 282

Literature Review, 283
References, 286
Exercises, 288

8   Program Comprehension   **289**

   8.1   General Idea, 289
   8.2   Basic Terms, 291
         8.2.1   Goal of Code Cognition, 291
         8.2.2   Knowledge, 291
         8.2.3   Mental Model, 293
         8.2.4   Understanding Code, 296
   8.3   Cognition Models for Program Understanding, 298
         8.3.1   Letovsky Model, 298
         8.3.2   Shneiderman and Mayer Model, 301
         8.3.3   Brooks Model, 303
         8.3.4   Soloway, Adelson, and Ehrlich Model, 308
         8.3.5   Pennington Model, 310
         8.3.6   Integrated Metamodel, 312
   8.4   Protocol Analysis, 315
   8.5   Visualization for Comprehension, 317
   8.6   Summary, 321
   Literature Review, 321
   References, 322
   Exercises, 324

9   Reuse and Domain Engineering   **325**

   9.1   General Idea, 325
         9.1.1   Benefits of Reuse, 327
         9.1.2   Reuse Models, 327
         9.1.3   Factors Influencing Reuse, 328
         9.1.4   Success Factors of Reuse, 329
   9.2   Domain Engineering, 329
         9.2.1   Draco, 331
         9.2.2   DARE, 331
         9.2.3   FAST, 331
         9.2.4   FORM, 331
         9.2.5   KobrA, 332
         9.2.6   PLUS, 332
         9.2.7   PuLSE, 332
         9.2.8   Koala, 332
         9.2.9   RSEB, 332
   9.3   Reuse Capability, 333
   9.4   Maturity Models, 334
         9.4.1   Reuse Maturity Model, 334

9.4.2   Reuse Capability Model, 336

9.4.3   RiSE Maturity Model, 338

9.5   Economic Models of Software Reuse, 340

9.5.1   Cost Model of Gaffney and Durek, 346

9.5.2   Application System Cost Model of Gaffney and Cruickshank, 348

9.5.3   Business Model of Poulin and Caruso, 350

9.6   Summary, 352

Literature Review, 352

References, 353

Exercises, 356

Glossary   **359**

Index   **379**

PREFACE

karmany eva dhikaras te; ma phalesu kadachana; ma karmaphalahetur bhur; ma te sango stv akarmani.

Your right is to work only; but never to the fruits thereof; may you not be motivated by the fruits of actions; nor let your attachment to be towards inaction.

—Bhagavad Gita

We have been witnessing stellar growth of the global software industry for three decades. As this century progresses the industry is engaged in fixing defects and enhancing and adding new features to the existing software applications. In fact, more resources are spent on software maintenance than on actual software development. The imbalance between software development and maintenance is opening up new business opportunities for software off-shoring companies. It is also generating much research interest to develop methods and tools for improving software evolution and maintenance (SEAM).

Twenty-five years ago, the software industry was a much smaller one, and the academia used to offer a single, comprehensive course entitled *Software Engineering* to educate undergraduate students in the nuts and bolts of software development and maintenance. Although software maintenance has been a part of the classical software engineering literature for decades, the subject has not been widely incorporated into the mainstream undergraduate curriculum. A few universities have started offering an *option* in software engineering comprising four specialized courses, namely, *Requirements Specification*, *Software Design*, *Software Testing and Quality Assurance*, and *Software Evolution and Maintenance*. In addition, some universities have introduced full undergraduate and graduate degree programs in software engineering.

Our survey of the subject of software evolution and maintenance reveals that a large body of work exists in disparate form, including research papers, technical reports, and reports of working groups. Moreover, there are many excellent books focusing on specific aspects of a course in software maintenance and evolution. However, there is no single book that presents the materials in a comprehensive manner. Absence of a comprehensive textbook explaining most of the aspects of software evolution and maintenance creates several problems for instructors and students alike. For example, an instructor needs to refer to many sources to prepare lecture materials. Consequently, it takes much time on the part of the instructor, and students do not have access to all those sources. Our goal is to introduce the students and the instructors to a set of well-rounded educational materials covering the fundamental developments in software evolution and common maintenance practices in the industry. We intend to provide students a single, comprehensive textbook covering most of the topics in evolution and maintenance with much detail so that it is very easy to get a handle on SEAM without reading a number of books and articles in this subject. We have not tried to specifically address their research challenges. Instead, we have presented the evolution theory and practice as a broad stepping stone which will enable the students and practitioners to understand and develop maintenance practices for complex software system.

We decided to write this book based on our teaching, research, and industrial experiences in software maintenance. For the past 20 years, Sagar has been teaching software engineering, including software testing and maintenance on a regular basis; Piyu managed software quality assurance teams in industry for the maintenance of routers, switches, wireless data networks, storage networks, and intrusion prevention appliances. Our combined experience has helped us in selecting and structuring the contents of this book to make it suitable as a text.

WHO SHOULD READ THIS BOOK?

We have written this book to introduce students, researchers, and software profession-als to the fundamental developments in evolution models and common maintenance practices for software. Undergraduate students in software engineering, computer science, and computer engineering will be introduced to the subject matter in a step-by-step manner. Practitioners too will benefit from the structured presentation and comprehensive nature of the materials. Graduate students can use it as a reference. After reading the whole book, the reader will have gained a thorough understanding of the following topics:

- Laws of software evolution and the means to control them
- Evolution and maintenance models, including maintenance of commercial off-the-shelf systems
- Reengineering techniques and processes for migration of legacy information systems

- Impact analysis and change propagation techniques
- Program comprehension and refactoring
- Reuse and domain engineering models

Each chapter gives a clear understanding of a particular topic in software evolution by discussing the main ideas with examples. It starts by explaining the basic concepts about the topic, thereby ensuring a common base of understanding; next, it expands the presentation by drilling the important aspects deeper.

HOW SHOULD THIS BOOK BE READ?

This book consists of several independent topics in SEAM glued together. Chapters 1, 2, and 3 provide basic understanding of the subject matters. Therefore, the first three chapters must be read in order. Next, depending upon the interest of the reader, one can choose any chapter to study without any difficulty. However, we recommend the reader to study Chapters 4 and 5 together in that order. This is because Chapter 4 ("Reengineering") introduces basic concepts of reengineering, reverse engineering, and data reverse engineering, whereas Chapter 5 ("Legacy Information Systems") discusses the migration of a system after it is reengineered. Therefore, in our opinion, the ordering will facilitate easier understanding of the materials, especially for those who are new to software evolution.

Notes for instructors

The book can be used as a text in an introductory course in SEAM. It is desirable to cover all the chapters in an introductory course in SEAM. When used as a recommended text in a software engineering course, the following selected portions can help students imbibe the essential concepts in software evolution and maintenance:

- Chapter 1: All the sections
- Chapter 2: Sections 2.1 and 2.3
- Chapter 3: Sections 3.1, 3.2, 3.3, 3.4, 3.5 and 3.8
- Chapter 4: Sections 4.1 and 4.2
- Chapter 5: Sections 5.1 and 5.2
- Chapter 6: All the sections
- Chapter 7: Sections 7.1 and 7.2
- Chapter 8: Sections 8.1 and 8.2
- Chapter 9: Section 9.1

Supplementary materials for instructors are available at: http://ece.uwaterloo.ca/~snaik/mybook2.html

ACKNOWLEDGMENTS

While preparing this book, we received invaluable support of different kinds from many people, including researchers, the publisher, our family members, our friends, and our colleagues. First, we thank all the researchers who have been shaping this field ever since programs were started to be written. Without their published work, this book would not have seen the light of the day. Second, we thank our editors, namely, George Telecki, Michael Christian, and Whitney A. Lesch, who gave us much professional guidance and patiently answered our various questions. The first author, Piyu Tripathy, would like to thank his former colleagues at Cisco Systems, Airvana Inc., NEC Laboratories America Inc., and present colleagues at Knowledge Trust.

Finally, the supports of our parents, parents-in-law, and spouses deserve a special mention. I, Piyu Tripathy, thank my dear wife Leena, who has taken many household and family duties off my hands to give me time that I needed to write this book; I would like to thank my newly arrived daughter Inu for asking me inquisitive questions about this book, which helped me in writing this preface.

I, Sagar Naik, thank my loving wife Alaka for her invaluable support. I also thank my charming daughters, Monisha and Sameeksha, and exciting son, Siddharth, for their understanding while I was writing this book. Finally, I heartily acknowledge all the support that my elder brother Gajapati extended to me. We are very pleased that now we have more time for our families.

PRIYADARSHI (PIYU) TRIPATHY

Knowledge Trust
Bhubaneswar, India

KSHIRASAGAR (SAGAR) NAIK

University of Waterloo
Waterloo, Canada

LIST OF FIGURES

2.1   Groups or clusters and their types   29
2.2   Decision tree types. From Reference 15. © 2001 John Wiley &
        Sons   32
2.3   Overview of concept categories affecting software maintenance   38
2.4   Inputs and outputs of software evolution. From Reference 26.
        © 1988 John Wiley & Sons   45
2.5   S-type programs   47
2.6   P-type programs   48
2.7   E-type programs   49
2.8   E-type programs with feedback. From Reference 33. © 2006 John
        Wiley & Sons   50
2.9   Onion model of FOSS development structure   59
2.10   Growth of the major subsystems (development releases only) of
        the Linux OS. From Reference 57. © 2000 IEEE   61
3.1   Traditional SDLC model. From Reference 1. © 1988 John Wiley
        & Sons   84
3.2   The quick fix model. From Reference 2. © 1990 IEEE   85
3.3   The iterative enhancement model. From Reference 2. © 1990
        IEEE   85
3.4   The full reuse model. From Reference 2. © 1990 IEEE   86
3.5   The simple staged model for the CSS life cycle. From
        Reference 6. © 2000 IEEE   88
3.6   The versioned staged model for the CSS life cycle. From
        Reference 6. © 2000 IEEE   90
3.7   The staged model for the FLOSS system. From Reference 9.
        © 2007 ACM   91

3.8	The change min-cycle. From Reference 12. © 2008 Springer	92
3.9	Seven phases of IEEE maintenance process. From Reference 26. © 2004 IEEE	95
3.10	Problem identification phase	96
3.11	Analysis phase	97
3.12	Design phase	97
3.13	Implementation phase	98
3.14	System test phase	98
3.15	Acceptance test phase	99
3.16	Delivery phase	100
3.17	ISO/IEC 14764 iterative maintenance process. From Reference 26. © 2004 IEEE	102
3.18	Process implementation activity	102
3.19	Problem and modification activity	103
3.20	Modification implementation activity	105
3.21	Maintenance review/acceptance activity	106
3.22	Migration activity	107
3.23	Retirement activity	109
3.24	Technical dimensions of SCM systems	113
3.25	An evolution of a file with two branches	114
3.26	A process for implementing SCM	117
3.27	State transition diagram of a CR	120
4.1	Levels of abstraction and refinement. From Reference 5. © 1992 IEEE	136
4.2	Conceptual basis for the reengineering process. From Reference 5. © 1992 IEEE	137
4.3	General model of software reengineering. From Reference 5. © 1992 IEEE	138
4.4	Horseshoe model of reengineering. From Reference 7. © 1998 IEEE	139
4.5	Conceptual basis for reengineering strategies. From Reference 5. © 1992 IEEE	142
4.6	Source code reengineering reference model. From Reference 15. © 1990 IEEE	147
4.7	The interface nomenclature. From Reference 15. © 1990 IEEE. "(N)-" represents the Nth layer	147
4.8	Software reengineering process phases. From Reference 14. © 1992 IEEE	150
4.9	Replacement strategies for recoding	152
4.10	Relationship between reengineering and reverse engineering. From Reference 6. © 1990 IEEE	154
4.11	A block of code to compute the sum and product of all the even integers in the range $[0, N)$ for $N \geq 3$	159
4.12	The backward slice of code obtained from Figure 4.11 by using the criterion $S < [7]; \text{sum} >$	159

4.13 The forward slice of code obtained from Figure 4.11 by using the
     criterion $S < [3]$; product $>$ 160
4.14 Relationship between decompilation and traditional
     reengineering. From Reference 83. © 2007   165
4.15 General architecture of the DBRE methodology. From
     Reference 95. © 1997 IEEE   169
4.16 Basic structure of reverse engineering tools. From Reference 6.
     © 1990 IEEE   171
5.1 Forward wrapper. From Reference 10. © 2006 ACM   190
5.2 Backward wrapper. From Reference 10. © 2006 ACM   190
5.3 Levels of encapsulation. From Reference 11.
     © 1996 IEEE   191
5.4 Modules of a wrapping framework   193
5.5 Portfolio analysis chi-square chart   198
5.6 Database first approach. From Reference 19. © 1999 IEEE   203
5.7 Database last approach. From Reference 19. © 1999 IEEE   204
5.8 Composite database approach. From Reference 19. © 1999 IEEE   205
5.9 Application gateway. From Reference 19. © 1999 IEEE   206
5.10 Information system gateway. From Reference 19. © 1999 IEEE   207
5.11 Migrating TempStore in Butterfly methodology. From
     Reference 19. © 1999 IEEE   211
5.12 The iterative system architecture methodology during
     reengineering. From Reference 29. © 2003 IEEE   214
5.13 The iterative migration process. From Reference 29. © 2003 IEEE   215
6.1 Impact analysis process. From Reference 6. © 2008 IEEE   226
6.2 Traceability in software work products. From Reference 22.
     © 1991 IEEE   229
6.3 Underlying graph for maintenance. From Reference 22. © 1991
     IEEE   230
6.4 Determine work product impact. From Reference 22. © 1991
     IEEE   231
6.5 Simple directed graph of SLOs. From Reference 12. © 2002 IEEE   232
6.6 In-degree and out-degree of SLO1. From Reference 12. © 2002
     IEEE   232
6.7 Example of a call graph. From Reference 26. © 2003 IEEE   234
6.8 Execution trace   235
6.9 Example program. From Reference 31. © 1990 ACM   236
6.10 Program dependency graph of the program in Figure 6.9   236
6.11 Dynamic program slice for the code in Figure 6.9, text case
     $X = -1$, with respect to variable Y 237
6.12 Intramodule and intermodule change propagation. From
     Reference 36. © 2001 John Wiley & Sons   239
6.13 Change propagation model. From Reference 10. © 2004 IEEE   243
6.14 Change propagation flow for a simple example. From
     Reference 10. © 2004 IEEE   244

6.15   Program   253
7.1   Class diagram of a local area network (LAN) simulator. From
       Reference 6. © 2007 Springer   260
7.2   Applications of two refactorings. From Reference 6. © 2007
       Springer   263
7.3   An example of a soft-goal graph for maintainability, with one leaf
       node. From Reference 11. © 2002 IEEE   264
7.4   An example of a program graph. From Reference 13. © 2006
       Elsevier   266
7.5   Program graph obtained after applying *push-down method*
       refactoring to the program graph of Figure 7.4. From
       Reference 13. © 2006 Elsevier   267
7.6   An example of a VRML diagram of two classes C1 and C2.
       Circles denote methods and squares denote attributes   269
7.7   Illustration of the push-down method refactoring: (a) the class
       diagram before refactoring; (b) the class diagram after refactoring   272
7.8   An example of parameterizing a method. There are four methods
       in (a), whereas there is one method in (b) with one parameter   273
7.9   Factors which can influence software structure. From
       Reference 2. © 1989 IEEE   274
7.10   Broad classification of approaches to software structuring   275
7.11   System sandwich approach to software restructuring. The arrows
       represent the flow of data and/or commands   278
7.12   Illustration of system level remodularization. Bullets represent
       low level entities. Dotted shapes represent modules. Arrows
       represent progression from one level to the next   279
7.13   Illustration of entity level remodularization. Bullets represent low
       level entities. Dotted shapes represent modules   279
7.14   Dendogram representation of Figure 7.12   282
8.1   Gaining general knowledge and software-specific knowledge   292
8.2   Letovsky's program comprehension model   298
8.3   Shneiderman and Mayer program comprehension model   302
8.4   An overview of Brooks comprehension model   304
8.5   Soloway, Adelson, and Ehrlich comprehension model   309
8.6   Pennington model   310
8.7   Integrated Metamodel. From Reference 1. © 1995 IEEE   313
9.1   Feedback between domain and application engineering   330
9.2   Reuse capability. From Reference 40. © 1993 IEEE   334

LIST OF TABLES

2.1   Evidence-Based 12 Mutually Exclusive Maintenance Types   30
2.2   Impact of the Types   31
2.3   Summary of Evidence-Based Types of Software Maintenance   33
2.4   Staged Model Maintenance Task   39
2.5   Laws of Software Evolution   50
2.6   System Data to be Used in Question 14   81
3.1   Template of a Maintenance Plan   101
3.2   Modification Request Task Steps   104
3.3   Option Task Steps   104
3.4   Documentation Task Steps   105
3.5   Review and Approval Task Steps   106
3.6   Migration Plan Task Steps   108
3.7   Operation and Training Task Steps   108
3.8   Retirement Plan Task Steps   110
3.9   Change Request Schema Field Summary   121
3.10 Engineering Change Document Information   124
4.1   Reengineering Process Variations   143
4.2   Tasks—Analysis and Planning Phase   151
4.3   Commonly Used Software Metrics   163
5.1   Common Quantifiable Benefit Metrics   200
5.2   Chicken Little Migration Approach   207
5.3   Phases of Butterfly Methodology   209
5.4   Migration Activities in Phase 1   209
5.5   Migration Activities in Phase 2   210
5.6   Migration Activities in Phase 3   210

5.7   Migration Activities in Phase 4   210
5.8   Migration Activities in Phase 5   211
6.1   Relationships Represented by a Connectivity Matrix   233
6.2   Relationships Represented by a Reachability Matrix   233
6.3   Relationship with Distance Indicators   234
6.4   Laws of Software Evolution   242
6.5   Performance of Change Propagation Heuristics for the Five
       Software Systems   247
8.1   Tasks and Activities Requiring Code Understanding   290
8.2   Code Cognition Models   290
9.1   Reuse Maturity Model   335
9.2   Critical Success Factors   337
9.3   RiSE Maturity Model Levels: Organizational Factors [42]   341
9.4   RiSE Maturity Model Levels: Business Factors [42]   343
9.5   RiSE Maturity Model Levels: Technological Factors [42]   344
9.6   RiSE Maturity Model Levels: Processes Factors [42]   345
9.7   Relative Costs of Development Activities   347
9.8   Relative Reuse Cost (b)   348

1

BASIC CONCEPTS AND PRELIMINARIES

Another flaw in the human character is that everybody wants to build and nobody wants to do maintenance.

—Kurt Vonnegut, Jr.

1.1 EVOLUTION VERSUS MAINTENANCE

In 1965, Mark Halpern introduced the concept of *software evolution* to describe the growth characteristics of software [1]. Later, the term "evolution" in the context of application software was widely used. The concept further attracted the attentions of researchers after Belady and Lehman published a set of principles determining evolution of software systems [2, 3]. The principles were very general in nature. In his landmark article entitled "The Maintenance 'Iceberg'," R. G. Canning compared software maintenance to an "iceberg" to emphasize the fact that software developers and maintenance personnel face a large number of problems [4]. A few years later, in 1976, Swanson introduced the term "maintenance" by grouping the maintenance activities into three basic categories: corrective, adaptive, and perfective [5]. In the early 1970s, IBM called them "maintenance engineers" or "maintainers" who had been making intentional modifications to running code that they had not developed themselves. The main reason for using nondevelopment personnel in maintenance work was to free up the software development engineers or programmers from support

---

Software Evolution and Maintenance: A Practitioner's Approach, First Edition.
Priyadarshi Tripathy and Kshirasagar Naik.

activities [6]. In this book, we will use maintainer, maintenance engineer, developer, and programmer interchangeably.

Bennett and Rajlich [7] researched the term "software evolution" and found that there is no widely accepted definition of the term. In addition, some researchers and practitioners used the phrases "software evolution" and "software maintenance" interchangeably. However, key semantic differences exist between the two. The two are distinguished as follows:

- The concept of *software maintenance* means preventing software from failing to deliver the intended functionalities by means of bug fixing.
- The concept of *software evolution* means a continual change from a lesser, simpler, or worse state to a higher or better state ([8], p. 1).

Bennett and Xu [9] made further distinctions between the two as follows:

- All support activities carried out *after* delivery of software are put under the category of *maintenance*.
- All activities carried out to effect changes in requirements are put under the category of *evolution*.

In general, maintenance and evolution are generally differentiated as follows [10]:

- Maintenance of software systems primarily means fixing bugs but preserving their functionalities. Maintenance tasks are very much planned. For example, bug fixing must be done and it is a planned activity. In addition to the planned activities, unplanned activities are also necessitated. For example, a new usage of the system may emerge. Generally, maintenance does not involve making major changes to the architecture of the system. In other words, maintenance means keeping an installed system running with no change to its design [11].
- Evolution of software systems means creating new but related designs from existing ones. The objectives include supporting new functionalities, making the system perform better, and making the system run on a different operating system. Basically, as time passes, the stakeholders develop more knowledge about the system. Therefore, the system evolves in several ways. As time passes, not only new usages emerge, but also the users become more knowledgeable. As Mehdi Jazayeri observed: "Over time what evolves is not the software but our knowledge about a particular type of software" ([12], p. 3).

While we are on the topic of maintenance, it is useful to glance at the maintenance of physical systems. Maintenance of physical systems often requires replacing broken and worn-out parts. For example, owners replace the worn-out tires and broken lamps of their cars. Similarly, a malfunctioning memory card is replaced with a good one. On the other hand, software maintenance is different than hardware maintenance. In hardware maintenance, a system or a component is returned to its original good state. On the other hand, in software maintenance, a software system is moved from its original erroneous state to an expected good state [13]. Software maintenance comprises all activities associated with the process of changing software for the purposes of:

- fixing bugs; and/or
- improving the design of the system so that future changes to the system are less expensive.

1.1.1 Software Evolution

Although the phrase "software evolution" had been used previously by other researchers, fundamental work in the field of software evolution was done by Lehman and his collaborators. Based on empirical studies [2, 14], Lehman and his collaborators formulated some observations and they introduced them as *laws of evolution*. The "laws" themselves have "evolved" from *three* in 1974 to *eight* by 1997 [15, 16]. Those laws are the results of studies of the evolution of large-scale proprietary or closed source software (CSS) systems. The laws concern a category of software systems called *E-type* systems. The eight laws are briefly explained as follows:

1. *Continuing change*. Unless a system is continually modified to satisfy emerging needs of users, the system becomes increasingly less useful.
2. *Increasing complexity*. Unless additional work is done to explicitly reduce the complexity of a system, the system will become increasingly more complex due to maintenance-related changes.
3. *Self-regulation*. The evolution process is self-regulating in the sense that the measures of products and processes, that are produced during the evolution, follow close to *normal* distributions.
4. *Conservation of organizational stability*. The average effective global activity rate on an evolving system is almost constant throughout the lifetime of the system. In other words, the average amount of additional effort needed to produce a new release is almost the same.
5. *Conservation of familiarity*. As a system evolves all kinds of personnel, namely, developers and users, for example, must gain a desired level of understanding of the system's content and behavior to realize satisfactory evolution. A large incremental growth in a release reduces that understanding. Therefore, the average incremental growth in an evolving system remains almost the same.
6. *Continuing growth*. As time passes, the functional content of a system is continually increased to satisfy user needs.
7. *Declining quality*. Unless the design of a system is diligently fine-tuned and adapted to new operational environments, the system's qualities will be perceived as declining over the lifetime of the system.
8. *Feedback system*. The system's evolution process involves multi-loop, multi-agent, multi-level feedback among different kinds of activities. Developers must recognize those complex interactions in order to continually evolve an existing system to deliver more functionalities and higher levels of qualities.

In circa 1988, Pirzada [17] was the first one to study the differences between the evolution of the Unix operating system developed by Bell Laboratories and the systems studied by Lehman and Belady [18]. Pirzada argued that the differences in academic and industrial software development could lead to differences in the evolutionary pattern. In circa 2000, after a gap of 12 years, empirical study of evolution of free and open source software (FOSS) was conducted by Godfrey and Tu [19]. The authors provided the trend of growth of the popular FOSS operating system Linux during 1994–1999. They showed the growth rate to be super-linear that is greater than linear. Robles et al. [20] later replicated the study of Godfrey and Tu and concluded that Lehman's laws Nos. 3, 4, and 5 do not hold for large-scale FOSS systems such as Linux. These studies reveal the changing nature of both software and software development processes. Lehman's studies mostly examined proprietary, monolithic systems developed by a team of developers within a company, whereas FOSS systems and their developments follow a different evolution paradigm.

Remark: FOSS is available to all with relaxed or nonexistent copyrights. FOSS is commonly used as a synonym for free software even though "free" and "open" have different semantics. The term "free" means the freedom to modify and redistribute the system under the terms of the original agreement, while "open" means accessibility to the source code.

1.1.2   Software Maintenance

More likely than not, there are defects in delivered software applications, because defect removal and quality control processes are not perfect. Therefore, maintenance is needed to repair those defects in released software. E. Burton Swanson [5] initially defined three categories of software maintenance activities, namely, *corrective*, *adaptive*, and *perfective*. Those definitions were later incorporated into the standard software engineering–software life cycle processes–Maintenance [21] and introduced a fourth category called *preventive* maintenance. The reader may note that some researchers and developers view preventive maintenance as a subset of perfective maintenance.

Swanson's classification of maintenance activities is intention based because the maintenance activities reflect the intents of the developer to carry out specific maintenance tasks on the system. In the intention-based classification of maintenance activities, the intention of an activity depends upon the motivations for the change. An alternative way of classifying modifications to software is to simply categorize the modifications in terms of activities performed [22]:

- *Activities to make corrections.* If there are discrepancies between the expected behavior of a system and the actual behavior, then some activities are performed to eliminate or reduce the discrepancies.

- *Activities to make enhancements.* A number of activities are performed to implement a change to the system, thereby changing the behavior or implementation of the system. This category of activities is further refined into three subcategories:

– enhancements that modify existing requirements;
– enhancements that create new requirements; and
– enhancements that modify the implementation without changing the requirements.

Chapin et al. [6] expanded the typology of Swanson into an evidence-based classification of 12 different types of software maintenance: training, consultive, evaluative, reformative, updative, groomative, preventive, performance, adaptive, reductive, corrective, and enhancive. The three objectives for classifying the types of software maintenance are as follows:

• It is more informative to classify maintenance tasks based on objective evidence that can be verified with observations and/or comparisons of software before and after modifications. This does not require accessing the knowledge of the personnel who originally developed the system.

• The granularity of the proposed classification can be made to accurately reflect the actual mix of activities observed in the practice of software maintenance and evolution.

• The classification groups are independent of hardware platform, operating system choice, design methodology, implementation language, organizational practices, and the availability of the personnel doing the original development.

Maintenance of COTS-Based Systems   Many present-day software systems are built from components previously developed for other systems or to be reused in many systems. In this approach, new components are developed by combining commercial off-the-shelf (COTS) components, custom-built (in-house) components, and open source software components. The components are obtained from a variety of sources and maintained by different vendors, possibly from different countries [23]. The motivations for performing software maintenance are the same for both component-based software systems (CBS) and custom-built software systems. However, there are noticeable differences between the activities in the two approaches. The major sources of the differences are as follows [24, 25]:

• *Skills of system maintenance teams.* Maintenance of CBS requires specialized skills to monitor and integrate COTS products. Those skills are different than the skills required to perform the more traditional maintenance functions: analyze and modify source code developed in-house. Maintainers view a CBS as a group of black-box components, and not as a compiled set of source code modules, thereby requiring a different set of maintenance skills. The differences in skills are neither pros nor cons, but it is important that the differences are taken into consideration for planning, staffing, and training.

- *Infrastructure and organization.* Running a support group for in-house products is necessary to manage a large product. This additional cost may be shared with other projects.

- *COTS maintenance cost.* This cost includes the costs of purchasing components, licensing components, upgrading components, and training maintenance personnel. From the perspective of a system's life cycle, much cost is shifted from in-house development to license and maintenance fees, thereby increasing the overall maintenance cost.

- *Larger user community.* COTS users are part of a broad community of users, and the community of users can be considered as a resource, which is a positive factor. However, being part of a community means having less control over changes and improvements to COTS products.

- *Modernization.* In general, vendors of COTS components keep pace with changing technology and continually update the components. As a result, the system does not become obsolete. However, the flip side is that the costs and risks of making changes keep increasing even if the application does not require any changes. In general, control over the evolution and maintenance of significant portions of the system is relinquished to third-party COTS developers. Those third-party developers may be motivated to pursue their own commercial self-interest. In addition, the third-party vendors control not only the nature of maintenance to be done on the products, but also when it is to be done. Therefore reliance on third-party products impacts both the type and timing of the maintenance performed by COTS-based developers. In a nutshell, unfortunately, upgrades to products are necessitated by technology and vendor economics.

- *Split maintenance function.* A COTS product is maintained by its vendor, whereas the overall system that uses the COTS product is maintained by the system's host organization. As a result, multiple, independent maintenance teams exist. The advantage of COTS-based development is that the system maintainers receive additional support from the COTS vendors. On the other hand, the drawback of the approach is that the different COTS pieces need tighter coordination, and the product vendors may stray in all directions with respect to functionality and standard.

- *More complex planning.* If a system depends upon multiple technologies and COTS products, the unpredictability and risk of change become high, and planning becomes complicated because coordination among a large number of vendors is more difficult.

1.2 SOFTWARE EVOLUTION MODELS AND PROCESSES

There is much confusion about the terms "software maintenance" and "software evolution." The confusion is partly due to a lack of attention paid to models for sustaining software systems and partly due to considering maintenance to be another activity in software development. For example, consider the classical Waterfall model for software development proposed by Winston Royce in circa 1970 [26]. The final phase of the Waterfall model is known as maintenance, which implies that software maintenance is a part of software development. In this regard it is worth quoting Norman Schneidewind [27]: "The traditional view of the software life cycle has done a disservice to maintenance by depicting it solely as a single step at the end of the cycle" (p. 304). Therefore, software maintenance should have its own software maintenance life cycle (SMLC) model [28]. A number of SMLC models with some variations are available in literature [8, 29–35]. Three common features of the SMLC models found in the literature are:

- understanding the code;
- modifying the code; and
- revalidating the code.

Other models view software development as *iterative* processes and based on the idea of *change mini-cycle* [7, 36–39] as explained in the following:

- *Iterative models.* The iterative models share the ideas that a complete set of requirements for a system cannot be completely understood, or the developers do not know how to build the full system. Therefore, systems are constructed in builds, each of which is a refinement of requirements of the previous build. A build is refined by considering feedback from users [40]. One may note that maintenance and evolution activities do not exist as distinct phases. Rather, they are closely intertwined.
- *Change mini-cycle models.* First proposed by Yau et al. [36] in the late 1970s, these models were recently re-visited by Bennet et al. [7] and Mens [41] among others. These models consist of five major phases: change request, analyze and plan change, implement change, verify and validate, and documentation change. In this process model, several important activities were identified, such as program comprehension, impact analysis, refactoring, and change propagation.

A different kind of software evolution model, called *staged model of maintenance and evolution*, has been proposed by Rajlich and Bennett [42]. The model is descriptive in nature, and its primary objective is to improve the understanding of how long-lived software evolves. The model considers four distinct, sequential stages of the lifetime of a system, as explained below:

1. *Initial development.* When the initial version of the system is produced, detailed knowledge about the system is fresh. Before delivery of the system, it undergoes many changes. Eventually, a system architecture emerges and soon it stabilizes.
2. *Evolution.* After the initial stability, it is easy to perform simple changes to the system. Significant changes involve higher cost and higher risk. In the period immediately following the initial delivery, knowledge about the system is still almost fresh in the minds of the developers. It is possible that the development team as a whole does not exist, because many original developers have taken up new responsibilities in the organization and some might have left

the organization. In general, for many systems, their lifespan are spent in this stage, because the systems continue to be of importance to the organizations.

3. *Servicing.* When the knowledge about the system has significantly decreased, the developers mainly focus on maintenance tasks, such as fixing bugs, whereas architectural changes are rarely effected. The developers do not consider the system to be a key asset. In this stage, the effects of changes are very difficult to predict. Moreover, the costs and risks of making changes are very significant.

4. *Phaseout.* When even minimal servicing of a system is not an option, the system enters its very final stage. The organization decides to replace the system for various reasons: (i) it is too expensive to maintain the system; or (ii) there is a newer solution available. Therefore, the organization develops an exit strategy to move from the current system to a new system. Moving from an existing, difficult-to-maintain system to a modern solution system has its own challenges involving wrapping and data migration. After the new system keeps running satisfactorily, sometimes in parallel with the old system, the old system is finally completely shut down.

Software Maintenance Standards   A well-defined process for software mainte-nance can be observed and measured, and thus improved. In addition, adoption of processes allows the dissemination of effective work practices more quickly than gaining personal experience. Process centric software maintenance is more of an engineering activity, with predictable time and effort constraints, and less of an art. Therefore, software maintenance standards have been formulated by ISO and IEEE. The maintenance standard document from ISO is called ISO/IEC 14764 [21] which is a part of the standard document ISO/IEC 12207 [43] for life cycle processes. The maintenance standard document from IEEE is called IEEE/EIA 1219 [44].

Both the standards describe processes for managing and executing activities for maintenance. The IEEE/EIA 1219 standard organizes the maintenance process in seven phases: problem identification, analysis, design, implementation, system test, acceptance test, and delivery. As a quick summary, the standard identifies the different phases and the sequence of their executions. Next, for each phase, the standard identifies the input and output deliverables, the supporting processes and the related activities, and a set of evaluation metrics. Both the standards, namely ISO/IEC 14764 and IEEE/EIA 1219, use the same terminology to describe software maintenance, with a little difference in their depictions. An iterative process has been described in ISO/IEC 14764 to manage and execute maintenance activities. The activities comprising the maintenance process are:

- process implementation;
- problem and modification analysis;
- modification implementation;
- maintenance review/acceptance;
- migration; and
- retirement.

Each of the aforementioned activities is made up of tasks described with specific inputs, outputs, and actions.

Software Configuration Management   Configuration management (CM) is the discipline of managing changes in large systems. The goal of CM is to manage and control the various extensions, adaptations, and corrections that are applied to a system over its lifetime. It handles the control of all products/configuration items and changes to those items. Software configuration management (SCM) is the configuration management applied to software systems. SCM is the means by which the process of software evolution is managed. SCM has been defined in the IEEE 1042 standard [45] as "software configuration management (SCM) is the discipline of managing and controlling change in the evolution of software systems." SCM provides a framework for managing changes in a controlled manner. The purpose of SCM is to reduce communication errors among personnel working on different aspects of the software project by providing a central repository of information about the project and a set of agreed upon procedures for coping with changes. It ensures that the released software is not contaminated by uncontrolled or unapproved changes. Early SCM tools had limited capabilities in terms of functionality and applicability. However, modern SCM systems provide advanced capabilities through which many different artifacts are managed. For example, modern SCM systems support their users in building an executable program out of its versioned source files. Moreover, it must be possible to regenerate old versions of the software system. In general, an SCM system has four different elements, each element addressing a distinct user need as follows [46, 47]:

- *Identification of software configurations.* This includes the definitions of the different artifacts, their baselines or milestones, and the changes to the artifacts.
- *Control of software configurations.* This element is about controlling the ways artifacts or configurations are altered with the necessary technical and administrative support.
- *Auditing software configurations.* This element is about making the current status of the software system in its life cycle visible to management and determining whether or not the baselines meet their requirements.
- *Accounting software configuration status.* This element is about providing an administrative history of how the software system has been altered, by recording the activities necessitated by the other three SCM elements.

1.3   REENGINEERING

Hongji Yang and Martin Ward [48] defined software evolution as " ... the process of conducting continuous software reengineering" (p. 23). Reengineering implies a single cycle of taking an existing system and generating from it a new system, whereas evolution can go forever. In other words, to a large extent, software evolution can be seen as repeated software reengineering. Reengineering is done to transform an existing "lesser or simpler" system into a new "better" system. Chikofsky and Cross II [49] define reengineering as "the examination and alteration of a subject system to reconstitute it in a new form and the subsequent implementation of the new form."

Therefore, reengineering includes some kind of reverse engineering activities to design an abstract view of a given system. The new abstract view is restructured, and forward engineering activities are performed to implement the system in its new form. The aforementioned process is captured by Jacobson and Lindström [50] with the following expression:

$$\text{Reengineering} = \text{Reverse engineering} + \Delta + \text{Forward engineering}.$$

Let us analyze the right-hand portion of the above equation. The first element "reverse engineering" is the activity of defining a more abstract and easier to understand representation of the system. For example, the input to the reverse engineering process is the source code of the system, and the output is the system architecture. The core of reverse engineering is the process of examination of the system, and it is not a process of change. Therefore it does not involve changing the software under examination. The third element "forward engineering" is the traditional process of moving from a high-level abstraction and logical, implementation-independent design to the physical implementation of the system. The second element "Δ" captures alterations performed to the original system.

While performing reverse engineering on a large system, tools and methodologies are generally not stable. Therefore, a high-level organizational paradigm enables repetitions of processes so that maintenance engineers learn about the system. Benedusi et al. [51] have proposed a repeatable paradigm, called Goals/Models/Tools, that describes reverse engineering in three successive stages, namely, Goals, Models, and Tools.

Goals. In this phase, one analyzes the motivations for setting up the process to identify the information needs of the process and the abstractions to be produced.

Models. In this phase, one analyzes the abstractions to construct representation models that capture the information needed for their production.

Tools. In this phase, software tools are defined, acquired, enhanced, integrated, or constructed to: (i) execute the Models phase and (ii) transform the program models into the abstractions identified in the Goals phase.

It is important to note that fact-finding and information gathering from the source code are keys to the Goal/Models/Tools paradigm. In order to extract information that is not explicitly available in source code, automated analysis techniques, such as *lexical analysis, syntactic analysis, control flow analysis, data flow analysis,* and *program slicing* are used to facilitate reverse engineering.

The increased use of data mining techniques in support systems have given rise to an interest in data reverse engineering (DRE) technology. DRE tackles the question of what information is stored and how this information can be used in a different context. DRE is defined by Peter Aiken as "the use of structured techniques to reconstitute the data assets of an existing system" [52]. The two vital aspects of the DRE process are to: (i) recover *data assets* that are useful or valuable and (ii) *reconstitute* the recovered data assets to make them more useful. Therefore, DRE can be regarded as adding value to the existing data assets, making it easier for organizations to conduct business efficiently and effectively.

1.4 LEGACY SYSTEMS

A legacy software system is an old program that continues to be used because it still meets the users' needs, in spite of the availability of newer technology or more efficient methods of performing the task. More often than not, a legacy system includes outdated procedures or terminology, and it is very difficult for new developers to understand the system. Organizations continue to use legacy systems because those are vital to them and the systems significantly resist modification and evolution to meet new and constantly changing business requirements [53, 54]. A legacy system falls in the *Phase out* stage of the software evolution model of Rajlich and Bennet described earlier. Organizations in business for a long time generally possess a sizable number of legacy systems. To manage legacy systems, a number of options are available. Some commonly chosen options are as follows [55, 56]:

- *Freeze.* An organization decides to perform no further work on a legacy system. This implies that either the services of the system are no longer needed or a new system completely replaces a legacy system.
- *Outsource.* An organization may decide that supporting legacy software—or for that matter any software—is not its core business. As an alternative, it may outsource the support service to a specialist organization.
- *Carry on maintenance.* In this approach, the organization continues to maintain the system for another period of time, despite all the difficulties in doing so.
- *Discard and redevelop.* In this approach, the application is redeveloped once again from scratch, using new hardware and software platforms, new software architecture and databases, and modern tools. When the new system is available, the legacy system is simply discarded.
- *Wrap.* In this approach, a legacy system is wrapped around with a new software layer, thereby hiding the unwanted complexity of the existing data, individual programs, application systems, and interfaces. The old system performs the actual computations, but users interact with the system in better ways. The notion of "wrapper" was first introduced by Dietrich et al. at IBM in the late 1980s [57]. Wrapping is a black-box reengineering task, because only the legacy interface is analyzed while ignoring the system's internals. A wrapper does

not directly modify the source code, but it indirectly modifies the software functionality of the legacy component. Wrapping lets organizations reuse well-tested components that they trust and leverage their massive investments in the system. As a result, the lifetime of the legacy system is increased. Many researchers have proposed techniques for wrapping legacy systems [58–60].

- *Migrate.* In this approach, an operational legacy system is moved to a new hardware and/or software platform, while still retaining the legacy system's functionality. The idea is to minimize any disruption to the existing business environment.

  Migration is the best alternative if wrapping is unsuitable and redevelopment is not acceptable due to substantial risk. Migration involves changes to the legacy system, including restructuring the system and enhancing the functionality of the system. However, it retains the basic functionality of the existing system without having to completely redevelop it. Migration projects require careful planning for smooth execution. Harry M. Sneed [61] suggested five steps for a good plan: project justification, portfolio analysis, cost estimation, cost-benefit analysis, and contracting. Project justification is the first step in any planning. Justifying the project requires analysis of the existing products, the maintenance process, and the business value of the applications. Portfolio analysis prioritizes applications to be reengineered according to their business value and technical quality. Cost estimation gives us an idea about the cost of the migration project. Cost-benefit analysis tells us the costs of the migration project and the expected returns. Contracting entails the identification of tasks and the distribution of efforts. Given the scale, complexity, and risk of failure of migration projects, a well-defined, easily implementable, detailed approach is essential to their success. Several migration approaches can be found in the literature: *Cold Turkey, Database First, Database Last, Composite Database, Chicken Little, Butterfly,* and *Iterative* [62–64].

1.5   IMPACT ANALYSIS

Impact analysis is the task of identifying portions of the software that can potentially be affected if a proposed change to the system is effected. The outcome of impact analysis can be used when planning for changes, making changes, and tracking the effects of changes in order to localize the sources of new faults. Impact analysis techniques can be categorized into two classes as follows [65]:

- *Traceability analysis.* In this approach, the high-level artifacts, such as requirements, design, code, and test cases related to the feature to be changed, are identified. A model of associations among artifacts, such that each artifact links to other artifacts, is constructed. This helps in locating the corresponding portions of the design, code, and test cases that need to be maintained.
- *Dependency analysis.* Dependency analysis attempts to assess the effects of a change on the semantic dependencies between program entities. This is achieved

by identifying the syntactic dependencies that may signal the presence of such semantic dependencies [66]. The two dependency-based impact analysis techniques are [67]: call graph-based analysis and dependency graph-based analysis. Dependency analysis is also known as source code analysis.

The following two additional notions are found to be keys to understanding impact analysis:

- *Ripple effect analysis.* Ripple effect analysis emphasizes the tracing repercussions in source code when the code is changed. It measures the impact of a change to a particular module on the rest of the program [68]. Impact can be stated in terms of the problems being created for the rest of the program because of the change. Analysis of ripple effect can provide information regarding what changes are occurring and where they are occurring. Measurement of ripple effect can provide knowledge about the system as a whole through its evolution: (i) the amount of increase or decrease of its complexity since the previous version; (ii) the levels of complexity of individual parts of a system in relation to other parts of the system; and (iii) the effect that a new module has on the complexity of a system as a whole when it is added.
- *Change propagation.* Change propagation activities ensure that a change made in one component is propagated properly throughout the entire system [69–71]. Misunderstanding, lack of experience, and unexpected dependencies are some reasons for failing to propagate changes throughout the development and maintenance cycles of source code. If a change is not propagated correctly, the project risks the introduction of new interface defects [72].

1.6 REFACTORING

Refactoring means performing changes to the structure of software to make it easier to comprehend and cheaper to make subsequent changes without changing the observable behavior of the system. A similar idea for non-object-oriented systems is called restructuring. Refactoring is achieved through removal of duplicate code, simplification of code, and moving code to a different class, among others. Without continual refactoring, the internal structure of software will eventually deform beyond comprehension, due to periodic maintenance. Therefore, regular refactoring helps the system to retain its basic structure [73]. In an agile software methodology, such as eXtreme Programming (XP), refactoring is continuously applied to: (i) make the architecture of the software stable; (ii) render the code readable; and (iii) make the tasks of integrating new functionalities into the system flexible.

An important characteristic of refactoring is that it must preserve the "observable behavior" of the system. Preservation of the observable behavior is verified by ensuring that all the tests passing before refactoring must pass after refactoring. Regression testing is used to ensure that the system did not deviate from the original system during refactoring. Refactoring does not normally involve code transformation to implement new requirements. Rather, it can be performed without adding new requirements to the existing system. Another aspect of refactoring is to enhance the internal structure of the system. In addition, the concept of program restructuring can be applied to transform legacy code into a more structured form and migrate it to a different programming language. That is, restructuring and refactoring can be used to reengineer software systems.

Refactoring techniques put emphasis on the development of a list of basic refactorings, which can be combined to form complex refactorings [74, 75]. The original list of basic refactorings contained transformations on object-oriented code: (i) add a class, method, or attribute; (ii) rename a class, method, or attribute; (iii) move an attribute or method up or down the hierarchy; (iv) remove a class, method, or attribute; and (v) extract chunks of code into separate methods. Most complex refactoring scenarios require small code changes for the refactorings to work correctly. Primitive refactorings are rarely used in isolation.

1.7 PROGRAM COMPREHENSION

The purpose of program comprehension is to understand an existing software system for planning, designing, coding, and testing changes. T. A. Corbi [76] observed in 1989 that *program comprehension* accounts for 50% of the total effort expended throughout the life cycle of a software system. Therefore, good understanding of the software is key to raising its quality by means of maintenance at a lower cost. In terms of concrete activities, program comprehension involves building mental models of an underlying system at different levels of abstractions, varying from low-level models of the code to very high-level models of the underlying application domain [77]. Mental models have been studied by cognitive scientists to understand how human beings know, perceive, make decisions, and construct behavior in a real world [78, 79]. In the domain of program comprehension, a mental model describes a programmer's mental representation of the program to be comprehended.

Program comprehension involves constructing a mental model of the program by applying various cognitive processes. A key step in developing mental models is generating hypotheses, or conjectures, and investigating their validity. Hypotheses are a way for a programmer to understand code in an incremental manner. After some understanding of the code, the programmer forms a hypothesis and verifies it by reading code. Verification of hypothesis results in either accepting the hypothesis or rejecting it. Sometimes, a hypothesis may not be completely correct because of incomplete understanding of code by the programmer. By continuously formulating new hypotheses and verifying them, the programmer understands more and more code and in increasing details.

One can apply several strategies to arrive at meaningful hypotheses, such as bottom–up, top–down, and opportunistic combinations of the two. A bottom–up strategy works by beginning with the code, whereas a top–down strategy operates by working from a high-level goal. A strategy is formulated by identifying actions to achieve a goal. Strategies guide two mechanisms, namely, chunking and cross-referencing to produce higher-level abstraction structures. Chunking creates new, higher-level abstraction structures from lower-level structures. Cross-referencing means being able to make links between elements of different abstraction levels. This helps in building a mental model of the program under study at different levels of abstractions. In general, understanding a program involves a knowledge base, which represents the expertise and background knowledge a programmer brings to the table, a mental model, and an assimilation process [80]. The assimilation process guides the programmer to look at certain pieces of information, such as a code segment or a comment, and move forward/backward while reading the code. The assimilation process can work in three ways: top–down, bottom–up, and opportunistic.

1.8 SOFTWARE REUSE

The 1968 NATO (North Atlantic Treaty Organization) conference on software engineering is viewed to have germinated the ever growing field of software engineering [81]. The conference focused on *software crises*—the problem of building large, reliable software systems in a controlled way. In that conference, the term *software crisis* was coined for the first time. Even in the first forum on software systems, *software reuse* was pronounced as a means for tackling software crisis. The idea of software reuse was first introduced by Dough McIlroy in a seminal paper [82] in 1968. He proposed to realize reuse by means of library components and automated ways for customizing components to varying degrees of robustness and precision.

Other significant early reuse research developments include David Parnas's idea of program families [83] and Jim Neighbors' introduction of the concepts of domain analysis [84]. A program family is a set of programs whose common properties are so extensive that it becomes advantageous to study the common properties of these programs before analyzing individual differences. On the other hand, domain analysis is an activity of identifying objects and operations of a class of similar systems in a particular problem domain.

Simply stated, software reuse means using existing software knowledge or artifacts during the development of a new system. Reusable assets can include both artifacts and software knowledge. Note that reuse is not constrained to source code fragments. Rather, Capers Jones identified four broad types of artifacts for reuse [85]:

- *Data reuse.* This involves a standardization of data formats. Reusable functions imply a standard data interchange format. Therefore, one of the critical precursors to full reusable software is that of reusable data.
- *Architectural reuse.* This consists of standardizing a set of design and programming conventions dealing with the logical organization of software. The goal is to define a complete set of functional elements which will be needed to create new systems from standard components.

- *Design reuse.* This deals with the reuse of abstract designs that do not include implementation details. These are then implemented specifically to fit the application requirements.
- *Program reuse.* This deals with reusing running code. The software units that are reused may be of different sizes. The whole of software system may be reused by incorporating it without change into other system (COTS product reuse).

Reusability is a property of software assets, which indicates the degree to which the software can be reused. For a software component to be reusable, it must exhibit the following characteristics: high cohesion, low coupling, adaptability, understandability, reliability, and portability. Those characteristics encourage the component's reuse in similar situations. There are two advantages of reusing previously written code [86–88]:

- *Better quality.* If previously tested modules are reused in a new software project, the reused modules are likely to have less faults than new modules. This reduces the overall failure rate of the new software.
- *Increased productivity.* Organizations can save time and other resources by reusing operational modules, thereby increasing their overall productivity. However, the quantum of increase depends upon the size and complexity of the components being reused and the overall size and complexity of the new software which reuses those components. The development cost of any software project is only about 40% of the total cost over its entire life cycle [89]. Significant maintenance benefit also results from reusing quality software. The empirical study conducted by Stephen R. Schach shows that the cost savings during maintenance, as a consequence of reuse, are nearly twice the corresponding savings during development [90].

1.9 OUTLINE OF THE BOOK

Having given the aforementioned brief introduction to software evolution and maintenance, now we provide an outline of the remaining chapters. Each chapter focuses on a specific topic in software evolution and maintenance, and it explains the topic by covering the technical, process, model, and/or practical aspects of the topic. Consequently, the reader gains a broad understanding of the main concepts in software evolution and maintenance.

In Chapter 2 we explain three major maintenance classification schemes based on intention, activity, and evidence. Then we describe Lehman's classification of properties of closed source software (CSS) of type S (Specified), P (Problem), and E (Evolving). The eight laws of software evolution for the E-type CSS system including empirical studies and its practical implications have been introduced. We discuss the origin of FOSS movement and the differences between CSS and

FOSS systems with respect to: (i) team structure; (ii) processes; (iii) releases; and (iv) global factors. In addition, we discuss the empirical research results about the Linux FOSS system to study the laws of evolution, originally proposed for CSS systems. We conclude this chapter with a brief discussion on maintenance of component off-the-shelf-based systems.

Chapter 3 introduces three types of evolution models, namely, reuse-oriented, staged, and change mini-cycle. Next, we discuss the IEEE/EIA 1219 and the ISO IEC 14764 maintenance processes. We explain a framework to make a plan for SCM to control software evolution processes. We close this chapter with a presentation of a state transition model to track the individual change requests as those flow through the organization.

Chapter 4 introduces the concepts of software reengineering based on three basic principles: abstraction, refinement, and alteration. We discuss five basic reengineering approaches: big bang, incremental, partial, iterative, and evolutionary. Next, we discuss two specific models for software reengineering: source code reengineering reference model and phase reengineering model. With the reengineering approaches and models in place, we introduce the concepts and objectives of reverse engineering with an introduction to the Goals/Models/Tools paradigm that divides a process for reverse engineering into three successive phases: Goals, Models, and Tools. In addition, we examine some low-level reverse engineering tasks such as decompilers and disassemblers. DRE for data-oriented applications is explained toward the end of the chapter.

Chapter 5 identifies the problems an organization faces in dealing with legacy information systems and discusses six viable solutions to the problems: freeze, out source, carry on, discard and redevelop, wrap, and migrate. We study four types of wrapping techniques in detail: database wrapper, system service wrapper, application wrapper, and function wrapper. In addition, we discuss five different levels of encapsulations: process level, transaction level, program level, module level, and procedural level. Next, we focus our attention on migration of information systems. First we discuss the migration issues, followed by 13 steps for migration planning to minimize the risk of modernization effort. We discuss seven available migration approaches: Cold Turkey, Database First, Database Last, Composite Database, Chicken Little, Butterfly, and Iterative.

Chapter 6 presents the fundamentals of impact analysis, including the related concepts of ripple effect and change propagation. The reader learns the strengths and limitations of impact analysis techniques. We have selected topics to provide a foundation for enduring value of impact analysis and change propagation.

In Chapter 7, we introduce to the reader different refactoring activities. Different formalisms and techniques to support these activities have been discussed. In addition, we discuss the initial work on software restructuring, such as elimination-of-goto, system sandwich, localization and information hiding, and clustering approaches.

Chapter 8 considers the issues and solutions that underpin program understanding during maintenance. We discuss different models proposed by different researchers. In addition, the concept of protocol analysis is introduced to the readers. The chapter ends with a brief discussion of visualization for software comprehension.

In Chapter 9, we introduce the readers to reuse and domain engineering. Software reuse has the potential to reduce the maintenance cost more than development cost of software projects. We present a taxonomy of reuse, followed by a detailed description of domain and application engineering concepts, including real domain engineering approaches: DARE, FAST, and Koala. Finally, we discuss maturity and cost models associated with reuse.

In the glossary section we have defined all the keywords that have been used in the book. The reader will find about 10 practice questions at the end of each chapter. A carefully chosen list of references is given at the end of each chapter for those who are more curious about the details of some of the topics. Finally, each of the following chapters contains a section on further reading. The further reading section provides pointers to more advanced materials concerning the topics of the chapter.

REFERENCES

[1] M. I. Halpern. 1965. Machine independence: its technology and economics. *Communications of the ACM*, 8(12), 782–785.

[2] L. A. Belady and M. M. Lehman. 1976. A model of large program development. *IBM Systems Journal*, 15(1), 225–252.

[3] M. M. Lehman. 1980. Programs, life cycles, and laws of software evolution. *Proceedings of the IEEE*, September, 1060–1076.

[4] R. G. Canning. 1972. The maintenance "iceberg". *EDP Analyzer*, 10(10), 1–14.

[5] E. B. Swanson. 1976. *The Dimensions of Maintenance*. Proceedings of the 2nd International Conference on Software Engineering (ICSE), October 1976, San Francisco, CA. IEEE Computer Society Press, Los Alamitos, CA. pp. 492–497.

[6] N. Chapin, J. F. Hale, K. M. Khan, J. F. Ramil, and W. G. Tan. 2001. Types of software evolution and software maintenance. *Journal of Software Maintenance and Evolution: Research and Practice*, 13, 3–30.

[7] K. H. Bennett and V. T. Rajlich. 2000, *Software Maintenance and Evolution: A Roadmap. ICSE, The Future of Software Engineering*, June 2000, Limerick, Ireland. ACM, New York. pp. 73–87.

[8] L. J. Arthur. 1988. *Software Evolution: The Software Maintenance Challenge*. John Wiley & Sons.

[9] K. H. Bennett and J. Xu. 2003. *Software Services and Software Maintenance*. Proceedings of the 7th European Conference on Software Maintenance and Reengineering, March 2003, Benevento, Italy. IEEE Computer Society Press, Los Alamitos, CA. pp. 3–12.

[10] M. W. Godfrey and D. M. German. 2008. *The Past, Present, and Future of Software Evolution*. Proceedings of the 2008 Frontiers of Software Maintenance (FoSM), October 2008, Beijing, China. IEEE Computer Society Press, Los Alamitos, CA. pp. 129–138.

[11] D. L. Parnas. 1994. *Software Aging*. Proceedings of 16th International Conference on Software Engineering, May 1994, Sorrento, Italy. IEEE Computer Society Press, Los Alamitos, CA. pp. 279–287.

[12] M. Jazayeri. 2005. *Species Evolve, Individuals Age*. Proceedings of 8th International Workshop on Principles of Software Evolution (IWPSE), September 2005, Lisbon, Portugal. IEEE Computer Society Press, Los Alamitos, CA. pp. 3–9.

[13] P. Stachour and D. C. Brown. 2009. You don't know jack about software maintenance. *Communications of the ACM*, 52(11), 54–58.

[14] M. M. Lehman, D. E. Perry, and J. F. Ramil. 1998. *On Evidence Supporting the Feast Hypothesis and the Laws of Software Evolution*. Proceedings of the 5th International Software Metrics Symposium (Metrics), November 1998. IEEE Computer Society Press, Los Alamitos, CA. pp. 84–88.

[15] M. M. Lehman and J. F. Ramil. 2006. Software evolution. In: *Software Evolution and Feedback* (Eds N. H. Madhavvji, J. F. Ramil, and D. Perry). John Wiley, West Sussex, England.

[16] M. M. Lehman, J. F. Ramil, P. D. Wernick, D. E. Perry, and W. M. Turski. 1997. *Metrics and Laws of Software Evolution—The Nineties View*. Proceedings of the 4th International Symposium on Software Metrics (Metrics 97), November 1997. IEEE Computer Society Press, Los Alamitos, CA, pp. 20–32.

[17] S. S. Pirzada. 1988. A statistical examination of the evolution of the Unix system. PhD Thesis, Department of Computing, Imperical College, London, England.

[18] M. M. Lehman and L. A. Belady. 1985. *Program Evolution: Processess of Software Change*. Academic Press, London.

[19] M. W. Godfrey and Q. Tu. 2000. *Evolution in Open Source Software: A Case Study*. Proceedings of the International Conference on Software Maintenance, October 2000. IEEE Computer Society Press, Los Alamitos, CA, pp. 131–142.

[20] G. Robles, J. J. Amor, J. M. Gonzalez-Barahona, and I. Herraiz. 2005. *Evolution and Growth in Large Libre Software Projects*. Proceedings of the 8th International Workshop on Principles of Software Evolution (IWPSE), September 2005, Lisbon, Portugal. IEEE Computer Society Press, Los Alamitos, CA. pp. 165–174.

[21] ISO/IEC 14764:2006 and IEEE Std 14764-2006. 2006. *Software Engineering–Software Life Cycle Processes–Maintenance*. Geneva, Switzerland.

[22] B. A. Kitchenham, G. H. Travassos, A. N. Mayrhauser, F. Niessink, N. F. Schneidewind, J. Singer, S. Takada, R. Vehvilainen, and H. Yang. 1999. Towards an ontologyy of software maintenance. *Journal of Software Maintenance and Evolution: Research and Practice*, 11, 365–389.

[23] G. Ramesh and R. Bhattiprolu. 2006. *Software Maintenance*. Tata McGraw-Hill, New Delhi.

[24] M. Vigder and A. Kark. 2006. *Maintaining Cots-Based Systems: Start with Design*. Proceedings of the 5th International Conference on Commercial-Off-The-Shelf (COTS)-Based Software Systems, February 2006, Orlando, Florida. IEEE Computer Society Press, Los Alamitos, CA. pp. 11–18.

[25] D. Hybertson, A. Ta, and W. Thomas. 1997. Maintenance of cots-intensive software systems. *Journal of Software Maintenance and Evolution: Research and Practice*, 9, 203–216.

[26] W. W. Royce. 1970. *Managing the Development of Large Software System: Concepts and Techniques*. Proceeding of IEEE WESCON, August 1970, pp. 1–9, Republished in ICSE, Monterey, CA, 1987, pp. 328–338.

[27] N. Schneidewind. 1987. The state of software maintenance. *IEEE Transactions on Software Engineering*, March, 303–309.

[28] N. Chapin. 1988. *Software Maintenance Life Cycle*. Proceedings of the International Conference on Software Maintenance (ICSM), October 1988, Phoenix, Arizona. IEEE Computer Society Press, Los Alamitos, CA, pp. 6–13.

[29] W. K. Sharpley. 1977. *Software Maintenance Planning for Embedded Computer Systems.* Proceedings of the IEEE COMPSAC, November 1977, IEEE Computer Society Press, Los Alamitos, CA, pp. 520–526.

[30] G. Parikh. 1982. The world of software manitenance. In: *Techniques of Program and System Maintenance* (Ed. G. Parikh), pp. 9-13. Little, Brown and Company, Boston, MA.

[31] J. Martin and C. L. McClure. 1983. *Software Maintenance: The Problem and Its Solution.* Prentice-Hall, Englewood Cliffs, NJ.

[32] S. Chen, K. G. Heisler, W. T. Tsai, X. Chen, and E. Leung. 1990. A model for assembly program maintenance. *Journal of Software Maintenance: Research and Practice*, March, pp. 3–32.

[33] D. R. Harjani and J. P. Queille. 1992. *A Process Model for the Maintenance of Large Space Systems Software.* Proceedings of the International Conference on Software Maintenance (ICSM), November 1992, Orlando, FL. IEEE Computer Society Press, Los Alamitos, CA. pp. 127–136.

[34] S. S. Yau, R. A. Nicholi, J. Tsai, and S. Liu. 1988. An integrated life-cycle model for software maintenance. *IEEE Transactions on Software Engineering*, August, pp. 1128–1144.

[35] S. S. Yau and I. S. Collofello. 1980. Some stability measures for software maintenance. *IEEE Transactions on Software Engineering*, November, pp. 545–552.

[36] S. S. Yau, J. S. Collofello, and T. MacGregor. 1978. *Ripple Effect Analysis of Software Maintenance.* COMPSAC, Chicago, Illinois. IEEE Computer Society Press, Piscataway, NJ. pp. 60–65.

[37] B. W. Boehm. 1988. A spiral model of software development and maintenance. *IEEE Computer*, May, pp. 61–72.

[38] V. R. Basili. 1990. Viewing maintenance as reuse-oriented software development. *IEEE Software*, January, pp. 19–25.

[39] R. G. Martin. 2002. *Agile Software Development: Principles, Patterns, and Practices.* Prentice-Hall.

[40] T. Gilb. 1988. *Principles of Software Engineering Management.* Addison-Wesley, Reading, MA.

[41] T. Mens. 2008. Introduction and roadmap: history and challenges of software evolution. In: *Software Evolution* (Eds. T. Mens and S. Demeyer). Springer Verlag, Berlin.

[42] V. T. Rajlich and K. H. Bennett. 2000. A staged model for the software life cycle. *IEEE Computer*, July, pp. 2–8.

[43] ISO/IEC 12207:2006 and IEEE Std 12207-2006. 2008. *System and Software Engineering–Software Life Cycle Processes.* Geneva, Switzerland.

[44] IEEE Standard 1219-1998. 1998. *Standard for Software Maintenance.* IEEE Computer Society Press, Los Alamitos, CA.

[45] IEEE Std 1042-1987. 1988. *IEEE Guide to Software Configuration Management.* IEEE, Inc., New York, NY.

[46] K. Narayanaswamy and W. Scacchi. 1987. Maintaining configuration of evolving software systems. *IEEE Transactions of Software Engineering*, March, 13(3), 324–334.

[47] D. Leblang. 1994. The CM challenge: configuration management that works. In: *Configuration Management*, Chapter 1 (Ed. W. F. Tichy). John Wiley, Chichester.

[48] H. Yang and M. Ward. 2003. *Successful Evolution of Software Systems.* Artech House, Boston, MA.

[49] E. J. Chikofsky and J. H. Cross II. 1990. Reverse engineering and design recovery. *IEEE Software,* January, pp. 13–17.

[50] I. Jacobson and F. Lindström. 1991. *Re-engineering of Old Systems to an Object-oriented Architecture.* Proceedings of the ACM Conference on Object Oriented Programming Systems Languages and Applications, October 1991. ACM Press, New York, NY, pp. 340–350.

[51] P. Benedusi, A. Cimitile, and U. De Carlini. 1992. Reverse engineering processes, design document production, and structure charts. *Journal of Systems Software,* 19, 225–245.

[52] P. Aiken. 1996. *Data Reverse Engineering: Staying the Legacy Dragon.* McGraw-Hill, Boston, New York, NY.

[53] K. H. Bennett. 1995. Legacy systems: coping with success. *IEEE Software,* January, pp. 19–23.

[54] M. Brodie and M. Stonebraker. 1995. *Migrating Legacy Systems.* Morgan Kaufmann, San Mateo, CA.

[55] A. Cimitile, H. Müller, and R. Klosch (Eds.) 1997. *Pulling Together.* Proceedings of the International Conference on Software Engineering, Workshop on Migration Strategies for Legacy Systems, Available as Technical Report TUV-1841-97-06 from Technical University University of Vienna, Vienna, Austria.

[56] K. Bennett, M. Ramage, and M. Munro. 1999. *Decision Model for Legacy Systems.* IEEE Proceedings on Software, June, pp. 153–159.

[57] W. C. Dietrich Jr., L. R. Nackman, and F. Gracer. 1989. Saving a legacy with objects. *Proceedings of the 1989 ACM OOPSLA Conference on Object-Oriented Programming,* 24(10), 77–83. ACM SIGPLAN Notices, ACM, New York, NY.

[58] H. M. Sneed. 1996. *Encapsulating Legacy Software for Use in Client/Server Systems.* 3rd Working Conference on Reverse Engineering, Washington, DC. IEEE Computer Society Press, Los Alamitos, CA. pp. 104–119.

[59] S. Comella-Dorda, K. Wallnau, R. C. Seacord, and J. Robert. 2000. *A Survey of Black-box Modernization Approaches for Information Systems.* Proceedings of the International Conference on Software Maintenance, October, 2000, San Jose, CA. IEEE Computer Society Press, Los Alamitos, CA. pp. 173–183.

[60] F. P. Coyle. 2000. Legacy integration—changing perpectives. *IEEE Software,* March/April, 37–41.

[61] H. M. Sneed. 1995. Planning the reengineeirng of legacy systems. *IEEE Software,* January, pp. 24–34.

[62] J. Bisbal, D. Lawless, B. Wu, J. Grimson, V. Wade, R. Richardson, and D. O'Sullivan. 1997. A survey of research into legacy system migration. Technical Report TCD-CS-1997-01, Computer Science Department, Trinity College, Dublin, January, pp. 39.

[63] M. Battaglia, G. Savoia, and J. Favaro. 1998. *Renaissance: A Method to Migrate from Legacy to Immortal Software Systems.* Proceedings of Second Euromicro Conference on Software Maintenance and Reengineering, 1998, Florence, Italy. IEEE Computer Society Press, Los Alamitos, CA. pp. 197–200.

[64] A. Bianchi, D. Caivano, V. Marengo, and G. Visaggio. 2003. Iterative reengineering of legacy systems. *IEEE Transactions on Software Engineering,* March, 225–241.

[65] S. A. Bohner and R. S. Arnold. 1996. An introduction to software change impact analysis. In: *Software Change Impact Analysis* (Eds. S. A. Bohner and R. S. Arnold). IEEE Computer Society Press, Los Alamitos, CA.

[66] A. Podgurski and L. Clrke. 1990. A formal model of program dependencies and its implications for software testing, debugging, and maintenance. *IEEE Transactions of Software Engineering*, September, 16(9), 965–979.

[67] M. J. Harrold and B. Malloy. 1993. A unified interprocedural program representation for maintenance environment. *IEEE Transactions of Software Engineering*, 19(6), 584–593.

[68] S. Black. 2008. Deriving an approximation algorithm for automatic computation of ripple effect measures. *Information and Software Technology*, 50, 723–736.

[69] V. Rajlich. 1997. *A Model for Change Propagation Based on Graph Rewriting.* Proceedings of the International Conference on Software Maintenance (ICSM), October 1997, Bari, Italy. IEEE Computer Society Press, Los Alamitos, CA. pp. 84–91.

[70] A. E. Hassan and R. C. Holt. 2004. *Predicting Change Propagation in Software Systems.* Proceedings of the International Conference on Software Maintenance (ICSM), October 2004, Chicago, USA. IEEE Computer Society Press, Los Alamitos, CA. pp. 284–293.

[71] N. Ibrahim, W. M. N. Kadir, and S. Deris. 2008. *Comparative Evaluation of Change Propagation Approaches Towards Resilient Software Evolution.* Proceedings of the Third International Conference on Software Engineering Advances, pp. 198–204.

[72] D. E. Perry and W. M. Evangelist. 1987. *An Empirical Study of Software Interface Faults— An Update.* Proceedings of the Twentieth Annual Hawaii International Conference on Systems Sciences, January 1987, Volume II, pp. 113–126.

[73] M. Fowler. 1999. *Refactoring: Improving the Design of Existing Programs.* Addison-Wesley.

[74] W. F. Opdyke. 1992. Refactoring: A program restructuring aid in designing object-oriented application framework. PhD thesis, University of Illinois at Urbana-Champaign.

[75] S. Demeyer. 2008. Object-oriented reengineering. In: *Software Evolution* (Eds. T. Mens and S. Demeyer). Springer Verlag, Berlin.

[76] T. A. Corbi. 1989. Program understanding: challenge for the 1990s. *IBM Systems Journal*, 28(2), pp. 294–306.

[77] H. A. Müller. 1996. *Understanding Software Systems Using Reverse Engineering Technologies: Research and Practice.* Department of Computer Science, University of Victoria. Available at http://www.rigi.csc.uvic.ca/uvicrevtut/uvicrevtut.html.

[78] P. N. Johnson-laird. 1983. *Mental Model.* Harvard University Press, Cambridge, MA.

[79] K. J. W. Craik. 1943. *The Nature of Explanation.* Cambridge University Press, Cambridge, UK.

[80] S. Letovsky. 1986. *Cognitive Processes in Program Comprehension.* Proceedings of the First Workshop in Empirical Studies of Programmers, pp. 58–79.

[81] P. Nauer, B. Randell, and J. N. Buxton (Eds). 1969. Software engineering. Report on a Conference by the NATO Science Committee, NOATO Scientific Affairs Division, Brussels, Belgium, Available through Petrocelli-Charter, New York.

[82] M. D. McIlroy. 1969. *Mass Produced Software Components.* Proceedings of Software Engineering Concepts and Techniques, 1968 NATO Conference on Software Engineering (Eds. P. Naur, B. Randell, and J. N. Buxton), pp. 138–155. Petrocelli-Charter, New York, NY.

[83] D. L. Parnas. 1976. On the design and development of program families. *IEEE Transactions of Software Engineering*, 2(1), 1–9.

[84] J. M. Neighbors. 1980. Software construction using components. Technical Report 160, Department of Information and Computer Sciences, University of California, Irvine.

[85] T. C. Jones. 1984. Reusability in programming: a survey of the state of the art. *IEEE Transactions of Software Engineering*, 10(5), 488–494.

[86] J. E. Gaffney and T. A. Durek. 1989. Software reuse - key to enhanced productivity: some quantitative models. *Information and Software Technology*, 31(5), 258–267.

[87] R. D. Banker and R. J. Kauffman. 1991. Reuse and productivity in integrated computer-aided software engineering: an emprical study. *MIS Quarterly*, 15(3), 374–401.

[88] V. R. Basili, L. C. Brand, and W. L. Melo. 1996. Machine independence: Its technology and economics. *Communications of the ACM*, 39(10), pp. 104–116.

[89] Gartner Group Inc. 1991. Software engineering strategies. Strategic Analysis Report, Stamford, CT, April.

[90] S. R. Schach. 1994. The economic impact of software reuse on maintenance. *Journal of Software Maintenance and Evolution: Research and Practice*, July/August, 6(4), pp. 185–196.

EXERCISES

1. Discuss the differences between software evolution and software maintenance.

2. Explain why a software system which is used in a real-world environment must be changed to not become progressively less useful.

3. What are some characteristics of maintaining software as opposed to new software systems?

4. You are asked to make a change to a system that leaves its functional specification unchanged but affects the design and source code of the system. This can be any of the four types of maintenance mentioned earlier except one. Identify the exception and justify your answer.

(a) Corrective maintenance

(b) Adaptive maintenance

(c) Perfective maintenance

(d) Preventive maintenance

5. Discuss the major differences between COTS-based software development and traditional in-house software development activities.

6. One of the key sources of risks in COTS-based development is the reliance on one or more third-party software vendors. However, this dependence can also present new challenges for the evolution of such systems. Which of the following evolution challenges can be directly attributed to reliance on the vendor?

(a) Lack of control over when errors in components are fixed.

    (b) Number and complexity of inter-component interfaces.

    (c) Diversity of inter-component interfaces.

    (d) Lack of experience and tools for evolving COTS-based systems.

7. What are the objectives of SCM?

8. A feature of any complex change to an existing software system is that it is likely to introduce new defects, even if the aim of the change is to remove defects. When considering whether or not to implement a change request, should this feature be considered as a cost, benefit, or risk associated with the change request?

9. System A is a mission critical legacy system that captures and stores detailed data on product sales. Data from system A must be regularly extracted and loaded into a new system (B), which is to be used to help managers understand the changes in sales patterns from week to week. Initial estimates suggest that the data for 1 week can be extracted and transformed in around 3 hours. What migration frequency would you choose for this new application?

    (a) Migrate on update.

    (b) Migrate daily, every evening at 2.00 A.M.

    (c) Migrate weekly, every Sunday evening at 2.00 A.M.

    (d) Migrate monthly, on the last Sunday of every month at 2.00 A.M.

10. What are some of the risks of not doing an impact analysis before effecting a change?

11. What actions can be taken to minimize the impact of fixing defects?

12. What problems do maintainers face when rewriting or reengineering a piece of code? What are the causes of those problems?

13. Explain the term hypotheses in the context of program understanding.

14. What benefits can be derived from reusing software?

2

TAXONOMY OF SOFTWARE MAINTENANCE AND EVOLUTION

Evolution is not a force but a process. Not a cause but a law.

—John Morley

2.1 GENERAL IDEA

In the early 1970s, the term "maintenance" was used to refer to tasks for making intentional modifications to the existing software at IBM. Those who performed maintenance tasks had not carried out the software development work. The idea behind having a different set of personnel to carry out maintenance work was to free the development engineers from support activities. The aforementioned model continued to influence the activities that are collectively known as "software maintenance." In circa 1972, in his landmark article "The Maintenance 'Iceberg'," R. G. Canning [1] used the iceberg metaphor to describe the enormous mass of potential problems facing practitioners of software maintenance. Practitioners took a narrow view of maintenance as correcting errors and expanding the functionalities of the system. In other words, maintenance consisted of two kinds of activities: correcting errors and enhancing functionalities of the software. Hence, maintenance can be inappropriately seen as a continuation of software development with an extra input—the existing software system [2].

The ISO/IEC 14764 standard [3] defines software maintenance as "... the totality of activities required to provide cost-effective support to a software system. Activities

Software Evolution and Maintenance: A Practitioner's Approach, First Edition.
Priyadarshi Tripathy and Kshirasagar Naik.
© 2015 John Wiley & Sons, Inc. Published 2015 by John Wiley & Sons, Inc.

are performed during the pre-delivery stage as well as the post-delivery stage" (p. 4). Post-delivery activities include changing software, providing training, and operating a help desk. Pre-delivery activities include planning for post-delivery operations. During the development process, maintainability is specified, reviewed, and controlled. If this is done successfully, the maintainability of the software will improve during the post-delivery stage. The standard further defines software maintainability as "... the capability of the software product to be modified. Modification may include corrections, improvements or adaptation of the software to changes in environment, and in requirements and functional specification" (p. 3).

A major difference exists between software maintenance and software development: maintenance is event driven, whereas development is requirements driven [4]. A process for software development begins with the objective of designing and implementing a system to deliver certain functional and nonfunctional requirements. On the other hand, a maintenance task is scheduled in response to an event. Reception of a *change request* from a customer is a kind of event that can trigger software maintenance. Similarly, recognition of the needs to fix a set of bugs is considered another kind of event. Events originate from both the customers and from within the developed organization. Generally, the inputs that invoke maintenance activities are unscheduled events; execution of the actual maintenance activities might be scheduled according to a plan, but the events that initiate maintenance activities occur randomly. A maintenance activity accepts some existing artifacts as inputs and generates some new and/or modified artifacts.

Now we further explain the idea of a maintenance activity taking in an input and producing an output. In general, an investigation activity is the first activity in a maintenance process. In an investigation activity, a maintenance engineer evaluates the nature of the events, say, a change request (CR). Finding the impact of executing the CR is an example of investigation activity. Upon completion of the first activity, the organization decides whether or not to proceed with the modification activity.

In the following subsections, we explain maintenance activities from three viewpoints:

- Intention-based classification of software maintenance activities;
- Activity-based classification of software maintenance activities; and
- Evidence-based classification of software maintenance activities.

2.1.1   Intention-Based Classification of Software Maintenance

In the intention-based classification, one categorizes maintenance activities into four groups based on what we intend to achieve with those activities [5–7]. Based on the Standard for Software Engineering–Software Maintenance, ISO/IEC 14764 [3], the four categories of maintenance activities are corrective, adaptive, perfective, and preventive as explained in the following.

Corrective maintenance. The purpose of corrective maintenance is to correct failures: processing failures and performance failures. A program producing a wrong output is an example of processing failure. Similarly, a program not being able to meet real-time requirements is an example of performance failure. The process of corrective maintenance includes isolation and correction of defective elements in the software. The software product is repaired to satisfy requirements. There is a variety of situations that can be described as corrective maintenance such as correcting a program that aborts or produces incorrect results. Basically, corrective maintenance is a *reactive* process, which means that corrective maintenance is performed after detecting defects with the system.

Adaptive maintenance. The purpose of adaptive maintenance is to enable the system to adapt to changes in its data environment or processing environment. This process modifies the software to properly interface with a changing or changed environment. Adaptive maintenance includes system changes, additions, deletions, modifications, extensions, and enhancements to meet the evolving needs of the environment in which the system must operate. Some generic examples are: (i) changing the system to support new hardware configuration; (ii) converting the system from batch to online operation; and (iii) changing the system to be compatible with other applications. A more concrete example is: an application software on a smartphone can be enhanced to support WiFi-based communication in addition to its present Third Generation (3G) cellular communication.

Perfective maintenance. The purpose of perfective maintenance is to make a variety of improvements, namely, user experience, processing efficiency, and maintainability. For example, the program outputs can be made more readable for better user experience; the program can be modified to make it faster, thereby increasing the processing efficiency; and the program can be restructured to improve its readability, thereby increasing its maintainability. In general, activities for perfective maintenance include restructuring of the code, creating and updating documentations, and tuning the system to improve performance. It is also called "maintenance for the sake of maintenance" or "reengineering" [8].

Preventive maintenance. The purpose of preventive maintenance is to prevent problems from occurring by modifying software products. Basically, one should look ahead, identify future risks and unknown problems, and take actions so that those problems do not occur. For example, good programming styles can reduce the impact of change, thereby reducing the number of failures [9]. Therefore, the program can be restructured to achieve good styles to make later program comprehension easier. Preventive maintenance is very often performed on safety critical and high available software systems [10–13]. The concept of "software rejuvenation" is a preventive maintenance measure to prevent, or at least postpone, the occurrences of failures due to continuously running the software system. *Software rejuvenation* is a proactive fault management technique aimed at cleaning up the system internal state to prevent the occurrence of more severe crash in the future. It involves occasionally terminating an application or a system, cleaning its internal state, and restarting it. Rejuvenation may increase the downtime of the application; however, it prevents the occurrence of more severe and costly failures. In a safety critical environment, the necessity of performing preventive maintenance is evident from the example of control software for Patriot missile: "On 21 February, the office sent out a warning that 'very long running time' could affect the targeting accuracy. The troops were not told, however, how many hours 'very long' was or that it would help to switch the computer off and on again after 8 hours." (p. 1347 of Ref. [14]). The purpose of software maintenance activities of preventive maintenance of a safety critical software system is to eliminate hazard or reduce their associated risk to an acceptable level. Note that a *hazard* is a state of a system or a physical situation which, when combined with certain environment conditions, could lead to an accident. A hazard is a prerequisite for an accident or mishap.

2.1.2 Activity-Based Classification of Software Maintenance

In the intention-based classification of maintenance activities, the intention of an activity depends upon the reason for the change [7]. On the other hand, Kitchenham et al. [4] organize maintenance modification activities based on the maintenance activity. The authors classify the maintenance modification activities into two categories: corrections and enhancements.

- *Corrections.* Activities in this category are designed to fix defects in the system, where a defect is a discrepancy between the expected behavior and the actual behavior of the system.
- *Enhancements.* Activities in this category are designed to effect changes to the system. The changes to the system do not necessarily modify the behavior of the system. This category of activities is further divided into three subcategories as follows:
  - enhancement activities that modify some of the existing requirements implemented by the system;
  - enhancement activities that add new system requirements; and
  - enhancement activities that modify the implementation without changing the requirements implemented by the system.

Now one can find a mapping between Swanson's terminology and Kitchenham's terminology. Enhancement activities which are necessary to change the implementations of existing requirements are similar to Swanson's idea of perfective maintenance. Enhancement activities, which add new requirements to a system, are similar to the idea of adaptive maintenance. Enhancement activities which do not impact requirements but merely affect the system implementation appear to be similar to preventive maintenance.

2.1.3 Evidence-Based Classification of Software Maintenance

The intention-based classification of maintenance activities was further refined by Chapin et al. [15]. The objectives of the classification are as follows:

- base the classification on objective evidence that can be measured from observations and comparisons of software before and after modifications;
- set the coarseness of the classification to truly reflect a representative mix of observed activities;

- make the classification independent of the execution and development environments: hardware, operating system (OS), organizational practices, design methodology, implementation language, and personnel involved in maintenance.

Modifications performed, detected, or observed on four aspects of the system being maintained are used as the criteria to cluster the types of maintenance activities:

- the whole software;
- the external documentation;
- the properties of the program code; and
- the system functionality experienced by the customer.

Classification of maintenance activities is based on changes in the aforementioned four kinds of entities. Evidence of changes to those entities is gathered by comparing the appropriate portions of the software *before* the activity with the appropriate parts *after* the execution of the activity. In general, software maintenance or evolution involves many activities that may result in some kind of modifications to the software. A dominant categorization of activities emerges from all the modifications made, detected, or observed. The classification proposed by Chapin [16] was exhaustive in nature. His mutually exclusive types were grouped into clusters as illustrated in Figure 2.1. The definitions of the 12 types of maintenance activities are given in Table 2.1.

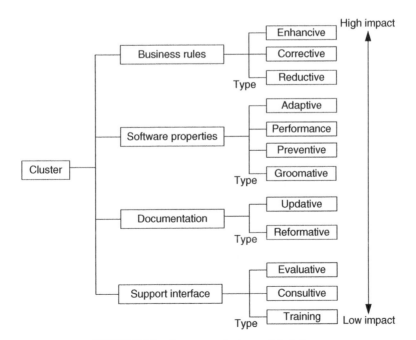

FIGURE 2.1   Groups or clusters and their types

TABLE 2.1 Evidence-Based 12 Mutually Exclusive Maintenance Types

Types of Maintenance	Definitions
Training	This means training the stakeholders about the implementation of the system.
Consultive	In this type, cost and length of time are estimated for maintenance work, personnel run a help desk, customers are assisted to prepare maintenance work requests, and personnel make expert knowledge about the available resources and the system to others in the organization to improve efficiency.
Evaluative	In this type, common activities include reviewing the program code and documentations, examining the ripple effect of a proposed change, designing and executing tests, examining the programming support provided by the operating system, and finding the required data and debugging.
Reformative	Ordinary activities in this type improve the readability of the documentation, make the documentation consistent with other changes in the system, prepare training materials, and add entries to a data dictionary.
Updative	Ordinary activities in this type are substituting out-of-date documentation with up-to-date documentation, making semi-formal, say, in UML to document current program code, and updating the documentation with test plans.
Groomative	Ordinary activities in this type are substituting components and algorithms with more efficient and simpler ones, modifying the conventions for naming data, changing access authorizations, compiling source code, and doing backups.
Preventive	Ordinary activities in this type perform changes to enhance maintainability and establish a base for making a future transition to an emerging technology.
Performance	Activities in performance type produce results that impact the user. Those activities improve system up time and replace components and algorithms with faster ones.
Adaptive	Ordinary activities in this type port the software to a different execution platform and increase the utilization of COTS components.
Reductive	Ordinary activities in this type drop some data generated for the customer, decreasing the amount of data input to the system and decreasing the amount of data produced by the system.
Corrective	Ordinary activities in this type are correcting identified bugs, adding defensive programming strategies and modifying the ways exceptions are handled.
Enhancive	Ordinary activities in this type are adding and modifying business rules to enhance the system's functionality available to the customer and adding new data flows into or out of the software.

TABLE 2.2   Impact of the Types

Impact on Software	Impact on Business Low ← – – – – – → High	Cluster and Type
Low		**Support interface**
↑	◇ ◇ ◇ ◇ ◇	Training
|	◇ ◇ ◇ ◇	Consultive
|	◇ ◇	Evaluative
|		**Documentation**
|	◇ ◇	Reformative
|	◇ ◇	Updative
|		**Software properties**
|	◇ ◇	Groomative
|	◇ ◇ ◇	Preventive
|	◇ ◇ ◇	Performance
|	◇ ◇	Adaptive
|		**Business rules**
|	◇	Reductive
|	◇ ◇ ◇	Corrective
↓	◇ ◇ ◇ ◇ ◇ ◇	Enhancive
High		

Source: From Reference 15. © 2001 John Wiley & Sons.

The impacts of the different types or clusters of maintenance activities are summarized in Table 2.2. The first dimension of the impact of the evolution is the customer's ability to perform its business functions effectively while continuing to use the system. The impact is represented as low or high. The number of diamonds in a row indicates the more probable range of impact on the business process of the customer. As an example, if the software is enhanced with new functionalities, then the customer is more likely to be able to achieve its business goals than modifications on noncode documentation. The second dimension is the software itself. This is arranged from top to bottom. As an example, rewriting a few pages of a user's manual has almost no impact on the software compared to rewriting a block of code to fix a defect. Figure 2.1 illustrates the relationship among the different types of activities in terms of impacts.

Decision Tree-Based Criteria   The classification of maintenance activities have been illustrated in Figure 2.1. The classification is based on modifications performed —modifications deliberately done, modifications observed, modifications manifested, and modifications detected—in various physical and conceptual entities:

- A—the whole software system.
- B—the program code.
- C—the functionalities experienced by customers.

The idea of objective evidence about activities is key to making the classification. The fundamental acts of observation of behavior and comparison of behavior of two entities reveal the evidence, and evidence of change-producing activities serves as the criteria. Note that observation is performed on the artifacts and the activities operating on them. On the other hand, comparison is performed on the relevant parts of the software before and after a maintenance activity is performed. Activities are classified into different types by applying a two-step decision process:

- First, apply criteria-based decisions to make the clusters of types.
- Next, apply the type decisions to identify one type within the cluster.

Figure 2.2 summarizes the aforementioned two steps in a hierarchical manner. The decision tree shown in Figure 2.2 is an objective evidence-based classification of maintenance types. The three-criteria decision involving A, B, and C lead to the right types of cluster. The decisions characterize the types within each cluster. In a maintenance process, we are interested in the impacts of maintenance activities not only on the software but also the business processes of the software. Due to the impact characteristics summarized in Table 2.2, one reads Figure 2.2 by beginning on the left-hand side and moving toward the right for increasing impact on the software and/or the business processes. First, clusters of maintenance types are identified by using the type (namely, A, B, and C) decisions. Next, the types within a cluster are

Types of software maintenance

Notes:
Types is read from left to right, bottom to top.
Questions have been listed in Table 2.2.
Italics show the type name when the type decision at the left of it is 'Yes'
For "cc", read "change to code"
* indicates the default type in the cluster.

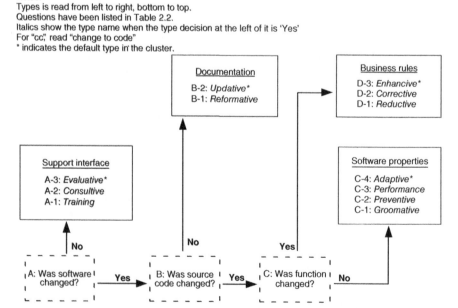

FIGURE 2.2   Decision tree types. From Reference 15. © 2001 John Wiley & Sons

TABLE 2.3   Summary of Evidence-Based Types of Software Maintenance

Criteria	Type Decision Question	Type
A-1	To train the stakeholders, did the activities utilize the software as subject?	Training
A-2	As a basis for consultation, did the activities employ the software?	Consultive
A-3	Did the activities evaluate the software?	Evaluative
B-1	To meet stakeholder needs, did the activities modify the noncode documentation?	Reformative
B-2	To conform to implementation, did the activities modify the noncode documentation?	Updative
C-1	Was maintainability or security changed by the activities?	Groomative
C-2	Did the activities constrain the scope of future maintenance activities?	Preventive
C-3	Were performance properties or characteristics modified by the activities?	Performance
C-4	Were different technology or resources used by the activities?	Adaptive
D-1	Did the activities constrain, reduce, or remove some functionalities experienced by the customer?	Reductive
D-2	Did the activities fix bugs in customer-experienced functionality?	Corrective
D-3	Did the activities substitute, add to, or expand some functionalities experienced by the customers?	Enhancive

identified by using type decisions. To make type decisions, one asks questions about a specific evidence. A type is only applicable if the answer to the type decision question is "Yes." For specific type decision questions, the reader is referred to Table 2.3. Sometimes, an objective evidence may be found to be ambiguous. In that case, clusters have their designated default types for use. The overall default type is evaluative if there are ambiguities in an activity. Ambiguities can be present in observations and the available documentation evidence. Trivially, no type of software maintenance has been conducted if observations indicate that no activities are performed on the software, except merely executing it.

Since software maintenance involves many activities, a variety of questions are answered to determine their types, as illustrated in Figure 2.2, in the structure of a decision tree. All the three cluster decision criteria A, B, and C shown in the three dotted boxes of Figure 2.2 and, listed below as well, must be asked:

- A: Was software changed?
- B: Was source code changed?
- C: Was function changed?

A "No" response to any of the aforementioned questions leads to a cluster, where one or more type decisions result in an "Yes." As an example, if the answer to question

A is "No," then at least one question in the box labeled "Support interface" produces a "Yes" answer. In addition, if the answer to question C is "Yes," then at least one question in the box labeled "Business rules" produces a "Yes" answer. The basic idea is to move upward from the bottom of the rightmost column of leaves in Figure 2.1 as far up as possible. The aforementioned traversal is similar to traversing the tree shown in Figure 2.2. Next, we explain the four kinds of clusters, namely, *support interface*, *documentation*, *software properties*, and *business rules* one by one.

Support Interface Cluster   This cluster relates to the modifications on how service and/or maintenance personnel interact with stakeholders and customers. The support interface cluster is invoked if the answer to the A criteria decision question "Was software changed?" is a "No." It consists of maintenance type decision in the order of A-1, A-2, and A-3, because of their increasing impact. The default type here is *Evaluative*. In the following, we explain the three type decisions one by one.

- *Type decision A-1.* "To train the stakeholders, did the activities utilize the software as subject?" is the A-1-type decision. In the training type, common activities include: (i) in-class lessons for customers and (ii) a variety of training spanning from on-site to web-based training using training materials from the documentations. The idea is to provide training to the stakeholders in the details of the system that has been implemented by the software.
- *Type decision A-2.* This type decision is "As a basis for consultation, did the activities employ the software?," and it is of *consultive* type. This type decision is commonly performed as it involves such activities as estimating the cost of the planned maintenance task, providing support from a help desk, helping customers in preparing a CR, and making specific knowledge about the system or resources available to others in the organization.
- *Type decision A-3.* This decision, which is of *evaluative* type, is "Did the activities evaluate the software?" A-3 is a commonly used decision as it includes the following activities: searching, examining, auditing, diagnostic testing, regression testing, understanding the software without modifying it, and computing different types of metrics.

Documentation Cluster   For the A criterion decision, if assessment of the objective evidence is "Yes," then it implies that the software was modified. Next, we analyze the B decision, which is about source code. The documentation cluster is invoked by a "No" answer to the B criterion question "Did the activities change the code?" It concerns modifications in the documentation except source code. The cluster comprises two decisions, namely, B-1 and B-2. Documentation cluster activities normally appear after the software interface cluster.

- *Type decision B-1.* The B-1 decision is "To meet stakeholder needs, did the activities modify the noncode documentation?" Ordinary activities in *reformative* type improve the readability of the documentation, change the documentation to incorporate the effects of modifications in the manuals, pre-pare training materials, and change the style of the documentation for noncode entities. In other words, it involves reformulation of documentation for noncode entities by modifying its style while preserving the code.

- *Type decision B-2.* The B-2 decision is "To conform to implementation, did the activities modify the noncode documentation?" This *updative* type involves activities for replacing out-of-date documentation with up-to-date documenta-tion, making semi-formal models to describe current source code, and combin-ing test plans with the documentation, without modifying the code. Out of the two types, the default type is *update*.

Software Properties Cluster   The code is said to be modified if the B criterion decision produces a "Yes" outcome. Next, one analyzes decision C which queries about modifications in the functionality of the system observed by the user. The software properties cluster is invoked by a "No" answer to the C criteria decision "Did the activities change the customer-experienced functionality?" This cluster comprises four type decisions, namely, C-1, C-2, C-3, and C-4, with increasing impact in that order. The cluster concerns modifications in the attributes of the software without involving modifications in the functionality delivered by the software. Activities in this group commonly follow the documentation cluster and the support interface cluster. The default type here is *adaptive*, and the details of the type decisions in this cluster are as follows:

- *Type decision C-1.* "Was maintainability or security changed by the activities?" is the C-1-type decision, and it is of *groomative* type. The decision involves "anti-regression" activities for source code grooming, such as substituting algorithms and modules with better ones, modifying conventions for data naming, making backups, changing access authorizations, altering code understandability, and recompiling the code.
- *Type decision C-2.* C-2 is a *preventive* type decision asking the question "Did the activities constrain the scope of future maintenance activities?" This type of activities makes modifications to the code without changing either the exist-ing functionality experienced by the customers or the resources utilized or the existing technology. The impacts of such activities are generally not visible to the customer. The common activities are making changes to improve maintain-ability.
- *Type decision C-3.* "Were performance properties or characteristics modified by the activities?" is a C-3-type decision, and it is of *performance* type. This involves improving system up time, substituting algorithms and modules with the ones with better efficiency, reducing the demand for storage, and improving the system's robustness and reliability. The customer often observes the changes in those properties.
- *Type decision C-4.* "Were different technology or resources used by the activ-ities?" is a C-4-type decision, and it is an *adaptive* type. This type includes

activities such as porting the software to a new execution platform, increased utilization of commercial off-the-shelf (COTS), changing the supported communication protocols, and moving to object-oriented technologies. Those activities can change customer-perceivable system properties, but similar to C-1, C-2, and C-3, type C-4 does not modify the functionality experienced by the customers. Type C-4 is the default in this group.

Business Rules Cluster   This cluster is invoked by a "Yes" answer to the C criteria decision question "Did the activities change the customer-experienced functionality?" This cluster comprises the D-1, D-2, and D-3-type decisions. These types of activities occur most frequently, and activities from other clusters are needed to support these activities. This cluster involves the user- and business-level functionalities.

- *Type decision D-1.* Type decision D-1 is "Did the activities constrain, reduce, or remove some functionalities experienced by the customers?" and it is of *reductive* type. This type of activities delete portions or all of the modules to constrain or remove some business rules. When organizations merge, their business rules undergo such actions as elimination, restriction, and reduction.
- *Type decision D-2.* Type decision D-2 is "Did the activities fix bugs in customer-experienced functionality?" The major tasks fix defects, introduce defensive programming, and modify the ways exceptions are handled.
- *Type decision D-3.* Type decision D-3 is "Did the activities substitute, add to, or expand some functionalities experienced by the customers?," and it is of *enhancive* type. This type implements modifications by enhancing the business rules to support more functionalities of the system. The major tasks are to add new subsystems and algorithms and modify the current ones to enhance their scope. The changes may affect customer experience of system functionality. D-3 is the default type in this group.

Example: A maintenance engineer, after analyzing all the documentation along with the program code, modified the program code for one component without modifying other documentation, built the rewritten component, executed the regression test suite, checked it into the version control, and embedded it into the production system. The only consequence the customer observed was improved latency. Question: Identify the type of software maintenance performed by the engineer [15].

From the activities reported it is apparent that criteria A and B evaluate to "Yes," whereas criterion C evaluates to "No." The given evidence leads to a "Yes" decision for the *performance* type in the Software Properties cluster. In addition, the evidence leads us to the *evaluative* type in the cluster Support Interface. In Figure 2.1, we identify the two types, namely, *performance* and *evaluative*, and note that the first type is higher up than the second one. Because *performance* type is higher up than *evaluative* type, one expects evidence of the *consultive, training, reformative, updative, preventive,* and *groomative* type, but not of the *adoptive, enhancive, corrective,* or *reductive* types. Therefore, *performance* is the dominant maintenance type for this example.

2.2   CATEGORIES OF MAINTENANCE CONCEPTS

In the previous section, we discussed different views of software maintenance. In this section, we describe some ways to organize maintenance activities. Organization of maintenance activities is conceptually similar to the organization of activities for software development. However, maintenance activities focus on product correction and adaptation, whereas development activities transform high-level requirements into working code. In this section, the key factors influencing the maintenance process are identified.

The domain concepts that influence software maintenance process can be classified into four categories:

- the product to be maintained;
- the types of maintenance to be performed;
- the maintenance organization processes to be followed; and
- the peopleware involved, that is, the people in the maintenance organization and in the customer/client organization.

The four categories and the concepts that influence the maintenance process have been illustrated in Figure 2.3. The concepts in each category are defined to understand the relationships among maintenance concepts. Next, we describe the characteristics of these concepts and their impacts on maintenance activities. This categorization enables one to know to what degree methods, tools, and skills for maintenance differ from those for software development [4]. In the following subsections, we explain the four dimensions of maintenance as depicted in Figure 2.3.

2.2.1   Maintained Product

The *maintained product* dimension is characterized by three concepts: *product, product upgrade,* and *artifacts.* We explain the characteristics of these concepts and their impacts on maintenance process.

 Product. A product is a coherent collection of several different artifacts. Source code is the key component of a software product. Other artifacts of interest include print manuals and online help.

 Product upgrade. Baseline is an arrangement of related entities that make up a particular software configuration. Any change or upgrade made to a software

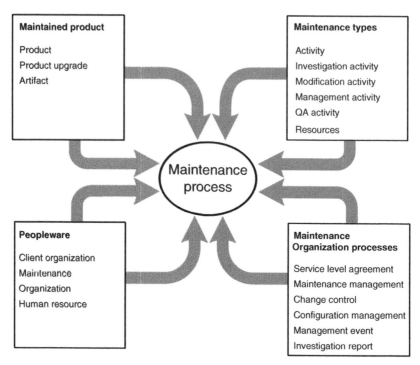

FIGURE 2.3   Overview of concept categories affecting software maintenance

product relates to a specific baseline. Note that an upgrade can create a new version of the system being maintained, a patch code for an object, or even a notice explaining a restriction on the use of the system. A restriction notice can be a release note saying that the product may not work with a specific version of a hardware.

Artifact. A number of different artifacts are used in the design of a software product and, similarly, a number of artifacts simultaneously exist along side a software product. One can find the following types of artifacts: textual and graphical documents, component off-the-shelf products, and object code components. Textual documents are readily understood by human readers: requirements specifications, plans, designs, and source code listings.

The key elements of the *maintained product* are size, age, application type, composition, and quality. The key characteristics of the aforementioned elements affecting maintenance performance are explained below.

The *size* of a software system affects the number of personnel needed to maintain the system. A small-size product can be maintained by a single person, whereas a medium-size product needs a team. However, for a large product one may need multiple maintenance teams. Maintenance activities on relatively large systems are generally less efficient than activities on small systems, because in a large product it is more difficult to: (i) conduct root cause analysis of some problems and (ii) identify ripple effects on the modules to support large enhancements.

The age of a software product, also known as *software geriatrics*, is the number of calendar years elapsed since its first release. The age of a software product can affect maintenance activities in various ways [17, 18]. It is difficult to maintain too old products for the following reasons: (i) it is difficult to find maintenance personnel for too old products, because of changes in development technologies; (ii) finding tools, namely, compilers and code analyzers, for very old systems is difficult; and (iii) the original or up-to-date development documentation may not be available for old products.

The life cycle stages of a software product have been listed in the first column of Table 2.4. The maintenance life cycle starts after the initial development and ends when the product is withdrawn from the market, as discussed in Section 3.3. The second column represents the corresponding maintenance tasks for each stage of maintenance. The third column represents typical size of user population associated with the product in that stage of its life cycle. It may be noted that large enhancements at the evolution stage can cause several patch releases at the servicing stage, considering the need for fixing faults (See Lehman's fifth law "conservation of familiarity.") Table 2.4 shows different types of maintenance tasks performed by an organization that are related to the maturity of a system.

Knowledge about the *application domain* influences productivities of software development and maintenance activities [19]. For example, a computer engineer will have stronger knowledge of IP (Internet Protocol) networking than an aerospace engineer. Hence, a computer engineer will be more productive in maintaining an IP network, whereas an aerospace engineer will be more productive in maintaining a software product to design airplane wings. In addition, application domains put constraints on maintenance of products and artifacts. For example, while maintaining a safety critical system, such as air traffic control, one must preserve—and, even increase—the product's reliability. On the other hand, in another application domain the concept of time-to-market may cause early deployment of a newer version of a system. Therefore, different application domains affect the same aspect of maintenance to different degrees.

The level of abstraction of the *product component* determines the skills required by the maintenance personnel and the tools they need to support the component. If the product has been derived from an in-house design, the maintenance personnel

TABLE 2.4   Staged Model Maintenance Task

Life Cycle Stage	Maintenance Task	User Population
Initial development	–	–
Evolution	Corrections, enhancements	Small
Servicing	Corrections	Growing
Phaseout	Corrections	Maximum
Closedown	Corrections	Declining

need access to the Computer-Aided Software Engineering (CASE) tools used by the software developers. On the other hand, if the product is composed of COTS components obtained from third parties, the maintenance engineers need integration and acceptance testing skills, and the required skills include development of supporting components such as *wrapper, glue,* and *tailoring.*

The *product quality* initially delivered to the customer places constraints on the subsequent maintenance activities. Intuitively, good quality artifacts are easier to maintain than poor quality ones. In the absence of communication between maintenance personnel and the original developers, quality of the product essentially determines the level of difficulty of maintaining the product. Documentation is often poor or even nonexistent for old products so maintenance personnel need specialized tools to reengineer the system.

2.2.2   Maintenance Types

We discussed different types of maintenance activities in Section 2.1. In this subsection, different types of maintenance activities are defined, followed by the impacts of those activities on maintenance performance.

> *Activity.* A number of different broad classes of maintenance activities are performed on software products, including investigation, modification, management, and quality assurance. An activity may be composed of several smaller sub-activities. Usually, an activity accepts some artifacts as inputs and produces new or changed artifacts. In the following, we briefly explain the four kinds of activities.
>
> *Investigation activity.* This kind of activities evaluate the impact of making a certain change to the system.
>
> *Modification activity.* This kind of activities change the system's implementation.
>
> *Management activity.* This kind of activities relate to the configuration control of the maintained system or the management of the maintenance process.
>
> *Quality assurance activity.* This kind of activities ensure that modifications performed on a system do not damage the integrity of the system. For example, regression testing is an example of quality assurance activities.

Maintenance personnel require different levels of understanding of the product by means of development tools so that they can execute the different maintenance modifications. For example, a corrective maintenance activity requires the ability to find the precise location of the faulty code and perform localized modifications. The maintenance engineers need to reproduce the bug in the test environment and may want to use tools to step through the suspected portion of code. On the other hand, an activity for quality or functionality enhancement requires a broad comprehension of large portions of the system. In addition, the maintenance engineer needs the development environment, such as version control, to check out and check in the code. The maintenance engineer may require re-engineering tools if the documentation is poor. The size and priority of the change are important features that impact the productivity and efficiency of the activities. Specifically, an enhancement with a large scope will involve a large number of maintenance personnel and it will incur more communication and coordination overhead. The priority of a maintenance activity affects the length of time needed for the change to be delivered to clients.

The efficiency and quality of investigation activities depend upon the knowledge of the maintenance engineers possess about the current status of the release, outstanding issues, and any planned modifications about the portion of the system involved. The effectiveness of the configuration control mechanism and control of the change process impact the availability of those information. To identify the status of each system component, a good configuration control process is required.

2.2.3 Maintenance Organization Processes

Two different levels of maintenance processes are followed within a maintenance organization:

- the individual-level maintenance processes followed by maintenance personnel to implement a specific CR and
- the organization-level process followed to manage the CRs from maintenance personnel, users, and customers/clients; this higher level of process is referred to as the maintenance organization process.

The software maintenance concepts defined below are used to modify one or more artifacts to implement a CR:

Development technology. This refers to the technology that was used to develop the original system and its constituent artifacts. The development technology constraints the maintenance procedures.

Paradigm. This refers to the philosophy adopted at the time of developing the original system. Some examples are procedural paradigm and object-oriented paradigm. This too constraints the possible maintenance procedures.

Procedure. A procedure can be a method, a technique, or a script. From a set of procedures, one is chosen to perform a specific activity.

Method. A method is a general, systematic procedure giving clear steps and heuristics to implement some activities.

Technique. A technique is a less rigorously defined procedure to realize an activity.

Script. A script is a general guideline to construct or amend a specific type of document.

Artifacts include plans, documents, system representations, and source and object code items. Artifacts are created during the software development process and changed during maintenance. A multitude of different scripts, techniques, and methods are used to create and change such artifacts. The performance of maintenance activities are impacted by the selection of development paradigm and development technology. It is also impacted by the degree of automation of procedures. In general, development paradigm and development technologies put limitations on maintenance activities and skill requirements. For example, if the service-oriented architecture (SOA) paradigm is used for the software development process, then the maintenance engineers must be well versed with the SOA.

Next, we briefly define the concepts of the maintenance organization processes and then discuss the impact of these concepts on maintenance.

Service-level agreement (SLA). This is a contract between the customers and the providers of a maintenance service. Performance targets for the maintenance services are specified in the SLA.

Maintenance management. This process is used to manage the maintenance service, which is not the same as managing individual CRs. An organization process is set up and run by the senior management. They create a structure of the maintenance team so that service-level agreement can be executed. In addition to fulfilling the roles of regular processes, such as project management and quality assurance, maintenance management handles events, change control, and configuration control.

Event management. The stream of events, namely, all the CRs from various sources, received by the maintenance organization, is handled in an event management process.

Change control. Evaluation of results of investigations of maintenance events is performed in a process called change control. Based on the evaluation, the organization approves a system change.

Configuration management. A system's integrity is maintained by means of a configuration management process. Integrity of a product is maintained in terms of its modification status and version number.

Maintenance organization structure. This is the hierarchy of roles assigned to maintenance personnel to perform administrative tasks.

Maintenance event. This is a problem report or a CR originating from within the maintenance organization or from the customers.

Investigation report. This is the outcome of assessing the cause and impacts of a maintenance event.

Three major elements of a maintenance organization are event management, configuration management, and change control system, as explained before in this section. A maintenance organization handles maintenance requests from users, customers, and maintainers. If any of the three elements is not adequate, maintenance will be inefficient and product quality is likely to be compromised. The efficiency of maintenance activities is highly influenced by support tools. There are many tools, namely, ManageEngine and Zendesk, to assist event management. The type and volume of CRs affect the performance of the maintenance organization. As an example, if many defects are reported in a short time, there may not be enough resources to carry out modifications.

After an initial investigation of a CR, a management process is put in place for approving change activities. Approval of a CR is normally the responsibility of a change control board. A change control board is organized as a formal process with meetings between maintenance managers, clients, users, and customers. A proposed modification activity is scheduled only after the modification is approved by the board and an SLA is signed with the client. The level of formality adopted in change control board procedures can affect the quality and efficiency of performing changes. A formal change control board generally slows down the maintenance process but is better at protecting the integrity of the systems being maintained.

SLAs describe the maintenance organization's performance targets. It can be used by maintenance personnel as a guidance to meet customer's expectations. SLAs should be based on results rather than effort, and maintenance organizations must be prepared to meet their SLAs. In general, maintenance organizations use three different support levels to organize the staff:

- *Level 1*. This group files problem reports and identifies the technical support person who can best assist the person reporting a problem.
- *Level 2*. This level includes experts who know how to communicate with users and analyze their problems. These people recommend quick fixes and temporary workarounds.
- *Level 3*. This level includes programmers who can perform actual changes to the product software.

Note that not all maintenance works cause changes in the system. In many situations, users may need advice on how to continue to use the system or in what ways they can bypass a problem.

2.2.4 Peopleware

Maintenance activities cannot ignore the human element, because software production and maintenance are human-intensive activities. The three people-centric concepts related to maintenance are as follows:

Maintenance organization. This is the organization that maintains the product(s).

Client organization. A client organization uses the maintained system and it has a clear relationship with the maintenance organization. The said relationship is described in the SLA.

Human resource. Human resource includes personnel from the maintenance and client organizations. Maintenance organization personnel include managers and engineers, whereas client organization personnel include customers and users. The management negotiates with the customers to find out the SLA, scheduling of requirement enhancements, and cost.

In general, maintenance tasks are perceived to be less challenging, and, hence, less well rewarded than original work. Often maintenance tasks are partly assigned to newly recruited programmers, which has a significant impact on productivity and quality. A novice programmer may introduce new defects while resolving an incident because of an absence in understanding the whole system. Normally, more skilled maintenance personnel produce more and better quality works.

Separation between development staff and maintenance staff impacts the maintenance process. On one hand, there is no real separation between maintenance and development. In such a scenario, the product undergoes continual evolution. The developers incorporate maintenance activities into a continuing process for planned enhancements. In this case, the tools and procedures are the same for both the development and maintenance activities. On the other hand, there are maintenance organizations which operate with minimal interactions with the development departments. Occasionally, the maintenance group may not be located in the same organization that produced the software. In such a scenario, maintenance engineers may need specially designed tools. Maintenance managers need to focus on the aforementioned issues when signing SLAs. Finally, the following user and customer issues affect maintenance:

- *Size.* The size of the customer base and the number of licenses they hold affect the amount of effort needed to support a system.
- *Variability.* High variability in the customer base impacts the scope of maintenance tasks.
- *Common goals.* The extent to which the users and the customer have common goals affects the SLAs. Ultimately, customers fund maintenance activities. If the customers do not have a good understanding of the requirements of the actual users, some SLAs may not be appropriate to the end users.

2.3   EVOLUTION OF SOFTWARE SYSTEMS

The term *evolution* was used by Mark I. Halpern in circa 1965 to define the dynamic growth of software [20]. It attracted more attention in the 1980s after Meir M. Lehman proposed eight broad principles about how certain types of software systems evolve [21–24]. Bennett and Rajlich [25] researched the term "software evolution," but found no widely accepted definition of the term. However, some researchers and

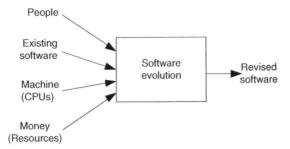

FIGURE 2.4   Inputs and outputs of software evolution. From Reference 26. © 1988 John Wiley & Sons

practitioners used the term software evolution as a substitute for the term software maintenance. Lowell Jay Arthur distinguished the two terms as follows:

- *Maintenance* means preserving software from decline or failure.
- *Evolution* means a continuously changing software from a worse state to a better state (p. 1 of Ref. [26]). Software evolution is like a computer program, with inputs, processes, and outputs (p. 246 of Ref. [26]) (See Figure 2.4).

Keith H. Bennett and Jie Xu [27] use "maintenance" for all post-delivery support, whereas they use "evolution" to refer to perfective modifications—modifications triggered by changes in requirements. Ned Chapin defines software evolution as:

"the applications of software maintenance activities and processes that generate a new operational software version with a changed customer-experienced functionality or properties from a prior operational version, where the time period between versions may last from less than a minute to decades, together with the associated quality assurance activities and processes, and with the management of the activities and processes" (p. 21 of Ref. [15]).

The majority of software maintenance changes are concerned with evolutions triggered by user requests for changes in the requirements. The following are the key properties of software evolution as desired by the stakeholders:

- Changes are accomplished quickly and in a cost-effective manner.
- The reliability of the software should not be degraded by those changes.
- The maintainability of the system should not degrade. Otherwise, future changes will be more expensive to carry out.

Software evolution is studied with two broad, complementary approaches, namely, *explanatory* and *process improvement*, and those describe the *what* and *how* aspects, respectively, of software evolution.

- *Explanatory (what/why).* This approach attempts to explain the causes of software evolution, the processes used, and the effects of software evolution. The explanatory approach studies evolution from a *scientific* view point. In this approach, the *nature* of the evolution phenomenon is studied, and one strives to understand its driving factors and impacts.

- *Process improvement (how)*. This approach attempts to manage the effects of software evolution by developing better methods and tools, namely, design, maintenance, refactoring, and reengineering. The process improvement approach studies evolution from an *engineering* view point. It focuses on the more pragmatic aspects that assist the developers in their daily routines. Therefore, methods, tools, and activities that provide the means to direct, implement, and control software evolution are at the core of the process improvement approach.

2.3.1   SPE Taxonomy

The abbreviation SPE refers to S (Specified), P (Problem), and E (Evolving) programs. In circa 1980, Meir M. Lehman [24] proposed an SPE classification scheme to explain the ways in which programs vary in their evolutionary characteristics. The classification scheme is characterized by: (i) how a program interacts with its environment and (ii) the degree to which the environment and the underlying problem that the program addresses can change. He observed a key difference between software developed to meet a fixed set of requirements and software developed to solve a real-world problem which changes with time. The observation leads to the identification of types S (Specified), P (Problem), and E (Evolving) programs. In the following, we explain the SPE concepts in detail.

S-type programs: S-type programs have the following characteristics:

- All the nonfunctional and functional program properties that are important to its stakeholders are *formally* and *completely* defined.
- Correctness of the program with respect to its formal specification is the *only* criterion of the acceptability of the solution to its stakeholders.

A formal definition of the problem is viewed as the specification of the program. S-type programs solve problems that are fully defined in abstract and closed ways. Examples of S-type programs include calculation of the lowest common multiple of two integers and to perform matrix addition, multiplication, and inversion [28]. The problem is completely defined, and there are one or more correct solutions to the problem as stated. The solution is well known, so the developer is concerned not with the correctness of the solution but with the correctness of the implementation of the solution. As illustrated in Figure 2.5, the specification directs and controls the programmers in creating the program that defines the desired solution. The problem statement, the program, and the solution may relate to a real world—and the real world can change. However, if the real world changes, the original problem turns into a completely *new problem* that must be respecified. But then it has a *new program* to provide a solution. It may be possible and time saving to derive a new program from

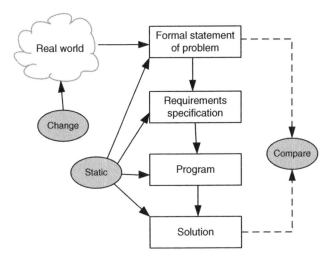

FIGURE 2.5   S-type programs

the old one, but it is a *different* program that defines a solution to a *different* problem. The program remains almost the same in the sense that it does not accommodate changes in the problem that generates it [29]. In the real world, S-type systems are rare. However, it is an important concept that evolution of software does not occur under some conditions.

P-type programs: With many real problems, the system outputs are accurate to a constrained level of precision. The concept of correctness is difficult to define in those programs. Therefore, approximate solutions are developed for pragmatic reasons. Numerical problems, except computations with integers and rational numbers, are resolved through approximations. For example, consider a program to play chess. Since the rules of chess are completely defined, the problem can be completely specified. At each step of the game a solution might involve calculating the various moves and their impacts to determine the next best move. However, complete implementation of such a solution may not be possible, because the number of moves is too large to be evaluated in a given time duration. Therefore, one must develop an approximate solution that is more practical while being acceptable.

In order to develop this type of solution, we describe the problem in an abstract way and write the requirement specification accordingly. A program developed this way is of P-type because it is based on a practical abstraction of the problem, instead of relying on a completely defined specification. Even though an exact solution may exist, the solution produced by a P-type program is tampered by the environment in which it must be produced. The solution of a P-type program is accepted if the program outcomes make sense to the stakeholder(s) in the world in which the problem is embedded. As illustrated in Figure 2.6, P-type programs are more dynamic than S-type programs. P-type programs are likely to change in an incremental fashion. If the output of the solution is unacceptable, then the problem abstraction may

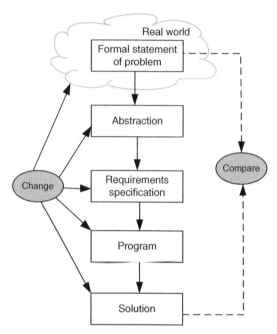

FIGURE 2.6   P-type programs

be changed and the requirements modified to make the new solution more realistic. Note that the program resulting from the changes cannot be considered a new solution to a new problem. Rather, it is a modification of the old solution to better fit the existing problem. In addition, the real world may change, hence the problem changes.

E-type programs: An E-type program is one that is embedded in the real world and it changes as the world does. These programs mechanize a human or society activity, make simplifying assumptions, and interface with the external world by requiring or providing services. An E-type system is to be regularly adapted to: (i) stay true to its domain of application; (ii) remain compatible with its executing environment; and (iii) meet the goals and expectations of its stakeholders [30].

Figure 2.7 illustrates the dependence of an E-type program on its environment and the consequent changeability. The acceptance of an E-type program entirely depends upon the stakeholders' opinion and judgment of the solution. Their descriptions cannot be completely formalized to permit the demonstration of correctness, and their operational domains are potentially unbounded. The first characteristic of an E-type program is that the outcome of executing the program is not definitely predictable. Therefore, for E-type programs, the concept of correctness is left up to the stakeholders. That is, the criterion of acceptability is the stakeholders' satisfaction with each program execution [31]. An E-type program's second characteristic

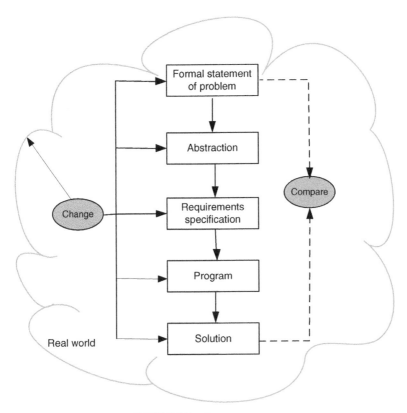

FIGURE 2.7   E-type programs

is that program execution changes its operational domain, and the evolution process is viewed as a feedback system [32]. Figure 2.8 [33] succinctly illustrates the feedback process.

2.3.2   Laws of Software Evolution

Lehman and his colleagues have postulated eight "laws" over 20 years starting from the mid-1970s to explain some key observations about the evolution of E-type software systems [34, 35]. The laws themselves have evolved from three in 1974 to eight by 1997, as listed in Table 2.5. The eight laws are the results of empirical studies of the evolution of large-scale proprietary software—also called closed source software (CSS)—in a variety of corporate settings. The laws primarily relate to perfective maintenance. These laws are largely based on the concept of feedback existing in the software environment. Their description of the phenomena are intertwined, and the laws are not to be studied separately. The numbering of the laws has no significance apart from the sequence of their development.

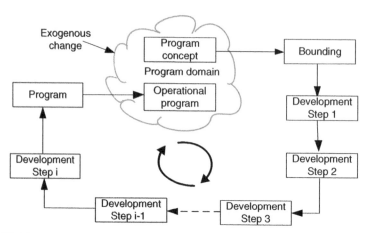

FIGURE 2.8 E-type programs with feedback. From Reference 33. © 2006 John Wiley & Sons

TABLE 2.5 Laws of Software Evolution

Names of the Laws	Brief Descriptions
I. Continuing change (1974)	E-type programs must be continually adapted, else they become progressively less satisfactory.
II. Increasing complexity (1974)	As an E-type program evolves, its complexity increases unless work is done to maintain or reduce it.
III. Self-regulation (1974)	The evolution process of E-type programs is self-regulating, with the time distribution of measures of processes and products being close to normal.
IV. Conservation of organizational stability (1978)	The average effective global activity rate in an evolving E-type program is invariant over the product's lifetime.
V. Conservation of familiarity (1978)	The average content of successive releases is constant during the life cycle of an evolving E-type program.
VI. Continuing growth (1991)	To maintain user satisfaction with the program over its lifetime, the functional content of an E-type program must be continually increased.
VII. Declining quality (1996)	An E-type program is perceived by its stakeholders to have declining quality if it is not maintained and adapted to its environment.
VIII. Feedback system (1971–1996)	The evolution processes in E-type programs constitute multi-agent, multi-level, multi-loop feedback systems.

Source: Adapted from Lehman et al. [34]. ©1997 IEEE.

Lehman's laws were not meant to be used in a mathematical sense, as, say, Newton's laws are used in physics. Rather, those were intended to capture stable, long-term knowledge about the common features of changing software systems, in the same sense social scientists use laws to characterize general principles applying to some classes of social situations [30]. The term "laws" was used because the observed phenomena were beyond the influence of managers and developers. The laws were an attempt to study the nature of software evolutions and the evolutionary trajectory likely taken by software.

First Law *Continuing change: E-type programs must be continually adapted, else they become progressively less satisfactory.* Many assumptions are embedded in an E-type program. A subset of those assumptions may be *complete* and *valid* at the initial release of the product; that is, the program performed satisfactorily even if not all assumptions were satisfied. As users continue to use a system over time, they gain more experience, and their needs and expectations grow. As the application's environment changes in terms of the number of sophisticated users, a growing number of assumptions become *invalid*. Consequently, new requirements and new CRs will emerge. In addition, changes in the real world will occur and the application will be impacted, requiring changes to be made to the program to restore it to an acceptable model. When the updated and modified program is reintroduced into the operational domain, it continues to satisfy user needs for a while; next, more changes occur in the operation environment, additional user needs are identified, and additional CRs are made. As a result, the evolution process moves into a vicious cycle.

Second Law *Increasing complexity: As an E-type program evolves, its complexity increases unless work is done to maintain or reduce it.* As the program evolves, its complexity grows because of the imposition of changes after changes on the program. In order to incorporate new changes, more objects, modules, and sub-systems are added to the system. As a consequence, there is much increase in: (i) the effort expended to ensure an adequate and correct interface between the old and new elements; (ii) the number of errors and omissions; and (iii) the possibility of inconsistency in their assumptions. Such increases lead to a decline in the product quality and in the evolution rate, unless additional work is performed to arrest the decline. The only way to avoid this from happening is to invest in preventive maintenance, where one spends time to improve the structure of the software without adding to its functionality.

Third Law *Self-regulation: The evolution process of E-type programs is self-regulating, with the time distribution of measures of processes and products being close to normal.* This law states that large programs have a dynamics of their own; attributes such as size, time between releases, and the number of reported faults are approximately invariant from release to release because of fundamental structural and organizational factors. In an industrial setup E-type programs are designed and coded by a team of experts working in a larger context comprising a variety of management entities, namely, finance, business, human resource, sales, marketing, support, and user process. The various groups within the large organization apply constraining information controls and reinforcing information controls influenced by past and present performance indicators. Their actions control, check, and balance the resource usage, which is a kind of feedback-driven growth and stabilization mechanism. This establishes a self-controlled dynamic system whose process and product parameters are normally distributed as a result of a huge number of largely independent implementation and managerial decisions [36].

Fourth Law *Conservation of organizational stability: The average effective global activity rate in an evolving E-type program is invariant over the product's lifetime.* This law suggests that most large software projects work in a "stationary" state, which means that changes in resources or staffing have small effects on long-term evolution of the software. To a certain extent management certainly do control resource allocation and planning of activities. However, as suggested by the third law, program evolution is essentially independent of management decisions. In some instances, as indicated by Brooks [37], situations may arise where additional resources may reduce the effective rate of productivity output due to higher communication overhead or decrease in process quality. In reality, activities during the life cycle of a system are not exclusively decided by management but by a wide spectrum of controls and feedback inputs [38].

Fifth Law *Conservation of familiarity: The average content of successive releases is constant during the life cycle of an evolving E-type program.* As an E-type system evolves, both developers and users must try to develop mastery of its content and behavior. Thus, after every major release, established familiarity with the application and the system in general is counterbalanced by a decline in the detail knowledge and mastery of the system. This would be expected to produce a temporary slow down in the growth rate of the system as it is recognized that the system must be cleaned up to simplify the process of re-familiarization. In practice, adding new features to a program invariably introduces new program faults due to unfamiliarity with the new functionality and the new operational environment. The more changes are made in a new release, the more faults will be introduced. The law suggests that one should not include a large number of features in a new release without taking into account the need for fixing the newly introduced faults. Conservation of familiarity implies that maintenance engineers need to have the same high level of understanding of a new release even if more functionalities have been added to it.

Sixth Law *Continuing growth: To maintain user satisfaction with the program over its lifetime, the functional content of an E-type program must be continually increased.* It is useful to note that programs exhibit finite behaviors, which implies that they have limited properties relative to the potential of the application domain. Properties excluded by the limitedness of the programs eventually become a source of performance constraints, errors, and irritation. To eliminate all those negative attributes, it is needed to make the system grow.

It is important to distinguish this law from the first law which focuses on "Continuing Change." The first law captures the fact that an E-type software's operational domain undergoes continual changes. Those changes are partly driven by installation and operation of the system and partly by other forces; an example of other forces is human desire for improvement and perfection. These two laws—the first and the sixth—reflect distinct phenomena and different mechanisms. When phenomena are observed, it is often difficult to determine which of the two laws underlies the observation.

Seventh Law *Declining quality: An E-type program is perceived by its stakeholders to have declining quality if it is not maintained and adapted to its environment.* This law directly follows from the first and the sixth laws. An E-Type program must undergo changes in the forms of adaptations and extensions to remain satisfactory in a changing operational domain. Those changes are very likely to degrade the performance and will potentially inject more faults into the evolving program. In addition, the complexity (e.g., the cyclomatic measure) of the program in terms of interactions between its components increases, and the program structure deteriorates. The term for this increase in complexity over time is called *entropy*. The average rate at which software entropy increases is about 1–3 per calendar year [17]. There is significant decline in stakeholder satisfaction because of growing entropy, declining performance, increasing number of faults, and mismatch of operational domains. The aforementioned factors also cause a decline in software quality from the user's perspective [39]. The decline of software quality over time is related to the growth in entropy associated with software product aging [18] or code decay [8]. Therefore, it is important to continually undertake preventive measures to reduce the entropy by improving the software's overall architecture, high-level and low-level design, and coding.

Eighth Law *Feedback system: The evolution processes in E-type programs constitute multi-agent, multi-level, multi-loop feedback systems.* Several laws of software revolution refer to the role of information feedback in the life cycles of software. The eighth law is based on the observation that evolution process of the E-type software constitutes a multi-level, multi-loop, multi-agent feedback system: (i) multi-loop means that it is an iterative process; (ii) multi-level refers to the fact that it occurs in more than one aspect of the software and its documentation; and (iii) a multi-agent software system is a computational system where software agents cooperate and compete to achieve some individual or collective tasks. Feedback will determine and constrain the manner in which the software agents communicate among themselves to change their behavior [40].

Remark: There are two types of aging in software life cycles: software process execution aging and software product aging. The first one manifests in degradation in performance or transient failures in continuously running the software system. The second one manifests in degradation of quality of software code and documentation due to frequent changes. The following aging-related *symptoms* in software were identified by Visaggio [41]:

- *Pollution.* Pollution means that there are many modules or components in a system which are not used in the delivery of the business functions of the system.
- *Embedded knowledge.* Embedded knowledge is the knowledge about the application domain that has been spread throughout the program such that the knowledge cannot be precisely gathered from the documentation.

- *Poor lexicon.* Poor lexicon means that the component identifiers have little lexical meaning or are incompatible with the commonly understood meaning of the components that they identify.
- *Coupling.* Coupling means that the programs and their components are linked by an elaborate network of control flows and data flows.

Remark: The code is said to have decayed if it is very difficult to change it, as reflected by the following three key responses: (i) the cost of the change, which is effective only on the personnel cost for the developers who implement it; (ii) the calendar or clock time to make the changes; and (iii) the quality of the changed software. It is important to note that code decay is antithesis of evolution in the sense that while the evolution process is intended to make the code better, changes are generally degenerative thereby leading to code decay.

2.3.3 Empirical Studies

Empirical studies are aimed at acquiring knowledge about the effectiveness of processes, methods, techniques, and tools used in software development and maintenance. Similarly, the laws of software evolution are prime candidates for empirical studies, because we want to know to what extent they hold. In circa 1976, Belady and Lehman [22] studied 20 releases of the OS/360 operating system. The results of their study led them to postulate five laws of software evolution: continuing change, increasing complexity, self-regulation, conservation of organizational stability, and conservation of familiarity. Those laws were further developed in an article published in 1980 [24]. Yuen [36, 42] further studied their five laws of evolution. He re-examined three different systems from Belady and Lehman [22] and several other systems and examined a variety of dependent variables. The number and percentage of modules handled are examples of dependent variables. After re-examining the data from previous studies, he observed that the characteristics observed for OS/360 did not necessarily hold for other systems. Specifically, the first two laws were supported, while the remaining three laws were not. Yuen, a collaborator of Lehman, notes that these three laws are more based upon those of human organizations involved in the maintenance process rather than the properties of the software itself.

Later, in a project entitled FEAST (Feedback, Evolution, And Software Technology), Lehman and his colleagues studied evolution of releases from four CSS systems: (i) two operating systems (OS/360 of IBM and VME OS of ICL); (ii) one financial system (Logica's FW banking transaction system); and (iii) a real-time telecommunication system (Lucent Technologies). Their results are summarized as a set of growth curves, as described by Lehman, Perry, and Ramil [43]. The studies suggest that during the maintenance process a system tracks a growth curve that can be approximated either as linear or inverse square [44]. The inverse square model represents the growth phenomena as an inverse square of the continuing effort. Those trends increase the confidence of validity of the following six laws: Continuing change (I), Increasing complexity (II), Self-regulation (III), Conservation of familiarity (V),

Continuing growth (VI), and Feedback system (VII). Confidence in the seventh law "Declining quality" is based on the theoretical analysis, whereas the fourth law "Conservation of organizational stability" is neither supported nor falsified based on the metric presented. In 1982, there was an independent study by Lawrence [45], who took a statistical approach to observe some evidence supporting laws I and II, while laws III–V were not supported by the data.

Inverse square law. According to the fourth law, the incremental effort, denoted by E, expended on each release stays the same during the evolution of the system. It is assumed that the incremental effort expended on each release is almost the same during the system evolution. Let Δ_i denote the incremental change of the system size and assume that it is solely due to the effort E expended on the ith release. To relate E and Δ_i, we need to consider a conceptual factor s_i, which behaves in this context like mass in dynamic physical systems. A larger s_i implies a greater resistance to change, and a smaller Δ_i will be obtained from expending effort E. Thus, $\Delta_i = E/s_i$ is the first, simple relation that appears in the view. Assume that the size of the system is expressed in terms of *number of modules,* and complexity is expressed in terms of the *number of intermodule interactions.* By considering the number of intermodule interactions to be proportional to the square of the number of modules, one can obtain a relationship as follows: $\Delta_i = E/s_i^2$, which is called the *inverse square law.* We assume that the law is valid and obtain the following expressions:

$$s_1 = s_1$$
$$s_2 = s_1 + E/s_1^2$$
$$s_3 = s_2 + E/s_2^2$$
$$\dots$$

By means of substitution we get:

$$s_1 = s_1$$
$$s_2 = s_1 + E/s_1^2$$
$$s_3 = s_2 + E/s_2^2 = s_1 + E\left(1/s_1^2 + 1/s_2^2\right)$$
$$\dots$$

Similarly, we get:

$$E_1 = \frac{s_2 - s_1}{1/s_1^2}$$
$$E_2 = \frac{s_3 - s_1}{1/s_1^2 + 1/s_2^2}$$
$$\dots$$

where the right-hand sides of the equations contain data about releases and nothing else. Thus, one can compute the mean of n values of E as $\overline{E} = (\sum_{i=1}^{n} E_i)/n$. $\overline{E}$ can be interpreted as the mean effort required per release, which can be considered to be a good approximation of the "constant" effort throughout the system evolution. Employing $\overline{E}$, system evolution is described by using the inverse square law as follows:

$$s_1 = s_1$$

$$s_2 = s_1 + \overline{E}/s_1^2$$

$$s_3 = s_2 + \overline{E}/s_2^2$$

$$\cdots$$

$$s_n = s_{n-1} + \overline{E}/s_{n-1}^2$$

The aforementioned relationship is consistent with the view that increasing complexity, captured in the second law, restrains growth. The inverse square law has an interesting property. By showing that the model closely matches the evolution pattern of a system, one may accurately predict the size of the subsequent releases after the data about the first few releases are available.

2.3.4 Practical Implications of the Laws

Based on the eight laws, Lehman suggested more than 50 rules for management, control, and planning [35] of software evolution. Those 50+ rules are put into three broad categories: assumptions management, evolution management, and release management [46].

Assumptions management. Several assumptions are made by different personnel involved throughout the life cycle of a project. When a software project fails, the primary source of failure can be traced back to those assumptions. It is generally found that some of those assumptions were never valid in the first place, or it is more likely that some of the assumptions became invalid as a result of changes outside the software system. Therefore, management of assumptions plays a key role in successful execution of projects involving E-type software. The following is a list of activities for managing assumptions.

- Identify and capture the assumptions pertinent to the project. The difficulty lies in completely identifying all the assumptions.
- Initiate periodic reviews to assess any need to correct or update the list of assumptions.
- Review and revalidate the assumptions whenever a change occurs in the specification, design, implementation, or operational domain.

- Where software operates in a rapidly changing environment, complement detailed assumption review process with re-writing of appropriate components of the software.
- Develop and use tools to track all the above activities.

Evolution management. In this section, the discussion has mainly referred to the evolution of software as reflected in a series of releases or upgrades. Recommendation relating to evolution and maintenance process includes the following list of items:

- Consistently assess and pursue antiregressive work such as complexity control, restructuring, and full documentation. The phrase antiregressive work means the work to be performed to reduce a program's complexity with no modifications to the user perceived functionality delivered by the system. As part of the development and maintenance responsibility, carry out antiregressive activities. This may not have an immediate impact on stakeholders, but this will facilitate future evolvability.
- Ensure that documentation includes identification and recording of assumptions.
- Assess the trends in the evolutions of the functional and nonfunctional requirements of the software product in advance. Review those trends during the release planning while taking the operational domain into consideration.
- Involve application and operational domain specialists in the assessment.
- Use tools to support data collection, modeling, and related activities.
- Acquire, plot, model, and interpret historical evolution metrics to project trends, patterns, growth, and their rate of changes in order to improve planning and processes.
- When validating incremental growth, assess the impact on the unchanged parts of the system and assumptions.
- Establish baselines of key measures over time to support evolution and maintenance planning and control.

Release management. A software release can be categorized as *safe, risky*, or *unsafe* according to the condition described as follows. Let m be the mean of the incremental growth m_i of the system in going from release i to release $i + 1$ and s be the standard deviation of the incremental growth. The release is *safe* if the content of the ith desired release (say, m_i) is less than or equal to m. The release is said to be *risky* if the content of the desired release is greater than m but less than $m + 2s$. Finally, the release is *unsafe* if the content of the desired release is close to or greater than $m + 2s$. Based on the aforementioned concepts of safety, concrete activities for release management are as follows:

- Ensure that the release is *safe*.
- When the release is not *safe*, then distribute the growth across several releases to make individual releases safe.

- If excessive functional increments are unavoidable, plan for follow-on clean-up releases with a focus on fixing defects and updating documentation.
- Follow established software engineering principles, namely, information hiding to minimize spread of changes between system elements.
- By allocating resources, put emphasis on antiregressive work, namely, restructuring, eliminating dead code, and reengineering.
- Consider the alternation of enhancement and extension with clean-up and restructuring releases.

The model discussed in this section concentrated on systems developed under industrial software process paradigm, namely, Closed Source Software (CSS) and extension of the waterfall model. The discussion has mainly referred to the evolution of software as reflected in a series of releases or upgrades. But general validity of the laws of Lehman in the context of newer paradigms, such as open source, agile programming, and COTS-based development, cannot be taken for granted. Hence, we discuss the evolution of free and open source software (FOSS) systems next.

2.3.5 Evolution of FOSS Systems

FOSS is a class of software that is both free software and open source. It is liberally licensed to grant users the right to use, copy, study, change, and improve its design through availability of its source code. The FOSS movement is attributed to Richard M. Stallman, who started the GNU project in circa 1984, and a supporting organization, the Free Software Foundation [47]. It is often emphasized that free software is a "matter of liberty not price" [48]. FOSS—also referred to as FLOSS (Free/Libre/Open Sources Software)—systems have attracted much academic and commercial interests due to the accessibility to large amounts of code and other free artifacts. Gradually, more and more software systems were developed by Open Source Community (OSC). Compared with CSS development methods, FOSS have lots of new characteristics. Eric Raymond concisely documented the FOSS approach in an article entitled "The Cathedral and the Bazaar" [49]. In this section, we briefly describe the differences between the evolutions of FOSS-based software and CSS-based software in terms of: (i) team structure; (ii) process; (iii) releases; and (iv) global factors [50–52].

Team structure. In traditional CSS development, organizations often have dedicated groups to carry out evolution tasks. These groups are staffed with specialist maintenance personnel. In contrast, FOSS development is very different. Even though several FOSS communities have core teams to manage evolution activities on a daily basis, most works are done voluntarily.

An onion model of FOSS development has been illustrated in Figure 2.9 [53, 54]. According to this model, a core sustainable community consists of a small group of key members, additional contributing developers, and a large number of active users who report defects. The outer layer represents those users who are not actively involved in the development process. The onion model has three primary

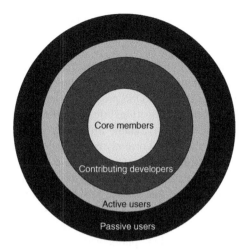

FIGURE 2.9   Onion model of FOSS development structure

characteristics: (i) a small core team; (ii) contributing developers add and maintain features; and (iii) active users take ownership of system testing and defect reporting. In the FOSS evolution model, numerous nomadic volunteers work together as a community. Therefore, one should consider the change of people in the evaluation of evolution of FOSS-based software.

Process. The FOSS development process is lighter than CSS development process followed in companies, where requirement documents and design specifications are indispensable. There are strict rules about coding style, documentation, and defect fixes. On the other hand, in FOSS development, requirement specification and detailed design documentations take a back seat, at least from the user's perspectives.

Though there are standards for coding and documenting, these are less relaxedly adhered compared to traditional CSS development. In FOSS development, source code comprises the main artifact for disseminating knowledge among the developers. Therefore, FOSS activities are largely confined to coding and testing. To overcome the ensuing difficulties due to not following a document-driven development process, an array of supplementary information is provided: release notes, defect databases, configuration management facilities, and email lists. For some projects, some developers act as the "gate keepers" for any revision to the code. Each project community makes their own rules to regulate the submission of bug fixes and new functionalities. Systematic testing is not always present compared to CSS-based projects. However, in FOSS projects, due to the large number of developers and beta-testers, almost all the issues can be quickly characterized and the fix is obvious to someone. As observed by Eric S. Raymond [49], "given enough eyeballs, all bugs are shallow." This is known as *Linus's Law*: the more widely available the source code is for public testing, scrutiny, and experimentation, the more rapidly all forms of defects are discovered.

Remark: Linus's law was attributed to a Finnish software engineer, Linus Benedict Torvals by Eric S. Raymond. He was the lead of the Linux kernel project and later became the chief architect of the Linux operating system and the project coordinator.

Releases. A key attribute of FOSS is that code is shared with almost no constraints. Compared to CSS development, FOSS development generally do not have schedule for regular releases. However, larger FOSS projects do have stated goals and releases are generally scheduled in terms of functionalities to be delivered. In general, there are two related streams of source code: (i) a stable stream of code for distribution and (ii) a development stream. The latter one is currently being modified and improved. At some instant, the development stream becomes stable and is released. The development stream is frozen for a few days prior to a milestone release to identify critical problems. When it is determined that critical problems have been resolved and the code is indeed stable, then the code is released [55]. However, it is a common behavior in many FOSS projects to follow the rule: "release early, release often." The above rule means that the code is available to public well before it is stable.

Global factors. In the FOSS development paradigm, developers working on even a very small project might be living in many countries around the world, due to the pervasive use of the world-wide web (WWW). With globalization on the rise, the collaborators hail from many countries with a variety of cultural backgrounds. FOSS development becomes very challenging because of the need to coordinate the geographically distributed developers. Though many companies have their development teams spread out in many countries, most of the traditional companies develop systems with their local teams and, occasionally, the system is tested at an overseas location.

Empirical Studies of FOSS Evolution   In circa 1988, Pirzada [56] analyzed the dissimilarities between the systems studied by Lehman and Belady [32] and the evolution of the Unix operating system. It was argued that the differences between commercial development and development for academic purposes could lead to differences in their evolutionary trajectories. In circa 2000, empirical study of FOSS evolution was conducted by Godfrey and Tu [57]. They provided the trend of growth between 1994 and 1999 for the Linux operating system (OS), which is a popular FOSS system, and showed its rate of growth to be superlinear. Specifically, they found that the size of the Linux followed a quadratic growth trend, and at that time the OS was about 2+ million lines of code (LOCs). In circa 2002, Schach et al. [58] studied the evolution of 365 versions of Linux and showed that module coupling, that is interconnection of modules, has been growing exponentially. They argued that unless efforts to alleviate this situation is undertaken, the Linux OS would become unmaintainable. Their argument was fully consistent with Lehman's sixth and seventh laws. However, it appears to be at odds with the third and the fifth laws, which are self-regulation and conservation of familiarity, respectively. Robles et al. [59], while replicating Godfrey and Tu's study, concluded that Lehman's fourth law (conservation of organizational stability) does not fit well with large-scale FOSS systems such as Linux. This behavior of exponential growth may be considered as an anomaly as pointed out by Lehman et al. [60]. The evolutionary behavior of other

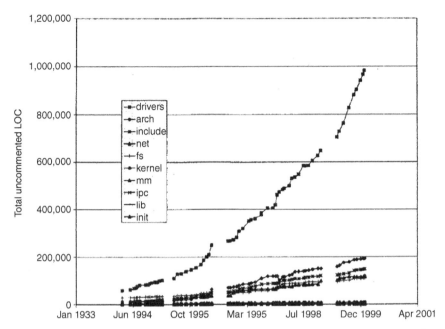

FIGURE 2.10   Growth of the major subsystems (development releases only) of the Linux OS. From Reference 57. © 2000 IEEE

FOSS systems such as *Gcc*, *Linux kernel*, *Apache*, *Brocade library*, and *Zlib* appears to follow Lehman's laws for software evolution [61, 62].

Godfrey and Tu observed that the growth rate was more for the device-driver subsystem of Linux as can be seen from Figure 2.10. As a matter of fact, the device-drivers appear to be mutually independent. Therefore, adding a new driver does not raise the subsystem's complexity. Another characteristic of Linux is that the system gives a false impression that it is larger than it really is. The "larger-than-real-size" impression is observed due to the fact that certain features, say, supporting different CPU types, are implemented with code replication (software clones).

Moreover, participation of an unrestricted pool of (novice) developers may explain this, that is, software clones. In order to have a better understanding of how a system is evolving, it is necessary to analyze and understand each subsystem within and across software releases irrespective of FOSS or CSS systems. This observation has been reported by Gall et al. based on the study of a CSS: a large telecommunication switching system [63].

2.4   MAINTENANCE OF COTS-BASED SYSTEMS

Component-based development has an intuitive underlying idea. Instead of developing a system by programming it entirely from scratch, develop it by using preexisting building blocks, components, and plug them together as required to built the target system. Components are nearly independent and replaceable parts of a system. Special components called Commercial-off-the-shelf (COTS) can be purchased on a component market. Often, these types of components are delivered without their source code. The use of COTS components is increasing in modern software development because of the following reasons: (i) there is significant gain in productivity due to reusing commercial components; (ii) the time to market the product decreases; (iii) the product quality is expected to be high, assuming that the COTS components have been well tested; and (iv) there is efficient use of human resources due to the fact that development personnel will be freed up for other tasks. However, many difficulties are to be overcome while using COTS compared to using in-house components. The black-box nature of COTS components prevents system integrators from modifying the components to better meet user's requirements. Moreover, the integrators have no visibility of the details of the components, their evolutions, or their maintenance; rather, they are solely dependent on the developers and suppliers of the components. The only source code being written and modified by the integrators is what is needed for integrating the COTS-based systems. This includes code for tailoring and wrapping the individual components, as well as the "glue" code required to put the components together [64]. Wrapper code X combined with another piece of code Y determines how code Y is executed. The wrapper acts as an interface between its caller and the wrapped code Y. Wrapping may be done for compatibility. A glue component is basically designed to combine the services from many components to provide a higher level of service. Component tailoring means enhancing the functionality of a component, and it is done by adding new elements to a component. Note that the source code is not changed by this activity. "Scripting" is an example of tailoring, because a program can be enhanced by having some event trigger a script.

Irrespective of a software system being in-house developed or COTS based, maintenance is the most expensive phase of the system's life cycle. There are key differences in the activities executed to maintain component-based software (CBS), even though the motivations behind system maintenance remain the same. The differences are due to the following major sources:

- Maintainers perceive a CBS system as an interacting group of large-scale black-box components, instead of a compiled set of source modules. The two views require different maintenance skill sets.
- Most of the source code implementing the wrapper, glue, and tailoring modules are used to integrate the system, instead of delivering services and functions.
- The maintenance organization largely loses control over the precise evolution of the system, because COTS developers focus on their own business interests.

2.4.1 Why Maintenance of CBS Is Difficult?

The cost of maintaining COTS-based software systems represent a significant fraction of the total cost of developing software products. Studies show that CBSs incur more maintenance cost than in-house built software [65]. As a first step, reduction of the cost of COTS-based software requires understanding of what makes CBSs maintenance difficult. In the following, we provide a list of those difficulties [66]. Next, we explain those difficulties one by one.

- Frozen functionality
- Incompatibility of upgrades
- Trojan horses
- Unreliable COTS components
- Defective middleware.

Frozen functionality. The functionalities of a COTS component are rendered to be frozen when the vendor stops enhancing the product or stops providing further product support. This occurs if the vendor or the supplier discontinues to support the component. The host system becomes unmaintainable due to the components becoming frozen. The host organization will have a serious problem if periodic updates are required to be performed on those components. The term host organization refers to an individual, group or organization that applies components as a part of some software system, called host system. To find a solution, an integrator is faced with the following options: (i) attempt to implement the frozen functionalities; (ii) acquire a new but similar component from a different vendor; and (iii) acquire the source code from the present vendor to maintain it. The first option is the most difficult choice, unless the host organization has the necessary domain knowledge. The second one is likely to be opted if there are competing alternative vendors. Otherwise, the third one is the only option available. In order to exercise the third option, the integrator should develop a good understanding of the domain to maintain the component source code.

Incompatibility of upgrades. The host organization integrates the components and upgrades the software product to meet the needs of its customers. If a modified component becomes inconsistent with the remaining components of the host system, then integration of the modified component with the host system may not be possible. For example, the new version of a component may require new data formats, which, in turn, requires modifications to be done to the contents and formats of the current files that were generated by earlier versions of the COTS software. The problem then becomes similar to the frozen functionality problem. Assuming that the solutions available to handle the frozen functionality problem are not available, then, as a fourth solution, one may build wrappers around a component to refrain it from exhibiting the incompatibility creating behavior. If wrappers alone are insufficient to eliminate incompatibilities, one can rewrite the "glue" connecting the newly possessed components with the existing ones. Finally, if wrappers and the modified "glue" do not solve the upgrade problem, then the integrator may consider downgrading the functionalities of the system. Not upgrading to the next version can produce the following consequences:

- There may not be continued vendor support for prior versions.
- The host organization may be unable to purchase more copies of the version in operation. Additional copies of a product may be needed when the system is being incrementally deployed.

Trojan horses. A software Trojan horse is a piece of code that has been programmed into a component to make it behave in a malicious way. For instance, deleting all files after switching to a privileged directory can be considered an example of Trojan horse functionality. Determining a functionality to be a Trojan horse is a difficult task. Making the Trojan horse dynamically context sensitive is one way to hide it. For instance, "delete all files" can be a valid command if it refers to entities in a temporary directory. On the other hand, it can have devastating consequences if it is executed in a system context. Therefore, deleting system files can be classified as Trojan horse behavior, whereas deleting temporary files is a normal function. Detection of malicious behavior is difficult enough even with full access to program code. Detection of suspicious actions in a running component will require capturing the requests emanating from the component and verifying their contexts. For COTS components, this can be done at the wrapper level. Note that this approach to detecting malicious behavior is too expensive, because too many calls and context checks are involved. In a running component, Trojan horses go largely undetected. It is an issue that programmers must be aware of while substituting an old component with a new one. Component substitution requires specialized procedures for testing and certifying COTS components. Each time some COTS products are changed, the components and the host system may have to be recertified.

Unreliable COTS components. The scenario of incompatible upgrades has been discussed before in this section. Now we consider unreliable COTS components. Though incompatibility and unreliability are related, there is a distinction between the two. Today, no uniform standard exists to test software components to certify their reliability [67]. By paying software certification laboratories (SCL) to grant software certificates, independent vendors partially shift their responsibility to the SCL. However, there are several ramifications of using services from SCLs: cost, liability issues, developer resources needed to access SCLs, and applicability to safety-critical systems [68]. It may be argued that products with better reliability can be produced with good processes, which can be graded with Capability Maturity Model (CMM), Test Process Improvement (TPI) model, and Test Maturity Model (TMM) [69]. However, process quality does not guarantee product quality, and a vendor may not reveal the maturity level of their process. Though software reliability models exist for decades [70], generic assumptions are made in those models about execution environments, rate of defect, severity of defects, and sizes of faults. Consequently, it is difficult to apply those models. The assumptions may not reflect the individual peculiarities of different environments. Therefore, the dependability of a component is not known to its customers. Even if a score for dependability is provided by the vendor, it is likely that the score was computed based on intricacies that do not broadly reflect the customer's execution environment.

Defective middleware. COTS components are primarily integrated by analyzing the syntax and semantics of their interfaces. However, the integrators have several means for integrating COTS components into a host system, and designing middleware is a straightforward approach. Whenever concerns exist regarding the behavior of a COTS component in the context of a whole system, it is prudent to write middleware to ensure that certain constraints are satisfied. For example, wrappers are a kind of middleware which can be used to constrain the functionalities of components. The main ideas in wrapper design is to: (i) restrict the inputs; (ii) perform preprocessing on the inputs; (iii) restrict the outputs of a component; or (iv) perform post-processing on the outputs. All those kinds of processing have the potential of modifying the semantics of a component. The key problem in designing wrappers is that it is not completely known what behavior to protect against. Querying the vendor could elicit some bits and pieces of information, but it is prudent to thoroughly test a component in its real environment. One can combine vendor supplied information with results of in-house testing to design better wrappers. But, wrappers can be complex, incomplete, and unreliable. Wrappers are discussed in Section 5.2 in great details.

2.4.2   Maintenance Activities for CBSs

It is necessary to identify the activities of the maintenance and management personnel to effectively manage COTS-based systems. Strategies can be formulated to facilitate those activities. Vigder and Kark [71] have surveyed several organizations maintaining systems with a significant portion of COTS elements. In their study, they identified the following cost-drivers:

- Component reconfiguration
- Testing and debugging
- Monitoring of systems
- Enhancing functionality for users
- Configuration management.

Component reconfiguration. Component reconfiguration means adding, removing, and replacing components of a system. The following actions lead to a system being reconfigured: (i) add new components to increase the capability of the system; (ii) delete components as requirements change; (iii) replace a component with a newer version; (iv) replace an old component with a better one; and (v) replace an in-house built component with COTS components. Often component vendors release software updates many times in a year. Therefore, integration of the enhanced components into the host system becomes an expensive task. The host organization continuously evaluates new component releases from the vendors. It establishes criteria by considering capabilities, risk, and cost to make a decision on system upgradation. If a decision is made to upgrade the system, then: (i) the components are analyzed within the context of the current host system and (ii) a new cycle for system integration and testing is planned. To determine the differences between the old version and the new version, system interfaces and behavior are tested. It is likely that the assumptions of the enhanced COTS system are not consistent with those of the other COTS elements. Hence, rigorous regression testing must be performed. In summary, performing component reconfiguration is a time-consuming process that requires an organization to move through a full release cycle: evaluate the product, obtain a design, perform integration, and execute system regression tests [72].

Testing and debugging. Every organization follows its own methodologies, strategies, processes, and techniques for performing testing and debugging on in-house developed code. However, testing and debugging of CBSs pose new challenges due to the absence of visibility into the internal details of third-party developed components. For example, fixing defects in an in-house developed system typically involves: (i) executing the system with a debugger to locate the problem and (ii) modifying the source code to fix the defects. On the other hand, maintenance personnel cannot modify source code of COTS components. Rather, they become dependent upon the component vendors to understand the internal details of the product. Consequently, maintenance personnel and COTS vendors frequently exchange detailed messages.

System monitoring. While a system is in operation, maintainers need to closely monitor the system to be able to better understand the system performance. Continuous monitoring enables the maintenance personnel to enhance the performance of the system, measure usage of resources, keep track of the anomalies in the system behavior, and perform root cause analysis of system failures. Monitoring for the purpose of maintenance is a difficult task because of the low visibility of the internal operations of COTS software.

Enhancing the functionalities for users. COTS products are designed and implemented in a broad sense so that those can be adapted in various applications. Integration personnel need to customize and tailor COTS functionality to satisfy their user community. Therefore, successful host systems exhibit the properties of efficient modifiability and tailorability to incorporate evolving and new user requirements. Tailoring involves a continual process of configuring and customizing of products, combining services of multiple products, and adding new components to products. In the absence of access to source code, tailoring is done by means of two techniques:

- write additional glue code to hold the system together and provide enhanced functionality; and
- use vendor supplied tailoring techniques to customize the products, because integration personnel have no access to program code.

Configuration management. Configuration management of CBS systems is done at two levels: (i) source-code level to manage the in-house software, namely, wrapper, glue, and tailoring developed by the personnel performing system integration and (ii) component level to manage COTS, procured from third-party vendors [73]. The following five activities are specifically done for CBS products:

- Track the versions of the COTS products, and retain the following details for each component in the version archive:
  - Save the name of the developer of the component if available.
  - Save the contact information of the person or organization supplying the component.
  - Archive the source code of the component if available.

- Archive the working versions of all tools, namely, compilers and linkers, necessary to rebuild a component.
- Make a detailed rationale for including the component in the system, including any previous use of the component and known facts about its quality attributes. For instance, BSD Unix was used by Sun Microsystems to build their proprietary OS. Therefore, the information "BSD Unix" is an instance of "previous use."
- Obtain the contact information of some of those using the component.

• Perform configuration management on the individually tailored COTS elements.

• Track the configuration history of a product at all its deployment sites.

• Find the compatible versions of the various COTS elements.

• Manage support and licenses for each COTS element.

Configuration management is a key activity over the life cycle of a large system. For COTS components, configuration management needs to be performed for each COTS software product and each platform on which the product is installed. The lists of those COTS software products and platforms are needed while (i) distributing software upgrades or fixes to multiple sites or (ii) restoring configurations that have been broken.

2.4.3   Design Properties of Component-Based Systems

The architecture of a CBS has significant impact on its maintainability. Component maintainability properties, such as minimal component coupling and visibility, cannot be enhanced after building a CBS. Rather, one must consider these properties at the time of the initial development of the CBS. The main areas influencing CBS maintainability are the choice of the components and the architecture and design used to perform system integration on the components.

Component Selection   Though system integrators do not design and implement individual components, they do have a say while components are selected to be integrated into the host system. The CBS integrator must consider the CBS evolution factor when designing criteria for component selection. A number of attributes of components effect the evolution and maintenance of CBSs. These attributes are discussed in what follows.

Openness of components. A component is considered to be open if it is designed to be visible, extensible, adaptable, and easily integrated into a variety of different host systems. In general, the more the openness of a component, the easier it is for integrators and maintainers to monitor, manage, extend, replace, test, and integrate. The factors that make a component open are adherence to standards, availability of source code, and ability to inter-operate with products from other vendors. Source code can be made available through original equipment manufacturer (OEM) partnership.

Tailorability of components. Tailoring the functionality of the components to meet the evolving user requirements is a kind of maintenance effort for CBS systems. One criterion for component selection can be whether or not the component can be tailored to satisfy the end users' requirements. Though components are seen as black-boxes, vendors can apply many techniques to make components tailorable. Examples of tailoring techniques are: scripting interfaces and extendible frameworks through the use of plug-ins and inheritance.

Available support community. Host system builders need much support from external organizations to build and maintain commercial products. The external support comes from the user community and the vendors. Noting that external support is key to system maintenance, the host system builders need to evaluate the support available during the component evaluation process.

Design Properties of Maintainable CBS   By analyzing and partly resolving the issues of maintainability in the design phase, one can build a system that facilitates the maintenance of CBSs. This requires the development of a set of criteria to evaluate maintainability. The following design attributes of a maintainable CBS have been identified by Vigder and Kark [71]:

- Encapsulated component collaborations
- Controlled component interfaces
- Controlled component dependencies
- Minimal component coupling
- Consistent failure handling
- High level of visibility
- Minimal build and deployment effort.

Encapsulated component collaborations. Collaborations are time-sequenced coordinated actions. Collaborations among components can involve many data and behavioral dependencies. A key design objective is to make collaborations explicit and encapsulate each collaboration within a single object, often called a *mediator*. A mediator can be implemented as part of the glue code, and it should be designed to (i) translate and transform data formats to enable data transfer and (ii) manage event sequencing for the components. By encapsulating collaborations the CBS will be more maintainable by supporting the following activities [74]:

- *Product reconfiguration.* It is much easier to understand and manage component dependencies by encapsulating component interactions within a separate object.
- *Troubleshooting.* Numerous problems in CBS are related to sequences of interactions among components. Problem isolation becomes easier if most of the interaction sequences happen within a single mediator.

- *Modifying and adding services.* By combining services from different components, mediators implement many business processes. Updating business processes become easier by confining services to mediators.
- *System monitoring.* Mediators can include instrumentation code for monitoring system behavior.

Controlled component interfaces. There are two main reasons to use integrator-controlled interfaces on COTS components: (i) facilitate component reconfiguration; and (ii) add visibility. As new components and component versions are combined with a system, an integrator-controlled interface can reduce the impact of frequent reconfigurations by means of isolation. In addition, management, instrumentation, and monitoring functionality can be included in an integrator. If integration personnel directly use interfaces supplied by vendors, they might face difficulties in: (i) reducing the consequences of reconfigurations and (ii) determining the dependencies between components. Integrators can use a number of approaches to turn interfaces into first-class objects and manipulate them. A first-class object is one that can be dynamically created, destroyed, or passed as an argument. One approach to creating a first-class object is designing a wrapper around all the components; a wrapper can be designed by using an adapter design pattern. The adapter design pattern translates one interface for a class into a compatible interface. An adapter allows classes to work together that normally could not because of incompatible interfaces, by providing its interface to clients while using the original interface. As the underlying component is modified, the ripple effect on the other components can be minimized. A second approach to creating a first-class object is to use standardized interfaces for COTS products.

Controlled component dependencies. The integrator identifies mutually dependent components and realizes strategies for controlling and managing those dependencies. Complex dependencies among components produce a fragile system. It becomes difficult to upgrade, add, and delete elements in a fragile system. To make maintenance easier for CBS systems, designers must reduce dependencies between components. Some dependencies are explicit and some are implicit. Flow of data through a visible interface is an example of direct dependency. Conflicting assumptions made by different software components are examples of implicit dependency. Dependencies can also result from resource contentions; an example of resource contention is when many components try to use the same TCP port number at the same time. Dependencies between COTS products include the following three broad kinds of dependencies:

- *Syntactic dependencies.* These occur when components make assumptions about the interface signature of the component.
- *Behavioral dependencies.* These occur when components are involved in two-way interactions or multi-way collaborations.
- *Resources dependencies.* These occur when multiple components compete for the same resources.

The designer must record, update, and verify all cross-component dependencies to perform risk analyses before a system upgrade involving those components. In addition, integrators can provide mechanisms for managing those dependencies: identification of deployment-time versions and verification of satisfaction of dependencies.

Minimal component coupling. It becomes more difficult to substitute a component if coupling of the component with other components is very high. Minimal component coupling is realized by: (i) constraining and controlling component access and (ii) isolating the resources used by separate components. A wrapper around a component can suppress undesired functionalities that introduce additional dependencies.

Consistent failure handling. In their tasks of testing, debugging, and monitoring system behavior, maintainers are assisted by failure handling. Therefore, integrators need consistent, complete, and effective means to detect and handle failures. A component can behave in an unpredictable manner if it is provided with faulty inputs. Therefore, it is important to identify and isolate faults sooner before they propagate as errors through other components. A consistent failure handling mechanism enables maintainers to detect errors when they occur, identify the root cause of the failure, and minimize the impact of the failure. For example, a consistent failure handling mechanism for any routines includes a *status* output argument, which is used to return error status codes. Status codes may be passed to another routine (viz. errormsgtext()) to extract an error message text from a message catalogue. Errors can be detected by the wrappers and handled in the glue code holding the system together.

High level of visibility. Visibility means that maintenance engineers are able to monitor the system, including the behavior of wrappers and glue components. Visibility can be added to the system by the integrators in several ways. Instrumentation and monitoring capabilities should be integrated into wrappers and glue code to support monitoring of interactions as part of the overall system design. Monitoring tools can support additional capabilities to gain visibility into a running system, namely, monitoring the input and output behavior of communication protocols with sniffer code.

Minimal build and deployment effort. CBSs are often built with many components that require frequent tailoring and reconfigurations. Therefore, the build process to install the software at all deployment sites is complex. On the other hand, it should be easily achievable to replace products or add new functionalities without going through an expensive build process. COTS elements may involve intricacies in their deployment processes, thereby contradicting the assumptions made by other products. As a result, the build itself can become an expensive and complex part of system maintenance [75, 76]. A build process becomes complicated if too many modules are new and have complex interfaces. A tool for version control is highly recommended for automating the build process.

2.5 SUMMARY

This chapter began with definitions of software maintenance from the perspectives of researchers, practitioners, and standardization groups. We differentiated development from maintenance: developing new software is a requirement-driven activity, whereas maintaining an existing system is event driven. For example, when a request for change is received, the maintenance organization may modify the system. Therefore, the inputs that drive maintenance changes are random events, originating, for example, from an user in the form of a CR. Software maintenance consists of two primary activities: correcting errors and enhancing functionality of the software. Hence, it can be seen as continued development.

We identified and explained the following maintenance activities:

- intention-based classification of software maintenance activities;
- activity-based classification of software maintenance activities; and
- evidence-based classification of software maintenance activities.

To explain intention-based classification of maintenance tasks, we introduced Swanson's approach [5] which defined three kinds of maintenance activities: corrective, adaptive, and corrective. On the other hand, the maintenance classification of Kitchenham et al. [4] consists of two broad kinds of activities for corrections and enhancements. The category for enhancement is subdivided into three types as follows: (i) modifications that change some of the current requirements; (ii) modifications that add new requirements to the system; and (iii) modifications that alter the implementation but not the requirements. The evidence-based classification of Chapin [16] consists of 12 types of software maintenance tasks: training, consultive, evaluative, reformative, updative, groomative, preventive, performance, adaptive, reductive, corrective, and enhancive.

Next we explained various concepts that influence software maintenance processes. Those concepts were studied under four categories: (i) maintained product; (ii) maintenance types; (iii) organization process; and (iv) peopleware. Then, we described the characteristics of those concepts and their impact on maintenance activities. This discussion clarifies the difference between maintenance methods/tools/skills from those used for software development.

Next, we studied various ways in which researchers define software evolution, and differentiated it from software maintenance. Keith H. Bennett and Jie Xu [27] use the term maintenance to refer to all post-delivery support activities, and evolution to perfective changes, that is, those driven by changes in requirements. In addition, the authors further state that evolution addresses both functional and nonfunctional requirements. On the other hand, Ned Chapin defines software evolution as the applications of software maintenance activities and processes that generate a new operational software version with a changed customer-experienced functionality or properties from a prior operational version [15].

We described Lehman's classification of properties of CSS of S-type (Specified), P-type (Problem), and E-type (Evolving). The S-type programs implement solutions to the problems that can be completely and unambiguously specified, for which, in theory at least, a program implementation can be proven correct with respect to the specification. The definition of S-type requires that the program be correct in the full mathematical sense related to the specification. A P-type program is based on a practical abstraction of the problem, rather than a completely defined specification. Even though the exact solution may exist, the solution produced by a P-type program is tampered by the environment in which it must be produced. The solution produced by a P-type program is acceptable if the results make sense to the stakeholder(s) in the world in which the problem is embedded. Finally, the distinctive attributes of E-type systems are as follows:

- The complex and large problems addressed by E-type systems cannot be completely and formally specified.
- The system has an incomplete model of the execution environment that embeds the program.
- The system makes a large number of simplifications and assumptions about the real world.
- Program execution modifies the operation domain.
- The development and evolution processes for E-type software are feedback driven.

Next, we discussed the following eight laws of software evolution for E-type CSS systems, including empirical studies and their practical implications.

 I. *Continuing change.* E-type programs must be continually adapted, else they become progressively less satisfactory.
 II. *Increasing complexity.* As an E-type program evolves, its complexity increases unless work is done to maintain or reduce it.
 III. *Self-regulation.* The evolution process of E-type programs is self-regulating, with the time distribution of measures of processes and products being close to normal.
 IV. *Conservation of organizational stability.* The average effective global activity rate in an evolving E-type program is invariant over the product's lifetime.
 V. *Conservation of familiarity.* The average content of successive releases is constant during the life cycle of an evolving E-type program.
 VI. *Continuing growth.* To maintain user satisfaction with the program over its lifetime, the functional content of an E-type program must be continually increased.
 VII. *Declining quality.* An E-type program is perceived by its stakeholders to have declining quality if it is not maintained and adapted to its environment.
 VIII. *Feedback system.* The evolution processes in E-type programs constitute multi-agent, multi-level, multi-loop feedback systems.

Next, we described the origin of FOSS movement and the differences between CSS and FOSS systems with respect to: team structure, process, releases, and global factors. In addition, we discussed the empirical research results about the Linux FOSS system to study the laws of evolution, originally proposed for CSS systems. We concluded this chapter with a discussion on maintenance of COTS.

LITERATURE REVIEW

The book by Dennis D. Smith ("Designing Maintainable Software," Springer, New York, 1999) is an excellent starting point for understanding the many issues related to maintenance. With theoretical reasoning and observation, the book explains how maintainers undergo problem solving. He provides helpful tips for maintainers regarding cognitive structures, naming conventions, and the use of truncation. Though the book does not cover evolution, it clearly explains software evolvability. Software maintenance is usually considered in terms of corrections, improvements, and enhancements. The article by Dewayne E. Perry ("Dimensions of Software Evolution" by D. E. Perry, International Conference on Software Maintenance, Victoria, BC, IEEE Computer Society Press, Los Alamitos, CA, September, 1994, p. 296–303) looks at the other three dimensions: domain, experience, and process to gain insights into the sources of software evolution. These three dimensions are interrelated in various ways and interact with each other in a number of ways. One will be able to understand and manage effectively the evolution of software systems only when there is a deep understanding of these dimensions. This idea was further extended by Ciraci et al. ("A Taxonomy for a Constructive Approach to Software Evolution," by S. Ciraci, P. Broek, and M. Aksit, Journal of Software, Vol. 2, No. 2, August, 2007, p. 84–96) to 24 feasible contexts for the software evolution. The taxonomy is based on the fact that a change in one of these sources (e.g., domain, process, or experience) has occurred or is expected to occur.

The typology of Swanson has been influential among researchers and practitioners [7]. However very few researchers and practitioners have followed Swanson's typology. Rather, others have given new meanings to those terms. For example, the standard proposed by IEEE [77] defines the three terms "corrective," "adaptive," and "perfective," which are not completely compatible with Swanson's. The article by Chapin et al. [15] clearly identifies and compares the differences in a tabular form along with the definitions of 12 maintenance types: training, consultive, evaluative, reformative, updative, groomative, preventive, performance, adaptive, reductive, corrective, and enhancive. The authors excluded the "perfective" type from their classification and coined a new term called "groomative." The reader is urged to study the article on preventive maintenance by Kajko-Mattsson [13]. The author did a comprehensive literature study on preventive maintenance both within software and hardware engineering. In addition, Kajko-Mattsson et al. [78] have discussed a comprehensive taxonomy of activities performed for the corrective type.

In the article by Jim Buckley et al. [79], the authors took a complementary view toward a taxonomy of maintenance by focusing more on the *how, when, what,* and *where* aspects of software changes. The article proposed four logical themes and 15 dimensions. The four logical themes are: (i) temporal properties (*When* is the change made?); (ii) object of change (*Where* is a change made?); (iii) system properties (*What* is being changed?); and (iv) change report (*How* is the change accomplished?). The 15 dimensions are: time to change, change history, change frequency, anticipation, artifacts, granularity, impact, change propagation, availability, activeness, openness, safety, degree of freedom, degree of formality, and change type.

The revised form of the SPE taxonomy, called SPE+, was proposed by Stephen Cook et al. [30] to address some ambiguities and weaknesses in the original taxonomy. For example, Lehman did not choose to characterize the P-type software.

Kemerer and Slaughter [80] showed that problems in software maintenance can be traced to an absence of understanding of: (i) the maintenance process and (ii) the cause–effect relationships between software maintenance practices and outcomes. Their study focused on the effort expended, modification performed, and cost incurred to evolve the software.

Many researchers are further studying new topics related to laws of software evolution. Readers interested in a more detailed discussion of the topic may read the following books:

N. H. Madhavji, J. F. Ramil, and D. E. Perry, Ed. *Software Evolution and Feedback – Theory and Practice*, John Wiley, West Sussex, England, 2006.

T. Mens and S. Demeyer, Ed. *Software Evolution*, Springer-Verlag, Berlin Heidelberg, 2008.

The first book focuses on the *what and why* aspects of software evolution, that is, on the *nature* of software evolution phenomenon with emphasis on nontechnical aspects, such as complexity theory, social interactions, and human psychology. This book provides a depth of material in the field of software evolution and feedback. Specifically, it describes the phenomenological and technological underpinnings of software evolution, and it explains the impact of feedback on development and maintenance of software. Part I (Chapters 1–16) is "evolution" centered, whereas part II (Chapters 17–27) is "feedback" centered, though both the topics are often discussed in the same chapter. Within these partitions, the chapters are organized from one more conceptual to more concrete contents.

The second book entitled "Software Evolution" focuses on the *how* aspects of software evolution: methods, activities, tools, and technology that give the means to manage software evolution. The book has been structured into three parts. The first part focuses on: (i) analysis of release histories and version repositories and (ii) improvement of evolution by fixing defects and eliminating redundancies in software. The second part explains how one can reengineer a legacy system into a modern system that is easier to maintain. The third part discusses the relation between evolution and other main subjects in software development.

Those interested in knowing more details about the comparative empirical study of FOSS and CSS may refer to the article by Paulson et al. [61]. The authors studied and compared the results of the evolution of three CSS and FOSS projects. The three well-known FOSS projects are the Linux kernel, the GCC compiler, and the Apache HTTP web server. The authors chose to consider only the kernel part of Linux because, apparently, the three CSS systems were more comparable with the kernel than the whole Linux system. The three CSS projects are from the embedded real-time system domain described as "software protocol stacks in wireless telecommunication device." The five hypotheses studied in this article were: (i) FOSS grows more quickly than proprietary, that is CSS, systems; (ii) FOSS systems foster more creativity; (iii) FOSS systems are less complex than CSS systems; (iv) fewer bugs are there in

FOSS systems and those can be more rapidly located and fixed; and (v) FOSS systems are better modularized. Out of those five hypotheses, only (ii) and (iv) were supported with measurements. The following measurements were used to test the hypotheses:

1. For hypothesis (i), count the number of lines of code added over time. This measurement captures the size (or growth) metric.

2. For hypothesis (ii), count the number of functions added over time. This measurement reflects the creativity shown over time.

3. For hypothesis (iii), measure the average complexity of all the functions and the average complexity of all the newly added functions.

4. For hypothesis (iv), count the number of functions changed to fix bugs and represent the number of functions changed to fix bugs as a percentage of the total number of functions.

5. For hypothesis (v), compute the correlation between the number of functions added and the number of functions changed.

REFERENCES

[1] R. G. Canning. 1972. The maintenance 'iceberg'. *EDP Analyzer*, 10(10), 1–14.

[2] T. M. Pigoski. 2001. *Chapter 6, Software Maintenance, SWEBOK: A Project of the Software Engineering Coordinating Committee (Trial Version 1.00)*. IEEE Computer Society Press, Los Alamitos, CA.

[3] ISO/IEC 14764:2006 and IEEE Std 14764-2006. 2006. *Software Engineering – Software Life Cycle Processes – Maintenance*. Geneva, Switzerland.

[4] B. A. Kitchenham, G. H. Travassos, A. N. Mayrhauser, F. Niessink, N. F. Schneidewind, J. Singer, S. Takada, R. Vehvilainen, and H. Yang. 1999. Towards an ontologyy of software maintenance. *Journal of Software Maintenance and Evolution: Research and Practice*, 11, 365–389.

[5] E. B. Swanson. 1976. *The Dimensions of Maintenance*. Proceedings of the 2nd International Conference on Software Engineering (ICSE), October 1976, San Francisco, CA. IEEE Computer Society Press, Los Alamitos, CA. pp. 492–497.

[6] B. P. Lientz and E. B. Swanson. 1980. *Software Maintenance Management*. Addison-Wesley, Reading, MA.

[7] E. B. Swanson and N. Chapin. 1995. Interview with E. Burton Swanson. *Journal of Software Maintenance and Evolution: Research and Practice*, 7(5), 303–315.

[8] S. G. Eick, T. L. Graves, A. f. Karr, J. S. Marron, and A. Mockus. 2001. Does code decay? Assessing evidence from change management data. *IEEE Transactions on Software Engineering*, January, 1–12.

[9] K. J. Lieberherr and I. M. Holland. 1989. *Tools for Preventive Software Maintenance*. Proceedings of International Conference on Software Maintenance (ICSM), October 1989, Miami, FL. IEEE Computer Society Press, Los Alamitos, CA. pp. 1–12.

[10] Y. Huang, C. Kintala, N. Kolettis, and N. D. Fulton. 1995. *Software Rejuvenation: Analysis, Module and Applications*. Proceedings of the 25th symposium on Fault Tolerant

Computing, June 1995, Pasadena, CA. IEEE Computer Society Press, Los Alamitos, CA. pp. 381–390.

[11] S. Garg, A. Puliafito, M. Telek, and K. Trivedi. 1998. Analysis of preventive maintenance in transactions based software systems. *IEEE Transactions on Computers*, January, 96–107.

[12] M. Grottke and K. S. Trivedi. 2007. Fighting bugs: remove, retry, replicate, and rejuvenate. *IEEE Computers*, February, 107–109.

[13] M. K. Mattsson. 2001. *Can We Learn Anything from Hardware Preventive Maintenance?* Seventh IEEE International Conference on Engineering of Complex Computer Systems, June 2001, Skovde, Sweden. IEEE Computer Society Press, Los Alamitos, CA. pp. 106–111.

[14] E. Marshall. 1992. Fatal error: how patriot overlooked a scud. *Science*, March 13, p. 1347.

[15] N. Chapin, J. F. Hale, K. M. Khan, J. F. Ramil, and W. G. Tan. 2001. Types of software evolution and software maintenance. *Journal of Software Maintenance and Evolution: Research and Practice*, 13, 3–30.

[16] N. Chapin. 2000. *Software Maintenance Types—A Fresh View*. Proceedings of the International Conference on Software Maintenance (ICSM), October 2000, San Jose, CA. IEEE Computer Society Press, Los Alamitos, CA. pp. 247–252.

[17] C. Jones. 2007. Geriatric issues of aging software. *CrossTalk: The Journal of Defense Software Engineering*, December, 4–8.

[18] D. L. Parnas. 1994. *Software Aging*. Proceedings of 16th International Conference on Software Engineering, May 1994, Sorrento, Italy. IEEE Computer Society Press, Los Alamitos, CA. pp. 279–287.

[19] K. Maxwell, L. V. Wassenhove, and S. Dutta. 1996. Software development productivity of European space, military and industrial applications. *IEEE Transactions on Software Engineering*, October, pp. 706–718.

[20] M. I. Halpern. 1965. Machine independence: its technology and economics. *Communications of the ACM*, 8(12), 782–785.

[21] R. F. Couch. 1971. Evolution of a toll mis – bell Canada. *Management Information Systems: Selected Papers from MIS Copenhagen 70—An IAG Conference* (Eds W. Goldberg, T. H. Nielsen, E. Johnson, and H. Josefsen), pp. 163–188. Auerbach Publisher Inc., Princeton, NJ.

[22] L. A. Belady and M. M. Lehman. 1976. A model of large program development. *IBM Systems Journal*, 15(1), 225–252.

[23] P. Wegner. 1978. *Research Direction in Software Technology*. Proceedings of the 3rd International Conference on Software Engineering (ICSE), May 1978, Atlanta, Georgia. IEEE Computer Society Press, Los Alamitos, CA. pp. 243–259.

[24] M. M. Lehman. 1980. Programs, life cycles, and laws of software evolution. *Proceedings of the IEEE*, September, 1060–1076.

[25] K. H. Bennett and V. T. Rajlich. 2000. *Software Maintenance and Evolution: A Roadmap*. ICSE, The Future of Software Engineering, June 2000, Limerick, Ireland. ACM, New York. pp. 73–87.

[26] L. J. Arthur. 1988. *Software Evolution: The Software Maintenance Challenge*. John Wiley & Sons.

[27] K. H. Bennett and J. Xu. *Software Services and Software Maintenance.* Proceedings of 7th European Conference on Software Maintenance and Reengineering, March 2003, Benevento, Italy. IEEE Computer Society Press, Los Alamitos, CA. pp. 3–12.

[28] M. M. Lehman and J. Ramil. 2002. Software evolution and software evolution processes. *Annals of Software Engineering,* 14, 275–309.

[29] S. L. Pfleeger. 1998. The nature of system change. *IEEE Software,* May/June, 87–90.

[30] S. Cook, R. Harrison, M. M. Lehman, and P. Wernick. 2006. Evolution in software systems: foundations of SPE classification scheme. *Journal of Software Maintenance and Evolution: Research and Practice,* 18, 1–35.

[31] M. M. Lehman. 1996. Feedback in the software evolution process. *Information and Software Technology,* 38, 681–686.

[32] M. M. Lehman and L. A. Belady. 1985. *Program Evolution: Processes of Software Change.* Academic Press, London.

[33] M. M. Lehman and J. F. Ramil. 2006. Software evolution. In: *Software Evolution and Feedback* (Eds N. H. Madhavvji, J. F. Ramil, and D. Perry). John Wiley & Sons, West Sussex.

[34] M. M. Lehman, J. F. Ramil, P. D. Wernick, D. E. Perry, and W. M. Turski. 1997. *Metrics and Laws of Software Evolution—The Nineties View.* Proceedings of 4th International Symposium on Software Metrics (Metrics 97), November 1997. IEEE Computer Society Press, Los Alamitos, CA. pp. 20–32.

[35] M. M. Lehman. 2001. Rules and tools for software evolution planning and management. *Annals of Software Engineering,* 11, 15–44.

[36] C. K. S. Chong Hok Yuen. 1987. *A Statistical Rational for Evolution Dynamics Concepts.* Proceedings of the International Conference on Software Maintenance, September 1987, Austin, Texas. IEEE Computer Society Press, Los Alamitos, CA. pp. 156–164.

[37] F. Brooks. 1993. *The Mythical Man Month* (2nd Ed.). Addison-Wesley, Reading, MA.

[38] M. M. Lehman. 1996. *Laws of Software Evolution Revisited.* Proceedings of the 5th European Workshop on Software Process Technology, Lecture Notes in Computer Science, Vol. 1149. Springer, London, pp. 108–124.

[39] D. A. Garvin. 1984. What does product quality mean? *Sloan Management Review,* Fall, 25–45.

[40] N. H. Madhavji, J. F. Ramil, and D. E. Perry (Eds). 2006. *Software Evolution and Feedback: Theory and Practice.* John Wiley & Sons, West Sussex.

[41] G. Visaggio. 2001. Ageing of a data-intensive legacy system: symptoms and remedies. *Journal of Software Maintenance and Evolution: Research and Practice,* 13, 281–308.

[42] C. K. S. Chong Hok Yuen. 1988. *On Analyzing Maintenance Process Data at the Global and Detailed Levels: A Case Study.* Proceedings of the International Conference on Software Maintenance, October 1988. Phoenix, Arizona. IEEE Computer Society Press, Los Alamitos, CA. pp. 248–255.

[43] M. M. Lehman, D. E. Perry, and J. F. Ramil. 1998. *On Evidence Supporting the Feast Hypothesis and the Laws of Software Evolution.* Proceedings of the 5th International Software Metrics Symposium (Metrics), November 1998. IEEE Computer Society Press, Los Alamitos, CA. pp. 84–88.

[44] W. M. Turski. 1996. Reference model for growth of software systems. *IEEE Transactions on Software Engineering,* August, 599–600.

[45] M. Lawrence. 1982. *An Examination of Evolution Dynamics*. Proceedings of International Conference on Software Engineering (ICSE), September 1982. IEEE Computer Society Press, Los Alamitos, CA. pp. 188–196.

[46] M. M. Lehman and J. F. Ramil. 2003. Software evolution—background, theory, practice. *Information Processing Letters*, 88(1–2), 33–44.

[47] S. Williams. 2002. *Free as in Freedom: Richard Stallman's Crusade for Free Software*. O'Reilly & Associates, Inc., Sebastopol, CA.

[48] R. M. Stallman, L. Lessig, and G. Gay. 2002. *Free Software, Free Society*. Free Software Foundation, Cambridge, MA.

[49] E. S. Raymond. 2001. *The Cathedral and the Bazaar: Musings on Linux and Open Source by an Accidental Revolutionary*. O'Reilly & Associates, Inc., Sebastopol, CA.

[50] Y. Wang, D. Guo, and H. Shi. 2007. Measuring the evolution of open source software systems with their communities. *ACM SIGSOFT Software Engineering Notes*, 32(6), pp. 1–7.

[51] J. F. Ramil, A. Lozano, and M. Wermelinger. 2008. Empirical studies of open source evolution. In: *Software Evolution* (Eds T. Mens and S. Demeyer). Springer, Berlin.

[52] W. Scacchi. 2006. Understanding open source software evolution. In: *Software Evolution and Feedback* (Eds N. H. Madhavvji, J. F. Ramil, and D. Perry), pp. 181–2026. John Wiley & Sons, West Sussex.

[53] K. Crowston and J. Howison. 2005. The social structure of free and open source software devellopment. *First Monday*, 10(2).

[54] M. Aberdour. 2007. Achieving quality in open source software. *IEEE Software*, 24(1), 58–64.

[55] A. Mockus, R. T. Fielding, and J. D. Herbsleb. 2002. Two case studies of open source software development: Apache and mozilla. *ACM Transactions on Software Engineering and Methodology*, July, 309–346.

[56] S. S. Pirzada. 1988. A statistical examination of the evolution of the Unix system. PhD Thesis, Department of Computing, Imperical College, London, England.

[57] M. W. Godfrey and Q. Tu. 2000. *Evolution in Open Source Software: A Case Study*. Proceedings of the International Conference on Software Maintenance (ICSM), October 2000. IEEE Computer Society Press, Los Alamitos, CA. pp. 131–142.

[58] S. R. Schach, B. Jin, D. R. Wright, G. Z. Heller, and A. J. Offutt. 2002. Maintainability of the linux kernel. *IEEE proceedings—Software*, 149(1), pp. 18–22.

[59] G. Robles, J. J. Amor, J. M. Gonzalez-Barahona, and I. Herraiz. 2005. *Evolution and Growth in Large Libre Software Projects*. Proceedings of Eighth International Workshop on Principles of Software Evolution (IWPSE), September 2005, Lisbon, Portugal. IEEE Computer Society Press, Los Alamitos, CA. pp. 165–174.

[60] M. M. Lehman, J. F. Ramil, and U. Sandler. 2001. *An Approach to Modelling Long-term Growth Trends in Software Systems*. Proceedings of the International Conference on Software Maintenance (ICSM), November 2001, Florence, Italy. IEEE Computer Society Press, Los Alamitos, CA, pp. 219–228.

[61] J. W. Paulson, G. Succi, and A. Eberlein. 2004. An empirical study of open-source and closed-source software products. *IEEE Transactions on Software Engineering*, April, 246–256.

[62] C. K. Roy and J. R. Cordy. 2006. *Evaluating the Evolution of Small Scale Open Source Software Systems*. 15th International Conference on Computing, Mexico City, November 2006. IEEE Computer Society Press, Los Alamitos, CA, Research in Computing Science, Vol. 23, pp. 123–136.

[63] H. Gall, M. Jazayeri, R. Klősch, and G. Trausmuth. 1997. *Software Evolution Observed Based on the Product Release History*. Proceedings of the International Conference on Software Maintenance (ICSM), October 1997, Bari, Italy. IEEE Computer Society Press, Los Alamitos, CA. pp. 160–166.

[64] M. R. Vigder and J. Dean. 1997. *An Architectural Approach to Building Systems from COTS Software Components*. Proceedings of the 22nd Annual Software Engineering Workshop, December 1997, Greenbelt, MA. pp. 99–113.

[65] D. Reifer, V. Basili, B. Boehm, and B. Clark. 2003. Eight lessons learned during cots-based systems maintenance. *IEEE Software*, September/October, 94–96.

[66] J. Voas. 1998. Maintaining components-based systems. *IEEE Software*, July/August, 22–27.

[67] S. Beydeda and V. Gruhn (Eds.) 2005. *Testing Commerical-off-the-Shelf Components and Systems*. Springer, Germany.

[68] J. Morris, G. Lee, K. Parker, G. Bundell, and C. Lam. 2001. Software component certification. *IEEE Computer*, September, pp. 30–36.

[69] K. Naik and P. Tripathy. 2008. *Software Testing and Quality Assurance: Theory and Practice*. John Wiley & Sons, Inc., Hoboken.

[70] C. V. Ramamoorthy and F. B. Bastani. 1982. Software reliability—status and perspectives. *IEEE Transactions on Software Engineering*, July, pp. 354–371.

[71] M. Vigder and A. Kark. 2006. *Maintaining Cots-based Systems: Start with Design*. Proceedings of the 5th International Conference on Commercial-Off-The-Shelf (COTS)-Based Software Systems, February 2006, Orlando, FL. IEEE Computer Society Press, Los Alamitos, CA. pp. 11–18.

[72] M. Vigder and J. Dean. 2000. Maintenance of cots-based systems. National Research Council of Canada, Institute for Information Technology, Ottawa, Ontario, Canada, NRC Report 43626, p. 6.

[73] D. J. Carney, S. A. Hissam, and D. Plakosh. 2000. Complex cots-based software practical steps for their maintenance. *Journal of Software Maintenance and Evolution: Research and Practice*, 12, 357–376.

[74] M. Krieger, M. Vigder, J. Dean, and M. Siddiqui. 2003. *Coordination in COTS-based Development*. Second International Conference on COTS-Based Software Systems (ICCBSS), February 2003, Ottawa, Canada, LNCS-2580. Springer, pp. 123–133.

[75] D. Garlan, A. Robert, and J. Ockerbloom. 1995. Architectural mismatch: why reuse is so hard. *IEEE Software*, November, 17–26.

[76] D. Garlan, A. Robert, and J. Ockerbloom. 2009. Architectural mismatch: why reuse is still so hard. *IEEE Software*, July/August, 66–69.

[77] IEEE Standard 1219-1998. 1998. *Standard for Software Maintenance*. IEEE Computer Society Press, Los Alamitos, CA.

[78] M. K. Mattsson, U. Westblom, S. Forssander, G. Andersson, M. Medin, S. Ebarasi, T. Fahlgren, S. E. Johansson, S. Tornquist, and M. Holmgren. 2001. *Taxonomy of*

Problem Management Activities. Proceedings of the 5th European Conference on Software Maintenance and Reengineering, March, 2001, lisbon, Portugal, IEEE Computer Society Press, Los Alamitos, CA. pp. 1–10.

[79] J. Buckley, T. Mens, M. Zenger, A. Rashid, and G. Kniesel. 2005. Towards a taxonomy of software change. *Journal of Software Maintenance and Evolution: Research and Practice*, 17(5), 309–332.

[80] C. F. Kemerer and S. Slaughter. 1999. An empirical approach to studying evolution. *IEEE Transactions on Software Engineering*, July/August, 493–509.

EXERCISES

1. Explain why it is important to make distinctions among the different types of software maintenance.

2. What are the causes of adaptive maintenance problems? What are the consequences of these problems?

3. Why should you fix something that is not broken? What are some reasons for performing perfective maintenance?

4. What are some common justifications for not doing perfective maintenance?

5. What is software aging? What are the common causes of software aging? How can those causes be eliminated? Discuss the answers in detail. (Hint: rejuvenate, software maintainability)

6. Explain the concept of software rejuvenation. Discuss the pros and cons of software rejuvenation.

7. Discuss the differences between hardware and software maintenance.

8. For each of the following situations, explain whether it is a hazard or a mishap.
   (a) Water in a swimming pool becomes electrified.
   (b) A room fills with carbon dioxide.
   (c) A car stops abruptly.
   (d) A long distance telephone company suffers an outage.
   (e) A nuclear weapon is destroyed in an unplanned manner.

9. Compare the software maintenance classification based on intention, activity, and evidence.

10. Explain the rationale behind Lehman's laws. Under what circumstances those laws may not hold?

11. What is software entropy? Explain its relationship with software aging.

12. What is code decay? Discuss the symptoms of code decay. What are the causes of code decay?

13. Explain the term software cloning and discuss its significance with respect to software evolution.

14. Explain the inverse square model of system evolution. For the system data given in Table 2.6, plot the graph for the actual and calculated (inverse square model) sizes for the system.

TABLE 2.6 System Data to be Used in Question 14

RSN	Size	RSN	Size	RSN	Size
1	977	8	1800	15	2151
2	1344	9	1595	16	2091
3	1390	10	1897	17	2095
4	1226	11	1832	18	2101
5	1246	12	1897	19	2312
6	1492	13	1902	20	2167
7	1581	14	2087	21	2315

Source: Data, taken from Reference 44. © 1996 IEEE.

15. Discuss the differences between FOSS and CSS software evolution system.

16. Suppose that you wish to construct a system by combining the functionality of two COTS-based products together. Requests must be handled by sending them first to one of the COTS products, and sending the results from that product to the second. The results from this second product can then be returned to the original requester. Which standard middleware component would you use in building this system?

    (a) glue
    (b) wrapper
    (c) mediator
    (d) tailoring

17. Identify the cluster and evidence maintenance type for the following scenario. Explain your answer.

    "A maintainer was assigned to install three upgraded COTS components, the first of which implements a hardware upgrade. Each COTS component was received from a different vender, but all are used in one system. In attempting to install a test version of the system, the maintainer found that one of the upgrades was incompatible with the other two, and that those other two would not work with the existing in-use version of the third. After considerable diagnostic test runs, and obtaining an "its your problem" response from the vendor of the third component, the maintainer got approval to write a wrapper for one of the upgraded COTS components in order to fit with the continued use of the existing version of the third component. After successful regression testing, the maintainer had the configuration management data updated and the new wrapper recorded. The change, since it would be nearly transparent to the customer, was put into production at the time of the next scheduled release of a version of the systems, and the document was updated."

3

EVOLUTION AND MAINTENANCE MODELS

People seldom improve when they have no other model but themselves to copy after.

—Oliver Goldsmith

3.1 GENERAL IDEA

The software production processes comprise a set of activities starting from conception to retirement. There are many software processes, differing primarily in their classifications of phases and activities. One traditional software development life cycle (SDLC) is shown in Figure 3.1, which comprises two discrete phases, namely, development and maintenance, the latter commonly approaching two-thirds of the product life span. As this diagram shows, about one-fourth to one-third of all software life cycle costs are attributed to software development, and the remaining cost is due to operations and maintenance. Note that the percentages in Figure 3.1 indicate relative costs. As listed below [1], software maintenance has unique characteristics, although many activities related to maintaining and developing software are similar:

- *Constraints of an existing system.* Maintenance is performed on an operational system. Therefore, all modifications must be compatible with the constraints of the existing software architecture, design, and code.
- *Shorter time frame.* A maintenance activity may span from a few hours to a few months, whereas software development may span 1 or more years.

Software Evolution and Maintenance: A Practitioner's Approach, First Edition.
Priyadarshi Tripathy and Kshirasagar Naik.
© 2015 John Wiley & Sons, Inc. Published 2015 by John Wiley & Sons, Inc.

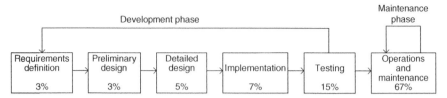

FIGURE 3.1 Traditional SDLC model. From Reference 1. © 1988 John Wiley & Sons

- *Available test data.* In software development, test cases are designed from scratch, whereas software maintenance can select a subset of these test cases and execute them as regression tests. Thus, the challenge is to select appropriate test cases from the existing test suite. In addition to the regression test cases, new test cases need to be created to adequately test the code changes.

Therefore, software maintenance should have its own software maintenance life cycle (SMLC) model as it involves many unique activities. On the other hand, software maintenance has got many similarities with software development, with a focus on product enhancement and correction, in addition to transforming requirements to software functionality. In this chapter, three maintenance models will be explained: reuse, simple staged, and change mini-cycle, representing, respectively, the old, relatively new, and still in research models. We examine in detail two standards, IEEE/EIA 1219 and ISO/IEC 14764, to manage and execute software maintenance activities.

Software maintenance is at the heart of an evolving software product. Evolution, change, and system configuration complicate maintenance activities. The software product which is released to a customer is in the form of executable code, whereas the corresponding "product" within the supplier organization is source code. Source code can be modified without affecting the executable version in use. Thus, strict control must be kept, otherwise exact source code representation of a particular executable version may not exist. In addition, documentation associated with the executable code must be compatible, otherwise the customer may not be able to understand the system. Therefore, tight documentation control is necessary. In other words, the set of products that are released to the customer must be controlled. Software configuration management (SCM) is the way by which the process of software evolution is controlled. SCM provides a framework for managing changes in an efficient way. The functionalities and best practices of SCM are discussed in this chapter. In addition, we discuss a state transition model of a modification (or, change) request, as it flows through the organization.

3.2 REUSE-ORIENTED MODEL

One obtains a new version of an old system by modifying one or several components of the old system and possibly adding new components. As a consequence, the new system is likely to reuse many components of the old system. A new version of

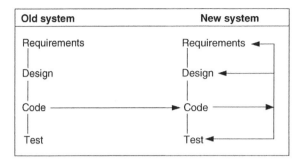

FIGURE 3.2   The quick fix model. From Reference 2. © 1990 IEEE

the system can be created after the maintenance activities are implemented on some of the old system's components. Based on this concept, three process models for maintenance have been proposed by Basili [2]:

- *Quick fix model.* In this model, necessary changes are quickly made to the code and then to the accompanying documentation (Figure 3.2).
- *Iterative enhancement model.* In this model, as illustrated in Figure 3.3, first changes are made to the highest level documents. Eventually, changes are propagated down to the code level.
- *Full reuse model.* In this model, as illustrated in Figure 3.4, a new system is built from components of the old system and others available in the repository.

The old system is reused by all of the three aforementioned models, and, therefore, those belong to the reuse-oriented paradigm. The models assume that the descriptions of the existing system are complete and consistent.

Quick fix model. This model embodies a commonly used approach to software maintenance. In this model, as illustrated in Figure 3.2, (i) source code is modified to

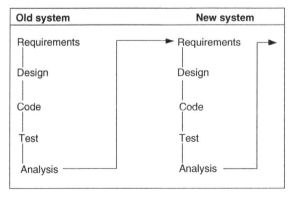

FIGURE 3.3   The iterative enhancement model. From Reference 2. © 1990 IEEE

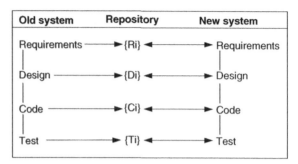

FIGURE 3.4   The full reuse model. From Reference 2. © 1990 IEEE

fix the problem; (ii) necessary changes are made to the relevant documents; and (iii) the new code is recompiled to produce a new version. Often changes to the source code are made with no prior investigation such as analysis of impact of the changes, ripple effects of the changes, and regression testing. Moreover, resource constraints often entail that modifications performed to the code are not documented.

Iterative enhancement model. This model is based on the Japanese principle of *Kaizen*, which means the incremental and progressive improvement of practices. Iterative and incremental development methodologies were practiced in early 1950s, before Winston Royce's Waterfall model [3] was widely used. An alternative approach to software maintenance is suggested by the iterative and incremental models. Those two models have the following ideas in common: (i) it is difficult to fully comprehend a large set of requirements for a system and (ii) developers may find it difficult to build the full system in one go. Therefore, a complete system is developed in progressively larger builds, where one build refines the requirements of the preceding build by taking user inputs into account [4]. The iterative enhancement model, explained in Figure 3.3, shows how changes flow from the very top-level documents to the lowest-level documents. The model works as follows:

- It begins with the existing system's artifacts, namely, requirements, design, code, test, and analysis documents.
- It revises the highest-level documents affected by the changes and propagates the changes down through the lower-level documents.
- The model allows maintainers to redesign the system, based on the analysis of the existing system.

Remark: The terms iteration and increment are liberally used when discussing iterative and incremental development. However, they are not synonyms in the field of software engineering. On the one hand, iteration implies that a process is basically cyclic, thereby meaning that the activities of the process are repeatedly executed in a structured manner. On the other hand, increment implies some quantifiable outcome of an iteration. Iterative development is based on scheduling strategies in which time is set aside to improve and revise parts of the system under development.

Incremental development is based on staging and scheduling strategies in which parts of the system are developed at different times and/or paces and integrated as they are completed.

The model is effectively a three-phase cycle: analysis, characterization of proposed enhancements, and redesign and implementation. A new build is constructed by starting with an analysis of the existing system's requirements, followed by design, coding, and testing. Next, documents at all levels, which are affected by the changes, are modified. Reuse, as explained in Chapter 9, is explicitly supported by the model. The model also accommodates the quick fix model. The iterative enhancement model gives us the key advantage that documentation is kept up-to-date with changes made to the code.

With replicated controlled experiments, Visaggio [5] compared the iterative model and the quick fix model with respect to maintainability. It has been shown that maintainability of systems degrade faster with the quick fix model. In addition, the iterative enhancement model enables organizations to perform maintenance modifications faster than those adopting the quick fix model. In general, an organization may adopt the quick fix model if they do not have time. Therefore, the latter observation is counterintuitive.

Full reuse model. The model illustrated in Figure 3.4 shows maintenance as a special case of reuse-based software development. The main assumption in this model is the availability of a repository of artifacts describing the earlier versions of the present and similar systems. Full reuse comprises two major steps:

- perform requirement analysis and design of the new system; and
- use the appropriate artifacts, such as requirements, design, code, and test from any earlier versions of the old system.

In the full reuse model, reuse is explicit and the following activities are performed:

- identify the components of the old system that are candidates for reuse;
- understand the identified system components;
- modify the old system components to support the new requirements; and
- integrate the modified components to form the newly developed system.

3.3   THE STAGED MODEL FOR CLOSED SOURCE SOFTWARE

Rajlich and Bennett [6] have defined a simple *staged* model to represent the traditional commercial Closed Source Software (CSS) life cycle. Their model comprises a sequence, as illustrated in Figure 3.5, of five stages:

- *Initial development.* Develop the first functioning version of the software.
- *Evolution.* The developers improve the functionalities and capabilities of the software to meet the needs and expectations of the customer.

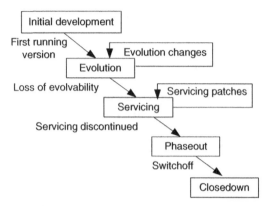

FIGURE 3.5   The simple staged model for the CSS life cycle. From Reference 6. © 2000 IEEE

- *Servicing.* The developers only fix minor and emergency defects, and no major functionality is included.
- *Phaseout.* In this phase, no more servicing is undertaken, while the vendors seek to generate revenue as long as possible.
- *Closedown.* The software is withdrawn from the market, and customers are directed to migrate to a replacement.

Initial development. Software developers build the first version of the system from scratch to satisfy the initial requirements. The initial development includes design, initial coding, and testing. Generally, no releases are made public to the customers in this stage. The first version may lack some functionality, but it lays two important foundations for future iterations, namely, *the software architecture* and *the team knowledge*:

- *The software architecture.* The components of the software, the interactions among them, and their desired properties, such as efficiency and functionality, continue to stay intact through the remains of the life cycle of the system.
- *The team knowledge.* During initial development, the software engineering team acquires knowledge about the application domain, user requirements, business process, data formats, algorithms, weaknesses and strengths of the software architectures, and execution environment. For the subsequent stages of the life-cycle of the software system, this knowledge is considered to be crucial.

Evolution. The software system moves to the evolution stage after the initial development is successful. Software developers extend the functionalities and capabilities of the system to meet the needs and expectations of the customers. In this stage: (i) quick patches and new releases are dispatched to the customers and (ii) feedback from the customers are received for additional enhancement to the software system.

Customer demands for additional functionalities and competitive products from other vendors cause the system to evolve. In addition, evolution of the system may occur due to changes in the operating environment and the business practice. An example of change in the business practice is to target enterprise markets instead of the service provider market segment. Sometimes, the developing company releases the software system right after the initial development. However, often a system is released in its evolution phase after it has undergone many quality improvement cycles. For example, reliability and stability are improved during a system's quality improvement cycle. The exact release date for the product is based on several factors such as timeliness, quality, innovation, and business goals of the company [7].

Servicing. For software to evolve easily, it has to have an appropriate architecture and the software team has to have the necessary expertise. When either architectural integrity or the expertise of the architecture is missing, the software ceases to easily evolve, and it makes a transition to its servicing stage. The system is viewed to have *aged* or *decayed* in the servicing stage. In this stage, the software is considered to have matured and simple modifications are made to the source code, without providing user perceivable enhancements. Changes in this stage are expensive and difficult. Therefore, software developers minimize the number of changes or use wrappers as a way to effect changes. Each of these changes further weakens the system architecture, thereby increasing the need for further servicing. Chapin et al. [8] refer to the servicing stage as the real maintenance phase. After considering the economic profitability of the system, a decision is made to transition the system from the evolution stage to the servicing stage. When new revenues from a software system do not justify the cost of performing modifications, the system is designated as a *legacy* system and it is no more evolved.

Phaseout. During the phaseout stage, the supplier may decide to not perform any more servicing. The software may still be in use, but because change requests (CRs) are no longer honored, it is becoming increasingly outdated. The users must work around the known deficiencies of the system more often. Going back to an earlier servicing stage becomes very difficult because of the increasingly large number of CRs. Eventually, the software system becomes a *legacy* system application.

Closedown. During the final shut down, the vendor pulls out the software product from the market and makes recommendations to the customers for alternative solutions. The supplier may have certain pending contractual responsibilities, namely legal obligations and source code retention. In the areas of outsourced software, source code retention is an important responsibility. As the software system moves from the phaseout to the closedown stage and if the software is still found to be businessworthy to its stakeholders, the system is called a legacy system. For a legacy system, it is prudent to move to a newer system which provides similar functionalities, without exhibiting the poor quality of the legacy system.

One version of the staged model for CSS is called *versioned staged model* and it has been illustrated in Figure 3.6. The model shown in Figure 3.6 has essentially the same stages as found in Figure 3.5, but separate evolution tracks from the initial development are found in Figure 3.6. The evolution process is the backbone of the model. Each evolution track includes servicing, phaseout, and closedown. At certain

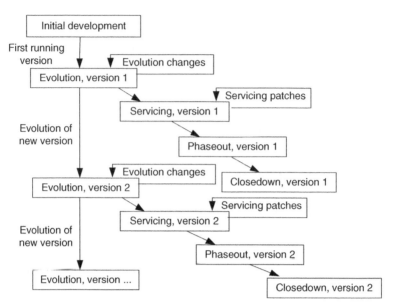

FIGURE 3.6   The versioned staged model for the CSS life cycle. From Reference 6. © 2000 IEEE

time frames, a version of the software is completed and released to the customers. The evolution of the software does not stop at that point; rather, it continues and eventually produces the next version. The released version is no longer evolved but only serviced. Many organizations use a scheme such as <product><version><release><build>, where version reflects the strategic changes made to the system during evolution, release reflects the servicing patches, and build reflects the, say, daily internal build of the software.

3.4   THE STAGED MODEL FOR FREE, LIBRE, OPEN SOURCE SOFTWARE

Capiluppi et al. [9] revised the staged model for its applicability to Free, Libre, Open Source Software (FLOSS) systems, as shown in Figure 3.7. The authors provide empirical evidence to justify the FLOSS model. The model benefits developers by characterizing FLOSS systems in terms of stages and indicating which stage the system is currently in and to which stage the system is more likely to transition.

Three major differences are identified between CSS systems and FLOSS systems. The first one is related to the availability of releases. CSS systems are available to the customers in a running condition after having been tested enough. On the other hand, a FLOSS system is posted on the versioning system repositories much before the official release. Therefore, binaries as well as source code can be downloaded not only by end users but by developers as well. The revised model shown in Figure 3.7 reflects

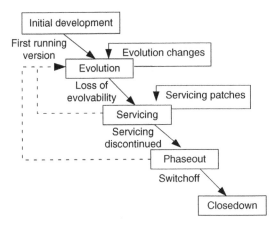

FIGURE 3.7   The staged model for the FLOSS system. From Reference 9. © 2007 ACM

the aforementioned difference between FLOSS and CSS systems. In Figure 3.7, the rectangle with the label "Initial development" has been visually highlighted because it can be the only initial development stage in the evolution of FLOSS systems. In other words, it does not have any evolution track for FLOSS systems.

The second difference concerns the transition from the evolution to the servicing stage. Based on the empirical data from several FLOSS systems, it was observed that a new development stage is reached following a phase without much enhancements. With some systems that were analyzed, after a transition from evolution to servicing, a new period of evolution was observed. This possibility is depicted in Figure 3.7 as a broken arc from the servicing stage to the evolution stage.

The third difference is a possibility of a transition from phaseout stage to evolution stage for FLOSS systems. A case study of a FLOSS system was illustrated by Capiluppi et al. [9]. In the said case study, a new team of developers took over the maintenance task that was abandoned by the previous developed team. In general, the active developers of FLOSS systems get frequently replaced by new developers. Therefore, the dashed line in Figure 3.7 exhibits this possibility of a transition from phaseout stage to evolution stage.

3.5   CHANGE MINI-CYCLE MODEL

Software change is a fundamental ingredient of software evolution and maintenance. Let us revisit the first law of software evolution which is stated as "A program undergoes continuing changes or becomes less useful. The change process continues until it becomes cost-effective to replace the program with a re-created version." The CCS staged model discussed earlier is based on the above fundamental premise. The difficulty of software changes distinguishes the two stages: evolution and servicing. Whereas substantial software changes are allowed in the evolution stage, in the Servicing stage limited changes are permitted. Note that iterative modification is

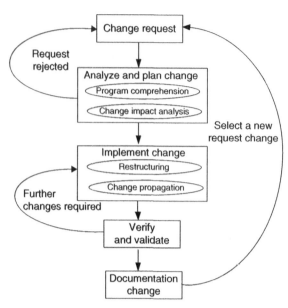

FIGURE 3.8 The change min-cycle. From Reference 12. © 2008 Springer

the primitive building block from which both the evolution and servicing stages are derived.

Software change is a process that may introduce new requirements to the existing system. In addition, there may be a need to alter the software system if the requirements are not correctly implemented. In order to capture this, an evolutionary model, known as *change mini-cycle* (Figure 3.8), was proposed by Yau et al. [10] in the late 1970s and revisited by other researchers, namely, Bennet et al. [11] and Mens [12]. The change mini-cycle model consists of five major phases: CR, analyze and plan change, implement change, verify and validate, and documentation change. In this process model, new significant activities were identified to reflect the fact that software changes are rarely isolated. Examples of those new activities are change impact analysis and change propagation. These activities continue to be the subjects of research.

Change request. A CR generally originates from the management, users of the software, or customers. A CR may take one of the following two forms: defect report and enhancement request.

- A defect report describes the defect and software system actions that are out of line with requirements.
- An enhancement request describes a change to the requirements, functionality, or quality of the system.

The above two items were in the focus of practitioner's concerns that can be traced back to the circa 1972 article "That maintenance 'iceberg'" by Canning [13].

According to the said article, practitioners observe maintenance narrowly as correcting errors and broadly as expanding and extending software functionality. In this book, CR refers to both the aforementioned views. The CR document must capture a minimal set of information about changes to software, hardware, and documentation.

Analyze and plan change. In the second phase, program comprehension and impact analysis are conducted. Program comprehension [14] is essential to understanding which parts of the software will be affected by a CR. Program comprehension is basically a process of acquiring useful information from source code. One such information is the location of the domain-specific concept in the source code [15, 16]. The code implementing the concepts may need to be changed in order to provide a solution to the CR. Concepts are units of human knowledge that can be processed by the human mind in one instance. As an example, let us consider the CR "Add a debit card payment issued by Chautauqua bank to the ATM system." In order to change the implementation, the maintenance engineer must locate those system components that implement the concepts "debit card," "payment," and "issued" embedded in the CR. The idea here is to identify the set of system components that are thought to be initially affected by the CR [17]. The identified system components are called Starting Impact Set (SIS) which is discussed in Chapter 6. A thorough discussion of program comprehension is given in Chapter 8.

Impact analysis is conducted to identify the potential consequences of a change and estimate the resources needed to accomplish the change [18]. By means of impact analysis, a software system is analyzed by maintenance personnel to identify the software components that will be affected by a CR. In this analysis, first decide if the components, which are neighbors of the SIS, also need to be modified due to the *ripple effect* [19]. A neighboring component is added to the set if it needs to be modified. For the newly added component, identify which of its neighboring components will be modified, and add them to the set. The process of identifying new components to be modified is repeated until it is found that a modification will not impact new neighboring components. The resulting set of components estimated to be modified is known as the estimated impact set (EIS). The objectives of impact analysis are as follows:

- to determine the set of system components to be affected, given the SIS identified by program comprehension activity;
- to develop accurate estimates of the resources needed to accomplish the implementation task; and
- to analyze the cost and benefits of the CR and make a decision on whether or not to implement the CR.

Software developers use the information gathered from impact analysis in planning how to implement a CR. Moreover, the goal of impact analysis is to minimize unexpected *side effects* of change. A side effect is an error or an undesirable behavior that occurs as a result of a modification in the software [20]. Chapter 6 discusses impact analysis in greater detail.

Implement change. The CR is implemented after the feasibility of a change is established. However, before the implementation of the CR, *restructuring* or *refactoring* of the software is performed in order to accommodate the requested modification. Refactoring is essentially the object-oriented variant of restructuring [21]. Restructuring is most often required in software maintenance; otherwise, systems lose structure. Restructuring is a means of restoring order to understand and change; the restructured product is less susceptible to error when future changes are made. Refactoring, discussed in Chapter 7, improves the software structure without changing their behavior.

Implementing a change comprises a number of steps, each focusing on one specific software component after the completion of refactoring. If a component is changed, it may cease to be compatible with the components with which it interacts. Therefore, non-essential changes must be made in the interacting components, thereby creating a ripple effect throughout the system. The aforementioned activity, generally called a change propagation activity [22, 23], ensures that a modification performed in one component is completely reflected throughout the entire system. Chapter 6 discusses change propagation in greater detail.

Verify and validate. In this phase the software system is verified and validated in order to assure that the integrity of the system has not been compromised. This activity includes code review, regression testing, and execution of new tests if necessary. Regression testing comprises a subset of the unit-, integration-, and system-level tests [24]. If the results are unsatisfactory, then the actualization of the request is rejected which in turn is investigated and further changes are implemented.

Documentation change. The final phase of the change mini-cycle deals with updating the program documentation. It is time to complete the documentation aspect which may include updating the requirements, functional specifications, and design specifications to be consistent with the code. In addition, user manuals and installation and troubleshooting guides are accordingly updated.

3.6 IEEE/EIA MAINTENANCE PROCESS

The IEEE/EIA 1219 standard [25] explains a process for executing and managing activities for software maintenance. The standard basically explains maintenance as a fundamental life cycle process and describes maintenance as the process of a software product undergoing "modification to code and associated documentation due to a problem or the need for improvement. The objective is to modify the existing software product while preserving its integrity" (p. 6–1 of Reference 26). The standard focuses on a seven-phase activity model of maintenance as illustrated in Figure 3.9. The seven phases are listed below:

- Identification of problems
- Analysis
- Design
- Implementation

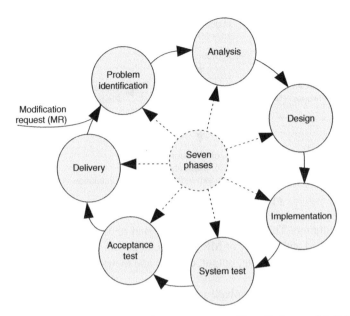

FIGURE 3.9   Seven phases of IEEE maintenance process. From Reference 26. © 2004 IEEE

- System test
- Acceptance test
- Delivery

Each of the seven activities have five associated attributes as follows:

- *Activity definition.* This refers to the implementation process of the activity.
- *Input.* This refers to the items that are required as input to the activity.
- *Output.* This refers to the items that are produced by the activity.
- *Control.* This refers to those items that provide control over the activity.
- *Metrics.* This refers to the items that are measured during the execution of the activity.

Problem identification. A request for change to the software is normally made by the users of the software system or the customers, and it starts the maintenance process. The request for change is submitted in the form of a modification request (MR) for a correction or for an enhancement. It may be noted that MR and CR are interchangeably used in maintenance literature. The maintenance (or sustaining) organization: (i) determines the type of request; (ii) determines the appropriate maintenance category – corrective, adaptive, or perfective; (iii) assigns a priority level; and (iv) assigns a unique identification number. Activities included in this phase are as follows: (i) reject or accept the MR; (ii) identify and estimate the resources needed to change the system; and (iii) put the MR in a batch of changes scheduled

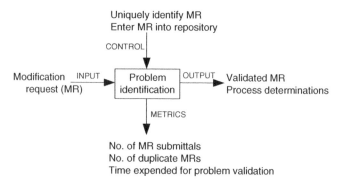

FIGURE 3.10 Problem identification phase

for implementation. The process of collecting and reviewing MRs, such as number of MR submitted and number of MR rejected, begins in this phase. For the problem identification phase, the input, output, control, and metrics have been summarized in Figure 3.10.

Analysis. The inputs to this phase are a validated MR, an initial resource estimation, repository information, and project documentation. Repository is the location in which all software-related artifacts are stored. The process is viewed to have two major components: feasibility analysis and detailed analysis. First, feasibility analysis is performed to (i) determine the impact of the change, (ii) investigate other possible solutions including prototyping, (iii) assess both short-term and long-term costs, and (iv) determine the benefits of making the change. After selecting a specific approach, the second phase of detailed analysis is undertaken. The second phase identifies (i) firm modification requirements, (ii) the software components involved, (iii) an overall test strategy, and (iv) an implementation plan. The standard puts emphasis on at least three levels of tests: unit, integration, and acceptance. In addition, regression tests are associated with each of the three levels of tests. Figure 3.11 summarizes input, control, metrics, and output for the analysis phase.

Upon completion of the analysis phase, a number of actions are taken: (i) risk analysis is performed; (ii) the preliminary resource estimate is updated; and (iii) by involving the customer, it is decided whether or not to proceed on to the next phase. If it is decided to move on to the next phase, the phase deliverables, including a detailed analysis report, are specified. The standard suggests several metrics to be gathered, such as the number of requirement changes, elapsed time, and the error rate generated.

Design. A modification to the system begins in this phase based on the information gathered up to this point. The information includes system and project documentation, the output of the analysis phase, existing software, and repository information. Activities of this phase are as follows: (i) identify the affected software components; (ii) modify the software components; (iii) document the changes; (iv) create a test suite for the new design; and (v) select test cases for regression testing. This phase provides a revised design baseline, revised test plans, an up-to-date detailed analysis report, revised risk analysis, and verified requirements. Figure 3.12 summarizes the input, output, metrics, and control for the design phase.

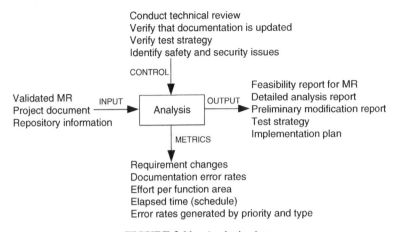

FIGURE 3.11   Analysis phase

Implementation. The design phase produces the primary inputs to this phase. The activities executed in this phase are: writing new code and performing unit testing, integrating changed code, conducting integration and regression testing, performing risk analysis, and reviewing the system for test readiness. To assess whether or not the system is ready for system-level testing, a review is performed in this phase. In this phase, risk analysis and reviews are periodically performed, rather than at the end of the phase. Multiple reviews need to be performed due to the fact that a large percentage of design, performance issues, risks, and cost are exposed while changing the system. All documentations, including the software, design, test, user, and training

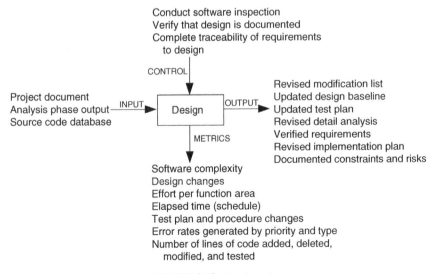

FIGURE 3.12   Design phase

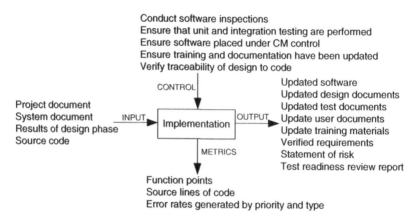

FIGURE 3.13 Implementation phase

information are updated. For the implementation phase, the input, output, metrics, and control are summarized in Figure 3.13.

System test. In this phase, tests are performed on the full system to ensure that the modified system complies with the original requirements as well as the new modifications. System-level testing comprises a broad spectrum of testing activities: functionality testing, robustness testing, stability testing, load testing, performance testing, security testing, and regression testing. Regression testing is conducted to validate that no new faults have been introduced. Quite often, during the maintenance process, the sustaining test engineers execute the system test cases [24]. Finally, the maintenance personnel verify whether or not the system is ready to perform acceptance testing. This phase accepts as its input a system test plan consisting of detailed test cases, test readiness review report, and an updated system. This phase provides a test report, a fully integrated tested system, and test readiness review report. For the system test phase, the input, output, metrics, and control are summarized in Figure 3.14.

Acceptance test. Acceptance testing is performed on a completely integrated system, and it involves customers, users, or their representatives. The main objective of

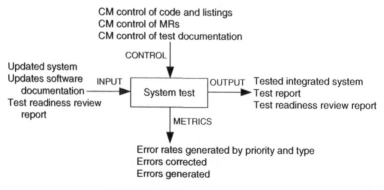

FIGURE 3.14 System test phase

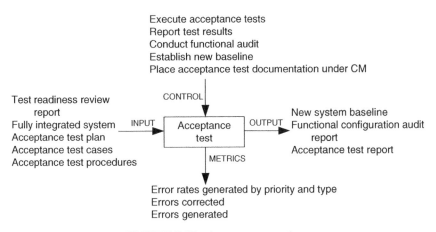

Execute acceptance tests
Report test results
Conduct functional audit
Establish new baseline
Place acceptance test documentation under CM

CONTROL

Test readiness review
   report
Fully integrated system   INPUT
Acceptance test plan
Acceptance test cases
Acceptance test procedures

Acceptance
test

OUTPUT   New system baseline
   Functional configuration audit
   report
   Acceptance test report

METRICS

Error rates generated by priority and type
Errors corrected
Errors generated

FIGURE 3.15   Acceptance test phase

acceptance testing is to assess the overall quality of the system, rather than actively identify defects. As an aside, on the other hand, the objective of system testing is to search for defects [24]. An important concept in acceptance testing is the customer's expectation from the system. The primary inputs to this phase are the test readiness review report, a fully integrated system, and a test plan with detailed test cases for acceptance testing. At the end of acceptance testing, a test report is generated. The report explains the status of the criteria that was agreed upon for successful completion of acceptance testing. The status report is communicated to the committee responsible for review. The customer chairs the review committee to evaluate the exit criteria and the test report to make sure that the system is ready for a release. For the acceptance test phase, the input, output, metrics, and control are summarized in Figure 3.15.

Delivery. In this phase, the changed system is released to customers for installation and operation. Included in this phase are the following activities: notify the user community, perform installation and training, and develop an archival version of the system for backup. For the delivery phase, the input, output, metrics, and control are summarized in Figure 3.16.

Guidelines on maintenance practices are also recommended by the standard in its appendices. For example, guidelines for maintenance practices include a guideline to make a maintenance plan; Table 3.1 shows the key sections of a maintenance plan.

3.7   ISO/IEC 14764 MAINTENANCE PROCESS

The document ISO/IEC 14764 [27] is an international standard for software maintenance, and it describes maintenance using the same concepts as IEEE/EIA 1219 except that they are depicted slightly differently. An iterative process to execute and manage maintenance activities is described in the document. The basic structure of an ISO process is made up of activities, and an activity is made up of tasks. To change

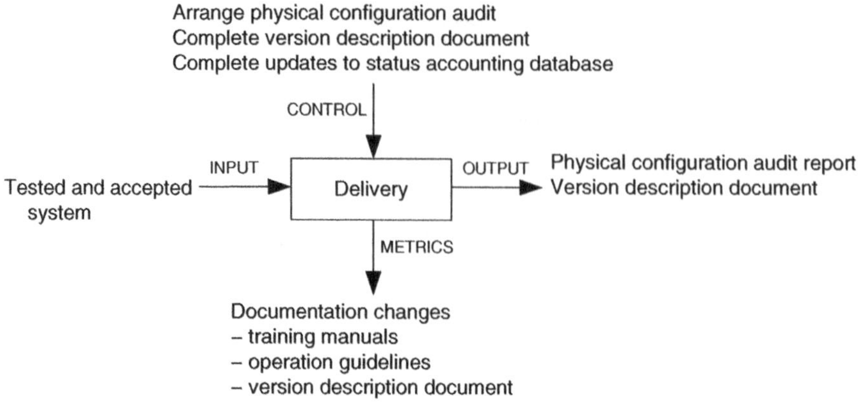

Arrange physical configuration audit
Complete version description document
Complete updates to status accounting database

CONTROL

INPUT   OUTPUT   Physical configuration audit report
Tested and accepted ──────▶ Delivery ──────▶ Version description document
system

METRICS

Documentation changes
– training manuals
– operation guidelines
– version description document

FIGURE 3.16   Delivery phase

an operational software without breaking its integrity, the necessary activities are described in the maintenance process.

Upon an activation of the maintenance process, plans and procedures are developed and resources are allocated to carry out maintenance. In response to a CR, code is modified in conjunction with the relevant documentation. Modification of the running software without losing the system's integrity is considered to be the overall objective of maintenance. The maintenance process enables the software product to migrate from its initial environment at its inception to new environments. The maintenance process is terminated upon the eventual decommissioning of the product, commonly known as being retired. The maintenance process comprises the following high-level activities:

1. Process implementation
2. Problem and modification analysis
3. Modification implementation
4. Maintenance review and acceptance
5. Migration
6. Retirement

The maintenance process activities developed by ISO/IEC are shown in Figure 3.17. Each of these activities is made up of tasks, and each task describes a specific action with inputs and outputs. A task specifies *what to do, but not* how to do [28]. Inputs refer to the items that are used by the maintenance activity to generate outputs. Effective controls are needed to provide useful guidance so that the maintenance activity produces the desired outputs. Outputs are objects generated by the maintenance activity. Support refers to the items that support the maintenance activity.

Process implementation. This activity establishes plans and procedures to be followed. A maintenance plan is made concurrently with the plan for development. Figure 3.18 graphically summarizes the process implementation activity with the

TABLE 3.1   Template of a Maintenance Plan

1. Introduction

This section outlines the goals, purpose, and general scope of the maintenance effort. Also, deviations from the standard are identified.

2. References

The documents that impose constraints on the maintenance effort are identified in this section.
In addition, other documents supporting maintenance activities are identified.

3. Definitions

All terms required to understand the maintenance plan are defined in this section.
If some terms are already defined in other documents, then references are provided to those documents.

4. Software Maintenance Overview

This section briefly describes the following aspects of the maintenance process:
4.1 Organization
4.2 Scheduling Priorities
4.3 Resource Summary
4.4 Responsibilities
4.5 Tools, Techniques, and Methods

5. Software Maintenance Process

This section describes the actions to be executed in each phase of the maintenance process. Each action is described in the form of input, output, process, and control.
5.1 Problem Identification/Classification and Prioritization
5.2 Analysis
5.3 Design
5.4 Implementation
5.5 System Testing
5.6 Acceptance Testing
5.7 Delivery

6. Software Maintenance Reporting Requirements

This section briefly describes the process for gathering information and disseminating it to members of the maintenance organization.

7. Software Maintenance Administrative Requirements

Describes the standard practices and rules for anomaly resolution and reporting.
7.1 Anomaly Resolution and Reporting
7.2 Deviation Policy
7.3 Control Procedures
7.4 Standards, Practices, and Conventions
7.5 Performance Tracking
7.6 Quality Control of Plan

8. Software Maintenance Documentation Requirements

Describes the procedures to be followed in recording and presenting the outputs of the maintenance process.

Source: From Reference 25. © 1998 IEEE.

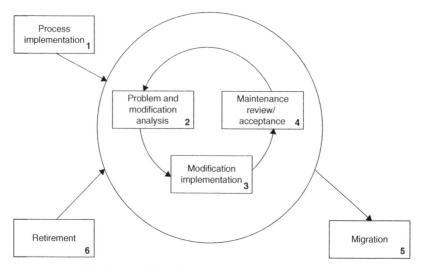

FIGURE 3.17   ISO/IEC 14764 iterative maintenance process. From Reference 26. © 2004 IEEE

input, output, control, and support items. The process implementation activity consists of three major tasks as explained in the following:

Maintenance plan: The maintenance plan describes a strategy to maintain the system, whereas the procedures for maintenance describe in details how to actually accomplish maintenance. The plan also describes how to: (i) organize and staff the maintenance team; (ii) assign responsibilities among team members; and (iii) schedule resources. The main idea is to provide cost-effective support to the maintenance team.

Modification requests: Users submit modification (or change) requests to communicate with the maintainer. The maintainer establishes procedures to receive, record, and track user requests for modifications and giving them feedback. The problem resolution process is initiated whenever an MR is received. MRs are

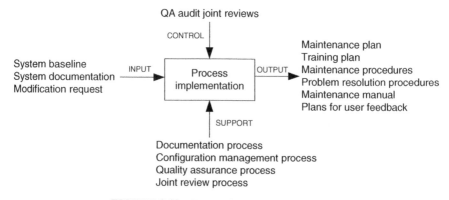

FIGURE 3.18   Process implementation activity

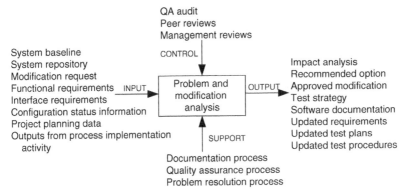

FIGURE 3.19   Problem and modification activity

classified by the maintainer as either problem reports (corrective) or enhancement (adaptive and perfective) requests. The maintenance process prioritizes and tracks these requests individually as different types of maintenance are there. A thorough discussion of MR workflow is given in Section 3.9.

Configuration management (CM): The software product and any changes made to it during its maintenance lifespan need to be controlled. Basically, change control is performed by enforcing and implementing an approved SCM process. The SCM process is implemented by developing and following a configuration management plan (CMP) and the corresponding procedures. It is discussed in detail in Section 3.8.

Problem and modification analysis. This activity is invoked after the software system transitions from development stage to maintenance stage, and it is called iteratively when the need for modification arises, as depicted in Figure 3.17. The maintainer analyzes the MR to identify its impact on the organization, the existing system, and the interfacing systems. Further, the maintainer (i) develops and documents potential solutions and (ii) obtains the approval from the upper management to implement the solutions. Figure 3.19 graphically summarizes the problem and modification analysis activity with the input, output, control, and support items. This activity comprises five tasks as discussed in the following paragraphs.

MR analysis: The maintainer analyzes the MR to determine the impact on the organization, hardware, the existing system, other interfacing systems, documentation, data structures, and humans (operators, maintainers, and users). The overall objective of impact analysis is to determine all the entities that are going to be modified and/or affected if the MR is going to be implemented. The steps of impact analysis are given in Table 3.2.

Verification: The maintainer must reproduce the problem and document the test results in the laboratory environment if the MR is corrective in order to determine the validity of the MR. For adaptive and perfective maintenance tasks, verification is not required. The maintainer designs a test strategy to verify and replicate the problem.

TABLE 3.2   Modification Request Task Steps

1. Decide whether or not the maintainer is adequately staffed to make the proposed changes.
2. Decide whether or not the maintenance program has received adequate budget.
3. Decide whether or not enough resources are available and whether the proposed change will effect some current or future projects.
4. Determine the operational issues to be considered.
5. Determine handling priority.
6. Classify the type of maintenance.
7. Determine the impact to current and future users.
8. Determine safety and security implications.
9. Identify ripple effects.
10. Determine any hardware or software constraints that may result from the proposed changes.
11. Estimate the values of the benefits of making the changes.
12. Determine the impact on existing schedules.
13. Document the risks resulting from the impact analysis.
14. Estimate the evaluation to be performed.
15. Estimate the cost of management to execute the modification.
16. Place developed artifacts under CM.

Options: The maintainer must outline two or more alternative solutions to the MR based on the analysis performed. The alternative solutions report must include the cost, effort, and schedule for implementing different solutions. The maintainer must perform the task steps shown in Table 3.3 to identify alternative solutions to the MR.

Documentation: The maintainer documents the MRs, the analysis results, and the implementation option report after the analysis is complete and the alternate solutions are identified. The maintainer may use the task steps shown in Table 3.4 to write this document.

Approval: The maintainer submits the analysis report to the appropriate authority in the organization to seek their approval for the selected change option. Upon approval, the maintainer updates the requirements if the MR is an enhancement (improvement).

TABLE 3.3   Option Task Steps

1. The MR is assigned a work priority.
2. Explore a work-around for the problem. If a work-around exists, provide it to the user.
3. Identify concrete requirements for the planned modification.
4. Calculate the magnitude and size of the planned modification.
5. Identify a variety of options to execute the planned modification.
6. Estimate the impacts of the options on the users and system hardware.
7. Analyze the risks of each option.
8. Document the outcomes of risk analysis for each of the proposed options.
9. Develop a widely acceptable plan to implement the modification.

TABLE 3.4   Documentation Task Steps

1. Ensure result analyses have been completed and documentations updated. If documentations do not exist, develop new documentation.
2. For accuracy, review the planned strategy to perform tests and review the schedule.
3. Review resource estimates for accuracy.
4. Revise the database for storing accounting status.
5. Describe a procedure to decide whether or not to approve the MR.

Modification implementation. In this activity, maintainers (i) identify the items to be modified and (ii) execute a development process to actually implement the modifications. The maintainer determines the type of documentation, software units, and version of the software that are to be changed. Though development becomes part of the modification activity, it is tailored to eliminate the activities that do not apply to maintenance effort, such as requirement elicitation and architectural design. To ensure that the modified or the newly added requirements are correctly implemented, test plans and procedures are included in the development process. In addition, it is ensured that the requirements that have not been modified are not affected by the new implementation. The inputs to this activity include all the analysis work performed in previous activities, and the output is a new software baseline. Figure 3.20 shows the modification implementation activity.

Maintenance review/acceptance. By means of this activity, it is ensured that (i) the changes made to the software are correct and (ii) changes are made to the software according to accepted standards and methodologies. The activity is augmented with the following processes: (i) a process for quality management; (ii) a process to verify the product; (iii) a process to validate the product; and (iv) a process to review the product. The maintenance plan should have documented how these supporting processes were tailored to address the characteristics of the specific software product. The inputs to this activity include the modified software and the test results. Figure 3.21 summarizes the maintenance/acceptance activity with the input,

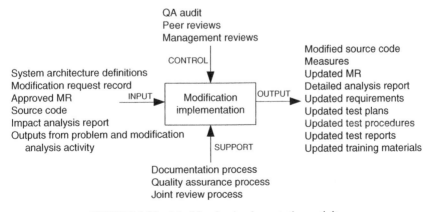

FIGURE 3.20   Modification implementation activity

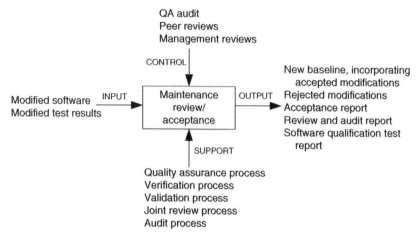

FIGURE 3.21   Maintenance review/acceptance activity

output, control, and support items. The process implementation activity consists of two major tasks: review and approval. The task steps for both review and approval are enumerated in Table 3.5.

Migration. This refers to the process of moving a software system from one technological environment to a different one that is considered to be better. Migration is effected in two broad phases: (i) identify the actions required to achieve migration and (ii) design and document the concrete steps to be executed to effect migration. Figure 3.22 summarizes the migration activity with the input, output, control,

---

TABLE 3.5   Review and Approval Task Steps

Review Task Steps
1. Track the MRs from requirement specification to coding.
2. Ensure that the code is testable.
3. Ensure that the code conforms to coding standards.
4. Ensure that only the required software components were changed.
5. Ensure that the new code is correctly integrated with the system.
6. Ensure that documentations are accurately updated.
7. CM personnel build software items for testing.
8. Perform testing by an independent test organization.
9. Perform system test on a fully integrated system.
10. Develop test report.

Approval Task Steps
1. Obtain quality assurance approval.
2. Verify that the process has been followed.
3. CM prepares the delivery package.
4. Conduct functional and physical configuration audit.
6. Notify operators.
7. Perform installation and training at the operator's facility.

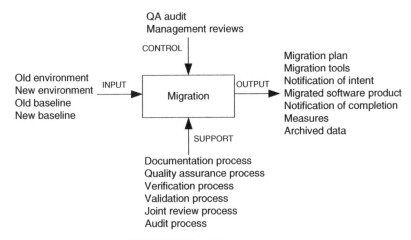

FIGURE 3.22   Migration activity

and support items. This activity comprises seven tasks discussed in the following paragraphs.

Migration standard: During the migration of a software product from an old to a new operational environment, the maintainer must ensure that any additional software products or data produced or modified adhere to standard ISO/IEC 12207 [29]. As a part of the standard tasks, the maintainer (i) identifies all the software elements or data that were changed or added and (ii) ensures that the tasks were performed according to standard ISO/IEC 12207.

Migration plan: For successful migration, a plan must be developed, documented, reviewed, and executed. The maintainer performs the task steps shown in Table 3.6 to write this document. The plan is developed in collaboration with the customers and it addresses the following:

- Requirements analysis and definition of migration
- Development of migration tools
- Conversion of software product and data
- Execution of migration
- Verification of migration
- Support backward compatibility with the old execution environment

Notification of intent: The maintainer explains to the users: (i) why support for the old environment has been discontinued; (ii) the new environment and when it will be supported; and (iii) the availability of other options, if there is any, upon the removal of the old environment.

Implement operations and training: Once a software product has been improved by modification and tested by the maintainer, it is installed in an operational environment to run concurrently with the old system. By running the old and the new system in parallel, users get an opportunity to become familiar with

TABLE 3.6   Migration Plan Task Steps

1. Analyze the requirements for migration.
2. Perform an impact analysis of migrating the software system.
3. Make a schedule to execute migration.
4. Determine all requirements for data collection to perform post-operation review.
5. Identify and record the migration effort.
6. Identify and reduce risks.
7. Identify the required tools to support migration.
8. Determine how the old environment is going to be supported.
9. Acquire and/or design new tools to support migration.
10. Partition software products and data for conversion in an incremental manner.
11. Prioritize the activities involving data conversion and software products.
12. Execute software products and data conversions.
13. Perform migration of software products and data to the new environment.
14. Operate the migrated system and the old system in parallel as much as possible.
15. Perform testing to ensure the success of migration.
16. Should there be a need, continue to provide support for the old environment.

TABLE 3.7   Operation and Training Task Steps

Parallel Operations Task Steps
1. Survey the site.
2. Install hardware equipment.
3. Install the software system.
4. Run basic tests to ensure that hardware and software have been correctly installed.
5. Run both the new and old systems in parallel, under the desired operational load.
6. Gather data from the old and the new systems.
7. Analyze the collected data.

Training Task Steps
1. Identify the requirements for migration training.
2. Schedule the requirements for migration training.
3. Review the migration training.
4. Update the plan to provide training.

the new system, so that transition from the old to the new system becomes smoother. In addition, this will create an environment for the maintainer to compare and understand the input/output relationships of the old and the new system. During this period training should also be provided to the users. The steps listed in Table 3.7 can be performed by the maintainer in this step.

Notification of completion: The maintainer notifies all the sites that the new system will become operational and that the old system can be shut down and uninstalled, after the completion of training and parallel operation of both the new and the old system for an appropriate number of hours. Essentially, the following task steps are performed by the maintainer:

1. Announce the migration.
2. Document the site-specific issues and make a plan to resolve them.
3. Archive the old system, including data and software.
4. Remove the old equipment.

Post-operation review: Following the installation and operation of a changed system, a review is performed to assess the impact of changing the system in the new environment. The review reports are sent to the competent parties for information, guidance, and further actions. The maintainer executes the following steps, as part of the task:

1. Analyze the results of running the two systems concurrently.
2. Identify potential risk areas.
3. Summarize the lessons learned.
4. Produce a report on impact analysis.

Data archival: Data associated with the old environment are made accessible to comply with the contractual requirements for data protection and audit. The maintainer performs the following steps as part of the task:

1. The old data and software are archived.
2. The old data and software are put on multiple media.
3. The media are saved in secure places.

Retirement. A software product is retired when it is viewed to have reached the end of its useful life. An economic-based analysis is performed to retire the product and it is included in the retirement plan. Sometimes the work performed by the product is no longer needed; therefore, the retired product is not replaced. In other cases, a new software product has already been developed to replace the current system. In either case, the software system must be removed from the service in an orderly manner. In addition, considerations are given to accessing data produced by the software to be retired. Figure 3.23

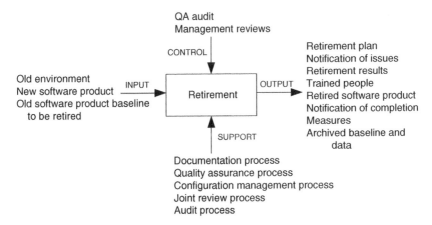

FIGURE 3.23   Retirement activity

TABLE 3.8 Retirement Plan Task Steps

1. Analyze the requirements to retire the systems.
2. Determine what impacts the retiring software will have.
3. Identify a product that will replace the software to be retired.
4. Make a schedule to retire the software.
5. Determine the need for residual support in the future.
6. Identify and describe the retirement effort.

summarizes the retirement activity with the input, output, control, and support items. All artifacts from the retirement activity are controlled with CM. This activity comprises five tasks discussed in the following paragraphs.

Retirement plan: In order to ensure a successful retirement, a retirement plan is developed, documented, reviewed, and executed. The maintainer performs the task steps shown in Table 3.8 to write this document. The plan is developed in collaboration with the customers to address the following:

- Transition to any new software system.
- Withdrawal of partial or full support after a grace period.
- Responsibility for any future contractual support.
- Archiving the software system, including all the documentation.
- Accessibility to archived data.

Notification of intent: The maintainer conveys to the users: (i) the reason for discontinuing support for the product; (ii) a note about the replacement or upgrade for the phased-out system, with an availability date; and (iii) a list of the other options available, if there is any, upon the removal of the old environment.

Implement parallel operations and training: If there is a replacement system for the software product to be retired, it is installed in an operational environment to run concurrently with the old system. By running the new and the old system in parallel, users will get an opportunity to become familiar with the new system so that transition from the old to the new system becomes smoother. In addition, this will create an environment for the maintainer to compare and understand the input/output relationships between the new system and the old system. In addition, training is provided to the users during this period.

Notification of completion: The maintainer notifies all the sites that the new system will become operational and that the old system can be shut down. The old system is generally shut down after the the new system is in operation for a certain length of time. The maintainer performs the following steps as part of the task:

1. Make an announcement about the changes.
2. Identify issues specific to individual sites and describe how those will be resolved.

3. Store the old data and software in an archive.

4. Disconnect and move out the old hardware infrastructure.

Data archival: Data associated or used with the old environment will be made accessible according to contractual requirements involving data protection and audit. The maintainer executes the following steps as part of this task:

1. Archive the old data and software.

2. Make multiple copies of the old data and software.

3. Keep the media in safe places.

3.8 SOFTWARE CONFIGURATION MANAGEMENT

Large, complex systems undergo many more changes than relatively small systems, and management of changes in large systems is nontrivial. Therefore, the concept of CM was developed to manage changes in large systems.

The goal of CM is to manage and control the numerous corrections, extensions, and adaptations that are applied to a system over its lifetime. It handles the control of all product items and changes to those items. On the other hand, SCM is applied to software products. In this case the product items include document, executable software, source code, hardware, and disks. SCM has been defined by Bersoff, Hendeson, and Siegel [30] as *the discipline of identifying the configuration of a system at discrete points in time for the purpose of systematically controlling changes to this configuration and maintaining the integrity and traceability of this configuration throughout the system life cycle.* SCM accrues two kinds of benefits to an organization as follows:

- SCM ensures that development processes are traceable and systematic so that all changes are precisely managed. Consequently, the product is always in a well-defined state [31].
- SCM enhances the quality of the delivered system and the productivity of the maintainers.

CM is an essential part of software development and maintenance environment. It ensures that the released software is not contaminated by uncontrolled or unapproved changes. The objectives of SCM are to:

- Uniquely identify every version of every software at various points in time.
- Retain past versions of documentations and software.
- Provide a trail of audit for all modifications performed.
- Throughout the software life cycle, maintain the traceability and integrity of the system changes.

Projects benefit from effective SCM as follows [32]:

1. Confusion is reduced and order is established.
2. To maintain product integrity, the necessary activities are organized.
3. Correct product configurations are ensured.
4. Quality is ensured and better quality software consumes less maintenance efforts.
5. Productivity is improved, because analysts and programmers know exactly where to find any piece of the software.
6. Liability is reduced by documenting the trail of actions.
7. Life cycle cost is reduced.
8. Conformance with requirements is enabled.
9. A reliable working environment is provided.
10. Compliance with standards is enhanced.
11. Accounting of status is enhanced.

3.8.1 Brief History

A need for CM was originally felt in the aerospace industry in the 1950s with the primary purpose of guaranteeing reproducibility of aircrafts and managing engineering changes (ECs). In the 1970s, large-scale computer software began to pose many of those same change management problems. It became apparent that software maintenance engineers could borrow CM techniques from the aerospace industry to manage software modifications. In the beginning, punch cards with different colors were used to indicate changes. In the late 1960s, to indicate changes to the UNIVAC-1100 EXEC-8 operating system, maintenance personnel used "corrective cards." At that time, development of operating systems benefited from SCM. In the 1970s and the 1980s, SCM emerged as a distinct discipline. With the advancements in user-friendly software development environments, namely, Unix, specialized computer software tools were built. For example, the Unix-based software tool *Make* [33] accepts descriptions of system configurations and can automatically construct the system from its descriptions. The source code control system (SCCS) [34] and the revision control system (RCS) [35] tools permit the maintainer to keep track of all the *textual* alterations made to a file.

Gradually, software products became candidates for configuration control. This resulted in a need to manage user workspaces, which was duly supported by newer SCM systems. In other words, SCM functionalities continued to evolve. Instead of storing the entire versions of software products, in the 1980s, delta algorithms based on text matching were developed to enable SCM tools to store just the differences among versions. In the 1990s, developers felt an increasing need to manage nontextual objects. Consequently, novel algorithms were developed for efficient storage and retrieval of nontextual objects. By the year 2000, due to disk storage becoming inexpensive, CPUs becoming fast, and nontextual objects becoming common, the storage of deltas became unimportant and many new tools simply used compression such as zip. These days SCM systems support the management of evolution of a broad range of software systems that are being modified by a large number of maintenance personnel working in different countries and utilizing a variety of machines.

3.8.2   SCM Spectrum of Functionality

These days a broad range of high-level functionalities are supported by SCM systems. Estublier et al. [31] classified the functionalities into three broad areas: product, tool, and process. Next, each area is decomposed into a number of technical dimensions as shown in Figure 3.24. Those technical dimensions are briefly explained in the following.

Identification. The items whose configurations need to be managed are identified in this function. The identified items include specification, design, documents, data, drawings, source code, executable code, test plan, test script, hardware components, and components of the software development environment, namely, compilers, debuggers, and emulators. Project plan and customer requirements should also be included. To accurately identify products, including their configuration and version levels, a schema of names and numbers is designed. Finally, for all configuration items and systems, a baseline configuration is established. If there is a need to make changes to the baseline, it is done so with the concurrence of the configuration control organization.

Version control. To avoid confusion during the process of artifact evolution, a new identifier is assigned to the artifact every time the artifact is modified. It is important to note that assigning a new identifier for every modification of the same artifact may hide important relations among the uniquely identified artifacts. As an example, one may be interested in recording a fact that a given artifact fixes a subset of defects

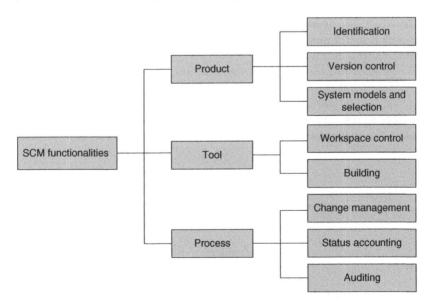

FIGURE 3.24   Technical dimensions of SCM systems

found in an earlier release. The aforementioned kind of relation can be recorded by means of the version control (VC) functionality of SCM by: (i) interpreting software artifacts as configuration items and (ii) identifying the relations, if there is any, among the configuration items.

The basic VC idea is to have two separate files: master copies and working copies. The former is stored in a centralized repository. Software developers check out working copies from the repository, modify the working copies, and, finally, check in the working copies into the repository. Checking in a file means committing to the changes made to the working copies. The VC system creates a new version in the repository every time a file is committed. As time passes, all versions of the file are stored in the repository. Storing multiple copies of a file does not excessively waste space. Therefore, storing many copies of a file does not excessively waste storage space. Conflicts can arise if many software developers want to use the same version of a file. However, conflicts can be resolved by means of two techniques: lock-modify-unlock and copy-modify-merge [36]. The former model requires developers to obtain a lock on the file they want to modify. While a developer is holding the lock on a file, no other developer can modify the file. However, it may be noted that a locked file can be checked out for viewing and compilation. When there is no need to further keep a file locked, the developer commits the modifications and the lock is released. On the other hand, developers are at liberty to change their working copies in the copy-modify-merge model. If different developers make conflicting changes, the VC system flags the conflicts so that the developers can resolve them.

In addition, VC must support parallel development by allowing branching of versions. For example, consider the scenario: (i) an organization is currently developing the next version of their already released application; and (ii) a report about a major defect is received from the end users. Now the development group has the option to retrieve the released version and create a branch, as illustrated in Figure 3.25, to fix the defect. The figure illustrates how a file evolves with two branches, where the main path is called trunk. As shown in the figure, branch changes are incorporated by merging with the trunk.

System models and selection. Files are discrete entities that contain descriptions of well-defined items of a project, namely, requirement specification, test cases, design, code, test results, and defect reports. However, it is neither efficient nor effective to manage a project file-by-file. Consequently, a need to support aggregate artifacts arises so that maintenancex personnel can enforce consistency in large projects by

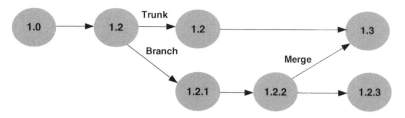

FIGURE 3.25   An evolution of a file with two branches

means of relationships among artifacts and attributes. Relationships among artifacts and attributes are captured by developing models which support the idea of software configurations. Intuitively, a configuration means an aggregate of versionable items. The general idea of configuration raises a need for enabling users to have selective access to parts and versions of such aggregated artifacts. By default, SCCS and RCS keep in the workspace the most recent version of the principal variant. Next, all artifacts that are exceptions to the default placement rule can be explicitly fetched by the user.

Workspace control. Workspaces are implemented by SCM systems to give users an isolated place. In their own workspaces, users perform the usual tasks of editing and managing their artifacts. Such an environment that enables the maintainer to make and test the changes in an isolated manner is called workspace. In an SCM system, software versions are stored in a repository that cannot be directly modified. Rather, when a need to modify some files arises, the files are copied into a workspace. One can realize a workspace in two ways: (i) it can be as simple as the home directory of the programmer who wants to modify the files and (ii) it can be a complex mechanism such as an integrated development environment and a database. In general, three basic functions are performed in a workspace:

- Sandbox: Checked out files are put in a workspace to be freely edited. In addition, it is not necessary to lock the original files in the repository.
- Building: An SCM system generally stores the differences between successive versions to save space. Therefore, the workspace expands the deltas into full-fledged source files. In addition, the workspace stores the derived binaries.
- Isolation: Every developer maintains at least one workspace. Therefore, the developer makes modifications to the source code, compiles the files, performs tests, and debugs code without impacting the works of other developers.

The aforementioned features are generally available in modern software development environments. SCM systems provide a centralized facility to manage these features.

Building. Efficiency is a key requirement of SCM systems so that developers can quickly build an executable file from the versioned source files. A second requirement of SCM systems is that it must enable the building of old versions of the system for recovery, testing, maintenance, or additional release purpose. Third, most SCM systems support building of software. The build process and their products are assessed for quality assurance. Outputs of the build process become quality assurance records, and the records may be needed for future reference. The *make* [33] application on the Unix operating system, originally developed by researchers at Bell Laboratories, is a classical example of a build process. The tool continues to remain popular for system building. For instance, commercial SCM systems such as *ClearCase* [37] continue to rely on variants of *make*.

Change management. SCM systems must: (i) enable users to understand the impact of modifications; (ii) enable users to identify the products to which a specific modification applies; and (iii) provide maintenance personnel with tools for change management so that all activities from specifying requirements to coding can be traced. In the beginning, CRs were managed in paper form. However, these days CRs are saved in the SCM repository and are linked with the actual modifications, in addition to being automated. This topic is further discussed in Section 3.9.

Status accounting. To be able to quantify the properties of the software being developed and the process being used, it is necessary to gather statistics—and it can be done at the SCM level. The primary purpose of status accounting is to: (i) keep formal records of already existing configurations and (ii) produce periodic reports about the status of the configurations. These records: (i) describe the product correctly; (ii) are used to verify the configuration of the system for testing and delivery; and (iii) maintain a history of CRs, including both the approved ones and the rejected ones. A history of CR includes the answers to the following questions:

- Why are changes made?
- When are the changes made?
- Who makes the changes?
- What changes are made?

Status accounting is useful in communicating important details of the project and configuration items to the stakeholders of the project. For example, maintenance personnel can view what files or fixes were part of what baseline systems. Another example is that project managers can trace completion of problem reports. Status accounting reduces the need to produce extensive reports, which include item *delta* report, transaction log, and modification log. Other common reports include resource usage, change in process, change in deviations, and status of all configuration items [38]. Examples of status accounting include the number of CR per software configuration item and the average time needed to implement a CR.

Auditing. SCM systems need to provide the following features: (i) roll back to earlier stable points and (ii) identify which modifications were performed, why those modifications were performed, and who performed those modifications. In other words, ideally, an SCM system behaves as a searchable archive of all things that happened in the past. By means of auditing, the organization maintains the integrity of the baselines and release configurations for all products. Two kinds of audits are performed before a software is released: audit for functional configuration and audit for physical configuration. The former determines whether or not the software satisfies the user requirement specification and the system requirement specification. On the other hand, the latter verifies if the reference and design documents accurately represent the software. Overall, a configuration audit tries to find answers to the following:

- To what extent are the requirements satisfied by the modified system?
- Does the software release under consideration reflect the MRs?

The activities to perform a configuration audit are as follows:

- Procedures and an audit schedule are defined.
- The personnel to perform the audits are identified.
- Established baselines are audited.
- Audit reports are generated.

3.8.3   SCM Process

There is a large gap between mere understanding of the capabilities of SCM and successfully applying SCM in practice. As it is the case with large software projects, planning is critical to the successful application of SCM. By means of a plan, a configuration baseline is established. Baselining is the process by which a given set of configurable items formally become publicly available at a standard location, such as in a repository, to the people who are authorized to use it. Following the identification of the initial configuration, a configuration control process, as illustrated in Figure 3.26 [32], is invoked. Figure 3.26 shows the three major SCM implementation activities: planning, baseline development, and configuration control.

Planning. Planning is begun with two activities: (i) defining the SCM process and (ii) establishing procedures to control and document changes. A key step during planning is the identification of the stakeholders. All those who influence a system's behavior and all those who are impacted by the system are stakeholders of the system [39]. The stakeholders in a CM are the maintainers, development engineers, sustaining test engineers, quality assurance auditors, users, and the management. The

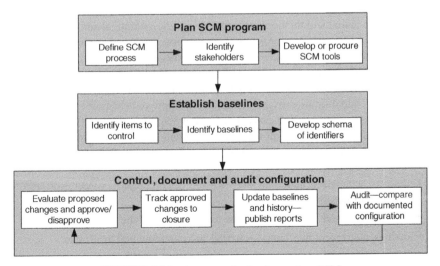

FIGURE 3.26   A process for implementing SCM

stakeholders are also known as configuration control board (CCB) members. Not all changes are reviewed by the board. Rather, small groups review and approve most of the changes. Therefore, those groups need to be identified in the planning phase. Various SCM tools are used to maintain configuration history and facilitate the SCM process flow. Examples of such tools are concurrent version system (CVS) and Clearcase [37].

Establishing baselines. Once an SCM program plan is in place, the next step in implementing effective SCM is to identify the items that are the subject of configuration control. Some examples of those items are code, data, and documents. With the configuration items identified, a software baseline library is established to make the set of configurable items publicly available. The library, called repository, is the heart of the SCM system. The repository is the central place that contains all configurations that have been made public. In other words, the repository has information about all the baselined items. The process of baseline (or re-baseline for a change) involves the following activities:

1. Create a snapshot of the current version of the product and its configuration items and allocate a configuration identifier to the entire configuration.
2. Allocate version numbers to the configuration items and check in the configuration.
3. Store the approved authority information as part of meta data in the repository.
4. Broadcast all the above information to the stakeholders.
5. To accurately identify the configuration version, design a schema of words, numbers, or letters for common types of configuration items. In addition, project requirements may dictate specific nomenclature.

Controlling, documenting, and auditing. After establishing a baseline, it is important to: (i) keep the actual and the documented configuration identical and (ii) ensure that the baseline complies with a project's configuration described in the requirements document. The aforementioned requirements of a baseline are realized by means of a four-step iterative process illustrated in Figure 3.26. The stakeholders specified in the SCM plan review and evaluate all changes to the configuration. After their evaluations, both approvals and disapprovals are documented. Approved changes are tracked until they are verified—and this is discussed in Section 3.9. Next, the appropriate baseline is revised in conjunction with all relevant documents, and reports are generated. At regular intervals, records and products are audited to verify that:

- there is acceptable matching between the documented configuration and the actual configuration;
- the configuration conforms with the requirements of the project; and
- documentations of all change activities are complete and up-to-date.

The three steps in the cycle, namely, controlling, documenting, and auditing, are repeatedly executed throughout the lifetime of the project.

3.9   CR WORKFLOW

A CR, also called an MR, is a vehicle for recording information about a system defect, requested enhancement, or quality improvement. In other words, defect reports or enhancement requests are documented as a CR. CRs are placed under the control of a change management system. Change management systems control changes by an automated system in the form of workflow. The basic objective of change management is to uniquely identify, describe, and track the status of each requested change. It is a methodology for controlling changes to evolving systems. The objectives of change management are as follows [1]:

- Provide a common method for communication among stakeholders.
- Uniquely identify and track the status of each CR. This feature simplifies progress reporting and provides better control over changes.
- Maintain a database about all changes to the system. This information can be used for monitoring and measuring metrics.

A CR describes the desires and needs of users which the system is expected to implement. While describing a CR, two factors need to be taken into account:

- Correctness of CRs: CRs need to be unambiguously described so that it is easy to review them for their correctness. The "form" of a CR is key to effective interactions between the software development organization and the users. The "form" should document essential information about changes to software, hardware, and documentation.
- Clear communication of CRs to the stakeholders: CRs need to be clearly communicated to the stakeholders, including the maintainers, so that those CRs are not interpreted in a different way. The people who might be collecting CRs may not be part of the maintenance group. For example, the marketing people may be collecting CRs. Therefore, there may not be direct communication between the teams actually carrying out the changes to the system and the end users.

It becomes counterproductive for different teams to interpret CRs differently. The results of interpreting a CR in different ways are as follows:

- The team carrying out actual changes to the system and the team performing tests may develop contradicting views about the new system's quality.
- The changed system may not meet the needs and desires of the end users.

CRs need to be represented in an unambiguous manner and made available in a centralized repository. Wide availability of CRs to all the stakeholders is likely to reveal differences in interpretations by different groups.

Next, a formal model is described to represent CRs for analysis and review. The life cycle of a CR has been illustrated in Figure 3.27, by means of a state-transition diagram. Each state represents a distinct stage in the life-cycle of a CR.

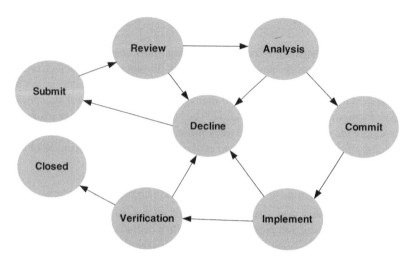

FIGURE 3.27   State transition diagram of a CR

The model shows the evolution of a CR via the following major states: *Submit, Review, Analysis, Commit, Implement, Verification,* and *Closed.* Specific actions are associated with each state, and the state of a CR is updated upon the completion of those actions. For several reasons, the status of a CR is changed to the *Decline* state from *Review, Analysis, Implement,* and *Verification.* For instance, the marketing team may conclude that realization of a CR may not fetch more business. The motivation for describing CRs by means of state diagrams is to enable their easy tracking. For ease of implementation and management of CRs, a general schema, as shown in Table 3.9, can be used. Once such a schema is implemented with a back-end database and a front-end graphical user interface, CRs can be stored in a database. Later, for the purposes of tracking and reporting the status of the CRs, queries are generated.

Submit state. This is the initial state of a newly submitted CR. Usually, end users, customers, and marketing managers are the prime sources of CRs. When a new CR is filed, the following fields, described in Table 3.9, are instantiated:

change_request_id
priority
description
maintenance_type
component
note
product
customer

Based on the priority level of a CR, it is moved from *Submit* to *Review.* Usually, a marketing manager assumes the responsibility of this initial handling of a CR, and he becomes the "owner" of the CR.

TABLE 3.9   Change Request Schema Field Summary

Field Name	Description
change_request_id	A unique identifier of the CR
title	A concise summary of the CR
description	A short description of the CR
maintenance_type	Classification of the maintenance type in terms of a member of {Corrective, Adaptive, Perfective, Preventive}
product	Product name
component	Component where the change is needed, or where the problem occurred
state	Present state of the CR in terms of a member of {Submit, Review, Analysis, Commit, Implementation, Verification, Closed, Declined}
customer	Name of the customer making the CR
problem_origin	The origin of the problem
impacts	Components that are affected by a change and its ripple effect
resolution	Documentation of what was changed, how, and why
note	Additional information provided by the submitter for subsequent decision making
software_release	The version number of the product release in which the CR is likely to be effective
committed_release	The version number of the product release in which the CR will be effective
priority	Priority of CR, which is an element of a set, namely, {normal, high}
severity	Severity of CR, which is an element of a set, namely, {normal, critical}
marketing_justification	The business justification for the CR to exist
time_to_implement	The time, in person-week, required to effect the change
eng_assigned	The engineering personnel assigned to analyze the CR
functional_spec_title	Title of the specification for functional requirements
functional_spec_name	Name of the file describing the functional requirements
functional_spec_version	This is the most recent version number of the specification of functional requirements
decline_note	The reason for declining the CR
ec_number	The identifier of the EC document
attachment	Attachment to further describe the CR (if any)
tc_id	Identifiers of test cases used in effecting the CR
tc_results	The result of testing: {Untested, Passed, Failed Blocked, Invalid}
verification_method	Record the methods of verification of the CR: analysis, testing, inspection, and/or demonstration
verification_status	The verification state of the CR: passed, failed, or incomplete
compliance	The level of compliance:{Non-compliance, Partial Compliance, or Compliance}

(*continued*)

TABLE 3.9 *(Continued)*

Field Name	Description
testing_note	Reports from the test personnel, possibly describing the demonstration given to the customers, analysis performed on the change, or inspection of the code performed by test personnel
defect_id	Defect identifier
	If "Failed" is assigned to the *tc_results* field, the defect identifier is associated with the failed test to indicate the defect causing the failure.
	The defect identifier is obtained from test database.

Review state. Generally, a manager for marketing handles the CR in the Review state by coordinating the following activities:

- It is possible that the newly generated CR is a duplicate of an existing CR. If it is found to be a duplicate of an existing CR, the request is moved to the *Decline* state with a short explanation and a link to the original CR. Should there be any ambiguity in the description of the CR, the submitter is asked to provide more details, which are recorded in the *note* and the *description* fields.
- Accept the assigned priority level of the CR or modify it.
- Re-evaluate the maintenance_type of the CR initially estimated by the submitter, and accept or modify it.
- Determine the level of severity of the CR: normal and critical. If it is critical, then the upper management may want to complete the review immediately. Note that a severity level and a priority level are independently assigned.
- To reflect the CR, determine a software release.
- Give a marketing rationale for the CR.
- For further actions, the CR is moved to the *Analysis* state.

In summary, the following fields are updated in the *Review* state:

priority
severity
maintenance_type
decline_note
software_release
marketing_justification
description and
note

Analysis state. In this stage, impact analysis is conducted to understand the CR and to estimate the time required to implement it. In addition, a high-level functional specification for the CR is prepared. If it is decided that it is not possible or desirable to implement the CR, then *Decline* becomes the next state of the CR. Otherwise, the CR is moved to the *Commit* state. In the *Commit* state, the program manager controls the CR by becoming its owner. While in the *Analysis* state, the owner, who is typically the director of software engineering, updates the following fields:

component

problem_origin

impacts

time_to_implement

attachment

functional_spec_title

functional_spec_name

functional_spec_version

eng_assigned

Commit state. The CR continues to stay in the *Commit* state before it is committed to a specific release of the product. In this state, the program manager is the owner of the CR. All the CRs that are desired to be in a specific software release are reviewed. Some CRs may be re-assigned to a later release after consultations with customers, the marketing division, and the director of software engineering. After committing a CR to a particular release, the CR is moved to the *Implement* state and all the functional specifications are frozen for development and test design purposes. In the *Commit* state: (i) the engineering team begins modifying the software component documentation, namely, data and control flow diagrams and schematics; (ii) test personnel review the CR and the associated functional specification to ensure that the CR is testable; (iii) test personnel write new test cases for the CR; and (iv) test personnel select regression tests. *Committed_release* is the only field updated in the *Commit* state.

Implement state. The *Implement* stage is controlled by the director of software engineering. A number of different scenarios can occur in this stage as follows:

- The CR can be declined if its implementation is infeasible.
- If the CR is infeasible in its current form, the director of software engineering may assign an EC number and provide an explanation, and the EC document is linked with the CR definition. Table 3.10 shows how to organize an EC document.
- If the CR or its modified version is doable, the software engineering group writes code and performs unit tests. The CR is moved from *Implement* to *Verification* after the product is available for system-level testing.

TABLE 3.10   Engineering Change Document Information

EC number	A unique number.
Requirement(s) affected	Identifiers of CRs and their titles.
Description of problem/issue	Brief description of the issue.
Description of change required	Description of changes needed to the original CR description.
Secondary technical impact	Description of the impact the EC will have on the system.
Customer impacts	Description of the impact the EC will have on the end customer.
Change recommended by	Name of the engineer(s).
Change approved by	Name of the approver(s).

Source: From Reference 24. © 2008 John Wiley & Sons.

In the *Implement* state the following fields are updated:

> *decline_note*
>
> *ec_number*
>
> *attachment*
>
> *resolution*

Verification state. In the *Verification* state, activities are largely controlled by the sustaining test manager. To assign a test verdict, verification can be performed by one or more methods: demonstration, analysis, inspection, and testing. If verification is performed by testing, then the software is executed with a set of tests. Inspection means reviewing the code to detect defects. Analysis is performed by means of statistical and/or mathematical tools. Demonstration implies showing the system in a live operation. A status of verification is provided in terms of the degree of compliance of the modified system to the CR: noncompliance, partial compliance, or full compliance. If the testing method is not used, then a note explains the details of the demonstration, the inspection, and/or the analysis performed.

Shortfalls in the realization of the CR, in the form of incomplete and even partly accurate implementation, are specified in an EC document. It is very difficult to correct any deviations or errors discovered at this stage. Therefore, a pragmatic approach to dealing with the deficiency is to produce an EC document, after negotiating with the customer, to revise the CR, and possibly generate a new CR for future considerations. As an extreme decision, the sustaining test manager may decline to accept the modifications made to the code an EC number and an explanation, followed by a state change to *Decline*. On the other hand, after ensuring that the implementation passed the required tests, the sustaining test manager moves the CR to the *Closed* phase. In the *Verification* state, the following fields are instantiated:

> *decline_note*
>
> *ec_number*
>
> *attachment*

verification_method
verification_status
compliance
tc_id
tc_results
defect_id
testing_note

Closed state. After successfully verifying that the CR has been incorporated into the software, the CR is moved from *Verification* to the *Closed* state. This is done by the owner of the CR in the *Verification* state who is, in general, the sustaining test manager.

Decline state. The *Decline* state is controlled by the marketing department. Due to one or more of the following causes, a CR happens to be in this state:

- Because of insufficient business impact of the CR, the marketing department decides to reject the CR.
- It is technically infeasible to implement the CR.
- The sustaining test manager concludes that changes made to the software to effect the CR could not be satisfactorily verified. An explanation is provided in the form of an EC number.

The CR may be moved to *Submit* by the marketing group after negotiating with the customer. Negotiations with the customer may lead to a reduction in the scope of the CR. The EC information is used as a basis for negotiation with the customer.

3.10 SUMMARY

This chapter began with three well-known reuse-oriented paradigms: quick fix, iterative enhancement, and full reuse. All the three models assume that a set of documents completely and accurately describe the existing system. The first model makes the necessary changes to the code first, followed by changes to the relevant documentations. The second model modifies the top-level documents impacted by the modifications and then propagates those changes down to the code level. The third model builds a new system from components of the old system and other components available in the repository.

Next, we studied a simple staged model for CSS development, which comprises five major stages: Initial development, Evolution, Servicing, Phaseout, and Closedown. In this view software life cycle, maintenance is actually a series of distinct stages, each with different activities. The software evolution process is the backbone of the model. It continues in an iterative fashion and eventually produces the next version of the software. We discussed its applicability to FLOSS systems model. The model benefits developers to characterize FLOSS systems in terms of stages, and identify the current stage of a system and the new stage to which it is more likely to move. Three major differences between CSS and FLOSS systems were identified and discussed.

Next, we described an evolutionary model known as change mini-cycle, which consists of five major phases: CR, analyze and plan change, implement change, verify and validate, and document change. In this model, several interesting activities were identified, such as program comprehension, impact analysis, refactoring, and change propagation, which continue to be the subjects of intense research.

With the three evolution models in place, we examined two standards: IEEE/EIA 1219 and ISO/IEC 14764. Both the standards describe the process for managing and executing software maintenance activities. Next, we discussed the management of system evolution by focusing on SCM. Next, a state-transition model was given to monitor individual CRs as those move through the software organization. Certain actions are completed in each state of the model. Finally, a sample schema to manage CRs was presented in detail.

LITERATURE REVIEW

In the classical Waterfall model for software development proposed by Royce in circa 1970 [40], the final phase is Operation and Maintenance. This model considers software maintenance as another task of software development. On the other hand, J. R. McKee, in his article "Maintenance as a function of design," *AFIP National Conference Proceeding*, 53, 1984, pp. 187–193, suggests software maintenance to be 2nd, 3rd, ... , nth round of development. In this regard it is worth quoting Norman Schneidewind from his article "The state of software maintenance," *IEEE Transactions on Software Engineering*, 13(3), 1987, pp. 303–309: "The traditional view of the software life cycle has done a disservice to maintenance by depicting it solely as a single step at the end of the cycle" (p. 304). Victor Basili [2] argues that software maintenance is continued development, using the same knowledge, methods, and tools used for software development. Based on this view he developed the reuse-oriented software development process. A more complicated idea of using SDLC is proposed by Barry Boehm ("Software engineering," *IEEE Transaction on Computers*, December 1976, pp. 1226–1241) based on his spiral model [41]. Ned Chapin, in his article "Software maintenance life cycle," *Proceedings of Conference on Software Maintenance*, Phoenix, Arizona, IEEE Computer Society Press, Los Alamitos, CA. 1988, pp. 6-13, argued that the SDLC model is not compatible with a software maintenance model. The use of SDLC will generate an inappropriate expectation set of metric requirements, such as effort needed, selection of tools, management support, and complexity of relevant task. Therefore, he prefers software maintenance to have its own SMLC model.

A number of proposals based on the SMLC model have been published with some variations among them. Three common features of SMLC models found in literature are: (i) understanding the code; (ii) modifying the code; and (iii) revalidating the software. In the following we list up those advocating the SMLC model:

G. Parikh. 1982. 'The world of software maintenance. In: *Techniques of Program and System Maintenance* (Ed. G. Parikh), pp. 9–13. Little, Brown and Company, Boston, MA.

J. Martin and C. L. McClure. 1983. *Software Maintenance: The Problem and Its Solution.* Prentice-Hall, Englewood Cliffs, NJ.

S. Chen, K. G. Heisler, W. T. Tsai, X. Chen, and E. Leung. 1990. A model for assembly program maintenance. *Journal of Software Maintenance: Research and Practice*, March, 3–32.

D. R. Harjani and J. P. Queille. 1992. *A Process Model for the Maintenance of Large Space Systems Software.* Proceedings of Conference on Software Maintenance, November 1992, Orlando, FL. IEEE Computer Society Press, Los Alamitos, CA. pp. 127–136.

W. K. Sharpley. 1977. *Software Maintenance Planning for Embedded Computer Systems.* Proceedings of the IEEE COMPSAC, November 1977, IEEE Computer Society Press, Los Alamitos, CA, pp. 520–526.

S. S. Yau, R. A. Nicholi, J. Tsai, and S. Liu. 1988. An integrated life-cycle model for software maintenance. *IEEE Transaction on Software Engineering*, August, 1128–1144.

S. S. Yau and I. S. Collofello. 1980. Some stability measures for software maintenance. *IEEE Transaction on Software Engineering*, November, 545–552.

L. J. Arthur. 1988. *Software Evolution: The Software Maintenance Challenge.* John Wiley & Sons, New York, NY, 1988.

The model proposed by Sharpley focused on corrective maintenance activities through problem verification, problem diagnosis, reprogramming, and baseline revalidation. On the other hand, Arthur's model is for corrective, adaptive, and perfective maintenance activities and consisted of several phases: (i) change management; (ii) impact analysis; (iii) system release planning; (iv) design change; (v) coding; (vi) testing; and (vii) system release.

Neal Febbraro and V. Rajlich presented an agile model of incremental change and development process that consists of repeated incremental change (*The Role of Incremental Change in Agile Software Processes*. Proceedings Agile, August 2007, Washington, D.C. IEEE Computer Science Press, Los Alamitos. pp. 92–103. At Iona Technologies, XP has been used successfully for maintenance of a Corba-based middleware product called Orbix, as reported in the article ("Using extreme programming in a maintenance environment," *IEEE Software*, November/December, 2001, pp. 42–50) by C. Poole and J. W. Huisman. According to Kent Beck, one of the proponents of XP, "Maintenance is really the normal state of an XP project" (*Extreme Programming Explained*. Addison-Wesley, Reading, MA, 1999).

By following a development process an organization develops new software products, whereas a maintenance process is seen as providing subsequent services. The line between services and products is not a crisp one. On the one hand, adaptive maintenance is viewed as a hybrid of services and product. On the other hand, corrective maintenance is a product-intensive service, and software operation can be considered a pure service. Basically, an intangible set of activities and/or benefits are bundled and sold as a service by an organization to its customers. Therefore, to deliver high-quality results from maintenance tasks, two quality dimensions must be considered: functional quality and technical quality. Maintenance services are improved by organizations by improving the: (i) technical quality of their work and (ii) functional quality of software maintenance. In this context it is valuable to read and practice the process proposed by Niessink and van Vliet in their article "Software maintenance from a service perspective," published in the *Journal of Software Maintenance: Research and Practice*, March/April 2000, pp. 103–120. Their process can be summarized in the form of four items:

1. Customer expectations are translated into maintenance service agreements.
2. Maintenance activities are planned and implemented by using the service agreements as a basis.
3. Planning and procedures guide the maintenance activities.
4. Manage the communication concerning the delivered services.

In addition, it is highly recommended for information technology (IT) professionals to study the following two standards:

1. The IT Service Capability Maturity Model, Version 1.0RC1, January 28, 2005, http://www.itservicecmm.org
2. The IT Infrastructure Library (ITIL)—An Introduction, Central Computer and Telecommunication Agency (CCTA), HMSO books, Norwich, England, 1993.

The British government developed ITIL through CCTA and it was maintained by the Netherlands IT Examinations Institute (EXIN). ITIL aims at establishing best standards and practices for IT service delivery. To explain the "best practices" in the delivery of IT service, nine sets of infrastructure library booklets have been developed. The nine sets of booklets cover two broad topics: (i) provision of IT services and management of IT infrastructure and (ii) environment. The former has been addressed in the first six sets of booklets, whereas the latter in the remaining three. Cabling, building, and service facilities are part of the environment. The IT service capability maturity model has much similarities with the Software CMM. IT services are delivered by installing, maintaining, managing, or operating the IT needs of a customer. In other words, software maintenance is one element of a whole gamut of the deliverable IT services.

The software maintenance maturity model SM^{mm} was designed by Alain April and Alain Abran (*Software Maintenance Management: Evaluation and Continuous Improvement*, Wiley-IEEE Computer Society Press, April 2008) as a customer-focused reference model for either (i) auditing the software maintenance capability of a software maintenance service supplier or outsourcer or (ii) improving internal software maintenance organizations. It includes 4 process domains, 18 key processes areas (KPAs), 74 roadmaps, and 443 practices. In addition, the reader is recommended to study the corrective maintenance maturity model article by Mira Kajko-Mattsson, "*Motivating the Corrective Maintenance Maturity Model (CM³)*. Seventh IEEE International Conference on Engineering of Complex Computer Systems, 2001, Skovde, Sweden. IEEE Computer Society Press, Piscataway, NJ. pp. 112–117."

Those who are interested in a much detailed treatment of SCM peruse the article by Estublier, Leblang, Hoek, Conradi, Clemm, Tichy, and Wiborg-Weber ("Impact of software engineering research on the practice of software configuration management," *ACM Transactions on Software Engineering and Methodology*, 14(4), October 2005, pp. 383–430). They discussed the evolution of SCM technology, with emphasis on the impact of industrial and university research.

REFERENCES

[1] L. J. Arthur. 1988. *Software Evolution: The Software Maintenance Challenge*. John Wiley & Sons, New York, NY.

[2] V. R. Basili. 1990. Viewing maintenance as reuse-oriented software development. *IEEE Software*, January, 19–25.

[3] C. Larman and V. R. Basili. 2003. Iterative and incremental development: a brief history. *IEEE Computer*, June, 47–55.

[4] T. Gilb. 1988. *Principles of Software Engineering Management*. Addison-Wesley, Reading, MA.

[5] G. Visaggio. 1999. Assessing the maintenance process through replicated controlled experiments. *The Journal of Systems and Software*, January, 187–197.

[6] V. T. Rajlich and K. H. Bennett. 2000. A staged model for the software life cycle. *IEEE Computer*, July, 2–8.

[7] E. Yourdon. 1995. When good enough software is best. *IEEE Software*, May, 79–81.

[8] N. Chapin, J. E. Hale, K. M. Khan, J. F. Ramil, and W. G. Tan. 2001. Types of software evolution and software maintenance. *Journal of Software Maintenance and Evolution: Research and Practice*, January/February, 3–30.

[9] A. Capiluppi, J. M. G. Barahona, I. Herraiz, and G. Robles. 2007. *Adapting the Staged Model for Software Evolution to Free/Libre/Open Source Software*. IWPSE, September 2007, Dubrovnik, Croatia. ACM, New York. pp. 79–82.

[10] S. S. Yau, J. S. Collofello, and T. MacGregor. 1978. *Ripple Effect Analysis of Software Maintenance*. COMPSAC, November 1978, Chicago, Illinois. IEEE Computer Society Press, Piscataway, NJ. pp. 60–65.

[11] K. H. Bennett and V. T. Rajlich. *Software Maintenance and Evolution: A Roadmap*. ICSE, The Future of Software Engineering, June 2000, Limerick, Ireland. ACM, New York. pp. 73–87.

[12] T. Mens. 2008. Introduction and roadmap: history and challenges of software evolution. In: *Software Evolution* (Eds T. Mens and S. Demeyer). Springer-Verlag, Berlin.

[13] R. G. Canning. 1972. That maintenance 'iceberg'. *EDP Analyzer*, October, 1–14.

[14] A. V. Mayrhauser and A. M. Vans. 1995. Program comprehension during software maintenance and evolution. *IEEE Computer*, August, 44–55.

[15] V. T. Rajlich and N. Wilde. 2002. *The Role of Concepts in Program Comprehension.* IWPC, June 2002, Paris, France. IEEE Computer Society Press, Piscataway, NJ. pp. 271–278.

[16] T. J. Biggerstaff, B. G. Mitbander, and D. E. Webster. 1994. Program understanding and the concept assignment problem. *Communications of the ACM*, May, 72–82.

[17] G. Antoniol, G. Canfora, G. Casazza, and A. De Lucia. 2000. *Identifying the Starting Impact Set of a Maintenance Request: A Case Study.* CSMR, February 2000, Zurich, Switzerland. IEEE Computer Society Press, Los Alamitos, CA. pp. 227–230.

[18] S. A. Bohner and R. S. Arnold. 1996. *Software Change Impact Analysis* (Eds S. A. Bohner and R. S. Arnold). IEEE Computer Society Press, Los Alamitos, CA.

[19] W. P. Stevens, G. J. Myers, and L. Constantine. 1974. Structured design. *IBM Systems Journal*, 13(2), 115–139.

[20] D. P. Freedman and G. M. Weinberg. 1981. A checklist for potential side effects of a maintenance change. In: *Techniques of Program and System Maintenance* (Ed. G. Parikh), pp. 93–100. QED Information Sciences Inc., Wellesley, MA, USA.

[21] T. Mens. 2004. A survey of software refactoring. *IEEE Transactions on Software Engineering*, February, pp. 126–139.

[22] V. T. Rajlich. 1997. *A Model for Change Propagation Based on Graph Rewriting.* ICSM, October 1997, Bari, Italy. IEEE Computer Society Press, Los Alamitos, CA. pp. 84–91.

[23] A. E. Hassan and R. C. Holt. 2004. *Predicting Change Propagation in Software System.* ICSM, September 2004, Chicago, Illinois. IEEE Computer Society Press, Los Alamitos, CA. pp. 284–293.

[24] S. Naik and P. Tripathy. 2008. *Software Testing and Quality Assurance: Theory and Practice.* John Wiley & Sons, Hoboken, NJ. pp. 93–100.

[25] IEEE Standard 1219-1998. 1998. *Standard for Software Maintenance.* IEEE Computer Society Press, Los Alamitos, CA.

[26] SWEBOK. 2004. *Guide to the Software Engineering Body of Knowledge.* IEEE Computer Scociety Press, Los Alamitos, CA.

[27] ISO/IEC 14764:2006 and IEEE Std 14764-2006. 2006. *Software Engineering - Software Life Cycle Processes - Maintenance.* Geneva, Switzerland.

[28] T. M. Pigoski. 1996. *Practical Software Maintenance.* John Wiley & Sons, New York, NY.

[29] ISO/IEC 12207:2006 and IEEE Std 12207-2006. 2008. *System and Software Engineering - Software Life Cycle Processes.* Geneva, Switzerland.

[30] E. Bersoff, V. Henderson, and S. Siegel. 1980. *Software Configuration Management—An Investment in Product Integrity.* Prentice Hall, Englewood Cliffs, NJ.

[31] J. Estublier, D. Leblang, A. V. Hock, R. Conradi, G. Clemm, W. Tichy, and D. Wiborg-Weber. 2005. Impact of software engineering research on the practice of software configuration management. *ACM Transactions on Software Engineering and Methodology*, October, 383–430.

[32] Software Technology Support Center. 2005. Configuration management fundamentals. *CrossTalk A Journal of Defense Software Engineering*, July, 10–15.

[33] S. Feldman. 1979. Make—a program for maintaining computer programs. *Software-Practice and Experience*, 9, 255–265.

[34] M. Rochkind. 1975. The source code control system. *IEEE Transactions on Software Engineering*, December, 364–370.

[35] W. Tichy. 1985. Rcs—a system for version control. *Software-Practice and Experience*, 15, 637–654.

[36] P. Louridas. 2006. Version control. *IEEE Software*, January–February, 104–107.

[37] ClearCase. 2009. *IBM Rational*, October. Available at http://www.ibm.com/software/awdtools/clearcase/.

[38] M. Ben-Menachem. 1994. *Software Configuration Management Guidebook*. McGraw-Hill, New York, NY.

[39] M. Glinz and R. J. Wieringa. 2007. Stakeholders in requirements engineering. *IEEE Software*, March–April, pp. 18–20.

[40] W. W. Royce. 1970. *Managing the Development of Large Software System: Concepts and Techniques*. Proceedings of IEEE WESCON, August 1970. pp. 1–9; Republished in 1987 by ICSE, Monterey, CA. 1987, pp. 328–338.

[41] B. W. Boehm. 1988. A spiral model of software development and maintenance. *IEEE Computer*, May, 61–72.

EXERCISES

1. Define the terms process, life-cycle, and model.

2. Discuss different ways of changing the following characteristics from one stage to another stage during the CSS life cycle model.
   (a) Staff expertise
   (b) Software architecture
   (c) Software decay
   (d) Economics

3. Discuss the similarities and differences between the staged models of CSS systems and FLOSS systems.

4. What is the difference between change propagation and change impact analysis?

5. Discuss the role of concept in program comprehension.

6. What is ripple effect? In what way is it different from side effect?

7. Explain why it is important to conduct program comprehension before impact analysis.

8. What are the advantages of the quick fix model and why is it still used?

9. Explain the differences between the incremental and the iterative development models?

10. What are the drawbacks of the iterative enhancement model?

11. Discuss the differences between the iterative enhancement and the full reuse models.

12. Discuss the major differences between the IEEE 1219 and the ISO/IEC 14764 standards for software maintenance procedure.

13. How would each of the following groups use the information contained in a CR?
   (a) Maintainers
   (b) Management
   (c) Quality assurance auditors
   (d) Sustaining test engineers
   (e) Customers

14. What are some of the factors that you would think about when reviewing a CR?

15. Why should a maintainer categorize CRs into different groups? What are some of the factors that should be considered when categorizing those CRs?

4

REENGINEERING

Neither situation nor people can be altered by the interference of an outsider. If they are to be altered, that alteration must come from within.

                                                                    —Phyllis Bottome

4.1 GENERAL IDEA

Reengineering is the examination, analysis, and restructuring of an existing software system to reconstitute it in a new form and the subsequent implementation of the new form. The goal of reengineering is to:

- understand the existing software system artifacts, namely, specification, design, implementation, and documentation; and
- improve the functionality and quality attributes of the system. Some examples of quality attributes are evolvability, performance, and reusability.

Fundamentally, a new system is generated from an operational system, such that the target system possesses better quality factors. The desired software quality factors include reliability, correctness, integrity, efficiency, maintainability, usability, flexibility, testability, interoperability, reusability, and portability [1]. In other words, reengineering is done to convert an existing "bad" system into a "good" system [2]. Of course there are risks involved in this transformation, and the primary risks are: (i) the

Software Evolution and Maintenance: A Practitioner's Approach, First Edition.
Priyadarshi Tripathy and Kshirasagar Naik.

target system may not have the same functionality as the existing system; (ii) the target system may be of lower quality than the original system; and (iii) the benefits are not realized in the required time frame [3]. Software systems are reengineered by keeping one or more of the following four general objectives in mind [4]:

- Improving maintainability
- Migrating to a new technology
- Improving quality
- Preparing for functional enhancement.

Improving maintainability. Let us revisit Lehman's second law, namely, *increasing complexity*: "As an E-type program evolves, its complexity increases unless work is done to maintain or reduce it." As systems grow and evolve, the cost of maintenance increases because changes become difficult and time consuming. Consequently, it is unrealistic to avoid reengineering in the long run. The system is redesigned with more explicit interfaces and more relevant functional modules. In addition, both external and internal documentations are made up-to-date. All those activities lead to better maintainability of the system.

Migrating to a new technology. Lehman's first law, namely, *continuing change*, states that "E-type programs must be continually adapted, else they become progressively less satisfactory." A program is continually adapted to make it compatible with its operating environment. In the fast-paced information technology industry, new—and sometimes cheaper—execution platforms include new features, which quickly make the current system outdated, and maybe more expensive. Compatibility of the newer system with the old one is likely to be an issue, because vendors have less motivation to provide support for older parts—both software and hardware—that become incompatible and more expensive. Moreover, as systems evolve, expertise of employees migrates to newer technologies, with fewer staff to maintain the old system. Consequently, organizations with perfectly working software that continues to meet their business needs are forced to migrate to a modern execution platform that includes newer hardware, operating system, and/or language.

Improving quality. Lehman's seventh law, namely *declining quality*, states that "Stakeholders will perceive an E-type program to have declining quality unless it is rigorously maintained and adapted to its environment." As time passes, users make increasingly more change requests to modify the system. Each change causes "ripple effects," implying that one change causes more problems to be fixed. As the system is continually modified as a result of maintenance activities, the reliability of the software gradually decreases to an unacceptable level. Therefore, the system must be reengineered to achieve greater reliability.

Preparation for functional enhancement. Lehman's sixth law, namely, *continuing growth*, states that "The functionality of an E-type program must be continually increased to maintain user satisfaction with the program over its lifetime." This law reflects the fact that all programs, being finite, limit the functionalities to a finite selection from a potentially unbounded set. Properties excluded by the bounds eventually become a source of performance limitations, dissatisfaction, and error. These properties in terms of functionalities must be implemented in the application to satisfy the stakeholders. In general, reengineering is not performed to support more functionalities of a system; rather, as a preparatory step to enhance functionalities, a system is reengineered. For example, if the objective is to transform programs from a procedural to an object-oriented form to distribute them in a client-server architecture, then, at the same time, plan to reduce the maintenance costs by using a language such that the system will be more amenable to changes.

4.2 REENGINEERING CONCEPTS

A good comprehension of the software development processes is useful in making a plan for reengineering. Several concepts applied during software development are key to reengineering of software. For example, *abstraction* and *refinement* are key concepts used in software development, and both the concepts are equally useful in reengineering. It may be recalled that abstraction enables software maintenance personnel to reduce the complexity of understanding a system by: (i) focusing on the more significant information about the system and (ii) hiding the irrelevant details at the moment. On the other hand, refinement is the reverse of abstraction. The principles of abstraction and refinement are explained as follows [5]:

> *Principle of abstraction.* The level of abstraction of the representation of a system can be gradually increased by successively replacing the details with abstract information. By means of abstraction one can produce a view that focuses on selected system characteristics by hiding information about other characteristics.
>
> *Principle of refinement.* The level of abstraction of the representation of the system is gradually decreased by successively replacing some aspects of the system with more details.

A new software is created by going downward from the top, highest level of abstraction to the bottom, lowest level. This downward movement is known as *forward engineering*. Forward engineering follows a sequence of activities: formulating concepts about the system to identifying requirements to designing the system to implementing the design. On the other hand, the upward movement through the layers of abstractions is called *reverse engineering*. Reverse engineering of software systems is a process comprising the following steps: (i) analyze the software to determine its components and the relationships among the components and (ii) represent the system at a higher level of abstraction or in another form [6]. Some examples of reverse engineering are: (i) decompilation, in which object code is translated into a high-level program; (ii) architecture extraction, in which the design of a program is derived; (iii) document generation, in which information is produced from, say, source code, for better understanding of the program; and (iv) software visualization, in which some aspect of a program is depicted in an abstract way.

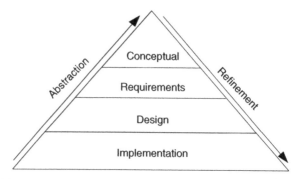

FIGURE 4.1   Levels of abstraction and refinement. From Reference 5. © 1992 IEEE

The concepts of abstraction and refinement are used to create models of software development as sequences of phases, where the phases map to specific levels of abstraction or refinement, as shown in Figure 4.1. The four levels, namely, conceptual, requirements, design, and implementation, are described one by one below:

- *Conceptual level.* At the highest level of abstraction, the software is described in terms of very high-level concepts and its reason for existence (*why?*). In other words, this level addresses the "why" aspects of the system, by answering the question: "Why does the system exist?"

- *Requirements level.* At this level, functional characteristics (*what?*) of the system are described at a high level, while leaving the details out. In other words, this level addresses the "what" aspects of the system by answering the question: "What does the system do?"

- *Design level.* At the design-refinement level, system characteristics (*what and how?*), namely, major components, the architectural style putting the components together, the interfaces among the components, algorithms, major internal data structures, and databases are described in detail. In other words, this level addresses more of "what" and "how" aspects of the system by answering the questions: (i) "What are the characteristics of the system?" and (ii) "How is the system going to possess the characteristics to deliver the functionalities?"

- *Implementation level.* This is the lowest level of abstraction in the hierarchy. At this level, the system is described at a very low level in terms of implementation details in a high-level language. In other words, this level addresses "how" exactly the system is implemented.

In summary, the refinement process can be represented as *why?* → *what?* → *what and how?* → *how?* and the abstraction process can be represented as *how?* → *what and how?* → *what?* → *why?*

A concept, a requirement, a design, and an implementation of a program usually denote different levels of abstraction. Moving from one level to another involves a process of crossing levels of abstraction. Usually a specification is more abstract than its implementation; therefore, the cycle of abstraction and refinement can be represented as follows: *concrete* → *more abstract* → *abstract* → *highly abstract* →

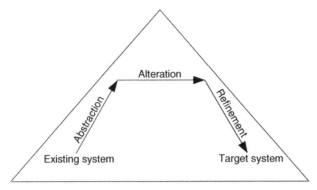

FIGURE 4.2   Conceptual basis for the reengineering process. From Reference 5. © 1992 IEEE

abstract → *less abstract* → *concrete*. Abstraction and refinement are important concepts, and these are useful in reengineering as well as in forward engineering.

In addition to the two principles of abstraction and refinement, an optional principle called *alteration* underlies many reengineering methods. The principle of alteration is defined as follows:

> *Principle of alteration.* The making of some changes to a system representation is known as alteration. Alteration does not involve any change to the degree of abstraction, and it does not involve modification, deletion, and addition of information.

Figure 4.2 shows the use of the three fundamental principles to explain reengineering characteristics. An important conceptual basis for the reengineering process is the sequence {abstraction, alteration, and refinement}. Reengineering principles are represented by means of arrows. Specifically, *abstraction* is represented by an up arrow, *alteration* is represented by a horizontal arrow, and *refinement* by a down arrow. The arrows depicting refinement and abstraction are slanted, thereby indicating the increase and decrease, respectively, of system information. It may be noted that alteration is nonessential for reengineering. Generally, the path from abstraction to refinement is via alteration. Alteration is guided by reengineering strategies as discussed in Section 4.3.2.

Another term closely related to "alteration" is *restructuring*, which was introduced in Chapter 3 and discussed in Chapter 7. In reengineering context, the term "restructuring" is defined as the transformation from one representation form to another at the same relative abstract level while preserving the subject system's external behavior [6]. Restructuring is often used as a form of preventive maintenance.

4.3   A GENERAL MODEL FOR SOFTWARE REENGINEERING

The reengineering process accepts as input the existing code of a system and produces the code of the renovated system. On the one hand, the reengineering process may be as straightforward as translating with a tool the source code from the given language to source code in another language. For example, a program written in BASIC can be translated into a new program in C. On the contrary, the reengineering process may be very complex as explained below:

- recreate a design from the existing source code;
- find the requirements of the system being reengineered;
- compare the existing requirements with the new ones;
- remove those requirements that are not needed in the renovated system;
- make a new design of the desired system; and
- code the new system.

Founded on the different levels of abstractions used in the development of software, Figure 4.3, originally proposed by Eric J. Byrne [5], depicts the processes for all abstraction levels of reengineering. This model suggests that reengineering is a sequence of three activities—reverse engineering, re-design, and forward engineering—strongly founded in three principles, namely, abstraction, alteration, and refinement, respectively.

A visual metaphor called *horseshoe*, as depicted in Figure 4.4, was developed by Kazman et al. [7] to describe a three-step architectural reengineering process. Three distinct segments of the horseshoe are the left side, the top part, and the right side. Those three parts denote the three steps of the reengineering process. The first step, represented on the left side, aims at extracting the architecture from the source code by using the abstraction principle. The second step, represented on the top, involves architecture transformation toward the target architecture by using the alteration principle. Finally, the third step, represented on the right side, involves the generation of the new architecture by means of refinement. One can look at the horseshoe bottom-up to notice how reengineering progresses at different levels of abstraction: source code, functional model, and architectural design.

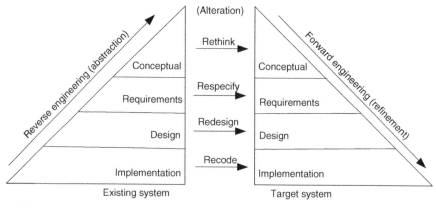

FIGURE 4.3   General model of software reengineering. From Reference 5. © 1992 IEEE

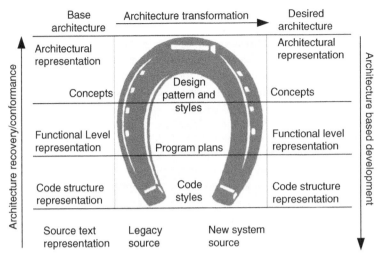

FIGURE 4.4   Horseshoe model of reengineering. From Reference 7. © 1998 IEEE

Now, we are in a position to revisit three definitions of reengineering.

- The definition by Chikofsky and Cross II [6]: Software reengineering is the analysis and alteration of an operational system to represent it in a new form and to obtain a new implementation from the new form. Here, a new form means a representation at a higher level of abstraction.
- The definition by Byrne [5]: Reengineering of a software system is a process for creating a new software from an existing software so that the new system is better than the original system in some ways.
- The definition by Arnold [3]: Reengineering of a software system is an activity that: (i) improves the comprehension of the software system or (ii) raises the quality levels of the software, namely, performance, reusability, and maintainability.

In summary, it is evident that reengineering entails: (i) the creation of a more abstract view of the system by means of some reverse engineering activities; (ii) the restructuring of the abstract view; and (iii) implementation of the system in a new form by means of forward engineering activities. This process is formally captured by Jacobson and Lindström [8] with the following expression:

$$\text{Reengineering} = \text{Reverse engineering} + \Delta + \text{Forward engineering.}$$

Referring to the right-hand side of the above equation, the first element, namely, "reverse engineering," is an activity to create an easier to understand and more abstract form of the system. The third element, namely, "forward engineering," is the traditional process of moving from a high-level abstraction and logical, implementation-independent design to the physical implementation of the system.

The second element "Δ" captures alterations made to the original system. Two major dimensions of alteration are change in functionality and change in implementation technique. A change in functionality comes from a change in the business rules [9]. Thus, a modification of the business rules results in modifications of the system. Moreover, change of functionality does not affect how the system is implemented, that is, how forward engineering is carried out. Next, concerning a change of implementation technique, an end-user of a system never knows if the system is implemented in an object-oriented language or a procedural language. Often, reengineering is associated with the introduction of a new development technology, for example, model-driven engineering [10]. A variant of reengineering in which the transformation is driven by a major technology change is called *migration*. Migration of legacy information systems (LIS) is discussed in Chapter 5.

Another common term used by practitioners of reengineering is *rehosting*. Rehosting means reengineering of source code without addition or reduction of features in the transformed targeted source code [11]. Rehosting is most effective when the user is satisfied with the system's functionality, but looks for better qualities of the system. Examples of better qualities are improved efficiency of execution and reduced maintenance costs. To modify a system's characteristics, alteration is performed at an abstraction level with much details about the characteristics. For example, if there is a need to translate the source code of a system to a new programming language, there is no need to perform reverse engineering. Rather, alteration, that is recoding, is done at the source code level. However, at a higher level of abstraction, say, architecture design, reverse engineering is involved and the amount of alterations to be done is increased. Similarly, to respecify requirements by identifying the functional characteristics of the system, reverse engineering techniques are applied to the source code.

4.3.1 Types of Changes

The model in Figure 4.3 suggests that an existing system can be reengineered by following one of four paths. The selection of a specific path for reengineering depends partly on the characteristics of the system to be modified. For a given characteristic to be altered, the abstraction level of the information about that characteristics plays a key role in path selection. Based on the type of changes required, system characteristics are divided into groups: rethink, respecify, redesign, and recode. It is worth noting that, on the one hand, modifications performed to characteristics within one group do not cause any changes at a higher level of abstraction. On the other hand, modifications within a particular group do result in modifications to lower levels of abstraction. For instance, one requirement is reflected in many design components, and one design component is realized by a block of source code. Hence, a small change in a design component may require several modifications to the code. However, the change to the design component should not influence the requirements. Next, the characteristics of each group are discussed in what follows.

Recode. Implementation characteristics of the source program are changed by recoding it. Source code level changes are performed by means of rephrasing and program translation. In the latter approach, a program is transformed into a program in a different language. On the other hand, rephrasing keeps the program in the same language [12].

Examples of translation scenarios are *compilation, decompilation*, and *migration*. By means of compilation, one transforms a program written in a high-level language into assembly or machine code. Decompilation is a form of transformation in which high-level source code is discovered from an executable program. In migration, a program is transformed into a program in another language while retaining the program's abstraction level. The language of the new program need not be completely different than the original program's language; rather, it can be a variation of the first language.

Examples of rephrasing scenarios are *normalization, optimization, refactoring*, and *renovation*. Normalization reduces a program to a program in a sublanguage, that is to a subset of the language, with the purpose of decreasing its syntactic complexity. Elimination of GOTO and module flattening in a program are examples of program normalization. Optimization is a transformation that improves the execution time or space performance of a program. Refactoring is a transformation that improves the design of a program by means of restructuring to better understand the new program.

Redesign. The design characteristics of the software are altered by redesigning the system. Common changes to the software design include: (i) restructuring the architecture; (ii) modifying the data model of the system; and (iii) replacing a procedure or an algorithm with a more efficient one.

Respecify. This means changing the requirement characteristics of the system in two ways: (i) change the form of the requirements and (ii) change the scope of the requirements. The former refers to changing only the form of existing requirements, that is, taking the informal requirements expressed in a natural language and generating a formal specification in a formal description language, such as the Specification and Description Language (SDL) or Unified Modeling Language (UML). The latter type of changes includes such changes as adding new requirements, deleting some existing requirements, and altering some existing requirements.

Rethink. Rethinking a system means manipulating the concepts embodied in an existing system to create a system that operates in a different problem domain. It involves changing the conceptual characteristics of the system, and it can lead to the system being changed in a fundamental way. Moving from the development of an ordinary cellular phone to the development of smartphone system is an example of Rethink.

4.3.2 Software Reengineering Strategies

Three strategies that specify the basic steps of reengineering are rewrite, rework, and replace. The three strategies are founded on three fundamental principles in software engineering, namely, abstraction, alteration, and refinement. The rewrite strategy is based on the principle of alteration. The rework strategy is based on the principles of abstraction, alteration, and refinement. Finally, the replace strategy is based on the principles of abstraction and refinement.

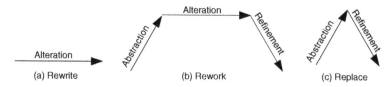

FIGURE 4.5   Conceptual basis for reengineering strategies. From Reference 5. © 1992 IEEE

Rewrite strategy. This strategy reflects the principle of alteration. By means of alteration, an operational system is transformed into a new system while preserving the abstraction level of the original system. For example, the Fortran code of a system can be rewritten in the C language. The rewrite strategy has been further explained in Figure 4.5a.

Rework strategy. The rework strategy applies all the three principles. First, by means of the principle of abstraction, obtain a system representation with less details than what is available at a given level. For example, one can create an abstraction of source code in the form of a high-level design. Next, the reconstructed system model is transformed into the target system representation, by means of alteration, without changing the abstraction level. Finally, by means of refinement, an appropriate new system representation is created at a lower level of abstraction. The main ideas in rework are illustrated in Figure 4.5b. Now, let us consider an example originally given by Byrne [5]. Let the goal of a reengineering project be to restructure the control flow of a program. Specifically, we want to replace the unstructured control flow constructs, namely GOTOs, with more commonly used structured constructs, say, a "for" loop. A classical, rework strategy-based approach to doing that is as follows:

- Application of abstraction: By parsing the code, generate a control flow graph (CFG) for the given system.
- Application of alteration: Apply a restructuring algorithm to the CFG to produce a structured CFG.
- Application of refinement: Translate the new, structured CFG back into the original programming language.

Replace strategy. The replace strategy applies two principles, namely, abstraction and refinement. To change a certain characteristic of a system: (i) the system is reconstructed at a higher level of abstraction by hiding the details of the characteristic and (ii) a suitable representation for the target system is generated at a lower level of abstraction by applying refinement. Figure 4.5c succinctly represents the replace strategy. Let us reconsider the GOTO example given by Byrne [5]. By means of abstraction, a program is represented at a higher level without using control flow concepts. For instance, a module's behavior can be described by its net effect, with no mention of control flow. Next, by means of refinement, the system is represented at a lower level of abstraction with a new structured control flow. In summary, the original unstructured control flow is replaced with a structured control flow.

4.3.3   Reengineering Variations

Three reengineering strategies and four broad types of changes were discussed in the preceding sections: (i) rewrite, rework, and replace are the three reengineering strategies and (ii) rethink, respecify, redesign, and recode are the four types of changes. The reengineering strategies and the change types can be combined to create different process variations. Three process factors cause variability in reengineering processes:

- the level of abstraction of the system representation under consideration;
- the kind of change to be made: rethink, respecify, redesign, and recode; and
- the reengineering strategy to be applied: rewrite, rework, and replace.

Possible variations in reengineering processes have been identified in Table 4.1. The table is interpreted by asking questions of the following type: If A is the abstraction level of the representation of the system to be reengineered and the plan is to make a B type of change, can I use strategy C? The table shows 30 reengineering

TABLE 4.1   Reengineering Process Variations

Starting Abstraction Level	Type Change	Reengineering Strategy		
		Rewrite	Rework	Replace
Implementation	Recode	Yes	Yes	Yes
level	Redesign	Bad	Yes	Yes
	Respecify	Bad	Yes	Yes
	Rethink	Bad	Yes*	Yes*
Design	Recode	No	No	No
level	Redesign	Yes	Yes	Yes
	Respecify	Bad	Yes	Yes
	Rethink	Bad	Yes*	Yes*
Requirement	Recode	No	No	No
level	Redesign	No	No	No
	Respecify	Yes	Yes	Yes
	Rethink	Bad	Yes*	Yes*
Conceptual	Recode	No	No	No
level	Redesign	No	No	No
	Respecify	No	No	No
	Rethink	Yes	Yes*	Yes*

Source: From Reference 5. © 1992 IEEE.
Yes—One can produce a target system.
Yes*—Same as Yes, but the starting degree of abstraction is lower than the uppermost degree of abstraction within the conceptual abstraction level.
No—One cannot start at abstraction level A, make B type of changes by using strategy C, because the starting abstraction level is higher than the abstraction level required by the particular type of change.
Bad—A target system can be created, but the likelihood of achieving a good result is low.

process variations. Out of the 30 variations, 24 variations are likely to produce acceptable solutions.

4.4   REENGINEERING PROCESS

An ordered set of activities designed to perform a specific task is called a *process*. For ease of understanding and communication, processes are described by means of process models. For example, in the software development domain, the Waterfall process model is widely used in developing well-understood software systems. Process models are used to comprehend, evaluate, reason about, and improve processes. Intuitively, process models are described by means of important relationships among data objects, human roles, activities, and tools. In this section, we discuss two process models for software reengineering.

Similarly, by understanding and following a process model for software reengineering, one can achieve improvements in how software is reengineered. The process of reengineering a large software system is a complex endeavor. For ease of performing reengineering, the process can be specialized in many ways by developing several variations. In a reengineering process, the concept of *approach* impacts the overall process structure. If a particular process model requires fine-tuning for certain project goals, those approaches need to be clearly understood. Five major approaches will be explained in the following subsections.

4.4.1   Reengineering Approaches

There are five basic approaches to reengineering software systems. Each approach advocates a different path to perform reengineering [13, 14]. Several considerations are made while selecting a particular reengineering approach:

- objectives of the project;
- availability of resources;
- the present state of the system being reengineered; and
- the risks in the reengineering project.

The five approaches are different in two aspects: (i) the extent of reengineering performed and (ii) the rate of substitution of the operational system with the new one. The five approaches have their own risks and benefits. In the following, we introduce the five basic approaches to software reengineering one by one.

Big Bang approach. The "Big Bang" approach replaces the whole system at once. Once a reengineering effort is initiated, it is continued until all the objectives of the project are achieved and the target system is constructed. This approach is generally used if reengineering cannot be done in parts. For example, if there is a need to move to a different system architecture, then all components affected by such a move must be changed at once. The consequent advantage is that the system is brought into its new environment all at once. On the other hand, the disadvantage of Big Bang is that the reengineering project becomes a monolithic task, which may not be desirable in all situations. In addition, the Big Bang approach consumes too much resources at once for large systems and takes a long stretch of time before the new system is visible.

Incremental approach. As the name indicates, by means of this approach a system is reengineered gradually, one step closer to the target system at a time. Thus, for a large system, several new interim versions are produced and released. Successive interim versions satisfy increasingly more project goals than their preceding versions. The desired system is said to be generated after all the project goals are achieved. The advantages of this approach are as follows: (i) locating errors becomes easier, because one can clearly identify the newly added components and (ii) it becomes easy for the customer to notice progress, because interim versions are released. The incremental approach incurs a lower risk than the "Big Bang" approach due to the fact that as a component is reengineered, the risks associated with the corresponding code can be identified and monitored. The disadvantages of the incremental approach are as follows: (i) with multiple interim versions and their careful version controls, the incremental approach takes much longer to complete; and (ii) even if there is a need, the entire architecture of the system cannot be changed.

Partial approach. In this approach, only a part of the system is reengineered and then it is integrated with the nonengineered portion of the system. One must decide whether to use a "Big Bang" approach or an "Incremental" approach for the portion to be reengineered. The following three steps are followed in the partial approach:

- In the first step, the existing system is partitioned into two parts: one part is identified to be reengineered and the remaining part to be not reengineered.
- In the second step, reengineering work is performed using either the "Big Bang" or the "Incremental" approach.
- In the third step, the two parts, namely, the not-to-be-reengineered part and the reengineered part of the system, are integrated to make up the new system.

The afore-described partial approach has the advantage of reducing the scope of reengineering to a level that best matches an organization's current need and desire to spend a certain amount of resources. A reduced scope implies that the selected portions of a system to be modified are those that are urgently in need of reengineering. A reduced scope of reengineering takes less time and costs less. A disadvantage of the partial approach is that modifications are not performed to the interface between the portion modified and the portion not modified.

Iterative approach. The reengineering process is applied on the source code of a few procedures at a time, with each reengineering operation lasting for a short time. This process is repeatedly executed on different components in different stages. During the execution of the process, ensure that the four types of components can coexist: old components not reengineered, components currently being reengineered, components already reengineered, and new components added to the system. Their coexistence is necessary for the operational continuity of the system. There are two advantages of the iterative reengineering process: (i) it guarantees the continued operation of the system during the execution of the reengineering process and (ii) the maintainers' and the users' familiarities with the system are preserved. The disadvantage of this approach is the need to keep track of the four types of components during the reengineering process. In addition, both the old and the newly reengineered components need to be maintained.

Evolutionary approach. Similar to the "Incremental" approach, in the "Evolutionary" approach components of the original system are substituted with reengineered components. However, in this approach, the existing components are grouped by functions and reengineered into new components. Software engineers focus their reengineering efforts on identifying functional objects irrespective of the locations of those components within the current system. As a result, the new system is built with functionally cohesive components as needed. There are two advantages of the "Evolutionary" approach: (i) the resulting design is more cohesive and (ii) the scope of individual components is reduced. As a result, the "Evolutionary" approach works well to convert an operational system into an object-oriented system. A major disadvantage of the approach is as follows: all the functions with much similarities must be first identified throughout the operational system; next, those functions are refined as one unit in the new system.

4.4.2   Source Code Reengineering Reference Model

The Source Code Reengineering Reference Model (SCORE/RM) is useful in understanding the process of reengineering of software. The model was proposed by Colbrook, Smythe, and Darlison [15]. The framework, depicted in Figure 4.6, consists of four kinds of elements: function, documentation, repository database, and metrication. The function element is divided into eight layers, namely, encapsulation, transformation, normalization, interpretation, abstraction, causation, regeneration, and certification. The eight layers provide a detailed approach to (i) rationalizing the system to be reengineered by removing redundant data and altering the control flow; (ii) comprehending the software's requirements; and (iii) reconstructing the software according to established practices. The top six of the eight layers shown in Figure 4.6 constitute a process for reverse engineering, and the bottom three layers constitute a process for forward engineering. Both the processes include causation, because it represents the derivation of requirements specification for the software.

Improvements in the software as a result of reengineering are quantified by means of the metrication element. The metrication element is described in terms of the relevant software metrics before executing a layer and after executing the same layer. The specification, constraints, and implementation details of both the old and the new versions of the software are described in the documentation element. The repository database is the information store for the entire reengineering process, containing the following kinds of information: metrication, documentation, and both the old and the

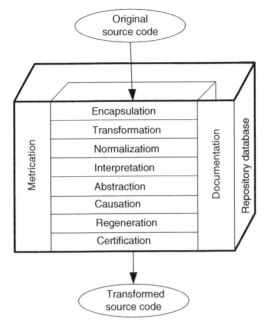

FIGURE 4.6   Source code reengineering reference model. From Reference 15. © 1990 IEEE

new source codes. The interfaces among the elements are shown in Figure 4.7. For simplicity, any layer is referred to as (N)-layer, while its next lower and next higher layers are referred to as $(N − 1)$-layer and the $(N + 1)$-layer, respectively. The three types of interfaces are explained as follows:

- Metrication/function: (N)-MF—the structures describing the metrics and their values.

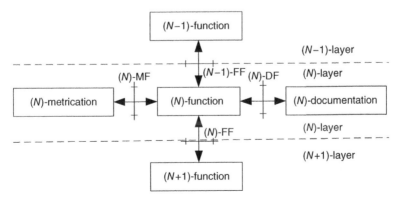

FIGURE 4.7   The interface nomenclature. From Reference 15. © 1990 IEEE. "(N)-" represents the Nth layer

- Documentation/function: (N)-DF—the structures describing the documentation.
- Function/function: (N)-FF—the representation structures for source code passed between the layers.

The functions of the individual layers are discussed in the following.

Encapsulation: This is the first layer of reverse engineering. In this layer, a reference baseline is created from the original source code. The goal of the reference baseline is to uniquely identify a version of a software and to facilitate its reengineering. The following functions are expected of this layer:

- *Configuration management.* The changes to the software undergoing mainte-nance are recorded by following a well-documented and defined procedure for later use in the new source code. This step requires strong support from upper management by allocating resources.
- *Analysis.* The portions of the software requiring reengineering are evaluated. In addition, cost models for the tangible benefits are put in place.
- *Parsing.* The source code of the system to be reengineered is translated into an intermediate language (IL). The IL can have several dialects, depending upon the relationship between the languages for the new code and the original code. All the reengineering algorithms act upon the IL representation of the source code.
- *Test generation.* This refers to the design of certification tests and their results for the original source code. Certification tests are basically acceptance tests to be used as baseline tests. The "correctness" of the newly derived software will be evaluated by means of the baseline tests.

Transformation: To make the code structured, its control flow is changed. This layer performs the following functions:

- *Rationalization of control flow.* The control flow is altered to make code struc-tured.
- *Isolation.* All the external interfaces and referenced software are identified.
- *Procedural granularity.* This refers to the sizing of the procedures, by using the ideas of high cohesion and low coupling.

Normalization: In this stage data and their structures are scrutinized by means of the following functions:

- *Data reduction.* Duplicate data are eliminated. To be consistent with the require-ments of the program, databases are modified.
- *Data representation.* The life histories of the data entities are now generated. The life histories describe how data are changed and reveal which control structures act on the data.

Interpretation: The process of deriving the meaning of a piece of software is started in this layer. The interpretation layer performs the following functions:

- *Functionalization.* This is additional rationalization of the data and control structure of the code, which (i) eliminates global variables and/or (ii) introduces recursion and polymorphic functions.
- *Program reading.* This means annotating the source code with logical comments.

Abstraction: The annotated and rationalized source code is examined by means of abstractions to identify the underlying object hierarchies. The abstraction layer performs the following functions:

- *Object identification.* The main idea in object identification is (i) separate the data operators and (ii) group those data operators with the data they manipulate.
- *Object interpretation.* Application domain meanings are mapped to the objects identified above. It is the different implementations of those objects that produce differences between the renovated code and the original code.

Causation: This layer performs the following functions:

- *Specification of actions.* This refers to the services provided to the user.
- *Specification of constraints.* This refers to the limitations within which the software correctly operates.
- *Modification of specification.* The specification is extended and/or reduced to accurately reflect the user's requirements.

Regeneration: Regeneration means reimplementing the source code using the requirements and the functional specifications. The layer performs the following functions:

- *Generation of design.* This refers to the production and documentation of the detailed design.
- *Generation of code.* This means generating new code by reusing portions of the original code and using standard libraries.
- *Test generation.* New tests are generated to perform unit and integration tests on the source code developed and reused.

Certification: The newly generated software is analyzed to establish that it is (i) operating correctly; (ii) performing the specified requirements; and (iii) consistent with the original code. The layer performs the following functions:

- *Validation* and *Verification.* The new system is tested to show its correctness.

- *Conformance.* Tests are performed to show that the renovated source code performs at the minimum all those functionalities that were performed by the original source code. It is not known what form the equivalence relationship must take, particularly when modification of the specification is likely to have occurred during reengineering.

4.4.3 Phase Reengineering Model

The phase model of software reengineering was originally proposed by Byrne and Gustafson [14] in circa 1992. The model comprises five phases: analysis and planning, renovation, target system testing, redocumentation, and acceptance testing and system transition, as depicted in Figure 4.8. The labels on the arcs denote the possible information that flows from the tail entities of the arcs to the head entities. A major process activity is represented by each phase. Tasks represent a phase's activities, and tasks can be further decomposed to reveal the detailed methodologies.

Analysis and planning. The first phase of the model is analysis and planning. Analysis addresses three technical and one economic issue. The first technical issue concerns the present state of the system to be reengineered and understanding its properties. The second technical issue concerns the identification of the need for the system to be reengineered. The third technical issue concerns the specification of the characteristics of the new system to be produced. Specifically, one identifies (i) the characteristics of the system that are needed to modified and (ii) the functionalities of the system that are needed to be modified. The identified modifications are analyzed and eventually integrated into the system. In addition, understand the expected characteristics of the new system to plan the required work.

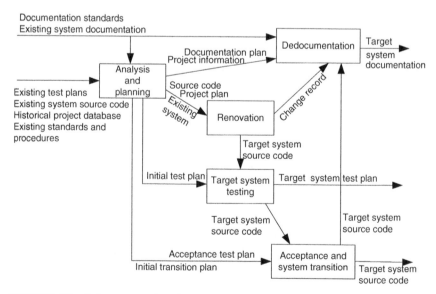

FIGURE 4.8 Software reengineering process phases. From Reference 14. © 1992 IEEE

TABLE 4.2   Tasks—Analysis and Planning Phase

Task	Description
Implementation motivations and objectives	List the motivations for reengineering the system. List the objectives to be achieved.
Analyze environment	Identify the differences between the existing and the target environments. Differences can influence system changes.
Collect inventory	Form a baseline for knowledge about the operational system by locating all program files, documents, test plans, and history of maintenance.
Analyze implementation	Analyze the source code and record the details of the code.
Define approach	Choose an approach to reengineer the system.
Define project procedures and standards	Procedures outline how to perform reviews and report problems. Standards describe the acceptable formats of the outputs of processes.
Identify resources	Determine what resources are going to be used; ensure that resources are ready to be used.
Identify tools	Determine and obtain tools to be used in the reengineering project.
Data conversion planning	Make a plan to effect changes to databases and files.
Test planning	Identify test objectives and test procedures, and evaluate the existing test plan. Design new tests if there is a need.
Define acceptance criteria	By means of negotiations with the customers, identify acceptance criteria for the target system.
Documentation planning	Evaluate the existing documentation. Develop a plan to redocument the target system.
Plan system transition	Develop an end-of-project plan to put the new system into operation and phase out the old one.
Estimation	Estimate the resource requirements of the project: effort, cost, duration, and staffing.
Define organizational structure	Identify personnel for the project, and develop a project organization.
Scheduling	Develop a schedule, including dependencies, for project phases and tasks.

Source: From Reference 14. © 1992 IEEE.

The economic issue concerns a cost and benefit analysis of the reengineering project. The economics of reengineering must compare with the costs, benefits, and risks of developing a new system as well as the costs and risks of maintaining an old system [16]. Planning includes (i) understanding the scope of the work; (ii) identifying the required resources; (iii) identifying the tasks and milestones; (iv) estimating the required effort; and (v) preparing a schedule. The tasks to be performed in this phase are listed in Table 4.2.

Renovation. An operational system is modified into the target system in the renovation phase. Two main aspects of a system are considered in this phase: (i) representation of the system and (ii) representation of external data. In general, the former

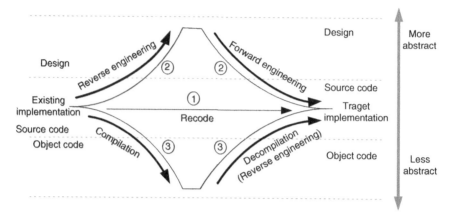

FIGURE 4.9   Replacement strategies for recoding

refers to source code, but it may include the design model and the requirement specification of the existing system. On the other hand, the latter refers to the database and/or data files used by the system. Often the external data are reengineered, and it is known as *data reengineering*. Data reengineering has been discussed in Section 4.8.

An operational system can be renovated in many ways, depending upon the objectives of the project, the approach followed, and the starting representation of the system. It may be noted that the starting representation can be source code, design, or requirements. Table 4.1 in Section 4.3.3 recommends several alternatives to renovate a system. Selection of a specific renovation approach is a management decision.

Let us consider an example of a project in which the objective is to recode the system from Fortran to C. Figure 4.9 shows the three possible replacement strategies. First, to perform source-to-source translation, program migration is used. Program migration accepts the source code for the system to be reengineered as input and produces new source code as output for the target system. Second, a high-level design is constructed from the operational source code, say, in Fortran, and the resulting design is reimplemented in the target language, C in this case. Finally, a mix of compilation and decompilation is used to obtain the system implementation in C: (i) compile the Fortran code to obtain object code and (ii) decompile the object code to obtain a C version of the program. For all the three approaches, the end effects are the same, but the tasks to be executed are different for each of the three replacement strategies.

Target system testing. In this phase for system testing, faults are detected in the target system. Those faults might have been introduced during reengineering. Fault detection is performed by applying the target system test plan on the target system. The same testing strategies, techniques, methods, and tools that are used in software development are used during reengineering. For example, apply the existing system-level test cases to both the existing and the new systems. Assuming that the two systems have identical requirements, the test results from both the scenarios must be the same.

Redocumentation. In the redocumentation phase, documentations are rewritten, updated, and/or replaced to reflect the target system. Documents are revised according to the redocumentation plan. The two major tasks within this phase are (i) analyze new source code and (ii) create documentation. Documents requiring revision are requirement specification, design documentation, a report justifying the design decisions, assumptions made in the implementation, configuration, user and reference manuals, on-line help, and the document describing the differences between the existing and the target systems. Different documents require different redocumentation tasks. A task for redocumentation comprises detailed subtasks to make a plan, actually update the document, and review the document.

Acceptance and system transition. In this final phase, the reengineered system is evaluated by performing acceptance testing. Acceptance criteria should already have been established in the beginning of the project. Should the reengineered system pass those tests, preparation begins to transition to the new system. On the other hand, if the reengineered system fails some tests, the faults must be fixed; in some cases, those faults are fixed after the target system is deployed. Upon completion of the acceptance tests, the reengineered system is made operational, and the old system is put out of service. System transition is guided by the prior developed transition plan.

4.5   CODE REVERSE ENGINEERING

Reverse engineering was first applied in electrical engineering to produce schematics from an electrical circuit. It was defined as the process of developing a set of specifications for a complex hardware system by an orderly examination of specimens of that system [17]. In the context of software engineering, Chikofsky and Cross II [6] defined *reverse engineering* as a process to (i) identify the components of an operational software; (ii) identify the relationships among those components; and (iii) represent the system at a higher level of abstraction or in another form. In other words, by means of reverse engineering one derives information from the existing software artifacts and transforms it into abstract models to be easily understood by maintenance personnel. The factors necessitating the need for reverse engineering are as follows [18]:

- The original programmers have left the organization.
- The language of implementation has become obsolete, and the system needs to be migrated to a newer one.
- There is insufficient documentation of the system.
- The business relies on software, which many cannot understand.
- The company acquired the system as part of a larger acquisition and lacks access to all the source code.
- The system requires adaptations and/or enhancements.
- The software does not operate as expected.

The above factors imply that a combination of both high-level and low-level reverse engineering steps need to be applied. High-level reverse engineering means creating

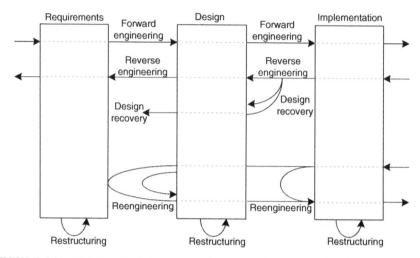

FIGURE 4.10   Relationship between reengineering and reverse engineering. From Reference 6. © 1990 IEEE

abstractions of source code in the form of design, architecture, and/or documentation. Low-level reverse engineering, discussed in Section 4.7, means creating source code from object code or assembly code.

Reverse engineering is performed to achieve two key objectives: *redocumentation of artifacts* and *design recovery*. The former aims at revising the current description of components or generating alternative views at the same abstraction level. Examples of redocumentation are pretty printing and drawing CFGs. On the other hand, the latter creates design abstractions from code, expert knowledge, and existing documentation [19]. In design recovery the domain knowledge, external information, and deduction or fuzzy reasoning are added to the observations of the subject system to identify meaningful higher-level abstractions beyond those obtained directly by examining the system itself. The relationship between forward engineering, reengineering, and reverse engineering is shown in Figure 4.10.

Although difficulties faced by software maintenance personnel gave rise to the idea of software reverse engineering, it can be used to solve problems in related areas as well. Six objectives of reverse engineering, as identified by Chikofsky and Cross II [6], are generating alternative views, recovering lost information, synthesizing higher levels of abstractions, detecting side effects, facilitating reuse, and coping with complexity. If source code is the only reliable representation of a system, following the IEEE Standard for Software Maintenance [20], one can perform reverse engineering on the system to understand it. Reverse engineering has been effectively applied in the following problem areas:

- redocumenting programs [21];
- identifying reusable assets [22–25];
- discovering design architectures [7, 26–30];

- recovering design patterns [31, 32];
- building traceability between code and documentation [33–35];
- finding objects in procedural programs [36];
- deriving conceptual data models [37–40];
- detecting duplications and clones [41–44];
- cleaning up code smells [45];
- aspect-oriented software development [46];
- computing change impact [47];
- transforming binary code into source code [48];
- redesigning user interfaces [49–51];
- parallelizing largely sequential programs [52];
- translating a program to another language [53, 54];
- migrating data [55];
- extracting business rules [9, 56, 57];
- wrapping legacy code [58];
- auditing security and vulnerability [59, 60]; and
- extracting protocols of network applications [61].

Six key steps in reverse engineering, as documented in the IEEE Standard for Software Maintenance [20], are:

- partition source code into units;
- describe the meanings of those units and identify the functional units;
- create the input and output schematics of the units identified before;
- describe the connected units;
- describe the system application; and
- create an internal structure of the system.

The first three of the six steps involve local analysis, because those are performed at the unit level. On the other hand, the remaining three steps involve global analysis, because those steps are performed at the system level. A high-level organizational paradigm is found to be useful while setting up a reverse engineering process, as advocated by Benedusi et al. [21, 62]. The high-level paradigm plays two roles: (i) define a framework to use the available methods and tools and (ii) allow the process to be repetitive. They propose a paradigm, namely, *Goals/Models/Tools*, which partitions a process for reverse engineering into three ordered stages: Goals, Models, and Tools.

Next, the three phases are explained one by one.

Goals. In this phase, the reasons for setting up a process for reverse engineering are identified and analyzed. Analyses are performed to identify the information needs of the process and the abstractions to be created by the process. The team setting up the process first acquires a good understanding of the forward engineering activities and the environment where the products of the reverse engineering process will be used. Results of the aforementioned comprehension are used to accurately identify (i) the information to be generated and (ii) the formalisms to be used to represent the information. For example, the design documents to be generated from source code are as follows:

- Low-level documents give both an overview and detailed descriptions of individual modules; detailed descriptions include the structures of the modules in terms of control flow and data structures.
- High-level documents give (i) a general description of the software product and (ii) a detailed description of its structuring in terms of modules, their interconnections, and the flow of information between modules.

Models. In this phase, the abstractions identified in the Goals stage are analyzed to create representation models. Representation models include information required for the generation of abstractions. Activities in this phase are:

- identify the kinds of documents to be generated;
- to produce those documents, identify the information and their relations to be derived from source code;
- define the models to be used to represent the information and their relationships extracted from source code; and
- to produce the desired documents from those models, define the abstraction algorithm for reverse engineering.

The important properties of a reverse engineering model are expressive power, language independence, compactness, richness of information content, granularity, and support for information-preserving transformation.

Tools. In this phase, tools needed for reverse engineering are identified, acquired, and/or developed in-house. Those tools are grouped into two categories: (i) tools to extract information and generate program representations according to the identified models and (ii) tools to extract information and produce the required documents. Extraction tools generally work on source code to reconstruct design documents. Therefore, those tools are ineffective in producing inputs for an abstraction process aiming to produce high-level design documents.

4.6 TECHNIQUES USED FOR REVERSE ENGINEERING

Fact-finding and information gathering from the source code are the keys to the Goal/Models/Tools paradigm. In order to extract information which is not explicitly available in source code, automated analysis techniques are used. The well-known analysis techniques that facilitate reverse engineering are *lexical analysis, syntactic analysis, control flow analysis, data flow analysis, program slicing, visualization,* and *program metrics.* In the following sections, we explain these techniques one by one.

4.6.1 Lexical Analysis

Lexical analysis is the process of decomposing the sequence of characters in the source code into its constituent lexical units. Various useful representations of program information are enabled by lexical analysis. Perhaps the most widely used program information is the cross reference listing. A program performing lexical analysis is called a lexical analyzer, and it is a part of a programming language's compiler. Typically it uses rules describing lexical program structures that are expressed in a mathematical notation called regular expressions. Modern lexical analyzers are automatically built using tools called lexical analyzer generators, namely, lex and flex (fast lexical analyzer) [63].

4.6.2 Syntactic Analysis

The next most complex form of automated program analysis is syntactic in nature. Compilers and other tools such as interpreters determine the expressions, statements, and modules of a program. Syntactic analysis is performed by a parser. Here, too, the requisite language properties are expressed in a mathematical formalism called context-free grammars. Usually, these grammars are described in a notation called Backus–Naur Form (BNF). In the BNF notation, the various program parts are defined by rules in terms of their constituents. Similar to syntactic analyzers, parsers can be automatically constructed from a description of the programmatical properties of a programming language. YACC is one of the most commonly used parsing tools [63].

Two types of representations are used to hold the results of syntactic analysis: *parse tree* and *abstract syntax tree.* The former is the more primitive one of the two. It is similar to the parsing diagrams used to show how a natural language sentence is broken up into its constituents. However, a parse tree contains details unrelated to actual program meaning, such as the punctuation, whose role is to direct the parsing process. For instance, grouping parentheses are implicit in the tree structure, which can be pruned from the parse tree. Removal of those extraneous details produces a structure called an *Abstract Syntax Tree* (AST). An AST contains just those details that relate to the actual meaning of a program. Because an AST is a tree, nodes of the tree can be visited in a pre-set manner, such as depth-first order, and the information contained in the node is delivered to the analyzer. Many tools have been based on the AST concept; to understand a program, an analyst makes a query in terms of the node types. The query is interpreted by a tree walker to deliver the requested information.

4.6.3 Control Flow Analysis

After determining the structure of a program, control flow analysis (CFA) can be performed on it [64]. The two kinds of CFA are *intraprocedural analysis* and *interprocedural analysis.* The former shows the order in which statements are executed within a subprogram, whereas the latter shows the calling relationship among program units. Intraprocedural analysis is performed by generating CFGs of subprograms. The idea of *basic blocks* is central to constructing a CFG. A basic block is a maximal sequence of program statements such that execution enters at the top of the block and leaves only at the bottom via a conditional or an unconditional branch statement. A basic block is represented with one node in the CFG, and an arc indicates possible flow of control from one node to another. A CFG can directly be constructed from an AST by walking the tree to determine basic blocks and then connecting the blocks with control flow arcs. A CFG shows an abstract view of the ways in which a subprogram can execute.

Interprocedural analysis is performed by constructing a call graph [65, 66]. Calling relationships between subroutines in a program are represented as a call graph which is basically a directed graph. Specifically, a procedure in the source code is represented by a node in the graph, and the edge from node f to g indicates that procedure f calls procedure g. Call graphs can be *static* or *dynamic*. A dynamic call graph is an execution trace of the program. Thus a dynamic call graph is exact, but it only describes one run of the program. On the other hand, a static call graph represents every possible run of the program.

4.6.4 Data Flow Analysis

Although CFA is useful, many questions cannot be answered by means of CFA. For example, CFA cannot answer the question: Which program statements are likely to be impacted by the execution of a given assignment statement? To answer this kind of questions, an understanding of definitions (def) of variables and references (uses) of variables is required. Normally, if a variable appears on the left-hand side of an assignment statement, then the variable is said to be defined. On the contrary, if a variable appears on the right-hand side of an assignment statement, then it is said to be referenced in that statement.

Data flow analysis (DFA) concerns how values of defined variables flow through and are used in a program [67]. CFA can detect the possibility of loops, whereas DFA can determine data flow anomalies [68]. One example of data flow anomaly is that an undefined variable is referenced. Another example of data flow anomaly is that a variable is successively defined without being referenced in between. DFA enables the identification of code that can never execute, variables that might not be defined before they are used, and statements that might have to be altered when a bug is fixed.

4.6.5 Program Slicing

Originally introduced by Mark Weiser, program slicing has served as the basis of numerous tools [69]. The slice of a program for a given variable at a given line of code is the portion of the program that gives a value to the variable at that point. Therefore, if one determines during debugging that the value of a variable at a specific

```
[1]      int i;
[2]      int sum = 0;
[3]      int product = 1;
[4]      for(i = 0; ((i < N) && (i % 2 = 0)); i++) {
[5]          sum = sum + i;
[6]          product = product * i;
         }
[7]      printf("Sum = ", sum);
[8]      printf("Product = ", product);
```

FIGURE 4.11 A block of code to compute the sum and product of all the even integers in the range $[0, N)$ for $N \geq 3$

line is incorrect, one may look at the corresponding program slice to find the faulty code. In Weiser's definition, a slicing criterion of a program P is $S < p; v >$ where p is a program point and v is a subset of variables in P. A *program slice* is a portion of a program with an execution behavior identical to the initial program with respect to a given criterion but may have a reduced size.

Weiser introduced the concept of *backward slice* [69]. A backward slice with respect to a variable v and a given point p comprises all instructions and predicates which affect the value of v at point p. Backward slices answer the question "What program components might effect a selected computation?" The dual of backward slicing is *forward slicing*, and it was proposed by Binkley et al. [70]. With respect to a variable v and a point p in a program, a forward slide comprises all the instructions and predicates which may depend on the value of v at p. Note that the statements in a forward program slice execute *after* the slicing criterion. Forward slicing answers the question "What program components might be effected by a selected computation?" [71].

As an example, let us consider the program shown in Figure 4.11 which is a block of code in C. The *backward slice*, given the slicing criterion $S < [7]; sum >$ is shown in Figure 4.12. For the slicing criterion $S < [3]; product >$, the forward program slice has been shown in Figure 4.13.

Besides detecting defects, program slicing is also used to extract business rules [57] and in refactoring which is discussed in Chapter 7. Tip's article [72] provides a comprehensive survey of program slicing techniques and their applications.

```
[1]      int i;
[2]      int sum = 0;
[4]      for(i = 0; ((i < N) && (i % 2 = 0)); i++) {
[5]          sum = sum + i;
         }
[7]      printf("Sum = ", sum);
```

FIGURE 4.12 The backward slice of code obtained from Figure 4.11 by using the criterion $S < [7]; sum >$

```
[3]      int product = 1;
[4]      for(i = 0; ((i < N) && (i % 2 = 0)); i++) {
[6]          product = product * i;
      }
[8]      printf("Product = ", product);
```

FIGURE 4.13   The forward slice of code obtained from Figure 4.11 by using the criterion $S < [3]$; product >

4.6.6 Visualization

Software visualization is a useful strategy to enable a user to better understand software systems. In this strategy, a software system is represented by means of a visual object to gain some insight into how the system has been structured. The visual representation of a software system impacts the effectiveness of the code analysis or design recovery techniques.

Two important notions of designing software visualization using 3D graphics and virtual reality technology are *visualizations* and *representations*. These two notions are introduced by Young and Munro [73] in order to evaluate the effectiveness of 3D software visualizations. The authors described a collection of desirable properties of both the concepts when building visualization software, which are summarized in this section.

- *Representation.* This is the depiction of a single component by means of graphical and other media.
- *Visualization.* It is a configuration of an interrelated set of individual representations-related information making up a higher-level component.

Essentially, graphical symbols are used to represent components. In a call graph, for example, the nodes and arcs are the representations, whereas the graph itself is the visualization. For effective software visualization, one needs to consider the properties and structure of the symbols used in software representation and visualization.

When creating a representation or evaluating its effectiveness, following key attributes are considered:

- *Individuality.* The individuality property means that different types of components should have different looking representations.
- *Distinctive appearance.* Even in a large visualization compacted into a small space, two representations should be quickly identifiable as being either dissimilar or identical. It may be necessary to increase the visual complexity of a representation in order to have an easily distinguishable appearance among a large number of representations.
- *High information content.* A representation should display some information about the corresponding component type. However, increased information content increases the visual complexity of the representation.
- *Low visual complexity.* Low visual complexity enhances the user's understanding of the representation, and it leads to better performance of the visualization

system. A representation should be easy to understand in addition to appearing *distinctive*. The possibility of a trade-off exists between viewing a system with a large number of simple representations and viewing the same system with fewer but complex representations.

- *Scalability of visual complexity.* It should be relatively easy to increase or reduce the amount of information presented to the user, depending upon the use context. Scalability enables the display of:
  - a small number of components by giving their maximum information; and
  - an overview of a collection of a large number of components, by revealing less about the components.
- *Flexibility for integration into visualizations.* Representations contain both extrinsic and intrinsic dimensions which can be used to encode information about components for quick visual understanding. On the one hand, position and motion are examples of extrinsic dimensions. On the other hand, shape, color, size, and angular velocity are examples of intrinsic dimensions. A representation with many intrinsic dimensions is rendered less flexible for adoption in a visualization.
- *Suitability for automation.* The ability to automate processes for generating representations and visualizations is key to the widespread adoption of visualization models in reengineering. Therefore, representations need to be designed with the objective of being usable in an automation process.

The following requirements are taken into account while designing a visualization:

- *Simple navigation.* Visualizations are designed with their users in mind. Visualizations are structured with added features to enable users to easily navigate through the visualization. Navigations are made simple so that users quickly become familiar with the details of the system.
- *High information content.* While not overwhelming the viewer, a visualization should show as much details as possible. A balance between high information content and low visual complexity needs to be retained.
- *Low visual complexity.* The complexity of the information presented in a visualization impacts the structural complexity of the visualization. By means of abstraction, the visual complexity can be reduced. For example, too much details about components need not be presented.
- *Varying levels of detail.* Users should have the option to view a variety of details, in the form of hierarchy, information content, and type of information. For example, initially, users expect to see the visualized system in its entirety. Gradually the user will begin exploring specific areas of interest. Visualization should support the user to view increasing levels of details as the user learns more about the components.
- *Resilience to change.* Visualizations need to be robust against small changes to the information content of the visualization. For example, small changes in information content should not lead to major changes in the structure of

visualization. Large changes to visualizations as a result of minor changes to the information content will simply require the user to spend more time on learning the structure once again.

- *Effective visual metaphors.* Metaphors enable users to easily understand software systems in terms of concepts already seen in everyday life. For example, in the city metaphor: (i) an object-oriented software system is represented as a collection of elements of a city and (ii) the city is traversed to enable the user to gain an understanding of the sense of locality. The user interacts with the city model to understand the program.

- *Friendly user interface.* Interactions with the visualizations should be intuitive without introducing undue overheads.

- *Integration with other information sources.* The elements of a software system and the elements of a visualization are different in look and details. Visualizations depict systems in a form which is very different than the elements that they represent. For example, a hexagon may represent a certain module. Therefore, being able to correlate the elements of a visualization with the original information is very important. For example, a red hexagon on a visualization, representing a module, can be linked to the module's actual source code.

- *Good use of interactions.* A highly interactive visualization is key to sustaining user interests in the system being comprehended. Those interactions should give the user several ways to understand the system: top view of the system, component view, interactions among components, and details of individual components.

- *Suitability for automation.* A visualization framework must be amenable to automation. Without automation, it is of no practical use.

4.6.7   Program Metrics

To understand and control the overall software engineering process, program metrics are applied. Table 4.3 summarizes the commonly used program metrics. The early program metric research focused on *complexity metrics*, and one of the most widely used complexity metrics is cyclomatic complexity [74]. The concept of function point (FP) was introduced in late 1970s by Albrecht [75] as an alternative metrics based on simple source line count. The aim of FP is to measure the amount of functionality delivered by a program. Intuitively, the more functionality a program has, the larger is the FP count. Based on a module's *fan-in* and *fan-out* information flow characteristics, Henry and Kafura [76] define a complexity metric, $C_p = (fan\text{-}in \times fan\text{-}out)^2$. Fan-in and fan-out have been explained in Table 4.3. A large fan-in and a large fan-out may be symptoms of a poor design.

In the 1990s, large-scale adoption of object-oriented (OO) programming techniques gave rise to some OO design metrics known as Chidamber and Kemerer (CK) metric suite [77]. Six performance metrics are found in the CK metric suite as follows:

- Weighted methods per class (WMC)—This is the number of methods implemented within a given class.

TABLE 4.3   Commonly Used Software Metrics

Metric	Description
Lines of code (LOC)	The number of lines of executable code
Global variable (GV)	The number of global variables
Cyclomatic complexity (CC)	The number of linearly independent paths in a program unit is given by the cyclomatic complexity metric [74].
Read coupling	The number of global variables read by a program unit
Write coupling	The number of global variables updated by a program unit
Address coupling	The number of global variables whose addresses are extracted by a program unit but do not involve read/write coupling
Fan-in	The number of other functions calling a given function in a module
Fan-out	The number of other functions being called from a given function in a module
Halstead complexity (HC)	It is defined as effort: $E = D * V$, where: $$\text{Difficulty: } D = \frac{n_1}{2} \times \frac{N_2}{n_2}; \text{ Volume: } V = N \times \log_2 n$$ Program length: $N = N_1 + N_2$; Program vocabulary: $n = n_1 + n_2$ n_1 = the number of distinct operators n_2 = the number of distinct operands N_1 = the total number of operators N_2 = the total number of operands
Function points	It is a unit of measurement to express the amount of business functionality an information system provides to a user [75]. Function points are a measure of the size of computer applications and the projects that build them

- Response for a class (RFC)—This is the number of methods that can potentially be executed in response to a message being received by an object of a given class. It is the number of methods implemented within a class plus the number of methods accessible to an object class due to inheritance.
- Lack of cohesion in methods (LCOM)—For each attribute in a given class, calculate the percentage of the methods in the class using that attributes. Next, compute the average of all those percentages, and subtract the average from 100%.
- Coupling between object class (CBO)—This is the number of distinct noninheritance-related classes on which a given class is coupled. A class is said to be coupled to another class if it uses methods or attributes of the other class.
- Depth of inheritance tree (DIT)—This is the length of the longest path from a given class to the root in the inheritance hierarchy.
- Number of children (NOC)—This is the number of classes that directly inherit from a given class.

The Chidamber–Kemerer metrics has been investigated in the context of fault proneness. Basili et al. [78] studied the fault proneness in software programs using eight student projects. They observed that the WMC, CBO, DIT, NOC, and RFC metrics were correlated with defects, while the LCOM metric was not correlated with defects. Kontogiannis et al. [42] developed techniques to detect clones in programs using five kinds of metrics:

- fan-out;
- the ratio of the total count of input and output variables to the fan-out;
- cyclomatic complexity;
- function points metric; and
- Henry and Kafura information-flow metric.

In their framework, the basic assumption is that if code fragments c_1 and c_2 are similar under a set of features measured by metric M, then metric values $M(c_1)$ and $M(c_2)$ will also be close. Similarity is gauged by Euclidean distance defined in the five-dimensional space of the above measures. Metric-based approach has been also applied to finding duplicated web pages or finding clones in web documents [79, 80].

4.7 DECOMPILATION VERSUS REVERSE ENGINEERING

A decompiler takes an executable binary file and attempts to produce readable high-level language source code from it. The output will, in general, not be the same as the original source code, and may not even be in the same language. Actual recovery of the original source code is not really possible. The decompiler does not provide the original programmers' annotations that provide vital instructions as to the functioning of the software. There are significant elements in most high-level languages that are just omitted during the compilation process, and it is impossible to recover those elements. Usually, there will be few, if any, comments or meaningful variable names, except for library function names. During compilation, one may enable some assertion code in the debug builds and disable it in the retail builds. Decompilation techniques were originally developed during the 1960s and the 1970s by Maurice Halstead, which form the basis for today's decompilers [81]. Disassemblers are programs that take a program's executable binary as input and generate text files that contain the assembly language code for the entire program or parts of it. Disassembly is a processor-specific process, but some disassemblers support multiple CPU architectures. The user requires a good knowledge of the specific machine's assembly language, and the output is voluminous for nontrivial programs.

Decompilation, or disassembly, is a reverse engineering process, since it creates representations of the system at a higher level of abstraction [6]. However, traditional reverse engineering from source code entails the recognition of "goals," or "plans," which must be known in advance [82]. For example, the "goal" can be to increase the overall comprehension of the program for maintenance.

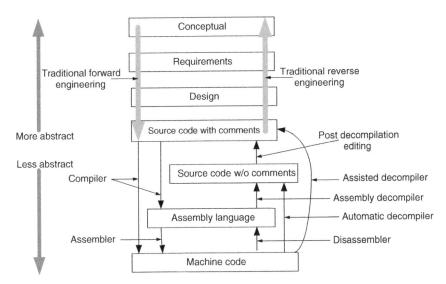

FIGURE 4.14   Relationship between decompilation and traditional reengineering. From Reference 83. © 2007

Decompilation provides the basis for comprehension, maintenance, and new development, with source code, but any high-level comprehension is provided by the reader [83]. Decompilation provides a limited kind of program comprehension. The relationship between decompilation and the traditional reengineering model of Byrne (see Figure 4.3) is depicted in Figure 4.14. As one can see, decompilation stops where architecture abstraction starts. Decompilation is certainly reverse engineering, since it is increasing the level of abstraction. However, compilation is not considered part of the forward engineering, since it is an automatic step.

Initially, decompilers aided program migration from one machine to another. As decompilation capabilities have increased, a wide range of potential applications emerged. Examples of new applications are recovery of lost source code, error correction, security testing, learning algorithms, interoperability with other programs, and recovery of someone else's source code (to determine an algorithm for example) [59]. However, not all uses of decompilers are legal uses. Most of the applications must be examined from the patent and/or copyright infringement point of view. It should be noted that it is never going to be possible to accurately predict beforehand whether or not a particular decompilation is going to be considered legal [84, 85]. License agreements may also bind the user to operate the program in a certain way and to avoid using decompilation or disassembly techniques on that program. It is recommended to seek legal counsel before starting any low-level reverse engineering project.

4.8   DATA REVERSE ENGINEERING

There has been considerable effort to develop concepts and methods to reengineer *data-oriented applications* [86, 87]. A data-oriented application is centered around a set of permanent files or a database. As a persistent data structure is the central part of the data-oriented applications, most approaches focus on database *schema analysis* [37, 39, 40, 88] (data reverse engineering (DRE)) and/or *schema translation and redesign* (data forward engineering) [39, 89, 90]. In addition, the procedural portions of *data-oriented applications* have to be adapted to the newly redesigned schema in order to complete the reengineering task.

Remark: A persistent data structure always preserves the previous version of itself when it is modified. A simple example of persistent data structure is the singly linked list. A data structure is partially persistent if all versions can be accessed but only the newest version can be modified.

DRE is defined as "the use of structured techniques to reconstitute the data assets of an existing system" [91, 92]. By means of structured techniques, existing situations are analyzed and models are constructed prior to developing the new system. The discipline in structured techniques makes the process of DRE economically viable. No doubt, data are valuable assets in all organizations. Student information, patient history, and billing addresses of customers are examples of data assets. The two vital aspects of a DRE process are (i) recover *data assets* that are valuable and (ii) *reconstitute* the recovered data assets to make them more useful. In other words, DRE increases the value of the existing data assets, making it more attractive for organizations to conduct business efficiently and effectively. In practice, the purpose of DRE is as follows [38, 93]:

- *Knowledge acquisition.* Knowledge acquisition is a method of learning. It includes elicitation, collection, analysis, modeling, and validation of information for software projects. The need for knowledge acquisition is pivotal to reverse engineering of *data-oriented applications*. The data portion—be it flat files or a relational database—must be clearly understood in a reverse engineering process.

- *Tentative requirements.* DRE of an operational system can identify the tentative requirements of the replacement system. DRE ensures that the functionality of the current system is not forgotten or overlooked.

- *Documentation.* DRE improves the documentation of existing systems, especially when the original developers are no longer available for advice. Maintenance of legacy software is assisted by the new documentation.

- *Integration.* DRE facilitates integration of applications, because (i) a logical model of encompassed software is a prerequisite for integration and (ii) a logical model of encompassed software presents a plausible model of how the program will function in certain environmental conditions.

- *Data administration.* As data are increasingly used as information, the data owner must be able to perform data administration easily and pragmatically.

DRE allows companies to manage data correctly and efficiently. Data administration, also known as data resource management, is an organizational function working in the areas of information systems that plans, organizes, describes, and controls data resources.

- *Data conversion.* One needs to understand the logical connection between the old database and the new one before converting the old data. Data conversion is the migration of the data instance from the old database to the new one.

- *Software assessment.* DRE represents one of the evaluation criteria for a software product, because DRE can be used to assess the database management system (DBMS) schema of the software [94]. A relational database contains a catalog that describes the various elements in the system. The catalog divides the database into sub-databases known as schemas. Within each schema are database objects—tables, views, and privileges. The catalog itself is a set of tables with its own schema name. Tables in the catalog cannot be modified directly; rather, those are modified indirectly with schema statements. The quality of the database design is an indicator of the quality of the software as a whole. Reverse engineering provides an unusual source of insight.

- *Quality assessment.* The overall quality of a software system can be assessed with DRE techniques, because a flawed design of a persistent data structure is likely to lead to faults in the software system. From data structure analysis, companies can decide whether or not to purchase and maintain COTS components.

- *Component reuse.* The concept of reuse has increasingly become popular amongst software engineers. DRE tools and techniques offer the opportunity to access and extract software components. Quite often these components need to be modified one way or another before they can be reused.

The complexity of reverse engineering *data-oriented applications* can be reduced because one can reverse engineer databases almost independent of the code. DRE deals only with data components of the *data-oriented applications.* Reverse engineering of a *data-oriented application,* including its user interface, begins with DRE. Recovering the specifications, that is the *conceptual schema* in database realm, of such applications is known as database reverse engineering (DBRE) [40]. A DBRE process facilitates understanding and redocumenting an application's database and files. The baselines for a generic DBRE methodology was proposed by Hainaut et al. [87], as discussed in the following.

By means of a DBRE process, one can recreate the complete logical and conceptual schemas of a database physical schema. The *conceptual schema* is an abstract, implementation-independent description of the stored data. Entity-relationship (ER) diagrams are commonly used as a schema notation. A conceptual schema, described with an ER diagram, comprises entities, relationships among entities, attributes of entities, and various constraints to capture an application's concepts and structures. On the one hand, a *logical schema* describes the data structures in concrete forms as those are implemented by the data manager. For example, the logical schema of a relational database precisely describes its tables, keys, and the data constraints. On the other hand, the *physical schema* of a database implements the logical schema by describing the physical constructs, namely, indices, and parameters, namely, page size and buffer management policy. Undoubtedly, deep understanding of the forward design process is needed to reverse engineer a database. The forward design process of a database comprises three basic phases as follows:

- *Conceptual phase.* In this phase, user requirements are gathered, studied, and formalized into a conceptual schema. The phase of conceptual schema has no impact on reverse engineering.

- *Logical phase.* In this phase, the conceptual schema is expressed as a simple model, which is suitable for optimization reasoning. Independent of the target DBMS, the model can be optimized. Next, it is translated according to the target model. The model can be further optimized according to data management system (DMS)-dependent rules.

- *Physical phase.* Now the logical schema is described in the data description language (DDL) of the DMS and the host programming language. The views needed by the application programs are expressed partly in DDL and partly in the host language.

A DBRE process is based on backward execution of the logical phase and the physical phase, beginning with the results of the physical phase. The process is divided into two main phases, namely, *data structure extraction* and *data structure conceptualization*. The two phases relate to the recovery of two different schemas: (i) the first one retrieves the present structure of data from their DDL/host language representation and (ii) the second one retrieves a conceptual schema that describes the semantics underlying the existing data structures. Figure 4.15 shows the general architecture of a reference DBRE methodology.

4.8.1   Data Structure Extraction

The complete DMS schema, including the structures and constraints, are recovered in this phase. In general, database systems provide a description of this schema in some machine processable form. Schemas are a rich starting point to begin a DBRE process. Schemas can be refined through further analysis of other components of the application such as subschema, screen and report layouts, procedures, and documentation. The problem is much more complex for standard files, for which no computerized description of their structure exists in most cases. For example, three standard files provided by Unix are Standard In, Standard Out, and Standard Error. Every running program under Unix starts with three standard opened files. By default, all inputs will come from the keyboard and all outputs (both normal and error output) will go to the screen. Each source program must be analyzed in order to detect partial structure of the files. For most real-world applications, *data structure elicitation* techniques are used to discover the constraints and structures

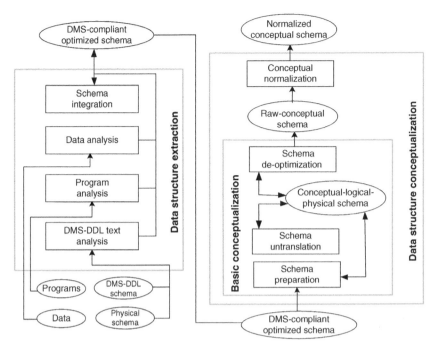

FIGURE 4.15 General architecture of the DBRE methodology. From Reference 95. © 1997 IEEE

that were implicitly incorporated into the implementation [40]. In this methodology, data structures are extracted by means of the following main processes:

DMS–DDL text analysis. Data structure declaration statements in a given DDL, found in the schema scripts and application programs, are analyzed to produce an approximate logical schema.

Program analysis. This means analyzing the source code in order to detect integrity constraints and evidences of additional data structures.

Data analysis. This means analyzing the files and databases to (i) identify data structures and their properties, namely, unique fields and functional dependencies in files and (ii) test hypothesis such as "could this field be a foreign key to this file?"

Schema integration. The analyst is generally presented with several schemas while processing more than one information source. Each of those multiple schemas offers a partial view of the data objects. All those partial views are reflected on the final logical schema via a process for *schema integration.*

4.8.2   Data Structure Conceptualization

In this phase, one detects and transforms or discards redundancies, DMS-dependent constructs, technical optimization, and nonconceptual structures. The phase comprises two sub-phases: *basic conceptualization* and *conceptual normalization*, as explained in the following.

> *Basic conceptualization.* In this sub-phase, relevant semantic concepts are extracted from an underlying logical schema, by solving two different problems requiring very different methods and reasoning: *schema untranslation* and *schema de-optimization.* It is important to note that first the schema is made ready by cleaning it before tackling those two problems.
>
> - *Making the schema ready.* First, the original schema might be using some concrete constructs, such as files and access keys, which might have been useful in the data structure extraction phase, but now can be eliminated. Second, some names can be translated to more meaningful names. Third, some parts of the schema might be restructured before trying to interpret them.
>
> - *Schema untranslation.* The existing logical schema is a technical translation of the initial conceptual constructs. Untranslation means identifying the traces of those translations, and replacing them by their original conceptual constructs.
>
> - *Schema de-optimization.* An optimized schema is generally more difficult to understand. Therefore, in a logical schema, it is useful to identify constructs included to perform optimization and replace those constructs.
>
> *Conceptual normalization.* The basic conceptual schema is restructured for it to have the desired qualities, namely, simplicity, readability, minimality, extensibility, and expressiveness. Examples of conceptual normalization are (i) replace some entity types by relationship types; (ii) replace some entity types by attributes; (iii) make the *is–a* relation explicit; and (iv) standardize the names.

4.9 REVERSE ENGINEERING TOOLS

In this section, we analyze a number of commercial and academic reverse engineering tools. Each of these tools has one or more distinct features compared to others. We put emphasis on the purpose of each tool and the functionality that it supports. It is important to note that software reverse engineering is a complex process that tools can only support, not completely automate. There is a need for a good deal of human intervention with any reverse engineering project. The tools can provide a new view of the product, as shown in Figure 4.16. The basic structure of reverse engineering tools, as outlined by Chikofsky and Cross II, is as follows:

- The software system to be reverse engineered is analyzed.
- The results of the analysis are stored in an information base.
- View composers use the information base to produce alternative views of the system.

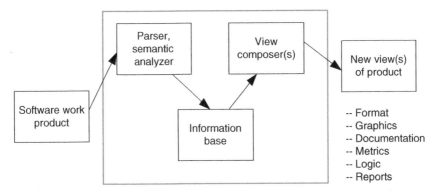

FIGURE 4.16   Basic structure of reverse engineering tools. From Reference 6. © 1990 IEEE

Ada SDA (System Dependency Analyzer) [96] is a tool that supports analysis and migration of Ada programs. It parses Ada code into an Object-Oriented Abstract Structural Type (OO-AST) and performs simple analysis. The analysis is focused on two areas, namely, portability check and architectural analysis. Portability check is carried out by searching for non-Ada routines, such as X/Motif in the program which are treated as *cliché*. The idea of *cliché* is explained after this paragraph. Architectural analysis involves determining what subunits and packages are used and the compilation dependency order.

Remark: A cliché is a frequently occurring pattern in a program, for example, data structures, algorithms, or domain-specific patterns. A *plan* is a representation of a cliché. Plan recognition involves recognizing cliché using plan. The recognition of plan is a symbolic pattern matching process [97]. To locate such patterns, what is needed is a search mechanism that is closer to the mental model of the software engineer. Program plans are abstract representations of source code fragments. Comparison methods are used to help recognize instances of program plans in a subject system. This process involves pattern matching at the programming language semantic level.

CodeCrawler [98] is a language-independent reverse engineering tool which combines metrics and software visualization [99]. CodeCrawler is written in Visualworks Smalltalk and it runs on every major platform. It uses two-dimensional displays to visualize software. Nodes represent software entities or abstraction of them, while the edges represent relationships between those entities. This tool combines the capability of showing software entities and their relationships with the capability of visualizing software metrics using *polymetric views*. CodeCrawler has been successfully used to reverse engineer several large industrial software systems.

DMS (Design Maintenance System) toolkit developed by Semantic Design, Inc. [100], is composed of a set of tools for carrying out reengineering of medium- or large-scale software systems. The capacities include analysis, porting, translation, interface changes, or other massive regular change and/or domain-specific program generation. This toolkit is the first implementation of the DMS, a software engineering environment that supports the incremental construction and maintenance of large application systems, driven by semantics and captured designs [101].

FermaT is the generic name for a set of tools designed by Software Migration Ltd. [102], specifically to support assembler code comprehension, maintenance, and migration. Based upon a unique IL called Wide Spectrum Language (WSL) and program transformation technique, FermaT is able to capture and manipulate the entire functionality of an assembler program, thereby significantly improving maintenance productivity and reducing cost [103]. These tools can be used to transform assembly language to C or COBOL.

GXL (Graph eXchange Language) [104] is an XML-based format for sharing data between tools. GXL represents typed, attributed, directed, ordered graphs which are extended to represent hyper-graphs and hierarchical graphs. An advantage of GXL is that one can exchange instance graphs together with their corresponding schema information in a uniform format. The language allows software reengineers to combine single-purpose tools especially for parsing, source code extraction, architecture recovery, data flow analysis, pointer analysis, program slicing, query techniques, source code visualization, object recovery, restructuring, refactoring, and remodularization into a single powerful reengineering workbench [105].

IDA Pro Disassembler and Debugger by Hex-Rays [106] is a powerful disassembler that supports more than 50 different processor architectures, including IA-32, IA-64 (Itanium), and AMD64. IDA also supports a variety of executable file formats such as PE (Portable Executable used in Windows), ELF (Executable and Linking Format, used in Linux), and even XBE, which is used on Microsoft's Xbox. IDA is a remarkably flexible product, providing highly detailed disassembly, along with a plethora of side features that assist with the reversing task. IDA is capable of producing a useful flowchart for a given function. In addition, it can produce call graphs that visually illustrate the flow of code of a loaded program. The graph can show internal subroutines and the links between every one of those subroutines. IDA also has several little features that make it very convenient to use, such as highlighting all instances of the currently selected operand. This makes it much easier to read disassembled listings and gain an understanding of how data flow within the code.

Hex-Rays Decompiler is a commercial decompiler plug-in for IDA Pro [107]. This plug-in adds a decompiler view to the other views available with the interactive disassembler. It converts executable programs into a human readable C-like pseudo code text. The output is not designed for recompilation; rather, it is used only for more rapid comprehension of what the function is doing. The output includes compound conditional operators (|| and &&), loops (for, while, and break), and function parameters and returns.

Imagix 4D [108] is useful in understanding legacy C, C++, and Java software. It enables users to quickly check software at multiple levels: high-level architecture, classes, and function dependencies. Users can explore their software's control structures, data usage, and inheritance. The tool is also useful in creating design documentation automatically.

IRAP (Input–Output Reengineering and Program Crafting) is a data reengineering tool developed by Spectra Research [109] that provides a semi-automated approach to recraft legacy software into an Intranet/Internet-enabled application without compromising program computational integrity. In particular, the input–output mechanism in a legacy software is migrated to the Intranet/Internet platform, and business rules are extracted from legacy software and reimplemented into an Intranet/Internet-enabled application. Currently, Spectra Research supports reengineering of file-base FORTRAN 77 and ANSI standard C programs.

JAD (JAva Decompiler) is a Java decompiler written in C++ [110]. JAD can be used for (i) recovering lost source code; (ii) exploring the sources of Java runtime libraries; and (iii) disassembling bytecode. Since Java files are compiled to bytecode, which is interpreted by a Virtual Machine, and not compiled to machine code like C programs, Java decompilers can decompile Java programs into compilable source code with near-perfect accuracy. JAD fails to decompile some nested loops and has difficulty in decompiling inline commands and inner functions.

ManSART [111] is a tool to recover the architecture of a given software system. Working primarily on source code, the tool semi-automatically constructs software structure by abstracting functionalities of the system.

McCabe IQ [112] is capable of predicting some key issues in maintaining large and complex business software applications: (i) locate error-prone sections of code and (ii) identify the risk of system failure. It also provides a rich graphical environment for analyzing the architectures of systems. In addition, it provides robust enterprise reporting, advanced reengineering capabilities, change analysis, and secure web-enabled test data collection. McCabe IQ is platform independent and supports a variety of languages such as C, C#, C++, Perl, PL1, COBOL, JAVA, and VB.NET.

PBS (Portable Bookshelf) is an implementation of the web-based concept called *Software Bookshelf* [113] for the presentation navigation of information representing large software systems. The *PBS Toolkit* [114] is a set of tools for the generation of a PBS Bookshelf, which captures, organizes, manages, and delivers comprehensive information about software systems. It provides an integrated suite of code analysis and visualization capabilities intended for software maintenance, reengineering, and migration. One accesses the Bookshelf via a set of web pages. A separate page is assigned to each subsystem of the target software, and the page hierarchy reflects the system decomposition. Because of the open nature of the structure of the Bookshelf, developers can directly access the source code and documentation by navigating the file system.

RE-Analyzer [115] is an automated, reverse engineering system providing a high level of integration with a computer-aided software engineering (CASE) tool developed at IBM. The RE-analyzer automatically reverse engineers source code into graphic and textual representations within a CASE tool supporting structured analysis methodology [116]. That is, it transforms source code into a set of data flow diagrams, state transition diagrams, and entity-relationship data models within the design database of a CASE tool. Since the resulting representations can be browsed and modified within the CASE tool environment, a broad range of software engineering activities is supported, including program understanding, reengineering, and redocumentation.

Reengineering Assistant (RA) aims to provide an interactive environment where software maintainers can reverse engineer source code into a higher abstraction level of representation. The earliest version of RA is called Maintenance Assistant (MA), which was first developed for program analysis purpose at the Centre for Software Maintenance, Durham University in 1989. By means of a unified reengineering framework, a rigorous approach to reverse engineering has been proposed by using a WSL [103]. Sound rules for creating abstractions have been developed within the framework, and a tool has been built for automation.

Rigi [117, 118] is a software tool for comprehending large software systems. Software comprehension is achieved by performing reverse engineering on the given system. The tool (i) extracts artifacts from the information space of the given system; (ii) organizes the artifacts to construct a model at a higher abstraction level; (iii) graphically presents the model; (iv) supports both automatic and user-defined clustering of source artifacts; and (v) supports hierarchically embedded views of different relations among the source artifacts. To understand Java code, a reverse engineering environment called Shimba [119] has been coupled with Rigi. Shimba can analyze the static and dynamic aspects of the system. A directed graph is used to show dependencies among static software artifacts extracted from Java byte code.

SEELA is a reverse engineering tool developed by Tuval Software Industries [120] to support the documentation and maintenance of structured source code. The tool performs top-down display of source code to enhance the readability of programs. Additional features available in the tool are a structure editor, a browser, and a source code documentation generator. It works with a variety of programming languages, including C, FORTRAN, Ada, and Cobol. The main motivation for designing SEELA was to bridge the gap between a system's design description and the source code.

4.10 SUMMARY

In this chapter, we introduced the concepts, processes, and techniques of software reengineering including the risks associated with it. In addition, four general software reengineering benefits were discussed: (i) improving maintainability; (ii) migrating to a newer technology; (iii) improving quality; and (iv) preparing for functional enhancement.

Next, we introduced the concept of software reengineering based on three basic principles: abstraction, refinement, and alteration. Then, we discussed a general model for software engineering proposed by Eric J. Byrne [5]. The model suggests that reengineering is a sequence of three major activities: reverse engineering, re-design, and forward engineering. The aforementioned sequence is founded in abstraction, alteration, and refinement. In addition, we discussed three reengineering strategies: rewrite, rework, and replace. These reengineering strategies specify the basic steps for reengineering methods. The rewrite strategy is founded on the principle of alteration; the rework strategy on the principles of abstraction, alteration, and refinement; and the replace strategy on the principles of abstraction and refinement. Different variations of the reengineering process based on three strategies—rewrite, rework, and replace—and four types of changes—re-think, re-design, re-specify, and re-code—were enumerated in a tabular form and critically analyzed.

We explained five basic reengineering approaches: big bang, incremental, partial, iterative, and evolutionary. Each approach advocates a path for reaching the same goal of producing the target system. A specific reengineering approach is chosen for a given project after careful considerations of the following key factors: (i) objectives of the project; (ii) resources available for the project; (iii) the current state of the system to be reengineered; and (iv) risks in executing the project. We described two reengineering models: (i) source code reengineering reference model (SCORE/RM) and (ii) phase reengineering model. On the one hand, the reference model is divided into eight layers providing a detailed approach to rationalizing the software, understanding its requirements and functions, and reconstructing the software system following established practices. On the other hand, the phase reengineering model comprises five stages: planning and analysis, renovation, target system testing, redocumentation, and acceptance testing and system transition. Tasks within the phases are further decomposed to express detailed methodologies.

With the reengineering approaches and models in place, we introduced the concepts and objectives of *reverse engineering*. Then we introduced the Goals/Models/Tools paradigm that divides a reverse engineering process into three ordered stages: Goals, Models, and Tools:

Goals. In the *Goals* stage, the motivations for setting up of a process for reverse engineering are analyzed. The goals of the analysis activity are to identify (i) the information that the process will need and (ii) the abstractions to be created by the process.

Models. In this stage, the abstractions identified in the first stage are analyzed to create representation models. Representation models include information needed for the generation of abstractions.

Tools. In this phase, one defines, acquires, and/or develops the software tools required to produce documents by means of reverse engineering. The tools are used in (i) executing the *Models* stage and (ii) transforming the program models into the abstraction models identified in the *Goals* stage.

Fact-finding and information gathering from source code are the keys to the Goal/Models/Tools paradigm. In order to extract information that is not explicitly available from source code, automated analysis techniques, such as *lexical analysis, syntactic analysis, control flow analysis, data flow analysis, program slicing, visualization*, and *metrics* are used to facilitate reverse engineering. We examined low-level reverse engineering such as decompilers and disassemblers. The relationship between decompilation and the traditional reengineering model was also discussed.

Next, we discussed DRE for *data-oriented applications*. In *data-oriented applications*, the complexity can be broken down by considering that the files or database can be reverse engineered almost independently of the procedural parts. DRE deals only with data components of the *data-oriented applications*. DRE is a process for understanding and redocumenting the files and/or database of an application. We discussed a generic methodology based on the work of Jean-Luc Hainaut and his colleagues.

Finally, we concluded this chapter with a description of several commercial and academic reverse engineering tools. During our discussion, we emphasized on the purpose of each tool and the functionality it supports.

LITERATURE REVIEW

The edited book by Robert S. Arnold entitled *Software Reengineering*, IEEE Computer Society Press, Los Alamitos, CA, 1993 is a collection of 52 selected articles. These articles will further enhance the reader's understanding of software reengineering technology. A wide variety of software engineering concepts, tools and techniques, case studies, risks, and benefits are presented in the book. The book includes an excellent annotated bibliography of software reengineering that were published before circa 1993.

Reverse engineering is an active area of research in computer science. Researchers and practitioners, who are interested in knowing more about this subject, are recommended to study the following two articles:

H. Müller, J. Jahnke, D. Smith, M. Storey, S. Tilly and K. Wong. 2000. *Reverse Engineering: A Roadmap*, International Conference on Software Engineering – Future of Software Engineering. IEEE Computer Society Press, Los Alamitos, CA. pp. 47–60.

G. Canfora and M. Di Penta. 2007. *New Frontiers of Reverse Engineering*, International Conference on Software Engineering – Future of Software Engineering. IEEE Computer Society Press, Los Alamitos, CA. pp. 326–341.

The first article above summarizes the reverse engineering research during the 1980s and the 1990s. The authors describe the research activities in data and code reverse engineering. In addition, they discuss research results for developing and evaluating tools for reverse engineering. The second article presents the main achievements in the area of reverse engineering, such as program analysis, architecture and design recovery, and visualization. In addition, the authors discuss future research directions in reverse engineering.

Program transformation has applications in many areas of software engineering including compilation, optimization, refactoring, software renovation, and reverse engineering. Program transformation is the act of changing one program into an equivalent program. The aim of program transformation is to increase programmer productivity by automating programming tasks, thus enabling programming at a higher level of abstraction, and increasing maintainability and re-usability. The article by Eelco Visser [12] gives a taxonomy of the application areas of program transformations, discusses considerations to be made in the implementation of program transformation systems, especially focusing on the specification of transformation strategies. A slightly different approach to program translation was proposed by Richard Waters, known as *program translation via abstraction and reimplementation* [53]. It is a two-step method: (i) the source program is analyzed in order to produce a high-level, language-independent description and (ii) the reimplementation process transforms the abstract description obtained in the first step into a program in the target language.

We discussed the Goals/Models/Tools paradigm proposed by Benedusi et al. [21] when setting up a reverse engineering process. In circa 2004, Spencer Rugaber and Kurt Stirewalt (Model-driven reverse engineering, *IEEE Software*, July/August, 2004, 45–52) proposed a model-driven reverse engineering (MDRE) process. MDRE uses a formal specification language called SLANG and automatic code generation to reverse the reverse engineering process. To illustrate the process, the authors use a numerical analysis application of finding the roots of nonlinear equations.

Clone detection in software systems is an active area of research within program analysis. Several interesting techniques have been developed besides metric-based techniques [42], such as AST-based and token-based techniques. The reader is recommended to study the survey article on this subject by Chanchal Kumar Roy and James R. Cordy (*A Survey on Software Clone Detection Research*, Technical Report No. 2007-541, School of Computing, Queen's University at Kingston, Ontario, Canada). Moreover, contrary to the common wisdom, C. Kasper and M. W. Godfrey (*'Cloning Considered Harmful' Considered harmful*, Proceedings of the 2006 Working Conference on Reverse Engineering. IEEE Computer Society Press, Los Alamitos, CA, 2006. pp. 9–18) argue that clones are not necessarily harmful, especially so if maintainers are aware of clones.

Those interested in knowing more about low-level reverse engineering may refer to the excellent book by Eldad Eilam entitled *Reversing: Secrets of Reverse Engineering* [59]. The author discussed several interesting topics related to reverse engineering such as (i) reverse engineering on the .NET platform, (ii) how to reverse engineer an operating system, (iii) how to decipher an undocumented file format, (iv) copy protect and digital rights management technologies, and (iv) theory and principle behind decompilers. Regarding the history of decompilers, the readers are recommended to visit the decompilation wiki page (http://www.program-transformation.org/Transform/DeCompilation).

Due to the use of persistent data structures in a large number of software systems, concepts and techniques in DRE have gained much attention. DRE evolves through two communities: database community and software engineering community [93]. DRE comprises two major activities, namely, data analysis and conceptual abstraction. The former tries to recover a structurally complete and semantically annotated logical data model, whereas the latter aims to map the logical data model to an equivalent conceptual design. The interested readers are recommended to study the articles by Jean-Luc Hainaut and his colleagues [40, 87, 88, 95]. In addition, the book by Jörg P. Wadsack entitled *Data-oriented Reengineering*, Sudwestdeutcher Verlag fur Hochschulschriften(SVH) AG, 2009 will further enhance the reader's understanding of data reengineering technology. The book presents a wide variety of reengineering approaches, concepts, tools and techniques, risks, and benefits. It discusses the processes that combine tools for reengineering the data as well as the applications.

The question of the extent to which low-level reverse engineering (decompilation or disassembly) can legitimately be carried out without the consent of the owner of copyright of the computer program has been the subject of debate and uncertainty for many years. The issue arises because any form of reverse engineering involves intermediate copying of the software being analyzed. Copyright protects the form of expression of ideas or information (but not the ideas or information in itself), conferring certain exclusive rights on the author or creator. A more contentious issue is whether exceptions to the copyright owner's exclusive rights should be recognized in order to permit copying which occurs in the course of reverse engineering of computer software. The article by Cristina Cifuentes and Anne Fitzgerald (The legal status of reverse engineering of computer software, *Annals of Software Engineering*, Vol. 9, 2000, pp. 337–351) summarize the state of the law in the United States, the European Union, and Australia in relation to exceptions to copyright infringement which permit reverse engineering. The authors also discussed the landmark cases of *Sega Enterprises Ltd versus Accolade, Inc. (Sega)* and *Atari Games Corp. versus Nintendo of America, Inc. (Atari)*.

REFERENCES

[1] J. A. McCall, P. K. Richards, and G. F. Walters. 1977. *Factors in Software Quality.* Vol. 1, ADA 049014, National Technical Information Service, Springfield, VA.

[2] D. Yu. 1991. A view on three r's (3rs): reuse, re-engineering, and reverse-engineering. *ACM SIGSOFT Software Engineering Notes*, 16(3), 69.

[3] R. S. Arnold. 1993. A road map guide to software reengineering technology In: *Software Reengineering* (Ed R. S. Arnold). IEEE Computer Society Press, Los Alamitos, CA.

[4] H. M. Sneed. 1995. Planning the reengineering of legacy systems. *IEEE Software*, January, 24–34.

[5] E. J. Byrne. 1992. *A Conceptual Foundation for Software Reengineering.* Proceedings of the International Conference on Software Maintenance, November 1992, Orlando, Florida. IEEE Computer Society Press, Los Alamitos, CA. pp. 226–235.

[6] E. J. Chikofsky and J. H. Cross II. 1990. Reverse engineering and design recovery. *IEEE Software*, January, 13–17.

[7] R. Kazman, S. Woods, and J. Carrière. 1998. *Requirements for Integrating Software Architecture and Reengineering Models: Corum ii.* Proceedings of Working Conference on Reverse Engineering (WCRE), Washington, DC. IEEE Computer Society Press, Los Alamitos, CA. pp. 154–163.

[8] I. Jacobson and F. Lindström. 1991. *Re-engineering of Old Systems to an Object-oriented Architecture.* Proceedings of the ACM Conference on Object Oriented Programming Systems Languages and Applications, October 1991. ACM Press, New York, NY. pp. 340–350.

[9] J. Shao and C. Pound. 1999. Extracting business rules from information systems. *BT Technology Journal*, 17(4), 179–186.

[10] D. C. Schmidt. 2006. Model-driven engineering. *IEEE Computer*, February, 25–31.

[11] J. Manzella and B. Mutafelija. 1992. *Concept of the Re-engineering Life-cycle.* Proceedings of the International Conference on System Integration, June 1992, Morristown, NJ. IEEE Computer Society Press, Los Alamitos, CA. pp. 566–570.

[12] E. Visser. 2005. A survey of strategies in rule-based program transformation. *Journal of Symbolic Computation*, 40(1), 831–873.

[13] L. H. Rosenberg and L. E. Hyatt. 1996. Software re-engineering. *SAYC-TR-95-1001*. Available at http://satc.gsfc.nasa.gov/support/reengrpt.PDF (accessed October 1996).

[14] E. J. Byrne and D. A. Gustafson. 1992. *A Software Re-engineering Process Model.* Proceedings of the Sixteenth Annual International Conference on Computer Software and Applications (COMPSAC), September 1992. IEEE Computer Society Press, Los Alamitos, CA. pp. 25–30.

[15] A. Colbrook, C. Smythe, and A. Darlison. 1990. *Data Abstraction in a Software Re-engineering Reference Model.* Proceedings of the International Conference on Software Maintenance, November 1990, San Diego, CA. IEEE Computer Society Press, Los Alamitos, CA. pp. 2–11.

[16] H. M. Sneed. 1991. Economics of software re-engineering. *Journal of Software Maintenance: Research and Practice*, September, 163–182.

[17] M. G. Rekoff Jr. 1985. On reverse engineering. *IEEE Transactions on Systems, Man, and Cybernetics*, March–April, 244–252.

[18] C. Cifuentes. 2001. Reverse engineering and the computing profession. *IEEE Computer*, December, 166–168.

[19] T. J. Biggerstaff. 1989. Design recovery for maintenance and reuse. *Computer*, July, 36–49.

[20] IEEE Standard 1219-1998. 1998. *Standard for Software Maintenance.* IEEE Computer Society Press, Los Alamitos, CA.

[21] P. Benedusi, A. Cimitile, and U. De Carlini. 1992. Reverse engineering processes, design document production, and structure charts. *Journal of Systems Software*, 19, 225–245.

[22] G. Canfora, A. Cimitile, and M. Munro. 1994. Reverse engineering and reuse engineering. *Journal of Software Maintenance and Evolution: Research and Practice*, 6(2), 53–72.

[23] B. Cheng and J. Jeng. 1997. Reusing analogous components. *IEEE Transactions on Knowledge and Data Engineering*, 9(2), 341–349.

[24] E. Burd and M. Munro. 1998. A method for the identification of reusable units through reengineering. *The Journal of Systems and Software*, 44(2), 121–134.

[25] G. Canfora, A. De Lucia, and M. Munro. An integrated environment for reuse reengineering C code. *The Journal of Systems and Software*, 42(2), 153–164.

[26] P. T. Breuer and K. Lano. 1991. Creating specification from code: reverse engineering techniques. *Software Maintenance: Research and Practice*, 3, 145–162.

[27] A. Lakhotia. 1997. A unified framework for expressing software subsystem classification technique. *The Journal od Systems and Software*, 36(3), 211–231.

[28] L. J. Holtzblatt, R. L. Piazza, H. B. Reubenstein, S. N. Roberts, and D. R. Harris. 1997. Design recovery for distributed systems. *IEEE Transactions on Software Engineering*, 23(7), 461–472.

[29] D. Jerding and S. Rugaber. 1997. *Using Visualization for Architectural Localization and Extraction.* 4th Working Conference on Reverse Engineering. IEEE Computer Society Press, Los Alamitos, CA. pp. 56–65.

[30] B. Schmerl, J. Aldrich, D. Garlan, R. Kazman, and H. Yan. 2006. Discovering architectures from running systems. *IEEE Transactions on Software Engineering*, 32(7), 454–466.

[31] G. Antoniol, G. Casazza, M. Di Penta, and R Fiutem. 2001. Object-oriented design patterns recovery. *Journal of Systems and Software*, 59(2), 181–196.

[32] N. Tsantalis, A. Chatzigeorgiou, G. Stephanides, and S. T. Halkidis. 2006. Design pattern detection using similarity scoring. *IEEE Transactions on Software Engineering*, 32(11), 896–909.

[33] G. Antoniol, G. Canfora, A. De Lucia, and E. Merlo. 2002. Recovering traceability links between code and documentation. *IEEE Transactions on Software Engineering*, 28(10), 970–983.

[34] G. Ebner and H. Kaindl. 2002. Tracing all around in reengineering. *IEEE Software*, May/June, pp. 70–77.

[35] A. Marcus and J. I. Maletic. 2003. Recovering documentation-to-source-code traceability links using latent semantic indexing. Proceedings of the 25th International Conference on Software Engineering, Portland, Oregon. IEEE Computer Society Press, Los Alamitos, CA. pp. 125–135.

[36] G. Canfora, A. Cimitile, and M. Munro. 1996. An improved algorithm for identifying objects in code. *Software – Practice and Experience*, 26(1), 25–48.

[37] W. J. Premerlani and M. R. Blaha. 1994. An approach for reverse engineering of relational databases. *Communications of the ACM*, 37(5), 42–49.

[38] M. R. Blaha. 1997. *Dimension of Database Reverse Engineering*. 4th Working Conference on Reverse Engineering. IEEE Computer Society Press, Los Alamitos, CA. pp. 176–183.

[39] J. H. Jahnke and J. Wadsack. 1999. *Integration of Analysis and Redesign Activities in Information System Reengineering*. Proceedings of the 3rd European Conference on Software Maintenance and Reengineering, October 1999. IEEE Computer Society Press, Los Alamitos, CA. pp. 160–168.

[40] J. Hainaut, J. Henrard, D. Roland, V. Englebert, and J. Hick. 1996. *Structure Elicitation in Database Reverse Engineering*. 3th Working Conference on Reverse Engineering. IEEE Computer Society Press, Los Alamitos, CA. pp. 131–139.

[41] B. S. Baker. 1995. *On Finding Duplication and Near-duplication in Large Software Systems*. Proceedings of the Working Conference on Reverse Engineering. IEEE Computer Society Press, Los Alamitos, CA. pp. 86–95.

[42] K. Kontogiannis, R. De Mori, E. Merlo, M. Galler, and M. Bernstein. 1996. Pattern matching for clone and concept detection. *Journal of Automated Software Engineering*, 3, 77–108.

[43] T. Kamiya, S. Kusumoto, and K. Inoue. 2002. Ccfinder: a multilinguistic token-based code clone detection system for large scale source code. *IEEE Transactions on Software Engineering*, 28(7), 654–670.

[44] R. Koschke. 2008. Identifying and removing software clones. In: *Software Evolution* (Eds T. Mens and S. Demeyer), pp. 15–36. Springer-Verlag, Berlin.

[45] E. van Emden and L. Moonen. 2002. *Java Quality Assurance by Detecting code Smells*. 9th Working Conference on Reverse Engineering, Richmond, VA. IEEE Computer Society Press, Los Alamitos, CA. pp. 97–107.

[46] M. Marin, A. van Deursen, and L. Moonen. 2004. *Identifying Aspects Using Fan-in Analysis*. Proceedings of the 11th Working Conference on Reverse Engineering. IEEE Computer Society Press, Los Alamitos, CA. pp. 132–141.

[47] R. S. Arnold and S. A. Bohner. 1993. Impact analysis—towards a framework for comparison. In: *Software Chnage Impact Analysis* (Eds S. A. Bohner and R. S. Arnold), pp. 34–43. IEEE Computer Society Press, Los Alamitos, CA.

[48] C. Cifuentes and K. J. Gough. 1995. Decompilation of binary programs. *Software – Practice and Experience*, 25(7), 811–829.

[49] E. Merlo, Y. Gagné P, J. F. Girard, K. Kontogiannis, L. J. Hendren, P. Panangaden, and R. de Mori. 1995. Reengineering user interfaces. *IEEE Software*, January, 64–73.

[50] C. Plaisant, A. Rose, B. Shneiderman, and A. Vanniamparampil. 1997. Low-effort, high-payoff user interface reengineering. *IEEE Software*, July–August, 66–72.

[51] H. M. Sneed and S. H. Sneed. 2006. Reverse engineering of system interfaces: a report from the field. 13th Working Conference on Reverse Engineering. IEEE Computer Society Press, Los Alamitos, CA. pp. 125–133.

[52] S. Bhansali, J. R. Hegemeister, C. S. Raghavendra, and H. Sivaraman. 1994. Parallelizing sequential programs by algorithm-level transformation. Proceedings of the 3rd Workshop on Program Comprehension, Washington, DC. IEEE Computer Society Press, Los Alamitos, CA. pp. 100–107.

[53] R. C. Waters. 1988. Program translation via abstraction and reimplementation. *IEEE Transactions on Software Engineering*, 14(8), 1207–1228.

[54] E. J. Byrne. 1991. Software reverse engineering: a case study. *Software – Practice and Experience*, 21(2), 1349–1364.

[55] G. Canfora, A. Cimitile, A. De Lucia, and G. A. Di Lucca. 2000. Decomposing legacy programs: a first step towards migrating to client-server platforms. *Journal of Systems and Software*, 54(2), 99–110.

[56] I. Jacobson, M. Ericsson, and A. Jacobson. 1995. *The Object Advantage – Business Process Re-engineering with Object Technology*. Addison-Wesley, Reading, MA.

[57] H. Huang, W. T. Tsai, S. Bhattacharya, X. Chen, Y. Wang, and J. Sun. 1998. Business rule extraction techniques for cobol programs. *Journal of Software Maintenance Research and Practice*, 10(1), 3–35.

[58] H. M. Sneed. 2000. Encapsulation of legal software: a technique for reusing legacy software components. *Annals Software Engineering*, 9, 293–313.

[59] E. Eilam. 2005. *Reversing: Secrets of Reverse Engineering*. Wiley, Indianapolis, IN.

[60] D. DaCosta, C. Dahn, S. Mancoridis, and V. Prevelakis. 2003. *Characterizing the 'Security Vulnerability Likelihood' of Software Function*. Proceedings, Conference on Software Maintenance. IEEE Computer Society Press, Los Alamitos, CA. pp. 266–275.

[61] M. Shevertalov and S. Mancoridis. 2007. *A Reverse Engineering Tool for Extracting Protocols of Networked Applications*. 14th Working Conference on Reverse Engineering, Vancouver, BC. IEEE Computer Society Press, Los Alamitos, CA. pp. 229–238.

[62] P. Benedusi, A. Cimitile, and U. De Carlini. 1989. *A Reverse Engineering Methodology to Reconstruct Hierarchical Data Flow Diagrams*. Proceedings of the International Conference on Software Maintenance, October 1989, Miami, FL. IEEE Computer Society Press, Los Alamitos, CA. pp. 180–189.

[63] D. Brown, J. Levine, and T. Mason. 1995. *lex & yacc*, 2nd Edition. O'Reilly Media Inc., Sebastopol, CA.

[64] M. S. Hecht. 1977. *Flow Analysis of Computer Programs*. Elsevier Science Inc., New York, NY.

[65] B. G. Ryder. 1979. Constructing the call graph of program. *IEEE Transactions on Software Engineering*, 5(3), 216–226.

[66] D. Callahan, A. Carle, M. W. Hall, and K. Kennedy. 1990. Constructing the procedure call multigraph. *IEEE Transactions on Software Engineering*, 16(4), 483–487.

[67] L. J. Osterweil and L. D. Fosdick. 1976. Dave – a validation, error detection, and documentation system for fortran programs. *Software – Practice and Experience*, October/December, 473–486.

[68] L. D. Fosdick and L. J. Osterweil. 1976. Data flow analysis in software reliability. *Computing Surveys*, September, 305–330.

[69] M. Weiser. 1984. Program slicing. *IEEE Transactions on Software Engineering*, 10(4), 352–357.

[70] D. Binkley, S. Horwitz, and T. Reps. 1995. Program integration for language with procedure calls. *ACM Transactions on Software Engineering and Methodology*, 4(1), 3–35.

[71] K. Gallagher and D. Binkley. 2008. *Program Slicing*. Proceedings of the 2008 Frontiers of Software Maintenance (FoSM), September 2008, Beijing, China. IEEE Computer Society Press, Los Alamitos, CA. pp. 58–67.

[72] F. Tip. 1995. A survey of program slicing techniques. *Journal of Programming Languages*, 3, 121–189.

[73] P. Young and M. Munro. 1998. *Visualising Software in Virtual Reality*. Proceedings of International Workshop on Working Conference on Program Comprehensive. IEEE Computer Society Press, Los Alamitos, CA. pp. 19–26.

[74] T. J. McCabe. 1976. A complexity measure. *IEEE Transactions on Software Engineering*, December, 308–320.

[75] A. J. Albrecht. 1979. *Measuring Application Development Productivity*. Process Joint SHARE/GUIDE/IBM Application Development Symposium, October 1979. Reprinted in 1981 in *Programming Productivity: Issues for the Eighties* (Ed. Capers Jones), No. EHO 186-7, pp. 34–43. Computer Society Press.

[76] S. M. Henry and D. G. Kafura. 1981. Software structure metrics based on information flow. *IEEE Transactions on Software Engineering*, 7(5), 510–518.

[77] S. R. Chidamber and C. F. Kemerer. 1994. A metric suite for object-oriented design. *IEEE Transactions on Software Engineering*, 20(6), 476–493.

[78] V. R. Basili, L. C. Briand, and W. L. Melo. 1996. A validation of object-oriented design metrics as quality indicators. *IEEE Transactions on Software Engineering*, 22(10), 751–761.

[79] G. A. Di Lucca, M. Di Penta, A. R. Fasolino, and P. Granato. 2001. *Clone Analysis in the Web Era: An Approach to Identify Cloned Web Pages*. Proceedings of 7th IEEE Workshop on Empirical Studies of Software Maintenance, November 2001, Florence, Italy. IEEE Computer Society Press, Los Alamitos, CA. pp. 107–113.

[80] G. A. Di Lucca, M. Di Penta, and A. R. Fasolino. 2002. *An Approach to Identify Duplicated Web Pages*. Proceedings of 26th International Computer Software and Applications Conference, August 2002, Oxford, England. IEEE Computer Society Press, Los Alamitos, CA. pp. 481–486.

[81] M. Halstead. 1962. *Machine Independent Computer Programming*. Spartan Books, Washington, DC.

[82] I. D. Baxter and M. Mehlich. 1997. Reverse Engineering Is Reverse Forward Engineering. 4th Working Conference on Reverse Engineering. IEEE Computer Society Press, Los Alamitos, CA. pp. 104–113.

[83] M. J. Van Emmerik. 2007. Static single assignment for decompilation. Ph.D. Thesis, School of Information Technology and Electrical Engineering, The University Queensland, Australia. Available at http://www.program-transformation.org/Transform/DecompilationAndReverseEngineering (accessed June 17, 2014).

[84] P. Samuelson and S. Scotchmer. 2002. The law and economics of reverse engineering. *The Yale Law Journal*, 111, 1575–1663.

[85] D. N. Pruitt. 2006. Beyond fair use: the right to contract around copyright protection of reverse engineering in the software industry. *Journal of Intellectual Property, Chicago-Kent College of Law*, 6(1), 66–86.

[86] J. A. Ricketts, J. C. DelMonaco, and M. W. Weeks. 1989. *Data Reengineering for Application Systems*. Proceedings of the International Conference on Software Maintenance, November 1989. IEEE Computer Society Press, Los Alamitos, CA. pp. 174–179.

[87] J. Hainaut, M. Chandelon, C. Tonneau, and M. Joris. 1993. *Contribution to a Theory of Database Reverse Engineering*. Proceedings of Working Conference on Reverse Engineering. IEEE Computer Society Press, Los Alamitos, CA. pp. 161–170.

[88] J. Hainaut, V. Englebert, J. Henrard, J. Hick, and D. Roland. 1995. *Requirements for Information System Reverse Engineering Support*. 2nd Working Conference on Reverse EngineeringToronto, ON. IEEE Computer Society Press, Los Alamitos, CA. pp. 136–145.

[89] J. Fong. 1997. Converting relational to object-oriented databases. *ACM SIGMOD Record*, 26(1), 53–58.

[90] S. Ramanathan and J. Hodges. 1997. Extraction of object-oriented structures from existing relational databases. *ACM SIGMOD Record*, 26(1), 59–64.

[91] P. Aiken. 1996. *Data Reverse Engineering: Staying the Legacy Dragon*. McGraw-Hill, Boston, New York.

[92] P. Aiken. 1998. Structured design. *IBM Systems Journal*, 37(2), 246–269.

[93] K. H. Davis and P. H. Aiken. 2000. *Data Reverse Engineering: A Historical Survey*. 7th Working Conference on Reverse Engineering. IEEE Computer Society Press, Los Alamitos, CA, pp. 70–78.

[94] M. Blaha. 1998. *On Reverse Engineering of Vendor Database*. 5th Working Conference on Reverse Engineering. IEEE Computer Society Press, Los Alamitos, CA, pp. 183–190.

[95] J. Hainaut, J. Hick, J. Henrard, D. Roland, and V. Englebert. 1997. *Knowledge Transfer in Database Reverse Engineering: A Supporting Case Study*. 4th Working Conference on Reverse Engineering. IEEE Computer Society Press, Los Alamitos, CA. pp. 194–203.

[96] G. Baratta-Perez, R. L. Conn, C. A. Finnell, and T. J. Walsh. 1994. Ada system dependency analyzer tool. *IEEE Computer*, February, 49–55.

[97] L. Wills and C. Rich. 1990. Recognizing a program's design: a graph-parsing approach. *IEEE Software*, January, 82–89.

[98] M. Lanza. 2007. Available at http://smallwiki.unibe.ch/codecrawler/. *CodeCrawler* (accessed August 2007).

[99] M. Lanza and S. Ducasse. 2003. Polymetric views – a lightweight visual approach to reverse engineering. *IEEE Transactions on Software Engineering*, Septemebr, 782–995.

[100] Semantic Design Inc. 1995–2008. *The DMS Software Reengineering Toolkit*. Available at http://www.semdesigns.com/products/dms/dmstoolkit.htm (accessed October 1995–2008).

[101] I. Baxter, P. Pidgeon, and M. Mehlich. 2004. Dms: *Program Transformations for Practical Scalable Software Evolution*. Proceedings of the 26th International Conference on Software Engineering, Scotland, UK. IEEE Computer Society Press, Los Alamitos, CA. pp. 625–634.

[102] Software Migration Ltd. 2007. *The FermaT Workbench*. Available at http://www.smltd.com/solutions.htm (accessed May 2007).

[103] H. Yang and M. Ward. 2003. *Successful Evolution of Software Systems*. Artech House, Boston, MA.

[104] R. C. Holt, A. Schürr, S. E. Sim, and A. Winter. 2006. Gxl: a graph-based standard exchange format for reengineering. *Science of Computer Programming*, 60(2), 149–170.

[105] R. Holt, A. Schürr, S. E. Sim, and A. Winter. 2002. *Graph Exchange Language Tools Version 1.0*. Available at http:/www.gupro.de/gxl/tools/tools.html (accessed July 2002).

[106] Hex-rays. 2007. *The IDA Pro Disassembler and Debugger*. Available at http://www.hex-rays.com/idapro (accessed February 2007).

[107] Hex-rays. 2008. *Hex-Rays Decompiler*. Available at http://www.hex-rays.com/decompiler.shtml. (accessed February 2008).

[108] Imagix corporation. 2007. *Reverse Engineering Quality Metrics, and Documentation Tool*. Available at http://www.imagix.com/products/products.html. (accessed October 2007).

[109] Spectra Research. 2008. *Software I/O Reengineering*. Available at http://www.spectra-research.com/inner/reeng.htm (accessed October 2008).

[110] P. Kouznetsov. 1997–2001. *Jad – The Fast JAva Decompiler*. Available at http://www.kpdus.com/jad.html (accessed June 17, 2014).

[111] M. P. Chase, S. M. Christey, D. R. Harris, and A. S. Yeh. 1998. *Managing Recovered Functions and Structure of Legacy Software Components*. 5th Working Conference on Reverse Engineering. IEEE Computer Society Press, Los Alamitos, CA, pp. 79–88.

[112] McCabe Software. 2008. *McCabe IQ Enterprise Edition*. Available at http://www.mccabe.com/iq_enterprise.htm (accessed October 2008).

[113] P. J. Finnigan, R. C. Holt, I. Kalas, S. Kerr, K. Kontogiannis, H. A. Müller, J. Mylopoulos, S. G. Perelgut, M. Stanley, and K. Wong. 1997. The software bookself. *IBM Systems Journal*, 36(4), 564–593.

[114] R. Holt. 1997. *Software Bookself: Overview and Construction*. Pbs Bookself. Available at http://www.swag.uwaterloo.ca/pbs (accessed March, 1997).

[115] A. B. O'Hare and E. W. Troan. 1994. Re-analyzer: from source code to structured analysis. *IBM Systems Journal*, 33(1), 110–130.

[116] E. Yourdon. 1989. *Modern Structured Analysis*. Prentice Hall, Englewood Cliffs, NJ, pp. 417–423.

[117] H. A. Müller. 1998. *Rigi User's Manual Version 5.4.4.* Available at http://www.rigi.csc.uvic.ca/pages/download.html.

[118] K. Wong, S. Tilley, H. A. Müller, and M. D. Storey. 1995. Structural redocumentation: a case study. *IEEE Software*, January, pp. 46–54.

[119] T. Systä, K. Koskimies, and H. Müller. 2001. Shimba—an environment for reverse engineering java software system. *Software Practice and Experience*, 31(4), 371–394.

[120] Tuval Software Industries. 2008. *SEELA: A Code Documentation Tool.* Available at http://www.speechover.com/index_files/about.htm (accessed October 2008).

EXERCISES

1. The potential reengineering risk areas are identified as follows: (i) process; (ii) reverse engineering; (iii) forward engineering; (iv) personal; (v) tools; and (vi) strategy. Explain these risk areas in detail.

2. Explain the principles of abstraction, refinement, and alteration in the context of software reengineering.

3. What are the differences among reengineering, reverse engineering, forward engineering, and rehosting?

4. Explain the differences between program translation and rephrasing. Discuss different types of program translation and rephrasing.

5. Discuss the differences between refactoring and renovation.

6. Explain the rework and replace reengineering strategies by giving concrete examples.

7. Discuss the pros and cons of different reengineering approaches.

8. Discuss the purpose of reverse engineering.

9. Explain the Goals/Models/Tools paradigm of software reverse engineering.

10. Explain the concepts of representation and visualization. Can a graphical object be both a representation within one context and a visualization within another? Explain it with an example.

11. Draw a CFG for the following sample code. Determine the cyclomatic complexity of the graph.

    (a) sum_of_all_positive_numbers(a, num_of_entries, sum)
    (b) sum = 0
    (c) init = 1
    (d)   while(init <= num_of_entries)
    (e)   if a[init] > 0

(f)   sum = sum + a[init]
         endif

(g)   init = init + 1
       endwhile

(h) end sum_of_all_positive_numbers

12. Obtain slices separately on *nw*, *nc*, *nl*, *inword*, and *c* of the following word count program.

```
[1]   #define   YES   1
[2]   #define   NO    0
[3]   main()
[4]   {
[5]       int c, nl, nw, nc, inword;
[6]       inword = NO;
[7]       nl = 0;
[8]       nw = 0;
[9]       nc = 0;
[10]      c = getchar();
[11]      while (c! = EOF) {
[12]          nc = nc + 1;
[13]          if (c == '\n')
[14]              nl = nl + 1;
[15]          if (c == ' '||c == '\n')||c == '\t')
[16]              inword = NO;
[17]          else if (inword == NO) {
[18]              inword = YES;
[19]              nw = nw + 1;
[20]          }
[21]          c = getchar();
[22]      }
[23]      printf("%d\n", nl);
[24]      printf("%d\n", nw);
[25]      printf("%d\n", nc);
[26]  }
```

13. Explain plan recognition.

14. Explain why decompilation is a reverse engineering process, whereas compilation is not a forward engineering process. Discuss the applications of decompilers. What technique can be used to avoid decompilation?

15. Discuss the purpose of DRE.

5

LEGACY INFORMATION SYSTEMS

When you have told anyone you have left him a legacy the only decent thing to do is to die at once.

—Samuel Butler

5.1 GENERAL IDEA

In Oxford English Dictionary (OED) the word "legacy" is defined as "A sum of money, or a specified article, given to another by will; anything handed down by an ancestor or predecessor." In software engineering, no standard definition of legacy exists; Bennett [1] used the following definition to define legacy systems: Legacy software systems are "large software systems that we don't know how to cope with but that are vital to our organization." This is the Phaseout stage of the *staged model* for CSS proposed by Rajlich and Bennett and discussed in Section 3.3 of Chapter 3. Similarly, Brodie and Stonebraker [2] define a legacy system as "any information system that significantly resists modification and evolution to meet new and constantly changing business requirements." Supporting both the definitions are a set of acceptable features of a legacy system:

- large with millions of lines of code;
- geriatric, often more than 10 years old;
- written in obsolete programming languages;

Software Evolution and Maintenance: A Practitioner's Approach, First Edition.
Priyadarshi Tripathy and Kshirasagar Naik.
© 2015 John Wiley & Sons, Inc. Published 2015 by John Wiley & Sons, Inc.

- lack of consistent documentation;
- poor management of data, often based on flat-file structures;
- degraded structure following years of modifications;
- very difficult, if not impossible, to expand;
- runs on old processors which are generally much slower; and
- the support team is totally reliant on the expertise and knowledge of expert individuals.

In addition, these information systems are mission-critical—that is, essential to the organization's business—and must be operational at all times. In summary, due to the lack of available skills and flexibility of the system, there is a strong urge to get rid of the legacy software system as soon as possible and start with something modern.

There are several categories of solutions for legacy information system (LIS) or simply legacy system. These solutions generally fall into six categories as follows [3, 4]:

- *Freeze*. The organization decides to not carry out further work on an LIS.
- *Outsource*. An organization may decide that supporting legacy (or any) software is not its core business. The organization may outsource it to a specialist organization offering this service.
- *Carry on maintenance*. Despite all the problems associated with supporting a software system, the organization decides to carry on maintenance for another period.
- *Discard and redevelop*. The organization throws all the software away and redevelops the application once again from scratch, using a new hardware platform and modern architecture tools and database. This approach removes the legacy problem in one stroke, but also removes a useful source of information for defining the requirements of the new system. The existing system is discarded in spite of it being stable, thoroughly debugged, and being a useful asset. One real issue in this approach is that the business requirements and technology are undergoing frequent changes. Therefore, at the end of a long development process, there is this danger that an organization gets a new system based on obsolete technology that no longer satisfies its business requirements. If the LIS cannot keep pace with changing business needs and if migration is not cost effective, then it is more appropriate to redevelop the system [5].
- *Wrap*. It is a black-box-based modernization technique: surround the LIS with a new layer of software to hide the complexity of the existing interfaces, applications, and data, with the new interfaces. Wrapping gives existing components a modern and improved appearance.
- *Migrate*. By means of migration a legacy system is ported to a modern platform, while retaining most of the system's functionality and introducing minimal disturbance in the business environment. Migration avoids the expensive and long process that generally characterize new development. Rather, reuse of portions

of the LIS, namely, implementation, design, specification, and requirements, is maximized. In addition, the target system runs in a different computing environment. In Section 5.3 migration is discussed in detail.

5.2   WRAPPING

In 1988, Dietrich et al. [6] first introduced the concept of a "wrapper" at IBM. Wrapping is a straightforward way to modify and enhance a legacy component. A wrapper does not directly modify the source code, but, instead, it indirectly modifies and changes the software functionality of the legacy component. Wrapping means encapsulating the legacy component with a new software layer that provides a new interface and hides the complexity of the old component. The encapsulation layer can communicate with the legacy component through sockets, remote procedure calls (RPCs), or predefined application program interfaces (API). Wrapping is a "black-box" reengineering activity because the interface of the legacy system is analyzed but not its internal details [7]. The wrapped component is viewed similar to a remote server; it provides some service required by a client that does not know the implementation details of the server. By means of a message passing mechanism, a wrapper connects to the clients. On the input front, the wrapper accepts requests, restructures them, and invokes the target object with the restructured arguments. On the output front, the wrapper captures outputs from the wrapped entity, restructures the outputs, and pushes them to the requesting entity. Well-tested components are reused by organizations via wrappers so as to reduce the maintenance cost. Consequently, legacy components can be invoked from the new state-of-the-art applications, thereby extending and enhancing the life of the legacy components [8]. However, this technique does not solve the problems with legacy systems.

5.2.1   Types of Wrapping

Orfali et al. [9] classified wrappers into four categories depending upon what is being wrapped. The four categories of wrappers are explained in the following.

- *Database wrappers.* Database wrappers serve as entry points to existing databases. Those wrappers enable clients implemented in today's object-oriented languages to access legacy databases. Database wrappers can be further classified into *forward wrappers* (*f-wrappers* in Figure 5.1) and *backward wrappers* (*b-wrappers* in Figure 5.2) [10]. The forward wrappers' approach, depicted in Figure 5.1, shows the process of adding a new component to a legacy system. The new component is developed with modern practices, whereas the legacy database and the legacy code are not modified. Therefore, by means of translation service involving both legacy data and queries, the wrapper integrates the new component with the legacy system. Those are called *forward wrappers* because they emulate new technology. The backward wrappers' approach has been depicted in Figure 5.2. In this approach, data are migrated first following the *Database first* approach discussed in Section 5.5.2. Next, new components

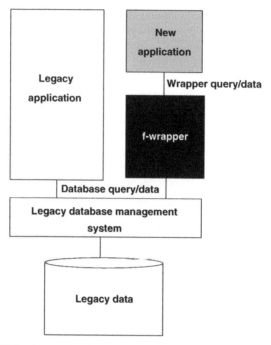

FIGURE 5.1   Forward wrapper. From Reference 10. © 2006 ACM

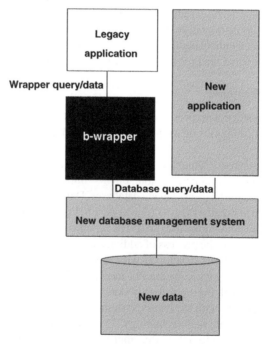

FIGURE 5.2   Backward wrapper. From Reference 10. © 2006 ACM

are developed that use the new database; the legacy components access the new data via wrappers. Those are called *backward wrappers* because they emulate the legacy technology on top of the new one.

- *System service wrappers.* This kind of wrappers support customized access to commonly used system services, namely, routing, sorting, and printing. A client program may access those services without knowing their interfaces.

- *Application wrappers.* This kind of wrappers encapsulate online transactions or batch processes. These wrappers enable new clients to include legacy components as objects and invoke those objects to produce reports or update files.

- *Function wrappers.* This kind of wrappers provide an interface to call functions in a wrapped entity. In this mechanism, only certain parts of a program—and not the full program—are invoked from the client applications. Therefore, limited access is provided by function wrappers.

5.2.2 Levels of Encapsulation

Legacy software has many levels of granularity: procedures are at the lowest level and processes are at the highest level. It may be noted that an entire application is not included in the granularity hierarchy, because an application is just a logical collection of processes executed at different times. Therefore, processes are considered to be at the highest level of granularity. Sneed [11] classified five levels (see Figure 5.3) of granularity at which one can access legacy software applications, as explained in the following:

Process level. A job is started on the server which accepts input data, accesses databases, and produces output data. The input data and output data are contained in files. The input files are created by the client program and are

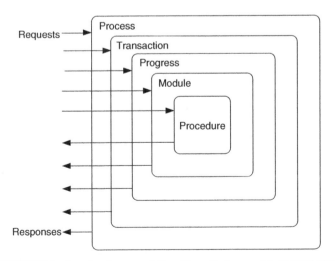

FIGURE 5.3   Levels of encapsulation. From Reference 11. © 1996 IEEE

transferred to the server by the wrapper by means of a standard file transfer utility. Upon the completion of the job, the wrapper takes over the output files to be forwarded to the client.

Transaction level. On the server, a virtual terminal is created that sends the terminal input map and receives the terminal output map. The wrapper is a program which simulates the user terminal. This type transaction level wrapping has become simple because modern transaction processors (i) take care of host-to-client communication and (ii) perform restart and recovery task, exception handling, rollback, and commit.

Program level. Via APIs, batch programs are called in a wrapper. The wrapper substitutes program inputs with data inputs coming in from the client application. In addition, outputs from the wrapped program are captured, reformatted, and sent to the client.

Module level. Legacy modules are executed using their standard interfaces. A significant deviation from the usual calls is that parameters are passed by value—and not by references. Therefore, first, the wrapper buffers the received values in its own address space. Next, the buffered values are passed on to the invoked module. Finally, the output values received from the invoked module are passed on to the client.

Procedure level. A procedure internal to the system is invoked as if the procedure was compiled separately. As a result, this special treatment of an internal procedure requires (i) constructing a parameter interface and (ii) if needed, initializing global variables before calling the procedure.

5.2.3 Constructing a Wrapper

A legacy system is wrapped in three steps as follows [12]:

- A wrapper is constructed.
- The target program is adapted.
- The interactions between the target program and the wrapper are verified.

A wrapper, constructed in the first step, is a program which receives input messages from the client program, transforms the inputs into an internal representation, and invokes the target system with the newly formatted messages. The wrapper intercepts the outputs produced by the target system, transforms them into a format understood by the client, and transfers them to the client. Conceptually, a wrapper comprises two interfaces and three event-driven modules as shown in Figure 5.4. The two interfaces are an internal interface and an external interface, and the three modules are message handler, interface converter, and I/O-emulator.

External interface. The interface of the wrapper that is accessed by the clients is called the external interface. The wrapper and its client generally communicate by passing messages. Messages normally comprise a header and a body. The header of a message contains control information: (i) identity of the sender; (ii) a time stamp; (iii) the transaction code; (iv) target program type; and (v) the identity of

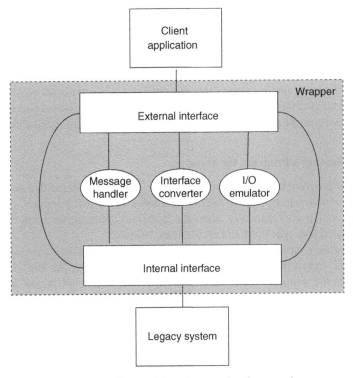

FIGURE 5.4   Modules of a wrapping framework

the transaction, program, procedure, or module to be invoked. The message body contains the input arguments. Similarly, the message body contains the output values in an output message. The values contained in a message are normally ASCII strings separated by a delimiter, say, a back slash ("\").

Internal interface. A wrapper's internal interface is the interface visible to the server. The internal interface is dependent upon the language and type of the wrapped entity. For example, if the wrapped entity is a job, the internal interface of the wrapper is a job control procedure, and the job control procedure is interpreted to execute the job. On the other hand, if the encapsulated entity is a program, procedure, transaction, or a module, the internal interface is a list of parameters in the language of the encapsulated software. Therefore, the internal interface is extracted from the source code of the encapsulated software. The parameters of the internal interface are specified in terms of the target language, thereby necessitating a translation from the input ASCII strings to the target types.

Message handler. The message handler buffers input and output messages, because requests from the client may occasionally arrive at a faster rate than they can be consumed. Similarly, outputs from the wrapped program may be produced at a faster rate than they can be sent to the client.

Interface converter. This entity converts the internal interface into the external interface and vice versa. In general, between the parameters of the two interfaces, there is a one-to-one mapping. In some cases, the mapping is one-to-many so the converter duplicates some parameters.

I/O-emulator. As the name suggests, the I/O-emulator intercepts the inputs to and outputs from the wrapped entity. Upon intercepting an input, the emulator fills the input buffer with the values of the parameters of the external interface. On the other hand, when it intercepts an output value, the emulator copies the contents of the output buffer into the parameter space of the external interface. Input/output functions of the original environment are emulated without affecting the encapsulated software.

5.2.4   Adapting a Program for Wrapper

A wrapped program is modified to some extent, and it is expected that the modified programs continue to operate in the normal mode. Therefore, programs are adapted with tools, rather than manually. Manual adaptations are prone to errors. Sneed [12] recommended four types of tools as discussed below.

Transaction wrapper. A transaction wrapper wraps a transaction processing program. If the transaction processing program supports panel input and output operations, then the wrapper converts the said input and output operations into calls to the wrapper. A panel is a particular arrangement of information grouped together for presentation to user.

Program wrapper. A batch processing program works on batches of file records. A batch processing program is handled by a wrapper by translating file input/output operations into wrapper calls. To access records on files, write and read statements in the batch processing programs are mapped to call statements in the wrapper. The program, instead of receiving a record from the file, receives the record from the wrapper. Similarly, output records are redirected to the wrapper.

Module wrapper. A module wrapper adapts the parameter interfaces of a subprogram that are called by reference. In the "called-by-reference" case, a parameter is an address in the address space of the calling program. If the inputs come from a program on another computer, a problem can arise in accessing the referenced location in the calling program. To solve the problem: (i) the interface of the wrapped module is modified so that values of the input parameters are put together in a single structure in a message buffer in the wrapper and (ii) a reference pointing to the message buffer in the wrapper is passed to the wrapped module.

Procedure wrapper. A procedure wrapper makes significant changes to the target program. New interfaces, not existing before, are created. A block of code that has been identified to be encapsulated as a method will get its separate invocation point with a parameter list and its separate exit point as well.

5.2.5   Screen Scraping

Screen scraping [13] is a common form of wrapping in which modern, say, graphical, interfaces replace text-based interfaces. The new interface can be a GUI (graphical user interface) or even a web-based HTML (hypertext markup language) client. Tools, such as Verastream from Attachmate [14], automatically generate the new screens.

Screen scraping is a short-term solution to a larger problem. Many serious issues are not addressed by simply mounting a GUI on a legacy system. For example, screen scraping (i) does not evolve to support new functions; (ii) incurs high maintenance cost; and (iii) ignores the problem of overloading. Overloading is simply defined as the ability of one function to perform different tasks. Screen scraping simply provides a straightforward way to continue to use a legacy system via a graphical user interface. At best it reduces the cost to train new employees. No new functionality is provided because not much code of the legacy system is overhauled.

5.3   MIGRATION

Migration of LIS is the best alternative, when wrapping is unsuitable and redevelopment is not acceptable due to substantial risk. However, it is a very complex process typically lasting 5–10 years [2]. If migration is successful, it gives long-term benefits. It offers better system understanding, easier maintenance, reduced cost, and more flexibility to meet future business requirements. Migration involves changes, often including restructuring the system, enhancing the functionality, or modifying the attributes. But, it retains the basic functionality of the existing system. In this section we discuss general guidelines for migrating a legacy system to a new target system. A brief overview of the migration steps is explained next.

Migration steps: LIS migration involves creation of a modern database from the legacy database and adaptation of the application program components accordingly [2, 15, 16]. A database has two main components: schema of the database and data stored in the database. Therefore, in general, migration comprises three main steps: (i) conversion of the existing schema to a target schema; (ii) conversion of data; and (iii) conversion of program.

Schema conversion. Schema conversion means translating the legacy database schema into an equivalent database structure expressed in the new technology. Both the schemas must convey the same semantics—that is, all the source data should be losslessly stored into the target database. The transformation of source schema to a target schema is made up of two processes. The first one is called DBRE and it aims to recover the conceptual schema that express the semantics of the source data structure, which is discussed in Section 4.8 of Chapter 4. The second process is straightforward and it derives the target physical schema from this conceptual schema: (i) an equivalent logical schema is obtained from the conceptual schema by means of transformations and (ii) a physical schema is obtained from the logical schema by means of transformations [15].

Data conversion. Data conversion means movement of the data instances from the legacy database to the target database. Data conversion requires three steps: extract, transform, and load (ETL) [17]. First, extract data from the legacy store. Second, transform the extracted data so that their structures match the format. In addition, perform data cleaning (a.k.a. *scrubbing or cleansing*) to fix or discard data that do not fit the target database [18]. Finally, load the transformed data in the target database.

Program conversion. In the context of LIS migration, program conversion means modifying a program to access the migrated database instead of the legacy data. The conversion process leaves the functionalities of the program unchanged. Program conversion depends upon the rules that are used in transforming the legacy schema into the target schema.

Testing and functionality: Migration engineers spent close to 80% of their time on testing the target system [19]. It is important to ensure that the outputs of the target system are consistent with those of the LIS. Therefore, new functionality is not to be introduced into the target system in a migration project. If both the LIS and the target system have the same functionality, it is easier to verify their outputs for compliance. However, to justify the project expense and the risk, in practice, migration projects often add new functionalities.

Cut over, also referred to as roll over: The last step of a migration project is the cut over from the LIS to the target system. The event of cutting over to the new system from the old one is required to cause minimal disruption to the business process. There are three kinds of transition strategies, as proposed by Simon [20]:

1. *Cut-and-run.* The simplest transition strategy is to switch off the legacy system and turn on the new system. Rolling over to the new system instantaneously in a single step is too risky because it would entail the entire information flow to be managed by a completely new system.
2. *Phased interoperability.* To reduce risks, cut over is gradually performed in incremental steps. In each step, replace a small number of legacy components—data or application—by their counterparts in the target system. For components to be independently migrated, this approach requires (i) the LIS to be partitioned into modules that perform different functions or (ii) the data into independent fragments.
3. *Parallel operation.* The target system and the LIS operate at the same time. During the period of simultaneous operation, tests are continuously performed on the target system; once the new system is considered to be reliable, the LIS is taken off service.

In practice, for a particular migration project, a transition strategy may be designed by combining all the three approaches, applied to different LIS components.

5.4   MIGRATION PLANNING

The success of any large project depends, to a large extent, upon good planning—and a migration project is not an exception. It is not easy to cut over and migrate several hundred databases and programs without interrupting the business of the organization. It is necessary to justify such a mission-critical project to the executive management. Management must be convinced that the organization will achieve significant benefits without excessively using resources. In addition, with poor or no planning, a lower-quality, much delayed product may be delivered at a higher cost.

The activity of planning for migration comprises several tasks. Seacord et al. [21] suggested that the following 13 steps be considered when planning a migration project:

Step 1: Perform portfolio analysis.

Step 2: Identify the stakeholders.

Step 3: Understand the requirements.

Step 4: Create a business case.

Step 5: Make a go or no-go decision.

Step 6: Understand the LIS.

Step 7: Understand the target technology.

Step 8: Evaluate the available technologies.

Step 9: Define the target architecture.

Step 10: Define a strategy.

Step 11: Reconcile the strategy with the needs of the stakeholder.

Step 12: Determine the resources required.

Step 13: Evaluate the feasibility of the strategy.

The objective of this plan is to minimize the risk of modernization effort leading to the development of a migration plan for the LIS. The remainder of the section expands on the these 13 steps.

Step 1: Perform portfolio analysis. In the first step, measures are established to evaluate the business value and technical quality of software systems; this is performed by means of portfolio analysis. Portfolio analysis establishes measures of technical quality and business value for a set of software systems. It is represented on a chi-square chart like the one shown in Figure 5.5. The vertical and horizontal axes of the chi-square chart are technical quality and business value, respectively.

Technical quality is computed as a weighted mean of various product and process metrics chosen by the user. Some example criteria for technical quality are ease of making changes, frequency of release notes, accuracy, performance of the system, error rate, cyclomatic complexity, and availability of training. The coefficients are ratios represented on a scale of 0–1. To obtain the coefficient values, first we need to define upper and a lower bounds for each quality metric. The upper and lower bounds are the maximum and minimum acceptable measures, respectively. Then the ratio is defined as [5]:

$$r = 1 - \left(\frac{actual\,measure - lower\_bound}{upper\_bound - lower\_bound} \right).$$

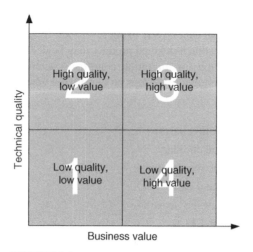

FIGURE 5.5   Portfolio analysis chi-square chart

The real challenge is to set the upper and lower bounds. It must be defined in terms of current industry standard or in terms of what other practitioners are doing. For example, cyclomatic complexity of value 12 can be considered as the upper bound [22].

The importance of an application or a system to an organization is measured in terms of business value. Some examples of the criteria to establish business value are level of usage, number of business goal satisfied, contribution to profit, user satisfaction, and annual revenue. Business value can be represented as a coefficient in the range [0, 1]. For example, if 100 is the maximum value of a certain criteria, and an application scores 30, then the coefficient of the said criteria is 0.30, which is obtained by dividing 30 by 100.

- *Quadrant 1.* A system with low technical quality and low business value is a prime candidate for substitution with a commercial product if one is available. These systems might be in use in the noncore sector of the organization.
- *Quadrant 2.* A system with high technical quality but low business value need not be replaced, migrated, or restructured.
- *Quadrant 3.* A system with high technical quality and high business value should be actively evolved. The system is in the Evolution stage of the *staged model* for CSS proposed by Rajlich and Bennett and discussed in Section 3.3 of Chapter 3.
- *Quadrant 4.* A system with low technical quality but high business value is a good candidate for redevelopment or migration to a new system.

Step 2: Identify the stakeholders. Stakeholders are the people or organizations that influence a system's behavior, or those who are impacted by the system. They typically include architects, developers, maintainers, managers, customers, and end users. The stakeholders ultimately judge the outcome and impact of the migration project. Each of the stakeholders bring their own perspectives to the table. Therefore, it is necessary to obtain their agreement and support.

Step 3: Understand the requirements. Requirements are a description of the needs and desires of stakeholders that a system is expected to implement. There are two challenges in defining requirements. First, ensure that the right requirements are captured. Second, express the requirements in such a way that the stakeholders can easily review and confirm their correctness. Therefore, it is essential to have an unambiguous representation of the requirements and have it made available in a centralized database so that all the stakeholders can review and validate the requirements [23]. Requirements can come from the LIS, business process reengineering, and stakeholders.

- *LIS.* Most requirements in a migration project are derived from the legacy system itself. The risk of deriving requirements from the subject system is that it may result in reimplementation of obsolete business practice.
- *Business process reengineering.* New requirements may come from business process reengineering (BPR). The objective of BPR is to improve the efficiency of business process. Business processes are embedded in existing information system, therefore it is logical to perform BPR before starting a legacy system migration project. Business processes need to be reevaluated, revalidated, and revisited before any migration works can begin.
- *Stakeholders.* Stakeholders generate new requirements, based on years of interactions with the LIS. These requirements are often recorded in outstanding change requests. Stakeholders often want to include technical advances as requirements.

Step 4: Create a business case. Based on a business case, executive management can decide whether or not the migration project will increase quality, reduce maintenance costs, and be financially viable. In general, a good business case provides the following information about the migration project:

- *Problem statement.* The problem statement describes the current LIS and highlights the inadequacies, inefficiencies, and weaknesses of the current situation.
- *Solution.* The business case must describe the solution at a high level. For example, the solution can be migrating the LIS to a new software/hardware architecture in an iterative manner. The solution should include an estimate of the cost, the effort needed, and a schedule. When calculating the effort in person-days, one can derive the minimum project duration using a variant of the COCOMO model [24], adjusted for the increased parallelism of the legacy migration project [5].
- *Risks.* Legacy migration projects benefit from identifying risk at an early stage. This allows to gain insight into and control of the project by enumerating things

TABLE 5.1   Common Quantifiable Benefit Metrics

Objective	Sample Quantifiable Benefit Metrics
Lower maintenance cost	Average cycle time to close problem reports
	Average labor hours to close problem reports
	Total staff census
	Average problem-report backlog
	Post-release fix rework hours
Add new functionality	Count of new functions added to the product
	Value added or revenue generated by new functions
Increase performance	Number of delivered operations, such as transactions, per unit time
Replace old equipment	Net annualized cost of purchase and maintenance
Recode in different languages	Number of modules in each programming language
Reuse of existing artifacts	Number of artifacts used in other products
Data rationalization	Number of redundant database objects removed
Integrate disjoint applications	Number of unified applications accessible to users
	Measures of usability and training time required for application suite

that can affect the effort and limit the resulting system. This will facilitate the management of the expectations of the stakeholders early, which is a crucial part of any successful migration effort. In addition, the business should also identify the assumptions in the migration project. Assumptions must be documented in case they later turn out to be incorrect or invalid. In either case, it may be necessary to reevaluate the business case.

- *Benefits.* This element of the business case identifies and, ideally, quantifies the benefits of the proposed solution, with an allowance for risks. Two ways to present benefits in a migration project are cost reductions and cost avoidance. Cost reduction refers to the actions taken immediately to reduce the costs. Cost avoidance relates to actions taken to reduce the cost in future. The initial cost of a migration project is high because of up-front investment in training, equipment, or redesign of the system. Therefore, it is helpful to include cost avoidance benefits by a *cost-benefit analysis*. In this analysis, the cost of migration effort is compared to the benefits of redeveloping and with the benefits of doing nothing at all. Moreover, one should find quantifiable benefits that can be measured. This requires the existence of a software metrics program to collect data. Table 5.1 lists sample quantifiable benefit metrics proposed by Tilley and Smith [25] that can serve as objective measures of migration project success.

Step 5: Make a go or no-go decision. Once a business case has been defined, it is reviewed by the stakeholders to reach an agreement. If the business case is unsatisfactory then the legacy migration project is terminated at this step.

Step 6: Understand the LIS. Understanding the LIS is essential to the success of any migration project. Techniques available to meet this challenge include program comprehension and reverse engineering. Reverse engineering and program comprehension are discussed in detail in Chapters 4 and 8, respectively.

Step 7: Understand the target technology. This activity can proceed in parallel with the activity of Step 6. It is important to understand the technologies that can be used in the migration effort and the technologies that have been used in the legacy system. In general, four types of technologies are of interest in the migration effort:

1. Languages and DBMS available, including COBOL, Java, eXtensible Markup Language (XML), and modern DBMS.
2. Distributed transaction models, including distributed communication and transaction technologies such as RPC or message queues. Key attributes of distributed communication protocol include support for direct or indirect, connectionless or connection-oriented, and asynchronous or synchronous communication.
3. Middleware technologies and standards that may be used to develop an information system, including message-oriented middleware (MOM), XML Messaging, Java 2 Enterprise Edition (J2EE), and Enterprise JavaBeans (EJB).
4. Tools that are available to assist in migration of the LIS to the new information system.

Step 8: Evaluate the available technologies. One must compare and contrast all the available technologies to evaluate their capabilities. If the capabilities overlap, then we must appraise these technologies to understand the quality of service they will provide in the migration process. To formulate the eventual architecture and design of the system, those evaluations are performed.

Step 9: Define the target architecture. The target architecture is the desired architecture of the new system. It models the stakeholders' vision of the new system. This usually requires descriptions using different views with different levels of granularity. The target architecture is likely to evolve during the migration process. Therefore, the target architecture is continually reevaluated and updated during the migration process.

Step 10: Define a strategy. A strategy defines the overall process of transforming the LIS to the new system. This includes migration methodology, that is schema conversion, data conversion, and program conversion, testing, and cut over. For a mission-critical legacy system, deploying the new system all at once is a risky procedure, therefore a legacy system is evolved incrementally to the new system. During the migration effort, many things can change: user requirements may change, additional knowledge about the system may be acquired, and the technology may change. Those changes must be accommodated by the migration effort. While accommodating those changes, a migration strategy needs to minimize risk, minimize development and deployment costs, support an aggressive but reliable schedule, and meet system quality expectations.

Step 11: Reconcile the strategy with the needs of the stakeholder. A consensus needs to be developed among stakeholders before implementing the migration plan. The migration strategy developed in the previous step must be reconciled with stakeholder needs. Therefore, this step includes briefing the stakeholders about the approach, reviewing the target architecture, and the strategy. The entire group evaluates the strategy and provides input for the final consensus profile.

Step 12: Determine the resources required. We estimate the resource need including cost of implementing the project. One can use the widely used cost estimation model called Constructive Cost Model II (COCOMO II). COCOMO II addresses nonsequential process models, reengineering work, and reuse-driven approach [26]. The COCOMO II model provides estimates of effort, schedule by phases, and staffing by phases and activities.

Step 13: Evaluate the feasibility of the strategy. After executing the first 12 steps, the management should have an understanding of the system under migration, the available technology options, a target architecture, migration strategy, cost of migration, and a schedule to effect migration. Based on available information, management determines whether or not the migration strategy is feasible. If the strategy is found to be viable, the migration plan is finalized. On the other hand, if it is unacceptable, a detailed report is produced. Based on the reasons stated in the report, one may revise the migration strategy until (i) a feasible approach can be identified or (ii) the migration strategy is determined to be infeasible and the project is terminated.

5.5   MIGRATION METHODS

In this section, seven approaches to migration have been explained [27–29]. No single approach can be applied to all kinds of legacy systems, because they vary in their scale, complexity, and risks of failure while migrating. The seven approaches are as follows:

- Cold turkey
- Database first
- Database last
- Composite database
- Chicken little
- Butterfly
- Iterative

5.5.1   Cold Turkey

The *Cold turkey* strategy [2] is also referred to as the Big Bang approach. It involves redesigning and recoding the LIS from the very beginning using a new execution platform, modern software architecture, and new tools and databases. For a reasonable sized system, this approach takes much time. The risk of failure is high for this approach to be seriously considered. For this approach to be adopted, one must guarantee that the renovated system will include many new features in addition to the functionality provided by the original legacy system. The risk of failure is increased due to the complexity of migration. While the legacy system is under a spell of long redevelopment, new technologies emerge and an organization's business focus could shift. Thus, organizations may perceive the redeveloped system to be not meeting their business goals. In addition, the technology used might have been outdated. However, this approach can be adopted, if a legacy system has stable, well-defined functionality and is small in size.

5.5.2 Database First

The *Database first* approach [30] is also known as *forward migration method* [31]. This method first migrates the database, including the data, to a modern DBMS, and then gradually migrates the legacy application programs and interfaces. The LIS simultaneously operates with the new system via a *forward gateway* while interfaces and legacy applications are being reengineered. Implemented as a software module, a gateway mediates among operational software components. This enables the LIS applications to access the database on the target side as shown in Figure 5.6. The forward gateway translates legacy application (old technology) calls to target (new database service) calls. Similarly, outputs of the reengineered database are translated for use by the legacy system.

A key benefit of the database first approach is that upon the completion of migration of the legacy data, one can start receiving productivity benefits by accessing the data.

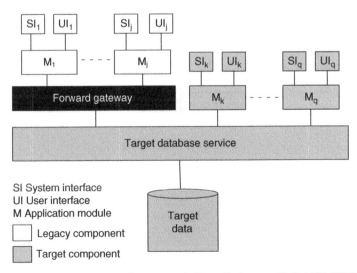

FIGURE 5.6 Database first approach. From Reference 19. © 1999 IEEE

The legacy system can operate concurrently with those applications and interfaces that have been migrated to the new system. Upon the completion of migration, the gateway will no longer be required. However, this approach has two major drawbacks. First, the approach is only applicable to a completely decomposable legacy system, where a clean interface to the legacy database exists. Second, the new database structure must be defined before migration can begin. The structure of the new database may be negatively impacted by the legacy database. Consequently, it becomes difficult to construct the forward gateway because of the dissimilarities between the legacy system and the target system in terms of database structure and technology.

Remark: An information system is said to be fully decomposable if the user and system interfaces, applications, and databases are considered to be distinct components connected by clearly defined interfaces. In a semidecomposable information system, only the user and the system interfaces are separate components; the database service and applications are inseparable. A nondecomposable information system is one where no functional components can be separated [2].

5.5.3   Database Last

The *Database last* approach [30] is also known as the *reverse migration method* [31]. It is suitable only for a fully decomposable LIS. In this approach, legacy applications are incrementally migrated to the target platform, but the legacy database stays on the original platform. Migration of the database is done last. Similar to the database first approach, interoperability of both the information systems is supported by means of a gateway. Target applications access the LIS database via a *reverse gateway*. As illustrated in Figure 5.7, the reverse gateway translates calls from the new applications and redirects them to the legacy database.

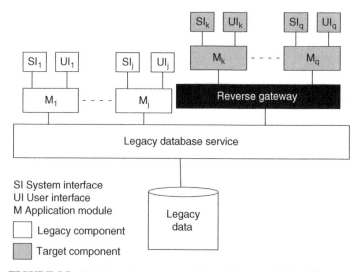

FIGURE 5.7   Database last approach. From Reference 19. © 1999 IEEE

There are two main issues with the database last approach. First, mapping from the schema of the target database to the legacy database can be slow, thereby impacting new applications. Second, several useful features of relational databases, namely, triggers, integrity, and constraints may not be exploited by the new applications, because those features might not be present in the legacy database.

5.5.4   Composite Database

The *composite database* approach [31] is applicable to fully decomposable, semide-composable, and nondecomposable LISs. However, in practice, a system may not strictly fit in one of those three categories. Most LISs have some decomposable components and some semidecomposable components, whereas the remaining components are nondecomposable.

In the composite database approach, the target information system is run in parallel with the legacy system during the migration process. In the beginning, the target system is a small one, but it grows in size as migration continues. Upon completion of the migration process, all the functionality of the old system are performed by the new system. While migration is continuing, as shown in Figure 5.8, the two systems form a composite information system, employing a combination of forward and reverse gateways. In this approach, data may be duplicated across both the databases: legacy and target. A transaction co-ordinators is employed to maintain data integrity. The co-ordinators intercepts update requests from both target and legacy applications and processes the requests to determine whether or not the requests refer to data replicated in both the databases. If replicated data are referred to, the update is propagated to both the databases using a two-phase commit protocol [32].

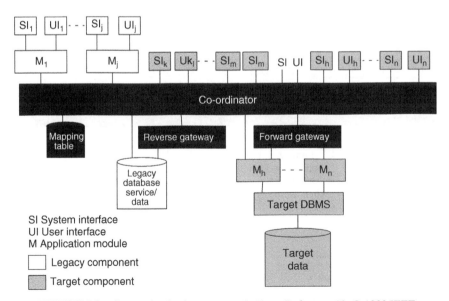

FIGURE 5.8   Composite database approach. From Reference 19. © 1999 IEEE

The task of analyzing a nondecomposable legacy component is difficult. A good way to analyze such a component is to identify its functionality. Next, the component can be newly developed from a specification of the functionality. As done in the database first and database last approaches, the composite database approach does not require a one-shot large migration of legacy data.

5.5.5   Chicken Little

The *Chicken little* strategy [2] refines the composite database strategy, by proposing migration solutions for fully decomposable, semidecomposable, and nondecomposable legacy systems with different kinds of gateways. The differences between those gateways are based upon (i) the locations of the gateways in the system and (ii) the degree of functionality of the gateways. All the gateways have the common goal of mediating between operational software components. Placement of the gateways is a critical factor that affects the complexity of the migration architecture, gateway, and the migration method.

For a fully decomposed LIS, a *database gateway* is located between the database service and the application modules, as explained in Sections 5.5.2 and 5.5.3. The said database gateway can be either a *forward gateway* or a *reverse gateway*. Both the *forward gateway* and the *reverse gateway* are also known as *database gateways*, since those encapsulate the entire database service and the database from the perspective of application modules. An *application gateway* is used for a semidecomposable LIS. This gateway has been illustrated in Figure 5.9, and it is located between user and system interfaces and the legacy application. It is called *application gateway* because it encapsulates from the applications down, from the perspective of interfaces. For nondecomposable systems an *information systems gateway* is located between user and other information systems and LIS. This gateway has been illustrated in

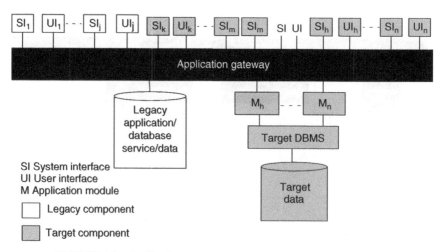

FIGURE 5.9   Application gateway. From Reference 19. © 1999 IEEE

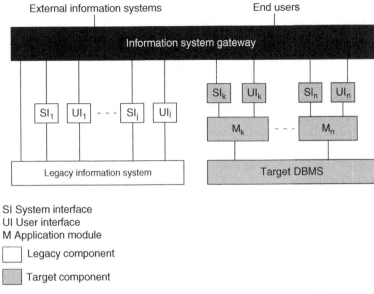

SI System interface
UI User interface
M Application module

☐ Legacy component

▨ Target component

FIGURE 5.10   Information system gateway. From Reference 19. © 1999 IEEE

Figure 5.10. The entire functionality of the legacy system is encapsulated in an information system gateway, whereas an application gateway encapsulates part of the legacy system, namely, only from application module down. An information system gateway is the primary means for dealing with the migration of user interface. It is recommended to use information gateway in all migration, due to the importance of user interface in migration of LIS. It may be noted that the strategy does not include a testing step. Executing a testing step, to ensure that the new system is equivalent to the legacy system, is useful before rolling over to the new system.

The Chicken little methodology proposes an 11-step generic strategy, as listed on Table 5.2, for migration projects. Each step handles a specific aspect of migration,

TABLE 5.2   Chicken Little Migration Approach

Step 1:	Incrementally analyze the LIS
Step 2:	Incrementally decompose the structure of the LIS
Step 3:	Design the interfaces of the target system in an incremental manner
Step 4:	Build the target applications in an incremental manner
Step 5:	Design the database in an incremental manner
Step 6:	Install the target environment in an incremental manner
Step 7:	Create and install the necessary gateways in an incremental manner
Step 8:	Migrate the databases in an incremental manner
Step 9:	Migrate the legacy applications in an incremental manner
Step 10:	Migrate the legacy interfaces in an incremental manner
Step 11:	Cut over to the target system in an incremental manner

and the methodology is designed to be incremental. For example, one step may handle database migration. The methodology can be fine tuned for individual legacy systems. The flow of steps is for each increment to be migrated, so the entire flow is repeated for each increment. Those 11 steps do not need to be performed in the given sequence, and some steps can be executed in parallel. In this methodology, using gateways, the legacy system and the target information system run concurrently during the entire process of migration. Initially, the size of the target system is small. However, with progress in migration, the target system becomes larger in size, and, finally, it is functionally indistinguishable from the old system. In the Chicken little methodology, data is stored in both the migrating legacy system and the evolving target system. Data consistency between the two systems is maintained by means of gateway co-ordinators.

5.5.6   Butterfly

The *Butterfly* methodology [33, 34] does not require simultaneous accesses of both the legacy database system and the target database system. Therefore, there is no need to make the two systems consistent. The target system is not operated in the production mode, at the time of reengineering the legacy system. In other words, the old system being reengineered remains operational during the migration stage. From the perspective of developing the target system, the semantics of data captured in schema are more important than the constantly changing data. Therefore, during the migration process, live data are not simultaneously stored in both the new system and the legacy system. For data migration, the Butterfly methodology introduces the following concepts [35]:

- Sample DataStore, Legacy SampleData, and Target SampleData
- TempStore
- Data-Access-Allocator
- Data-Transformer
- Termination-Condition and Threshold Value.

A representative subset of the legacy database is held in *Legacy SampleData*; the *Target SampleData* is derived from the *Legacy SampleData*. Based on the data model of the target system, *Sample DataStore* stores the *Target SampleData*. The *Sample DataStore* supports the initial development and testing of all components.

In order to migrate legacy data, the methodology uses a sequence of temporary datastores called *TempStores* (TS). During the migration process, the TempStores hold the results of manipulations on the legacy data. When migration of legacy data begins, the *Data-Access-Allocator* (DAA) directs those manipulations, and the results are stored by the DAA in the most recent TempStore. Similarly, the DAA retrieves the required data from the most recent TempStore.

To migrate the legacy data and the TempStores data to the target system, the methodology uses a *Data-Transformer* called *Chrysaliser*. Transformation of data

TABLE 5.3   **Phases of Butterfly Methodology**

Phase 1: Readiness for migration
Phase 2: Comprehend the semantics of the system to be migrated and develop schema(s) for the target database
Phase 3: Based upon the Target SampleData, construct a Sample DataStore
Phase 4: Except the data, migrate the components of the legacy system
Phase 5: Gradually migrate the legacy data
Phase 6: Roll over to the new system

from the legacy system and the TempStores is performed with a set of rules. Based on the earlier process of determining a target schema, the rules are designed. The schema of the target database is conceptually equivalent to the schema of the old database. To determine whether or not the new system is ready to be used, the concepts of *Termination-Condition* and *Threshold Value* are introduced. The *Threshold Value* is represented by a pre-determined value ϵ. Basically, ϵ represents the acceptable quantity of data remaining in the current TS. The condition *size (TS)* $\leq \epsilon$ implies that the time required to migrate the data is negligibly small to shutdown the legacy system without inflicting much disturbance on the core business. The condition to end migration, denoted by Termination-Condition, is satisfied when TS_n has been completely transformed and size $(TS_{n+1}) \leq \epsilon$ $(n \geq 0)$, where TS_n is the nth TempStore.

The following are the key attributes of the methodology. During migration, live data are stored at the LIS. The target system is not rolled over to live operation before fully migrating the system. The legacy data store is "frozen" to be read-only when data migration begins.

The DAA redirects manipulations of legacy data, and the results are saved in a series of temporary data stores called *TempStore(s)* (TS). If a legacy application needs to access legacy data, the DAA extracts data from the correct entity: the current *TempStore* or the legacy database. As shown in Table 5.3, migration of a legacy system is organized into six major steps, also called phases [34].

Phase 1: Readiness for migration. Considered to be important issues in the Butterfly methodology are user's requirements and determination of the target system. Table 5.4 [34] lists the main activities in the preparation phase. Success of these activities depends upon much co-operation among users, migration engineers, and LIS experts.

Phase 2: Comprehend the semantics of the system to be migrated and develop new schema(s) for the target database. Table 5.5 shows the activities performed

TABLE 5.4   **Migration Activities in Phase 1**

1.1 Identify the basic requirements of migration
    1.1.1 Identify the user requirements
    1.1.2 Identify the criteria to measure the success of the migration process
1.2 Design the architecture of the target system
1.3 Set up the target hardware platform

TABLE 5.5   Migration Activities in Phase 2

2.1 Comprehend the existing interfaces, determine redundancies in the existing interface, and determine the new interfaces

2.2 Comprehend the legacy applications, determine redundancies in the legacy applications, and identify the functional requirements of the new applications

2.3 Comprehend the existing legacy data, determine redundancies in the legacy data, and determine what legacy data to migrate

2.4 Identify and comprehend the interactions of the legacy system with its environment

2.5 Identify the requirements of migration

2.6 Design and develop the data redirector tool called DAA

2.7 Design the schema for the new data and identify the rules for mapping of data

TABLE 5.6   Migration Activities in Phase 3

3.1 Construct the Legacy SampleData.

3.2 Develop the Chrysaliser.

3.3 Construct the Sample DataStore by using the Target SampleData derived from the Legacy SampleData.

in this phase. The migration requirements are finalized in activity 2.5. However, not all requirements can be identified until the legacy system is fully understood. In this phase, the DAA tool is developed to redirect all manipulations of legacy data and data stored in TempStores.

Phase 3: Based upon the Target SampleData, construct a Sample DataStore. The activities of Phase 3 are listed on Table 5.6. Developing the Chrysaliser and determining the legacy SampleData are the main tasks in Phase 3. The Chrysaliser derives the Sample DataStore from the SampleData, and the Sample DataStore is used to test and develop the target system.

Phase 4: Except the data, migrate the components of the legacy system. The activities in Phase 4 are listed on Table 5.7. In this phase, forward software engineering principles and methods are used in the migration process. Constructed in Phase 2, the

TABLE 5.7   Migration Activities in Phase 4

4.1 Migrate legacy interface
    4.1.1 Migrate/develop a portion of the interface of the target system
    4.1.2 For correctness, test the target interface against Sample DataStore
    4.1.3 Validate the target interface against user's requirements

4.2 Migrate legacy applications
    4.2.1 Migrate/develop a target application
    4.2.2 Test the target application against Sample DataStore for corrections
    4.2.3 Validate the target application against the requirements

4.3 Migrate the reusable components of the legacy system

4.4 Integrate target components/system

4.5 Test target components/system

4.6 Validate target components/system against the user's requirements

4.7 Train the users on the new system

TABLE 5.8   Migration Activities in Phase 5

5.1 Integrate the Data-Access-Allocator into the legacy system.

5.2 Create TempStore TS_1 and set the access mode of the legacy datastore (TS_0) to read-only.

5.3 The contents of TS_0 are migrated into the new data store by means of the Chrysaliser. Accesses to the legacy data store are redirected by the DAA while migration is continuing, and results of the manipulations are stored in TS_1.

5.4 Create TempStore TS_2; then set TS_1 to read-only.

5.5 Through the Chrysaliser, migrate TS_1 into the target datastore(s). The DAA redirects all accesses to the legacy data, and all manipulation results are stored in TS_2.

5.6 Repeat Steps 5.4 and 5.5 for TS_{n+1} and TS_n until the *Termination-Condition* is satisfied.

5.7 Do not make changes to the legacy system. Transform TS_0 into the new, target datastore(s) by means of the Chrysaliser.

5.8 Train the users about the target system.

Sample DataStore is used in supporting the "design-develop-test" cycle for new target components. The interactions among the target system's components are verified in activity 4.4.

Phase 5: Gradually migrate the legacy data. Table 5.8 [35] lists the activities of Phase 5. Migration of legacy data is performed in Phase 5, and it is central to the Butterfly methodology. Legacy data are incrementally migrated by using TempStores, the Chrysaliser, and the DAA. It may be noted that the Chrysaliser element serves as a data transformer.

Once migration of legacy data is started, no changes are allowed to be performed on the legacy data store. As indicated in Figure 5.11, the DAA redirects manipulation

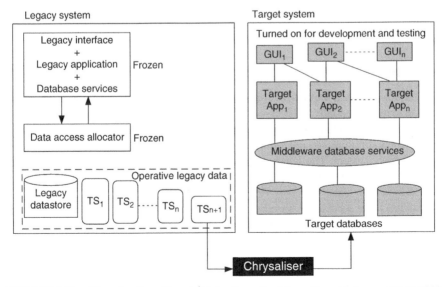

FIGURE 5.11   Migrating TempStore in Butterfly methodology. From Reference 19. © 1999 IEEE

operations of legacy data, and the results are saved in a series of TempStore(s) (TS). When a legacy application needs to access data, the DAA correctly decides which source—the correct TempStore or the legacy data—to retrieve the data from.

By means of a Data-Transformer, called Chrysaliser, data are migrated to the new system from the legacy store and the series of TempStores. A series of temporary stores (TS's) are used by the Chrysaliser in the data migration process. For example, all manipulations are stored in TS_1 when migrating the legacy data TS_0. Similarly, all manipulations are stored in TS_2 when migrating TS_1, and so on.

To determine when one can roll over to the new system, the Butterfly methodology introduces two concepts: a *Termination-Condition* and a *Threshold Value* (represented by ϵ). The allowable amount of data in the final TempStore TS_N is denoted by the pre-determined value ϵ. If size $(TS_N) \leq \epsilon$, where TS_N denotes the final TempStore, the time required to migrate the remaining data in TS_N is sufficiently small to allow the legacy system to be shutdown without creating any problem to the environment. Thus, during the migration process in this methodology, the legacy system is not inaccessible for a significant amount of time. Figure 5.11 depicts a data migration scenario, where it is shown that the Chrysaliser and DAA working together serve as a data migration engine.

Phase 6: Roll over to the new system. Roll over to the new system is the final phase of the Butterfly methodology. After the new system is built and the legacy data are migrated, the new system is ready for operation.

The main drawback of the Butterfly methodology is that the legacy database is used for reading only, whereas modifications are placed in a separate, temporary database. Consequently, when there is a need to access some data, the system reads both the databases—the old database and the target database—plus the temporary database. As a result, there is an increase in the time to access the required data. For data-oriented systems, an increase in access time is likely to degrade system performance. In addition, the legacy functions do not simultaneously operate with the newly added functions and the reengineered system.

5.5.7 Iterative

The iterative method implies that one component at a time is reengineered. Thus, the legacy system gradually evolves over a period of time. A component represents a physical piece of implementation of a system, including software [29]. The methodology enables simultaneous operations of the reengineered system and the components of the legacy system. The legacy database is gradually moved into a new database, rather than being frozen or duplicated. The components of the reengineered system access either the legacy database or the new database, based upon the location of the actual data to be accessed. This enables a gradual reengineering of the legacy system and the coexistence of the reengineered components with the legacy components. An iterative methodology partitions legacy data into two categories:

1. *Primary data.* Primary data are those data that are essential to an application's business functions.

2. *Residual data.* These data are not required to carry out the application's business functions, but are used by the legacy system. The legacy database holds the residual data until the code that needs to access them is reengineered.

Next, the primary and residual categories of data are explained in detail. Primary data comprise two kinds of data: *conceptual* and *structural* as follows:

- *Conceptual data.* These data describe concepts specific to the application's domain.
- *Structural data.* These data are needed to organize and support data structures that are used to correctly access the conceptual data.

Data in the *residual* category comprise those data in the legacy store which will eventually be discarded. The residual data are grouped into four categories: *control data, redundant structural data, semantically redundant data*, and *computationally redundant data*. By means of control data one procedure communicates to another procedure that a certain event has occurred. Some data are used to support the organization of the legacy system, but those data are not necessarily needed; those nonessential data are called redundant structural data, and those can be removed with an improved database design. The definition domain of some data is the same as the definition domain of other data, and two identical values in the two domains have the same meanings. Therefore, one of those two definition domains is semantically redundant. Some data is called computationally redundant if it can be derived from another data set in the same database.

Each component may be in one of the following states during the reengineering process:

- *Legacy.* This state means that the component has not been reengineered, which implies that it continues to be a legacy component.
- *Restored.* The structure of the component remains the same and it performs the same functions, but the component accesses data through the new Data Banker.
- *Reengineered.* The component has already been modified, and a desired level of quality has been achieved.
- *New.* The component was not part of the legacy system and has been newly added in order to introduce new functions.

System architecture. While reengineering is in progress, Figure 5.12 shows the system architecture of gradual evolution of a legacy system. It is illustrated that legacy, restored (temporary), and reengineered components are enclosed within a unique architecture. The original legacy components have been represented without shading, and those will gradually disappear as reengineering continues. The temporary components are shown with dotted shading, and in this case reengineering of procedures follow data reengineering. The components with dark shade will continue to

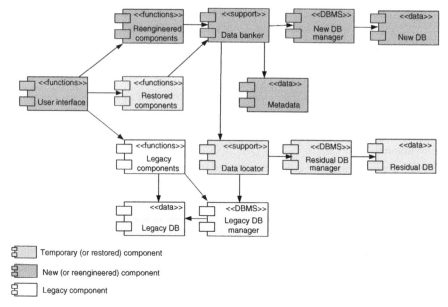

Temporary (or restored) component

New (or reengineered) component

Legacy component

FIGURE 5.12 The iterative system architecture methodology during reengineering. From Reference 29. © 2003 IEEE

exist to make up the reengineered system. The architecture lets the system to be normally used, while its components undergo modifications. In other words, the entity "User Interface" intercepts the external inputs and invokes the desired components which may be in various states: reengineered, restored, or legacy.

In Figure 5.12, the "Legacy DB manager" manages all accesses of the "Legacy DB" by the legacy components. The database with the new structure is represented by "New DB." "New DB" includes (i) all primary data for those functions which have been added to the new system in the process of reengineering and (ii) all primary data which have been migrated from the legacy DB. "Residual DB" stores the residual data from the legacy database, and "Residual DB Manager" is the corresponding data manager. The "Residual DB Manager" may be the DBMS of the legacy software system or the new database. The "Reengineered Components" and the "Restored Components" get data from "Data Banker." By means of "Metadata," "Data Banker" knows whether or not the required data is available in "New DB," "Residual DB," or "Legacy DB." If the "Data Banker" needs to access the "New DB," metadata are used to retrieve their physical locations. Next, "Data Banker" uses the knowledge of the physical data locations to obtain data from the "New DB Manager." In the aforementioned two cases, "Data Banker" routes the requests for data to the "Data Locator." The "Data Locator" interprets the information that the "Data Banker" has extracted from metadata and gets the required data from the "Residual DB Manager" or the "Legacy DB Manager."

Both the "Data Banker" and "Metadata" will continue to exist beyond the reengineering effort. The structure of "New DB" is known to "Metadata" and the services of

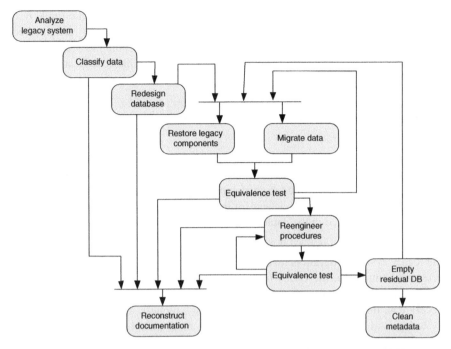

FIGURE 5.13   The iterative migration process. From Reference 29. © 2003 IEEE

the "New DB Manager" are known to "Data Banker." Therefore, if there are changes to the physical structure of the "New DB", only the contents of "Metadata" need to be modified. On the other hand, changes to the "New DB Manager" require changes to the "Data Banker" alone.

Migration process. The migration process diagram is shown in Figure 5.13 [29]. In the following, all the phases are discussed one by one.

Analyze legacy system: All the change requests having an influence on a component to be reengineered are put aside until the component is reengineered. Therefore, the system is partitioned into components so as to minimize their client–supplier relationships for two reasons: (i) to minimize the number of change requests (CRs) to be frozen and (ii) to minimize the time durations for which CRs are frozen. Hence, in the partitioning process, identify the legacy system's components which minimize the impact of reengineering the system.

For the ith component, n_i denotes the total number of change requests made so far, and $\Delta t_{j,i} = t_{j,i} - t_{j-1,i}$ denotes the time gap between two consecutive change requests. The j index captures successive change requests. MTMR$_i$ denotes the *mean time to maintenance request* for the ith component, and it is expressed as MTMR$_i = \sum_{j=1}^{n_i} \frac{\Delta t_{j,i}}{n_i}$. For all i, MTMR$_i$ values are used to partition the set of components that need to be reengineered. The historical archive of the system can be used to generate the values of n_i and $\Delta t_{j,i}$. When the expected time for reengineering the ith component,

RT_i is less than $MTMR_i$, then it is reasonable to assume that there are unlikely to be requests for change of ith component during the time it is being reengineered. Conversely, if RT_i is larger than $MTMR_i$, divide the ith component into smaller subcomponents, to prevent the requests for change that are likely to be made at this time during the process.

Classify data: Legacy data are classified as *primary* or *residual data*. All the data in the Legacy DB, which are nonduplicated, are recorded in a table produced by means of data classification.

Redesign database: The data classified before are restructured in this phase: (i) to reorganize them in the new database for more effective and efficient access; (ii) to eliminate all the defects in the legacy database; and (iii) to eliminate redundant data. While describing the mode of access for the new database, define the characteristics of the data to be stored in the database for Metadata.

Restore legacy components: After having reengineered the database, in this phase, the legacy system program is made compatible with the new database. To make the program compatible, the codes involved in accessing the data are identified. The identified code are replaced with new ones that call the Data Banker, rather than access data directly. Depending upon the client's request, after the adaptation, the system acts as follows:

1. If reengineered data are not involved in the request, invoke the procedures of the legacy system that access the legacy data.
2. Otherwise, invoke the procedures of the restored components that access the reengineered data.

The aforementioned behavior is not visible to users, who will continue to use the system as they did before with the legacy system due to the Data Banker component. On the other hand, if users access the reengineered data, the New DB or the Residual DB, will be physically accessed, instead of the Legacy DB. The appropriate choice is executed by the User Interface in Figure 5.12.

Migrate data: The legacy database is incrementally migrated to the new database, and nonessential data are put in the residual database. A data migration tool can be developed for this purpose. For each data file to be reengineered, the tool must read all the data it contains, copies them into the Residual DB or New DB based on the information contained in the Metadata.

Reengineer procedures: Functions are reengineered in this phase, thereby evolving them from the *restored* state to the *reengineered* state. Quality deficiencies of the procedures are analyzed and suitable remedies are introduced. Specifically, to conduct analysis, one performs the following tasks on individual components:

- Restructure the components to improve their maintainability. For example, application of the principle of information hiding improves maintainability.

- Identify the procedures that are clones of reengineered procedures, and replace those procedures with the reengineered procedures.
- Improve the algorithm used, for better maintainability and performance.
- Update the user interface.
- Update the module interfaces.
- Recall that some maintenance operations had been put on hold during reengineering. Execute those operations.
- Use a modern programming language in the project.

While executing the above tasks, original components of the legacy system are reused as much as possible for two reasons: (i) reduce the cost of reengineering and (ii) preserve the skills that the maintainers have developed. In addition, documentation of the system design is performed in this phase.

Equivalence tests: Equivalence testing ensures that, after migration, the system continues to execute the same way as it did before. Therefore, tests are conducted after procedure restoration and data migration. In addition, this phase allows the test plan documentation to be updated.

Empty residual DB: In iterative reengineering, some parts of the legacy database are migrated into the New DB, whereas the remaining parts move into the Residual DB. While performing reengineering in an iterative manner, data to be no longer used are removed from the Residual DB. Therefore, by the end of the reengineering process, the Residual DB will be completely empty. Consequently, the Residual Data Manager and the Data Locator components can be withdrawn from the system.

Iteration: The components of the legacy system are reengineered one at a time. After reengineering a selected component, the process is repeated for another component and so on, until the entire system has been reengineered.

Clean metadata: Upon completion of reengineering, Metadata only reflects the contents of the New DB. Therefore, metadata concerning Residual DB are no more needed; hence, those are eliminated from Metadata. In addition, all procedures in the Data Banker, which communicate with the Data Locator are removed.

Reconstruct documentation: Documentation reengineering proceeds concurrently with the actual migration. Up-to-date documentation can be performed throughout the reengineering process.

5.6 SUMMARY

This chapter began by identifying the problem an organization faces in dealing with LISs. Next, six viable solutions to the problem were discussed: freeze, outsourcing, carry on maintenance, discard and redevelop, wrap, and migrate.

Next, we studied wrapping techniques in detail. We explained four types of wrappers that practitioners use: database wrapper, system service wrapper, application wrapper, and function wrapper. In addition, we discussed five different levels of encapsulations: process level, transaction level, program level, module level, and procedural level. We introduced a three-step detailed procedure to construct wrappers:

- first, the wrapper is constructed;
- second, the target program is adapted; and
- finally, the interactions between the target programs and the wrapper are tested.

We concluded the wrapper discussion with an introduction to a specific wrapper known as screen scrapper. We then focused our attention on migration of LIS, starting with migration issues and a 13-step migration plan. Next, we discussed seven available migration approaches in detail.

LITERATURE REVIEW

Narsim Ganti and William Brayman (*The Transition of Legacy Systems to a Distributed Architecture*, John Wiley & Son Inc., Somerset, NJ, 1995) propose guidelines for migrating legacy systems to a distributed environment. LISs are analyzed to identify the systems having data and business logic of value in a distributed environment.

Harry Sneed [5] suggested to consider five steps when planning reengineering of legacy projects: (i) project justification, which analyzes the existing products, the maintenance process, and the business value of the applications; (ii) portfolio analysis, which prioritizes the applications to be reengineered based on their business value and technical quality; (iii) cost estimation, which calculates the cost of executing the project; (iv) cost-benefit analysis, which compares the costs and expected returns; and (v) contracting, which identifies the tasks and the distribution of efforts.

For researchers, we recommend part II of the edited book by Tom Mens and Serge Demeyer (*Software Evolution*, Springer, Berlin, Heidelberg, 2008). Part II of the book has three chapters focusing on migration or reengineering of a legacy software system that is no longer outdated and more easy to maintain and adapt. Ideally, data migration is the process of moving an organizations data from one device to another, without disabling or disrupting the running applications. An organization goes for data migration for a variety of reasons:

- upgradation or replacement of server or storage technology;
- consolidation of servers or storage devices;
- relocation of the data center; and
- optimization of server or storage, including load balancing.

Data upgrade, consolidation, migration, and integration differ in two ways:

Connectivity between data sources and targets. The movement of data from their sources to their targets can take three forms: (i) many-to-one; (ii) one-to-one; and (iii) many-to-many. The many-to-one scenario is called consolidation, the one-to-one scenario is called migration or upgrade, and the many-to-many scenario is called integration.

Diversity of source and target data models. Data movement is achieved by developing transforms and mappings between source data models and target data models. Therefore, data movements with more diversity will need more number of data models, and, hence, more development time.

REFERENCES

[1] K. H. Bennett. 1995. Legacy systems: coping with success. *IEEE Software*, January, pp. 19–23.

[2] M. Brodie and M. Stonebraker. 1995. *Migrating Legacy Systems*. Morgan Kaufmann, San Mateo, CA.

[3] A. Cimitile, H. Müller, and R. Klosch (Eds.). 1997. *Pulling Together*. Proceedings of the International Conference on Software Engineering, Workshop on Migration Strategies for Legacy Systems. Available as Technical Report TUV-1841-97-06 from Technical University University of Vienna, A-1040 Vienna, Austria.

[4] K. Bennett, M. Ramage, and M. Munro. 1999. Decision model for legacy systems. *IEE Proceedings on Software*, June, 153–159.

[5] H. M. Sneed. 1995. Planning the reengineering of legacy systems. *IEEE Software*, January, 24–34.

[6] W. C. Dietrich Jr., L. R. Nackman, and F. Gracer. 1989. *Saving a Legacy with Objects*. Proceedings of the 1989 ACM OOPSLA Conference on Object-Oriented Programming. ACM SIGPLAN Notices, ACM, New York, NY, Vol. 24, No. 10, pp. 77–83.

[7] S. Comella-Dorda, K. Wallnau, R. C. Seacord, and J. Robert. 2000. *A Survey of Black-box Modernization Approaches for Information Systems*. Proceedings of the International Conference on Software Maintenance, October 2000, San Jose, CA. IEEE Computer Society Press, Los Alamitos, CA. pp. 173–183.

[8] F. P. Coyle. 2000. Legacy integration—changing perpectives. *IEEE Software*, March/April, 37–41.

[9] R. Orfali, D. Harkey, and J. Edwards. 1995. *The Essential Distributed Objects Survival Guide*. John-Wiley & Sons, Hoboken, NJ.

[10] P. Thiran, J. Hainaut, G. Houben, and D. Benslimane. 2006. Wrapper-based evolution of legacy information systems. *ACM Transactions on Software Engineering and Methodology*, 15(4), 329–359.

[11] H. M. Sneed. 1996. *Encapsulating Legacy Software for Use in Client/Server Systems*. 3rd Working Conference on Reverse Engineering, Washington, DC. IEEE Computer Society Press, Los Alamitos, CA. pp. 104–119.

[12] H. M. Sneed. 2000. Encapsulation of legacy software: a technique for reusing legacy software components. *Annals of Software Engineering*, 9, 293–313.

[13] D. F. Carr. 1998. Web-enabling legacy data when resources are tight. *Internet World*, August.

[14] Attachmate. 2009. *Application Integration*. Available at http://www.attachmate.com/products/products.html. (accessed February, 2009).

[15] J. Hainaut, A. Cleve, J. Henrard, and J. Hick. 2008. Migration of legacy information systems. In: *Software Evolution* (Eds T. Mens and S. Demeyer), pp. 105–138. Springer-Verlag, Berlin.

[16] J. Henrard, J. Hick, P. Thiran, and J. Hainaut. 2002. *Strategies for Data Engineering*. 9th Working Conference on Reverse Engineering, Washington, DC. IEEE Computer Society Press, Los Alamitos, CA. pp. 211–220.

[17] R. Kimball and J. Caserta. 2004. *The Data Warehouse ETL Toolkit*. John Wiley & Sons, Hoboken, NJ.

[18] E. Rahm and H. Do. 2000. Data cleaning: problems and current approaches. *Data Engineering Bulletin*, 23(4), 3–13.

[19] J. Bisbal, D. Lawless, B. Wu, and J. Grimson. 1999. Legacy information systems: issue and directions. *IEEE Software*, September/October, 103–111.

[20] A. R. Simon. 1992. *System Migration—A Complete Reference*. Van Nonstrand Reinhold, New York, NY.

[21] R. C. Seacord, D. Plakosh, and G. Lewis. 2003. *Modernizing Legacy Systems*. Addison Wesley, Boston, MA.

[22] T. J. McCabe. 1976. A complexity measure. *IEEE Transactions on Software Engineering*, December, 308–320.

[23] K. Naik and P. Tripathy. 2008. *Software Testing and Quality Assurance: Theory and Practice*. John Wiley & Sons, Hoboken, NJ.

[24] B. Boehm. 1983. *Software Engineering Economics*. Prentice Hall, Englewood Cliffs, NJ.

[25] S. Tilley and D. Smith. 1996. *Perspective on Legacy System Reengineering*. Software Engineering Institute, Pittsburg, PA. p. 146.

[26] B. Boehm, C. Abts, A. Brown, S. Chulani, B. Clark, E. Horowitz, R. Madachy, D. Reifer, and B. Steece. 2000. *Software Cost Estimation with COCOMO II*. Prentice Hall, Englewood Cliffs, NJ.

[27] J. Bisbal, D. Lawless, B. Wu, J. Grimson, V. Wade, R. Richardson, and D. O'Sullivan. 1997. A survey of research into legacy system migration. *Technical Report TCD-CS-1997-01, Computer Science Department, Trinity College, Dublin*, January, 39.

[28] M. Battaglia, G. Savoia, and J. Favaro. 1998. *Renaissance: A Method to Migrate from Legacy to Immortal Software Systems*. Proceedings of Second Euromicro Conference on Software Maintenance and Reengineering, Florence, Italy. IEEE Computer Society Press, Los Alamitos, CA. pp. 197–200.

[29] A. Bianchi, D. Caivano, V. Marengo, and G. Visaggio. 2003. Iterative reengineering of legacy systems. *IEEE Transactions on Software Engineering*, March, 225–241.

[30] A. Bateman and J. Murphy. 1994. Migration of legacy system. *Working Paper CA-2894, School of Computer Applications, Dublin City University,* http://www.compapp.dcu.ie/CA_Working_Papers.

[31] M. Brodie and M. Stonebraker. 1993. Darwin: On the incremental migration of legacy information systems. *TR-022-10-92-165*, GTE Labs Inc. Available at http://info.gte .com/ftp/doc/tech-reports/tech-reports.html (accessed March 1993).

[32] D. Bell and J. Grimson. 1992. *Distributed Database Systems*. Addison-Wesely Longman Publishing Co., Boston, MA.

[33] B. Wu, D. Lawless, J. Bisbal, R. Richardson, J. Grimson, V. Wade, and D. O'Sullivan. 1997. *The Butterfly Methodology: A Gateway-free Approach for Migrating Legacy Information Systems*. Proceedings of the International Conference on Engineering of Complex Computer Systems, September 1997, Como, Italy. IEEE Computer Society Press, Los Alamitos, CA. pp. 200–205.

[34] B. Wu, D. Lawless, J. Bisbal, J. Grimson, V. Wade, D. O'Sullivan, and R. Richardson. 1997. *Legacy Systems Migration: A Method and its Tool-kit Framework*. Joint 1997 Asia Pacific Software Engineering Conference and International Computer Science Conference, December 1997, Hong Kong, China. IEEE Computer Society Press, Los Alamitos, CA. pp. 312–320.

[35] B. Wu, D. Lawless, J. Bisbal, J. Grimson, V. Wade, R. Richardson, and D. O'Sullivan. 1997. *Legacy Systems Migration: A Legacy Data Migrating Engine*. Proceedings of the 17th International Database Conference, October 1997, Brno, Czech Republic. IEEE Computer Society Press, Los Alamitos, CA. pp. 129–138.

EXERCISES

1. What is a legacy system? Discuss different types of solutions to the legacy problem.

2. Which of the following characteristics are part of the definition of a legacy system? Give reasons.
   (a) The system is very difficult to maintain.
   (b) The system has a great many users.
   (c) The system is performing a useful function for its organization.
   (d) The system has not been modified since it was installed.
   (e) The system has an old-fashioned terminal-style interface.

3. Explain the difference between migration and reengineering.

4. Explain the concept of wrapping. Why do you think it is not useful to modernize the LIS in long term?

5. What is a database wrapper? Discuss the difference between *b-wrapper* and *f-wrapper* with examples. How these two concepts can be used in migration?

6. Why is a screen scrapping technique not the solution to the real issue?

7. Calculate coefficient ratio for the following technical quality criteria:
   (a) Actual error rate is 3 per 1000 lines of code and the maximum and minimum error rates are 7 and 0 per 1000 lines of code, respectively.

(b) Actual Cyclomatic complexity is 22 per procedure and the maximum and minimum cyclomatic complexities are 50 and 10 per procedure, respectively.

8. Discuss the similarity and difference between Database first and Database last approach.

9. Why is the risk of failure for Cold turkey migration strategy high?

10. Which of the following is *not one* of the expected benefits of the Chicken little migration approach?

(a) Some improvement or new functionality can be delivered to the client in a relatively short timescale.

(b) If the current increment fails, then only a limited amount of rework needs to be done.

(c) The needs of all users can be satisfied in a short timescale.

(d) Cut over of each individual step is less risky.

11. Modify the Chicken little steps (see Table 5.2) for (i) forward migration method and (ii) reverse migration method.

12. What are the drawbacks of the Butterfly approach?

13. Describe the features of Iterative reengineering method that are similar to both Chicken little methodology and Butterfly methodology. What are the advantages of Iterative reengineering method?

6

IMPACT ANALYSIS

An error does not become truth by reason of multiplied propagation, nor does truth become error because nobody sees it.

—Mohandas Karamchand Gandhi

6.1 GENERAL IDEA

A change request (CR) activates an organization's process to modify a software system to carry out maintenance. The maintenance process is started by performing impact analysis. Impact analysis basically means identifying the components that are impacted by the CR [1]. Impact analysis enables understanding and implementing changes in the system. Potential effects of the proposed changes are made visible by performing impact analysis. In addition, it is used in estimating cost and planning a schedule. Before executing a change request, impact of the changes are analyzed for the following reasons [2].

- To estimate the cost of executing the change request. It incurs some cost to execute a change request so estimate the cost before effecting the change. If a change request can potentially impact large disjoint portions of the system, then reexamine the request. A large change is likely to incur higher cost and it may make the system inconsistent. Therefore, if the size of the change is large, reject the request in favor of a safer change.

Software Evolution and Maintenance: A Practitioner's Approach, First Edition.
Priyadarshi Tripathy and Kshirasagar Naik.
© 2015 John Wiley & Sons, Inc. Published 2015 by John Wiley & Sons, Inc.

- To determine whether some critical portions of the system are going to be impacted due to the requested change. If so, more resources are to be allocated to execute the change request.
- To record the history of change-related information for future evaluation of changes. By taking feedback from end-users, the overall quality of changes can be evaluated at a later stage.
- To understand how items of change are related to the structure of the software. This will enable maintenance engineers to better understand the current change request.
- To determine the portions of the software that need to be subjected to regression testing after a change is effected.

There are several ways of looking at impact analysis as follows.

- Richard Turver and Malcolm Munro [3] define impact analysis as the assessment of the impact of a change to the source code of a module on the other modules of the system. It determines the scope of a change and provides a measure of its complexity.
- Queille et al. [4] define impact analysis as the task of assessing the effects of making a set of changes to a software system.
- Bohner and Arnold [5] define impact analysis as identifying potential consequences of a modification or discovering the entities to be modified to accomplish a change.

All the three definitions emphasize the estimation of the potential impacts which is crucial in maintenance tasks, because what is actually changed will not be fully known until after the software change is complete.

Implementation of change requests impact all kinds of artifacts, including the source code, requirements, design documentation, and test scenarios. Therefore, impact analysis traceability information can be used in performing impact analysis [6]. Gotel and Finkkelstein [7] define traceability as the ability to describe and follow the life of an artifact in both the forward and backward directions. Bohner and Arnold [5] define traceability as the ability to trace between software artifacts generated and modified during the software product life cycle. Thus, traceability helps software developers understand the relationships among all the software artifacts in a project. After identifying the high level documents about the feature to be modified, by using the concept of traceability, the maintainer locates the entities that need to be changed. Examples of such entities are design and source code.

There are two broad kinds of traceability: (i) horizontal (external) traceability; and (ii) vertical (internal) traceability. Traceability of artifacts between different models is known as external traceability, whereas internal traceability refers to tracing dependent artifacts within the same model. Internal traceability primarily focuses on source code artifacts. In this context, the three classical impact analysis techniques, based on program dependency, are: call-graph-based analysis, static program slicing, and dynamic program slicing. For example, inserting changes in the code and performing forward slicing from the changed points yield a set of statements that may be affected by the changes.

A topic related to impact analysis is *ripple effect analysis*. Ripple effect means that a modification to a single variable may require several parts of the software system to be modified. The concept of ripple effect has relevance in software evolution because it concerns changes and their effects [8]. Analysis of ripple effect reveals what and where changes are occurring. Measurement of ripple effects can provide the following information about an evolving software system: (i) between successive versions of the same system, measurement of ripple effect will tell us how the software's complexity has changed; and (ii) when a new module is added to the system, measurement of ripple effect on the system will tell us how the software's complexity has changed because of the addition of the new module.

An implementation of a change request may consist of several steps; in each step, a specific module, identified during impact analysis, is visited and refactored. If a visited component is changed, it may no longer properly interact with other components. Therefore, additional changes are to be made in the neighboring components, which may trigger further changes throughout the software system. This process is called change propagation activity [9, 10]. The change propagation activity ensures that a change made in one component is propagated properly throughout the entire system. Maintenance engineers fail to correctly and completely propagate changes in a software system for a number of reasons: lack of experience, unexpected dependencies among code blocks, and misunderstanding of the design details. As a result, projects run the risk of generating new interface defects, if changes are incorrectly propagated [11].

6.2   IMPACT ANALYSIS PROCESS

Figure 6.1 depicts a process of impact analysis [5, 12]. The process begins by analyzing the CR, the source code, and the associated documentation to identify an initial set, called *starting impact set* (SIS), of software objects that are likely to be affected by the required change. To discover additional elements to be affected by the CR, the SIS is analyzed. The union of SIS and the new set generated by analyzing SIS is the *candidate impact set* (CIS) (a.k.a. estimated impacted set). An *actual impact set* (AIS) is obtained after the change is actually implemented. Given that one can implement a CR in many ways, the AIS set is not unique [13].

Impact analysis, which is an iterative process, has been illustrated in Figure 6.1. Newly impacted elements, not present in the CIS, may be identified while implementing a CR. A *discovered impact set* (DIS) represents the collection of all those newly discovered elements, and it indicates an underestimation of impacts of the change. Simultaneously, some members of CIS may not be actually impacted by the CR, and the group of those entities is known as *false positive impact set* (FPIS). FPIS indicates an overestimation of impacts. Ideally, AIS should be equal to $SIS \cup DIS \setminus FPIS$, where $\cup$ denotes set union and $\setminus$ denotes set difference. The error in impact

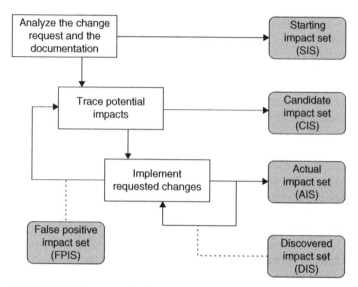

FIGURE 6.1   Impact analysis process. From Reference 6. © 2008 IEEE

estimation can be computed as $(|DIS| + |FPIS|)/|CIS|$. The various sets of components are formally defined as follows.

- *Starting Impact Set (SIS):* The initial set of objects (or components) presumed to be impacted by a software CR is called SIS.
- *Candidate Impact Set (CIS):* The set of objects (or components) estimated to be impacted according to a certain impact analysis approach is called CIS.
- *Discovered Impact Set (DIS):* DIS is defined as the set of new objects (or components), not contained in CIS, discovered to be impacted while implementing a CR.
- *Actual Impact Set (AIS):* The set of objects (or components) actually changed as a result of performing a CR is denoted by AIS.
- *False Positive Impact Set (FPIS):* FPIS is defined as the set of objects (or components) estimated to be impacted by an implementation of a CR but not actually impacted by the CR. Precisely, $FPIS = (CIS \cup DIS) \setminus AIS$.

In the process of impact analysis it is important to minimize the differences between AIS and CIS, by eliminating false positives and identifying true impacts. Several metrics are defined in the literature to evaluate the impact analysis process [6, 13, 14]. Here, we discuss two traditional information retrieval metrics: *recall* and *precision*.

- *Recall:* It represents the fraction of actual impacts contained in CIS, and it is computed as the ratio of $|CIS \cap AIS|$ to $|AIS|$. The value of recall is 1 when DIS is empty.

- *Precision:* It represents the fraction of candidate impacts that are actually impacted, and it is computed as the ratio of |CIS ∩ AIS| to |CIS|. For an empty FPIS set, the value of precision is 1.

Note that if AIS is equal to CIS, both recall and precision are computed to be equal to 1. However, this does not happen too often. Therefore, recall might be traded off in favor of precision and vice versa. For a larger CIS, the probability of identifying all actual impacts is higher; the down side is that many false positives are encountered. *Adequacy* and *effectiveness* are two key aspects of any impact analysis approach [14].

- *Adequacy:* Adequacy of an impact analysis approach is the ability of the approach to identify all the affected elements to be modified. Ideally, AIS ⊆ CIS. Adequacy is repressed in terms of a performance metric called *inclusiveness*, as follows.

$$Inclusiveness = \begin{cases} 1 & \text{if AIS} \subseteq \text{CIS} \\ 0 & \text{otherwise} \end{cases}.$$

The concept of adequacy is essential to assessing the quality of an impact analysis approach. An inadequate approach is in fact useless, as it provides the maintenance engineer with incorrect information. For example, if *inconclusive* is 0, the approach cannot be used because it does not provide the maintenance engineer with all the components to be analyzed. In this case, the actual modification will be certainly affected by errors.

- *Effectiveness:* The ability of an impact analysis technique to generate results, that actually benefit the maintenance tasks, is known as its effectiveness. *Effectiveness* is expressed in terms of three fine-grained characteristics as follows.
  - *Ripple-sensitivity*
  - *Sharpness*
  - *Adherence*

Ripple-sensitivity implies producing results that are influenced by *ripple effect*, which is discussed in Section 6.4. The set of objects that are directly affected by the change is denoted by DISO (directly impacted set of objects), and it is also known as primary impacted set. Similarly, the set of objects that are indirectly impacted by the change is denoted by IISO (indirectly impacted set of objects), and it is also known as the secondary impacted set. The cardinality of IISO is an indicator of ripple effect. The software maintenance personnel expect that the cardinality of IISO is not far from the cardinality of DISO. Therefore, the concept of *Amplification*, as defined below, is used as a measure of *Ripple-sensitivity*.

$$Amplification = \frac{|IISO|}{|DISO|} \longrightarrow 1,$$

where | . | denotes the cardinality operator.

Sharpness is the ability of an impact analysis approach to avoid having to include objects in the CIS that need not be changed. Sharpness is expressed by means of *Change Rate* as defined below.

$$ChangeRate = \frac{|CIS|}{|System|}.$$

It may be noted that CIS is included in "System", and *Change Rate* falls in the range from 0 to 1. For *Sharpness* to be high, we must have *Change Rate* $\ll 1$.

Adherence is the ability of the approach to produce a CIS which is as close to AIS as possible. A small difference between CIS and AIS means that a small number of candidate objects fail to be included in the actual modification set. Adherence is expressed by *S-Ratio* as follows:

$$S\text{-}Ratio = \frac{|AIS|}{|CIS|}.$$

If the impact analysis approach is adequate, AIS is included in CIS, and *S-Ratio* takes on values in the range from 0 to 1. Ideally, the *S-Ratio* is equal to 1.

6.2.1   Identifying the SIS

Impact analysis begins with identifying the SIS. The CR specification, documentation, and source code are analyzed to find the SIS. Larger software systems require more effort to identify the SIS. It takes more effort to map a new CR's "concepts" onto source code components (or objects) as discussed in Section 3.5. In the "concept assignment problem," one discovers human-oriented concepts and assigns them to their realization [15]. It is difficult to fully automate the concept assignment problem because programs and concepts do not occur at identical levels of abstractions, thereby necessitating human interactions.

There are several methods to identify concepts, or features, in source code [16]. The "grep" pattern matching utility available on most Unix systems and similar search tools are commonly used by programmers [17]. One can search for variable names and comments in the code by using the "grep" tool. Each block of source code found in the search process needs to be studied to generate more search queries to find more variables, functions, and comments. However, the tool has some deficiencies: it is based on the correspondence between the name for the concept assigned by the programmer and an identifier in the code. The technique often fails when the concepts are hidden in the source code, or when the programmer fails to guess the program identifiers.

The software reconnaissance methodology proposed by Wilde and Scully [18] is based on the idea that some programming concepts are selectable, because their execution depends on a specific input sequence [19]. Selectable program concepts are known as features. By executing a program twice, one can often find the source code implementing the features: (i) execute the program once with a feature and once without the feature; (ii) mark portions of the source code that were executed the first time but not the second time; and (iii) the marked code are likely to be in or close to the code implementing the feature.

Chen and Rajlich [20] proposed a dependency-graph-based feature location method for C programs. The component dependency graph is searched, generally beginning at the `main()`. Functions are chosen one at a time for a visit. The maintenance personnel reads the documentation, code, and dependency graph to comprehend the component before deciding if the component is related to the feature under consideration. The C functions are successively explored to find and understand all the components related to the given feature.

6.2.2 Analysis of Traceability Graph

Software maintenance personnel may choose to execute the CR differently, or they may not execute it at all, if the complexity and/or size of the traceability graph increases as a result of making the proposed change. Moreover, the complexity and size of the work products are expected to increase. Therefore, whenever change is proposed, it is necessary to analyze the traceability graphs in terms of its complexity and size to assess the maintainability of the system [21].

By means of an example, we explain the traceability links and graphical relationships among related work products (see Figure 6.2). The graph is constructed by examining each requirement, and then linking the requirements to the design component that implements it. Next, design components are linked with the corresponding modules of source code. In the final step, source code modules are linked with sets of test cases. The graph that is so constructed reveals the relationships among work products. Specifically, the graph shows the *horizontal traceability* of the system. The

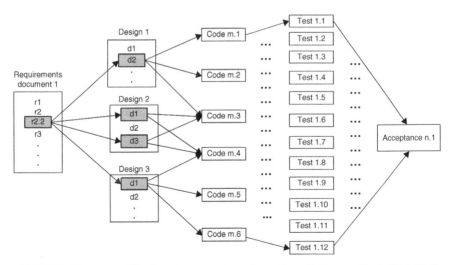

FIGURE 6.2   Traceability in software work products. From Reference 22. © 1991 IEEE

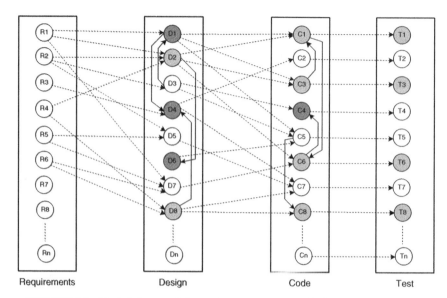

FIGURE 6.3   Underlying graph for maintenance. From Reference 22. © 1991 IEEE

graph has four categories of nodes: requirements, design, code, and test. Figure 6.3 is an example of the general appearance of such a graph. Each category of nodes is represented by a silo, and additional edges can be found within a silo. The edges within a silo represent *vertical traceability* for the kind of work product represented by the silo. Vertical traceability has been represented by solid lines, whereas horizontal traceability by dashed lines. For a node i in a graph, its in-degree in(i) counts the number of edges for which i is the destination node, and in(i) denotes the number of nodes having a direct impact on i. Similarly, the out-degree of node i, denoted by out(i), is the number of edges for which i is the source. Node i being changed, out(i) is a measure of the number of nodes which are likely to be modified.

If some changes are made to requirement object "R4," the results of horizontal traceability and vertical traceability from Figure 6.3 are shown in Figure 6.4. The horizontally traced objects have been shown as lightly shaded circles, whereas the vertically traced objects have darkly shaded circles.

As work products change, both the vertical traceability and horizontal traceability are likely to change. The change to vertical traceability is assessed by considering the complexity and size of the vertical traceability graph within each silo. A common measure of complexity of a graph is the well-known Cyclomatic complexity. Also, node count is a measure of size. It may be noted that vertical traceability metrics are *product metrics*—and those metrics reflect the effect of change on each product. To minimize the impact of a change, out-degrees of nodes need to be made small. For nodes with large out-degrees, one may partition the nodes to uniformly allocate dependencies across multiple nodes. Low in-degrees of nodes are an indication of a good design.

On the other hand, *process metrics* are useful in examining horizontal traceability. To understand changes in horizontal traceability, it is necessary to understand:

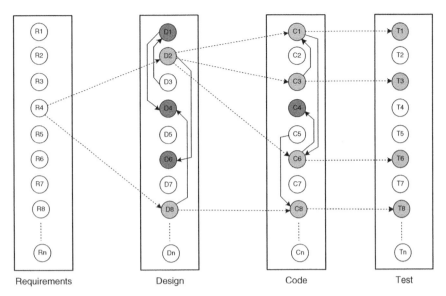

FIGURE 6.4   Determine work product impact. From Reference 22. © 1991 IEEE

(i) the relationships among the work products; and (ii) how work products relate to the process as a whole. In traceability graphs, the relationships among work products are denoted by dashed lines. For a pair of adjacent work products, one can examine the subgraph formed by the nodes of the work products and the dashed lines. Therefore, there exist three graphs: (i) the first one relating requirements to software design; (ii) the second one relating software design to source code; (iii) and the third one relating source code to tests. Next, size and complexity metrics are obtained for those three graphs to know about the work products and the effects of changes. One might conclude that if a proposed change results in increased size or complexity of the relationship between a pair of work products, the resulting system will be more difficult to maintain.

6.2.3   Identifying the Candidate Impact Set

A CIS is identified in the next step of the impact analysis process. The SIS is augmented with software lifecycle objects (SLOs) that are likely to change because of changes in the elements of the SIS. Changes in one part of the software system may have direct impacts or indirect impacts on other parts [12]. Both direct impact and indirect impact are explained in the following.

- *Direct impact:* A direct impact relation exists between two entities, if the two entities are related by a fan-in and/or fan-out relation.
- *Indirect impact:* If an entity *A* directly impacts another entity *B* and *B* directly impacts a third entity *C*, then we can say that *A* indirectly impacts *C*.

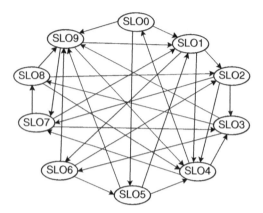

FIGURE 6.5   Simple directed graph of SLOs. From Reference 12. © 2002 IEEE

To understand those concepts, let us consider the directed graph in Figure 6.5 with ten SLOs, SLO0–SLO9. Each SLO represents a software artifact connected to other artifacts. The artifacts can be arbitrary entities, ranging from a requirement of the entire system to the definition of a variable. Dependencies among SLOs are represented by arrows. In the figure, SLO1 has an indirect impact from SLO8 and a direct impact from SLO9. The in-degree of a node i reflects the number of known nodes that depend on i. Figure 6.6 shows the four nodes—SLO0, SLO5, SLO7, and SLO9—that are dependent on SLO1, and the in-degree of SLO1 is four. In addition, the out-degree of SLO1 is three.

The connectivity matrix of Table 6.1 is constructed by considering the SLOs and the relationships shown in Figure 6.5. A reachability graph can be easily obtained from a connectivity matrix. A reachability graph shows the entities that can be

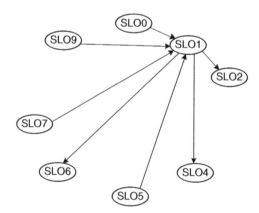

FIGURE 6.6   In-degree and out-degree of SLO1. From Reference 12. © 2002 IEEE

TABLE 6.1   Relationships Represented by a Connectivity Matrix

	SLO0	SLO1	SLO2	SLO3	SLO4	SLO5	SLO6	SLO7	SLO8	SLO9
SLO0		x				x				x
SLO1			x		x		x			
SLO2				x	x			x		
SLO3							x		x	x
SLO4	x			x				x		
SLO5		x			x					x
SLO6			x			x				x
SLO7		x		x					x	
SLO8			x		x					x
SLO9		x			x			x		

Source: From Reference 12. © 2002 IEEE.

impacted by a modification to an SLO, and there is a likelihood of overestimation. The dense reachability matrix of Table 6.2 has the risk of over-estimating the CIS. To minimize the occurrences of false positives, one might consider the following two approaches.

- Distance-based approach: In this approach, SLOs which are farther than a threshold distance from SLO *i* are considered not to be impacted by changes in SLOW *i*. In Table 6.3, the concept of distance has been introduced in the analysis. One can estimate the scope of the ripple by augmenting Warshall's algorithm [23] with data about the nodes traversed so far.
- Incremental approach: In this approach, the CIS is incrementally constructed [24]. For every SLO in the SIS, one considers all the SLOs interacting with it, and only SLOs that are actually impacted by the change request are put in the CIS. The identification process is recursively executed until all the impacted SLOs are identified.

TABLE 6.2   Relationships Represented by a Reachability Matrix

	SLO0	SLO1	SLO2	SLO3	SLO4	SLO5	SLO6	SLO7	SLO8	SLO9
SLO0		x	x	x	x	x	x	x	x	x
SLO1	x		x	x	x	x	x	x	x	x
SLO2	x	x		x	x	x	x	x	x	x
SLO3	x	x	x		x	x	x	x	x	x
SLO4	x	x	x	x		x	x	x	x	x
SLO5	x	x	x	x	x		x	x	x	x
SLO6	x	x	x	x	x	x		x	x	x
SLO7	x	x	x	x	x	x	x		x	x
SLO8	x	x	x	x	x	x	x	x		x
SLO9	x	x	x	x	x	x	x	x	x	

Source: From Reference 12. © 2002 IEEE.

TABLE 6.3   Relationship with Distance Indicators

	SLO0	SLO1	SLO2	SLO3	SLO4	SLO5	SLO6	SLO7	SLO8	SLO9
SLO0		1	2	3	2	1	2	2	3	1
SLO1	2		1	2	1	2	1	2	3	2
SLO2	2	2		1	1	3	2	1	2	2
SLO3	3	2	2		2	2	1	2	1	1
SLO4	1	2	3	1		2	2	1	2	2
SLO5	2	1	2	2	1		2	2	3	1
SLO6	3	2	1	2	2	1		2	3	1
SLO7	3	1	2	1	2	3	2		1	2
SLO8	3	2	1	2	1	3	3	2		1
SLO9	2	1	2	2	1	3	2	1	2	

Source: From Reference 12. © 2002 IEEE.

6.3   DEPENDENCY-BASED IMPACT ANALYSIS

In general, source code objects are analyzed to obtain vertical traceability information. Dependency-based impact analysis techniques identify the impact of changes by analyzing syntactic dependencies, because syntactic dependencies are likely to cause semantic dependencies. Two traditional impact analysis techniques [25] are explained in this section. The first technique is based on call graph, whereas the second one is based on dependency graph [25].

6.3.1   Call Graph

A *call graph* is a directed graph in which a node represents a function, a component, or a method, and an edge between two nodes A and B means that A may invoke B. Programmers use call graphs to understand the potential impacts that a software change may have [5]. An example call graph has been shown in Figure 6.7. Let P be a program, G be the call graph obtained from P, and p be some procedure in P. A key assumption in the call-graph-based technique is that some change in p has the potential to impact changes in all nodes reachable from p in G. Under this assumption, all the potential impact relationships in P can be calculated by applying the transitive closure relation. However, a procedure can have a variety of calling behavior, as follows: (i) a procedure $p1$ calls a second procedure $p2$, but $p2$ does not

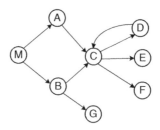

FIGURE 6.7   Example of a call graph. From Reference 26. © 2003 IEEE

M B r A C D r E r r r r x.
FIGURE 6.8   Execution trace

make any further calls; (ii) a procedure $p1$ calls a second procedure $p2$, and $p2$ calls a third procedure $p3$; or (iii) a procedure $p1$ calls a second procedure $p2$, and $p2$ makes calls to many other procedures.

Therefore, the call-graph-based approach to impact analysis suffers from many disadvantages as follows:

- A call graph represents the potential calls by a single procedure, while ignoring the dynamic aspects. Consequently, impact analysis based on call graphs can produce an imprecise impact set. For example, in Figure 6.7, one cannot determine the conditions that cause impacts of changes to propagate from M to other procedures.

- Generally, a call graph captures no information flowing via returns. Therefore, impact propagations due to procedure returns are not captured in the call-graph-based technique. Suppose that in Figure 6.7, E is modified and control returns to C. Now, following the return to C, it cannot be inferred whether impacts of changing E propagates into none, both, A, or B.

To address the aforementioned issues, researchers have considered more precise ways to assess the impact of changes, using information collected during execution of calls. Law and Rothermel [26] defined a technique called *path-based dynamic impact analysis* that uses *whole path profiling* [27] to estimate the effects of changes. In this approach, if a procedure p is changed, then one considers the impact that is likely to propagate along those executable paths that are seen to be passing through p. As a result, any procedure, that is invoked after p but still appears on the call stack after p terminates, is assumed to be potentially impacted. For the approach to work, the software system needs to be instrumented to collect information. However, it is not necessary to have access to the source code, because program binaries can be instrumented.

Let us consider an execution trace as shown in Figure 6.8. The trace corresponds to a program whose call graph is shown in Figure 6.7. In the figure, r and x represent function returns and program exits, respectively. Let procedure E be modified. The impact of the modification with respect to the given trace is computed by *forward* searching in the trace to find: (i) procedures that are indirectly or directly invoked by E; and (ii) procedures that are invoked after E terminates. One can identify the procedures into which E returns by performing *backward* search in the given trace. For example, in the given trace, E does not invoke other entities, but it returns into M, A, and C. Due to a modification in E, the set of potentially impacted procedures is $\{M, A, C, E\}$.

6.3.2   Program Dependency Graph

In the program dependency graph (PDG) of a program [28–30]: (i) each simple statement is represented by a node, also called a vertex; and (ii) each predicate expression is represented by a node. There are two types of edges in a PDG: data dependency edges

begin
| | |
S1:   *read(X)*
S2:   *if (X < 0)*
          then
S3: $Y = f_1 (X)$;
S4: $Z = g_1 (X)$;
          else
S5:   *if (X = 0)*
               then
S6: $Y = f_2 (X)$;
S7: $Z = g_2 (X)$;
               else
S8: $Y = f_3 (X)$;
S9: $Z = g_3 (X)$;
                    end_if;
               end_if;
S10:   *write(Y)*;
S11:   *write(Z)*;
     end.

FIGURE 6.9   Example program. From Reference 31. © 1990 ACM

and control dependency edges. Let v_i and v_j be two nodes in a PDG. If there is a data dependency edge from node v_i to node v_j, then the computations performed at node v_i are directly dependent upon the results of computations performed at node v_j. A control dependency edge from node v_i to node v_j indicates that node v_i may execute based on the result of evaluation of a condition at v_j. Let us consider the program shown in Figure 6.9 [31]. Functions f_i and g_i, where $i = 1$–3, are assumed to have no side effects. Figure 6.10 shows the PDG of the program shown in Figure 6.9. Data dependencies are shown as solid edges, whereas control dependencies are shown as dashed edges.

A static program slice is identified from a PDG as follows: (i) for a variable *var* at node *n*, identify all reaching definitions of *var*; and (ii) find all nodes in the PDG

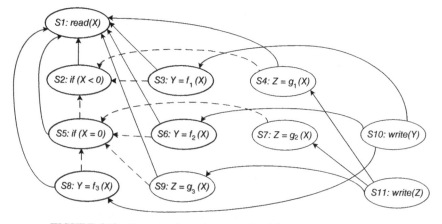

FIGURE 6.10   Program dependency graph of the program in Figure 6.9

which are reachable from those nodes. The visited nodes in the traversal process constitute the desired slice. Now we give an example of finding a static program slice. Consider the program in Figure 6.9 and variable Y at $S10$. First, find all the reaching definitions of Y at node $S10$—and the answer is the set of nodes $\{S3, S6,$ and $S8\}$. Next, find the set of all nodes which are reachable from $\{S3, S6,$ and $S8\}$—and the answer is the set $\{S1, S2, S3, S5, S6, S8\}$. In Figure 6.10, the nodes belonging in the slice have been identified in bold.

Referring to the static slice example discussed above, only one of the three assignment statements, $S3$, $S6$, or $S8$, may be executed for any input value of X. Consider the input value -1 for the variable X. For -1 as the value of X, only $S3$ is executed. Therefore, with respect to variable Y at $S10$, the dynamic slice will contain only $\{S1, S2,$ and $S3\}$. For -1 as the value of X, if the value of Y is incorrect at $S10$, one can infer that either f_i is erroneous at $S3$ or the "if" condition at $S2$ is incorrect. Thus, a dynamic slice is more useful in localizing the defect than the static slice.

Agrawal and Horgan [31] proposed some approaches to computing dynamic slices of programs. A simple approach to obtaining dynamic program slices is explained here. Given a test and a PDG, let us represent the execution history of the program as a sequence of vertices $< v_1, v_2, \ldots, v_n >$. The execution history *hist* of a program P for a test case *test*, and a variable *var* is the set of all statements in *hist* whose execution had some effect on the value of *var* as observed at the end of the execution. Note that unlike slicing where a slice is defined with respect to a given location in the program, dynamic slicing is defined with respect to the end of an execution history.

Now, in our example discussed before, the static program slice with respect to variable Y at $S10$ for the code shown in Figure 6.9 contains all the three statements— $S3$, $S6$, and $S8$. However, for a given test, one statement from the set $\{S3, S6,$ and $S8\}$ is executed. A simple way to finding dynamic slices is as follows: (i) for the current test, mark the executed nodes in the PDG; and (ii) traverse the marked nodes in the graph.

Figure 6.11 illustrates how a dynamic slice is obtained from the program in Figure 6.9 with respect to variable Y at the end of execution. For the case $X = -1$,

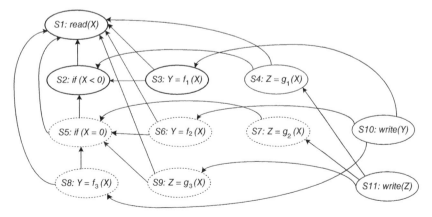

FIGURE 6.11 Dynamic program slice for the code in Figure 6.9, text case $X = -1$, with respect to variable Y

the executed nodes are: $<S1, S2, S3, S4, S10, S11>$. Initially, all nodes are drawn with dotted lines. If a statement is executed, the corresponding node is made solid. Next, beginning at node $S3$, the graph is traversed only for solid nodes. Node $S3$ is selected because the variable Y is defined at node $S3$. All nodes encountered while traversing the graph are represented in bold. The desired dynamic program slice is represented by the set of bold nodes $\{S1, S2, S3\}$.

6.4   RIPPLE EFFECT

Haney [32] introduced the concept of ripple effect in the early 1970s, and the concept of *module connection analysis* was described by means of matrix algebra. Matrix algebra was applied in the estimation of the total number of modifications required to stabilize a changing system. The probability that a change in one module would require a change in any other modules is recorded in a matrix. From the functional and performance perspectives, Yau, Collofello, and McGregor [33] defined the concept of ripple effect in 1978. They viewed ripple effect as a complexity measure to compare changes to source code. In the scheme of Yau et al., ripple effect is computed by means of *error flow analysis*. In error flow analysis, definitions of program variables involved in a change are considered to be potential sources of errors, and inconsistency can propagate from those sources to other variables in the program. The other sources of errors are successively identified until error propagation is no more possible. This work was later extended to include stability measure. Stability reflects the resistance to the potential ripple effect which a program would have when it is changed [34]. Stability analysis and impact analysis differ as follows. Stability analysis considers the total potential ripple effects rather than a specific ripple effect caused by a change. Design stability was studied by Yau and Collofello [35] by means of an algorithm, which computes stability based on design documentation. Specifically, one counts the number of assumptions made about shared global data structures and module interfaces. The key difference between design level stability and code level stability is as follows: design level stability does not consider change propagations within modules. In the next subsection we explain how to compute ripple effect, based on the works of Sue Black [36] and Yau et al. [33]. The basic idea is to identify the impact of a change to one variable on the program.

6.4.1   Computing Ripple Effect

Contained in module m_1 of Figure 6.12, consider the three lines of code referring to variables a, b, and d. A change in the value of b will impact a in line (1), and it will propagate to a in line (2). Variable a affects variable d in line (2) and this will propagate to variable d in line (3). Based on the above example, *intramodule change propagation* is defined as the propagation of changes from one source code line in a module to another source code line within the same module.

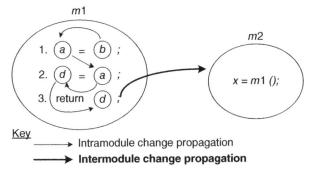

Key
→ Intramodule change propagation
➡ **Intermodule change propagation**

FIGURE 6.12   Intramodule and intermodule change propagation. From Reference 36. © 2001 John Wiley & Sons

A matrix V_m is used to represent the initial starting points for intramodule change propagation. The matrix records the following five conditions of the module's variable x for all x:

1. x is *defined* in an assignment statement;
2. x is *assigned* a value in a read input statement;
3. x is an *input* to an invoked module;
4. x is an *output* from an invoked module;
5. x is a *global* variable.

In V_m, variable definitions are uniquely identified. In case a variable is defined twice, then separate entries for each definition are included in V_m. Variable occurrences satisfying any of the five conditions—defined, assigned, input, output, and global— are denoted by "1"; otherwise, an occurrence is denoted by "0." In addition, the notation x_i^d means that the variable x has been defined at line (i). Similarly, the notation x_i^u means that the variable x has been used at line (i). In module m_1, variable a is global and it is considered to be defined. Matrix V_{m1} for the lines of code in m_1 is expressed as

$$V_{m1} = \begin{matrix} a_1^d & d_1^u & d_2^d & a_2^u & d_3^u \\ (1 & 0 & 1 & 1 & 0) \end{matrix}.$$

A zero–one (0–1) matrix Z_m indicates values of what variables propagate to other variables in the same module. Individual occurrences of variables are denoted by rows and columns of Z_m. It is to be noted that the value of a variable propagates from an occurrence in row i to an occurrence in column j. As an example, the propagation of the value of a occurring in line (2) to variable d occurring in the same line is recorded in the cell at row 4 and column 3—and not in the cell at row 3 column 4. The source code of module m_1 results in the following matrix:

$$
Z_{m1} = \begin{array}{c} \\ a_1^d \\ d_1^u \\ d_2^d \\ a_2^u \\ d_3^u \end{array}
\begin{array}{c} \begin{matrix} a_1^d & d_1^u & d_2^d & a_2^u & d_3^u \end{matrix} \\
\begin{pmatrix}
1 & 0 & 1 & 1 & 1 \\
1 & 1 & 1 & 1 & 1 \\
0 & 0 & 1 & 0 & 1 \\
0 & 0 & 1 & 1 & 1 \\
0 & 0 & 0 & 0 & 1
\end{pmatrix} \end{array}.
$$

It is easy to observe that Z_{m1} is both reflexive and transitive. The reflexive property implies that every variable propagates to itself, whereas transitivity means that if v_1 propagates to v_2 and v_2 propagates to v_3 then v_1 also propagates to v_3.

Propagation of values of variables in one module to variables in a different module is referred to as *intermodule change propagation*. Intermodule change propagation of values of a variable w occurs in the following ways:

1. If w is a global variable, then a change made to w by one module is seen by another module accessing w.
2. If w is an input parameter in a call to a second module, then values of w are propagated from the caller to the callee.
3. If w is an output parameter, then its value propagates from the module that makes an output to the module that accepts the output.

Now we examine the code segment in Figure 6.12. Variable d propagates to any module that calls m_1, because d appears in the return statement. If variable a is global, its appearance on the left-hand side of an assignment statement causes its value to be propagated to any module that uses variable a. Suppose that module m_1 is called by m_2, a is a global variable, and m_2 and m_3 use a. If values of the variable corresponding to row i propagate to the module corresponding to column j, then the (i,j)th entry of the zero–one matrix is set to 1. For all the variables of a module m_1, propagation of their values to other modules is captured by an X matrix, denoted by X_{m1} as follows:

$$
X_{m1} = \begin{array}{c} \\ a_1^d \\ d_1^u \\ d_2^d \\ a_2^u \\ d_3^u \end{array}
\begin{array}{c} \begin{matrix} m_1 & m_2 & m_3 \end{matrix} \\
\begin{pmatrix}
0 & 1 & 1 \\
0 & 0 & 0 \\
0 & 0 & 0 \\
0 & 0 & 0 \\
0 & 0 & 1
\end{pmatrix} \end{array}.
$$

The intermodule change propagation for variables occurring in m_1 is obtained by means of the Boolean product of the two matrices Z_{m1} and X_{m1}, as follows:

$$Z_{m1}X_{m1} = \begin{pmatrix} 1 & 0 & 1 & 1 & 1 \\ 1 & 1 & 1 & 1 & 1 \\ 0 & 0 & 1 & 0 & 1 \\ 0 & 0 & 1 & 1 & 1 \\ 0 & 0 & 0 & 0 & 1 \end{pmatrix} \begin{pmatrix} 0 & 1 & 1 \\ 0 & 0 & 0 \\ 0 & 0 & 0 \\ 0 & 0 & 0 \\ 0 & 0 & 1 \end{pmatrix} = \begin{pmatrix} 0 & 1 & 1 \\ 0 & 1 & 1 \\ 0 & 0 & 1 \\ 0 & 0 & 1 \\ 0 & 0 & 1 \end{pmatrix}.$$

In the Boolean product $Z_{m1}X_{m1}$, the "1" in row 2, column 3 indicates change in propagation from b_1^u to m_3; similarly, the "0" in row 3, column 2 indicates no change in propagation from d_2^d to m_2.

The Boolean product of V_{m1} and $Z_{m1}X_{m1}$ indicates the variable definitions that propagate from m_1 to other modules:

$$V_{m1}Z_{m1}X_{m1} = \begin{pmatrix} 1 & 0 & 1 & 1 & 0 \end{pmatrix} \begin{pmatrix} 0 & 1 & 1 \\ 0 & 0 & 0 \\ 0 & 0 & 0 \\ 0 & 0 & 0 \\ 0 & 0 & 1 \end{pmatrix} = \begin{pmatrix} 0 & 1 & 3 \end{pmatrix}.$$

Now, $V_{m1}Z_{m1}X_{m1}$ indicates that there are no change propagations to m_1, one change propagation to m_2, and three change propagations to m_3.

Concerning the complexity of making changes, the more complex a module is, the more the resources are needed to change the module. Therefore, a measure of complexity can be factored into the calculation of change propagation to obtain a measure of the complexity of modifying the definitions of variables. The well-known McCabe's cyclomatic complexity [37] can be integrated with the ongoing computation of change propagation. A C matrix of dimension $1 \times n$ is chosen to represent McCabe's cyclomatic complexity, where n is the number of modules:

$$C = \begin{matrix} m_1 \\ m_2 \\ m_3 \end{matrix} \begin{pmatrix} 1 \\ 1 \\ 1 \end{pmatrix}.$$

Because the complete codes for m_1, m_2, and m_3 have not been given, we assume their arbitrary complexity values for example purpose. The product of $V_{m1}Z_{m1}X_{m1}$ and C is

$$V_{m1}Z_{m1}X_{m1}C = \begin{pmatrix} 0 & 1 & 3 \end{pmatrix} \begin{pmatrix} 1 \\ 1 \\ 1 \end{pmatrix} = \begin{pmatrix} 4 \end{pmatrix}.$$

The complexity-weighted total propagation of variable definitions for m_1 is represented by $V_{m1}Z_{m1}X_{m1}C$. The quantity $V_{m1}Z_{m1}X_{m1}C/|V_{m1}|$, where $|V_{m1}|$ represents

TABLE 6.4   Laws of Software Evolution

Laws of Lehman	Relevance to Ripple Effect
I. Continuing change	Compare versions of program
	Highlight complex modules
	Measure stability over time
	Highlight areas ripe for restructuring/refactoring
II. Increasing complexity	Determine which module needs maintenance
	Measure growing complexity
III. Self-regulation	Helps measure rate of change of system
	Helps look at patterns/trends of behavior
	Determine the state of the system
IV. Conservation of organizational stability	Not relevant
V. Conservation of familiarity	Provide system change data
VI. Continuing growth	Measure impact of new modules on a system
	Help determine which modules to use in a new version
VII. Declining quality	Highlight areas of increasing complexity
	Determine which modules need maintenance
	Measure stability over time
VIII. Feedback system	Provide feedback on stability/complexity of system

Source: Adapted from Reference 8. © 2006 John Wiley & Sons

the total number of variable definitions in m_1, represents the mean complexity-weighted propagation of variable definition in m_1. In the aforementioned example, $|V_{m1}| = 3$, and it means that ripple in module m_1 is caused by three sources. For module m_1, the mean complexity-weighted propagation of variable is $4/3 = 1.33$. The general expression for calculating the ripple effect for a program (*REP*) is as follows [36]:

$$REP = \frac{1}{n} \sum_{m=1}^{n} \frac{V_m \cdot Z_m \cdot X_m \cdot C}{|V_m|},$$

where m = module and n = number of modules.

A tool called Ripple Effect and Stability Tool (REST) by Sue Black [38] automates the calculation of ripple effect by: (i) approximating intramodule change propagation; and (ii) excluding control flow within source code.

Sue Black examined some links between ripple effect measurement, as summarized in Table 6.4 [8], and Lehman's laws of software evolution, explained in Chapter 2.

6.5   CHANGE PROPAGATION MODEL

Change propagation means that if an entity, say, a function, is changed, then all related entities in the system are changed accordingly. Based on the work of Hassan

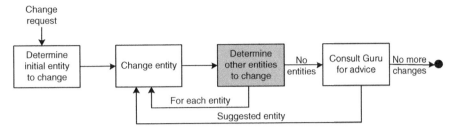

FIGURE 6.13   Change propagation model. From Reference 10. © 2004 IEEE

and Holt [10], a change propagation model has been illustrated in Figure 6.13. After receiving a change request, one identifies the initial entity in the system that needs to be changed. After changing the function, the maintainer must analyze the code to find out other, related entities to change. Then, those entities are actually modified to propagate the change. Similarly, the propagation process is repeated for each changed entity. A *Guru* is consulted when the maintenance engineer cannot identify more entities to modify. A *Guru* can be a senior developer or even a comprehensive test suite. If the *Guru* suggests that an entity be considered, then the entity is taken up for modification and the process for change propagation is applied to that entity. This iterative process is continued until all the desired entities have been changed. Eventually, the *change set* is determined for the change request and all entities in the *change set* are changed.

6.5.1   Recall and Precision of Change Propagation Heuristics

Gurus rarely exist and comprehensive test suites are generally incomplete in large maintenance projects. Therefore, software maintenance engineers need good change propagation heuristics, that is, good software tools that can guide them in identifying entities to propagate a change. The heuristic should possess a high precision attribute to be accurate and a high recall attribute to be complete. A heuristic with low precision will waste software maintainers' time, and maintainers will stop using them. On the other hand, if a heuristic has low recall, then software maintainers will miss to change some entities , thereby introducing defects.

We explained the concepts of *recall* and *precision* in Section 6.2. In this section, we explain the use of those two metrics to measure the change propagation heuristic by means of an example. Let us assume that Rohan wants to enhance an existing feature of a legacy information system. He first identifies that entity A needs to be changed. After changing A, a heuristic tool is queried for suggestions, and entities B and X are suggested by the tool. Next, B is changed and he determines that X should not be changed. Now the tool is given the information that B was changed, and the tool suggests that Y and W need to be changed. However, neither Y nor W need to be changed so no changes are performed on Y and W. After having used the tool, now Rohan consults a Guru, Krushna. Krushna indicates that C should be changed. Now, Rohan modifies C and queries the heuristic for additional entities to change.

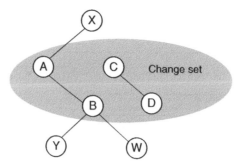

FIGURE 6.14   Change propagation flow for a simple example. From Reference 10. © 2004 IEEE

In response, D is suggested by the tool. Next, D is changed and Krushna is further queried. However, this time Krushna does not suggest any more entities for change. Now, Rohan stops changing the legacy system.

All the changed entities in the example represent the *change set* for this enhancement. The entities and their interrelationships have been shown in Figure 6.14. According to the heuristic, one edge is added from A to B and another edge from A to X. Since the change set contains A, the set contains both B and X. Similarly, edges are added from C to D, from B to Y, and from B to W. Now let us calculate the *recall* and *precision* for this example. The set of entities that are changed will be called *change set*; *change* = {A, B, C, D}. The set of entities suggested by the tool is called a *predicted* set. In the Rohan example, *predicted* = {B, X, Y, W, D}. The entities that were required to be predicted, but were found from Guru, are put in a set called the *occurred* set. In the Rohan example, *occurred* = {B, C, D}. The *occurred* set does not include A, which was initially selected by Rohan, because there is no need to predict it. That is, *occurred* = *change* − {*initial entity*}. Now, *recall* and *precision* for this example are computed as follows.

$$recall = \frac{|\ predicted \cap occurred\ |}{|\ occurred\ |} = \frac{2}{3} = 66\%$$

$$precision = \frac{|\ predicted \cap occurred\ |}{|\ predicted\ |} = \frac{2}{5} = 40\%$$

In the analysis of the above example to measure *recall* and *precision*, the authors, Hassan and Holt [10], made three assumptions.

- *Symmetric suggestions:* This assumption means that if the tool suggests entity F to be modified when it is told that entity E was changed, the tool will suggest entity E to be modified when it is told that entity F was changed. This assumption has been depicted in Figure 6.14 by means of undirected edges.

- *Single entity suggestions:* This assumption means that each prediction by a heuristic tool is performed by considering a *single entity* known to be in the *change set*, rather than multiple entities in the change set.
- *Query the tool first:* This assumption means that the maintainer (e.g., Rohan) will query the heuristic before doing so with the Guru (e.g., Krushna).

All the three assumptions together indicate that different orderings of selection and queries to a heuristic do not affect *precision* and *recall*.

6.5.2   Heuristics for Change Propagation

The "Determine Other Entities to Change" step in Figure 6.13 is executed by means of several heuristics. The set of entities that need to be changed as a result of a changed entity is computed in the aforementioned step. Modification records are central to the design of the heuristics. In general, source control repositories are used to keep track of all the changes made to files in the system. For each modification, a modification record stores the date and time of change, the name of the person making the change, the reason for the change, the code blocks that were changed, and names of the modified files. The changes can be recorded at the level of source code entities, namely, data type definitions, variables, and functions, to be able to track the following details.

- Modification, deletion, and addition of a source code entity.
- Alterations to dependencies between the changed entities and other entities in source code. For instance, it may be determined that a variable is no longer needed by a function.
- For each modification to the code, the corresponding modifications made to other files.

Each heuristic discussed in this section is characterized by: (i) data source; and (ii) pruning technique.

Heuristic Information Sources   A heuristic can use one of many information sources to predict the entities that need to be modified. The objectives of the heuristics are to: (i) ensure that the entities that need to be modified are predicted; and (ii) minimize the number of predicted entities that are not going to be modified. Some potential information sources are as follows.

Entity information: In a heuristic based on entity information, a change propagates to other entities as follows.
- If two entities changed together, then the two are called a *historical co-change* (HIS).
- Static dependencies between two entities may occur via what is called CUD relations: *call, use* and *define*. A *call* relation means one function calls another

function; a *use* relation means a variable is used by a function; and a *define* relation means a variable is defined in a function or it appears as a parameter in the function.

- The locations of entities with respect to subsystems, files, and classes in the source code are represented by means of a *code layout* (FIL) relation. Subsystems, files, and classes indicate relations between entities— generally, related entities simultaneously.

Developer information (DEV): In a heuristic based on developer information, a change propagates to other entities changed by the same developer. In general, programmers develop skills in specific subject matters of the system and it is more likely that they modify entities within their field of expertise.

Process information: In a heuristic based on process information, change propagation depends on the development process followed. A modification to a specific entity generally causes modifications to other recently or frequently changed entities. For example, a recently changed entity may be the reason for some system-wide modifications.

Textual information: In a heuristic based on name similarity, changes are propagated to entities with similar names. Naming similarities indicate that there are similarities in the role of the entities [39].

Pruning Techniques   A heuristic may suggest a large number of entities to be changed. Several techniques can be applied to reduce the size of the suggested set, and those are called pruning techniques, as explained in the following.

- *Frequency* techniques identify the frequently changing, related components. The number of entities returned by these techniques are constrained by a threshold. In a Zipf distribution, a small number of entities tend to change frequently and the remaining entities change infrequently.
- *Recency* techniques identify entities that were recently changed, thereby supporting the intuition that modifications generally focus on related code and functionality in a particular time frame.
- *Random* techniques randomly choose a set of entities, up to a threshold. In the absence of no frequency or recency data, one may use this technique.

6.5.3   Empirical Studies

Hassan and Holt [40] studied the performance of four heuristics—DEV, HIS, CUD, and FIL—using the development replay (DR) framework. To evaluate heuristics for change propagation, real change sets from the project's history are used in the DR framework. To evaluate a heuristic: (i) historical changes are played; and (ii) the *recall* and *precision* attributes are measured for every change set. They used five open software systems—NetBSD, FreeBSD, OpenBSD, Postgres and GCC— and the performance results are given in Table 6.5. The results show that historical co-change information is a practical indicator of change propagation. The authors

TABLE 6.5   Performance of Change Propagation Heuristics for the Five Software Systems

Application Name	Application Type	DEV		HIS		CUD		FIL	
		Recall	*Precision*	*Recall*	*Precision*	*Recall*	*Precision*	*Recall*	*Precision*
NetBSD	OS	0.74	0.01	0.87	0.06	0.37	0.02	0.79	0.16
FreeBSD	OS	0.68	0.02	0.87	0.06	0.40	0.02	0.82	0.11
OpenBSD	OS	0.71	0.02	0.82	0.08	0.38	0.01	0.80	0.14
Postgres	DBMS	0.78	0.01	0.86	0.05	0.47	0.02	0.77	0.12
GCC	C/C++ Compiler	0.79	0.01	0.94	0.03	0.46	0.02	0.96	0.06
	Average	0.74	0.01	0.87	0.06	0.42	0.02	0.83	0.12

Source: From Reference 10. © 2004 IEEE.

applied the pruning techniques discussed in Section 6.5.2 to improve *precision*, while maintaining high *recall*.

6.6   SUMMARY

We introduced three related concepts in this chapter: analysis of impacts of changes to the system, ripple effect, and change propagation. Impact analysis is defined as the task of discovering the effects of making a change to a software system. It reveals likely effects of the proposed change before the changes are actually implemented. The main motivation for performing impact analysis is to minimize unexpected side effects from an intended change to the system. On the other hand, ripple effect analysis emphasizes on the tracing of repercussions in source code when code is changed. The ripple effect measure can provide insights into the system through its evolution: (i) know the change in the system's complexity compared to the previous version; (ii) know the complexity of individual modules; (iii) know the change in complexity of a system after a new module is added. The change propagation activity ensures that a change made in one component is propagated properly throughout the entire system.

Next, we described the process of impact analysis process. In this framework, we explained four different types of software object (or, components) sets, namely, SIS, CIS, AIS, and FPIS. The AIS set is not unique because a modification can be effected in many ways.

In general, tools for impact analysis estimate SIS, CIS, and AIS, and we discussed guidelines to estimate those sets. In addition, we introduced several metrics to evaluate the impact analysis process. The two commonly used information retrieval metrics are recall and precision.

Precision is a measure of the performance of a retrieval technique to not return non-relevant items. The precision of a technique is equal to 1 if every entity returned by the technique is relevant to the query. However, a technique with precision equal to 1 runs the risk of missing relevant entities. Therefore, precision and recall should be considered.

The performance metric *recall* is the proportion of relevant entities, that is data or documents, retrieved by a technique from all available entities. The recall of a technique is equal to 1 if every relevant entity is retrieved. Theoretically, it is possible to achieve a recall value of 1 by returning every entity in the collection. In that sense, recall by itself is not a good measure. Therefore, recall needs to be considered with precision.

Next, we discussed traceability graph techniques to support impact analysis. Dependencies and relationships among software artifacts are understood by means of traceability links. After identifying the high level documents concerning the feature to be modified, traceability is used to locate the portions of software design, source code, and tests that are needed to be updated. Traceability is classified into two types: horizontal (external) and vertical (internal). In general, source code objects are used to provide vertical traceability, and dependency-based analysis techniques are used to identify dependencies among the source code objects. Dependency-based impact analysis techniques asses the effects of change by identifying syntactic dependencies that may indicate semantic dependencies, and we examined two such techniques which operate on call graphs and PDGs.

We provided a brief introduction to ripple effect and differentiated it from stability analysis. Then we described the ripple effect algorithm with a simple example. Next, we examined the link between Lehman's laws of software evolution and measurement of ripple effect.

Finally, we introduced the concept of change propagation and provided a model for it, and we discussed several heuristics. The heuristics were characterized by data sources and pruning techniques. Empirical results of these heuristics were presented.

LITERATURE REVIEW

The techniques for performing impact analysis are partitioned into two major categories: one group is based on dependency analysis and the other group is based on traceability analysis [5]. Dependency-based techniques attempt to assess the effects of a change on semantic dependencies between program entities. Semantic dependencies are identified by means of syntactic dependencies. The techniques used to identify syntactic dependencies include slicing techniques and transitive closure on call graphs. One can follow requirement traceability links between source code and documentation to locate features described in the requirements document. To identify an impact set for a change request, Turver and Munro [3] have proposed the idea of a ripple propagation graph for modeling documentation entities and their links to source code. Ibrahim et al. [41] developed a traceability tool, called Catia, to trace ripple effects. Bianchi et al. [42] experimented with many examples of traceability link using the ANALYST tool; their aim was to assess: (i) the effectiveness of these traceability links to support impact analysis in object-oriented environment; and (ii) the accuracy of the maintenance process.

Impact analysis based on transitive closure of call graphs has been discussed in an article by Law and Rothermel [26]. A change process was modeled as a sequence of snapshots by Rajlich [9]. One snapshot represents one moment in the change process. In this technique a program is represented by a directed graph, where nodes represent *entities* (e.g., classes). There are two kinds of directed edges in a graph: one kind of edges represents dependencies and the second kind of edges represents inconsistencies. For example, classes a and b are represented by two nodes with the same name. Inconsistency between nodes a and b is represented by a directed edge $I < a, b >$, where b is to be updated for any change to a. For each edge $I < a, b >$, either a depends upon b or b depends upon a.

Intuitively, a program graph is said to be consistent if there are no I-type of edges. Based on the above graph model, four kinds of change propagation strategies were applied: *top-down, random change-and-fix, strict change-and-fix,* and *bottom-up.* Luqi [43] uses graphs and sets to represent changes. Ajila [2] explicitly defines elements and relations between elements to be traced with intra-level and inter-level dependencies. Impact analysis based on transitive closure of call graphs is discussed by Law [26]. Similarly, Lindvall et al. [44] show tracing across phases again with intra-level and inter-level dependencies. The authors also discuss an impact analysis technique based on traceability data of an object-oriented system. Impact analysis for software architectures has been studied by Zhao et al. [45]. Based on an architectural slicing and chopping technique, they propose an approach to performing change impact analysis at the architectural level of software systems. Berg et al. [46] proposed a framework for the impact analysis of software artifacts across several phases of software development.

Computing ripple effects for object-oriented systems is a research topic of considerable interest. To compute ripple effect at design level for object-oriented systems, Elish and Rine have given an algorithm in Reference 47. To compute ripple effect at the code level in C++, Chaumun et al. [48] studied the impact of changes in a system. To perform regression testing of modules implemented as objected-oriented code, Li and Offut [49] performed impact analysis to identify those modules. By means of experiments on two software systems, Kabaili et al. [50] studied the relationship between coupling metrics and changeability. They concluded that coupling is a predictor of changeability.

REFERENCES

[1] L. J. Arthur. 1988. *Software Evolution: The Software Maintenance Challenge.* John Wiley & Sons, New York, NY.

[2] S. Ajila. 1995. Software maintenance: An approach to impact analysis of object change. *Software Practice and Experience*, 25(10), 1155–1181.

[3] R. J. Turver and M. Munro. 1994. An early impact analysis technique for software maintenance. *Journal of Software Maintenance and Evolution: Research and Practice*, 6(1), 35–52.

[4] J. P. Queille, J. F. Voidrot, N. Wilde, and M. Munro. 1994. *The Impact Analysis Task in Software Maintenance: A Model and a Case of Study.* Proceedings of the International

Conference on Software Maintenance (ICSM), October, 1994, Phoenix, Arizona, IEEE Computer Society Press, Los Alamitos, CA, pp. 234–242.

[5] S. A. Bohner and R. S. Arnold. 1996. An introduction to software change impact analysis. In: *Software Change Impact Analysis* (Eds S. A. Bohner and R. S. Arnold). IEEE Computer Society Press, Los Alamitos, CA.

[6] A De Lucia, F. Fasano, and R. Oliveto. 2008. *Traceability Management for Impact Analysis*. Proceedings of the 2008 Frontiers of Software Maintenance (FoSM), October, 2008, Beijing, China, IEEE Computer Society Press, Los Alamitos, CA, pp. 21–30.

[7] O. C. Z. Gotel and A. C. W. Finkelstein. 1994. *An Analysis of the Requirements Traceability Problem*. Proceedings of First International Conference on Requirements Engineering, 1994, pp. 94–101.

[8] S. Black. 2006. The role of ripple effect in software evolution. In: *Software Evolution and Feedback: Theory and Practice* (Eds N. H. Madhavji and J. F. Ramil and D. E. Perry). John Wiley, West Sussex, England.

[9] V. Rajlich. 1997. *A Model for Change Propagation Based on Graph Rewriting*. Proceedings of the International Conference on Software Maintenance (ICSM), October, 1997, Bari, Italy, IEEE Computer Society Press, Los Alamitos, CA, pp. 84–91.

[10] A. E. Hassan and R. C. Holt. 2004. *Predicting Change Propagation in Software Systems*. Proceedings of the International Conference on Software Maintenance (ICSM), October, 2004, Chicago, USA, IEEE Computer Society Press, Los Alamitos, CA, pp. 284–293.

[11] D. E. Perry and W. M. Evangelist. 1987. An Empirical Study of Software Interface Faults – An Update. Proceedings of the Twentieth Annual Hawaii International Conference on Systems Sciences, January, 1987, Volume II, pp. 113–126.

[12] S. A. Bohner. 2002. *Software Change Impacts: An Evolving Perspective*. Proceedings of the International Conference on Software Maintenance (ICSM), October, 2002, Phoenix, Arizona, IEEE Computer Society Press, Los Alamitos, CA, pp. 263–271.

[13] R. S. Arnold and S. A. Bohner. 1993. *Impact Analysis – Towards a Framework for Comparison*. Proceedings of the International Conference on Software Maintenance (ICSM), October, 1993, IEEE Computer Society Press, Los Alamitos, CA, pp. 292–301.

[14] A. R. Fasolino and G. Visaggio. 1999. *Improving Software Comprehension Through an Automated Dependency Tracer*. Proceedings of 7th International Workshop on Program Comprehension, 1999, IEEE Computer Society Press, Los Alamitos, CA, pp. 58–65.

[15] T. J. Biggerstaff, B. G. Mitbander, and D. E. Webster. 1994. Program understanding and the concept assignment problem. *Communications of the ACM*, May, 72–82.

[16] N. Wilde, M. Buckellew, H. Page, V. Rajlich, and L. Pounds. 2003. A comparison of methods for locating features in legacy software. *The Journal of Systems and Software*, 65, 105–114.

[17] S. E. Sim, C. L. A. Clarke, and R. C. Holt. 1998. *Archetypal Source Code Searches: A Survey of Software Developers and Maintainers*. Proceedings of International Workshop on Program Comprehension, 1998, IEEE Computer Society Press, Los Alamitos, CA, pp. 180–187.

[18] N. Wilde and M. Scully. 1995. Software reconnaissance: Mapping program features to code. *Journal of Software Maintenance and Evolution: Research and Practice*, 7, 49–62.

[19] V. T. Rajlich and N. Wilde. 2002. The role of concepts in program comprehension. IWPC, June, 2002, Paris, France, IEEE Computer Society Press, Piscataway, NJ, pp. 271–278.

[20] K. Chen and V. Rajlich. 2000. *Case Study of Feature Location Using Dependence Graph.* Proceedings of International Workshop on Program Comprehension, 2000, IEEE Computer Society Press, Los Alamitos, CA, pp. 241–249.

[21] S. L. Pfleeger and S. A. Bohner. 1990. *A Framework for Software Maintenance Metrics.* Proceedings of International Conference on Software Maintenance, 1990, IEEE Computer Society Press, Los Alamitos, CA, pp. 320–327.

[22] S. A. Bohner. 1991. *Software Change Impact Analysis for Design Evolution.* Proceedings of International Conference on Software Maintenance and Reengineering, 1991, IEEE Computer Society Press, Los Alamitos, CA, pp. 292–301.

[23] S. Warshall. 1962. A theorem on boolean matrices. *Journal of the ACM*, 9(1), 11–12.

[24] V. Rajlich and P. Gosavi. 2004. Incremental change in object-oriented programming. *IEEE Software*, 21(4), 62–69.

[25] M. J. Harrold and B. Malloy. 1993. A unified interprocedural program representation for maintenance environment. *IEEE Transactions of Software Engineering*, 19(6), 584–593.

[26] J. Law and G. Rothermel. 2003. *Whole Program Path-based Dynamic Impact Analysis.* Proceedings of the International Conference on Software Engineering (ICSE), May, 2003, IEEE Computer Society Press, Los Alamitos, CA, pp. 308–318.

[27] J. Larus. 1999. *Whole Program Paths.* Proceedings of the ACM Conference on Programming Language Design and Implementation, May, 1999, ACM Press, New York, pp. 1–11.

[28] J. Ferrante, K. J. Ottenstein, and J. D. Warren. 1987. The program dependence graph and its uses in optimization. *ACM Transactions on Programming Languages and Systems*, 9(3), 319–349.

[29] K. J. Ottenstein and L. M. Ottenstein. 1984. *The Program Dependence Graph in a Software Development Environment.* Proceedings of the ACM SIGSOFT/SIGPLAN Symposium on Practical Software Development Environments, May, 1984, Pittaburgh, Pennsylvania, April, 1984, SIGPLAN Notices, ACM Press, New York, Vol. 19, No. 5, pp. 177–184.

[30] S. Horwitz, T. Reps, and D. Binkley. 1990. Interprocedural slicing using dependence graphs. *ACM Transactions on Programming Languages and Systems*, 12(1), 26–60.

[31] H. Agrawal and J. R. Horgan. 1990. *Dynamic Program Slicing.* Proceedings of the ACM Conference on Programming Language Design and Implementation, June, 1990, SIGPLAN Notices, ACM Press, New York, Vol. 25, No. 6, pp. 246–256.

[32] F. M. Haney. 1972. *Module Connection Analysis – a Tool for Scheduling of Software Debugging Activities.* Proceedings of the AFIPS Fall Joint Computer Conference, 1972, AFIPS Press, Reston, VA, pp. 173–179.

[33] S. S. Yau, J. S. Collofello, and T. MacGregor. 1978. Ripple effect analysis of software maintenance. COMPSAC, November, 1978, Chicago, Illinois, IEEE Computer Society Press, Piscataway, NJ, pp. 60–65.

[34] S. S. Yau and J. S. Collofello. 1980. Some stability measures for software maintenance. *IEEE Transactions of Software Engineering* 6(6), 545–552.

[35] S. S. Yau and J. S. Collofello. 1985. Design stability measures for software maintenance. *IEEE Transactions of Software Engineering*, 11(9), 849–856.

[36] S. Black. 2001. Computing ripple effect for software maintenance. *Journal of Software Maintenance and Evolution: Research and Practice*, 13, 263–279.

[37] T. J. McCabe. 1976. A complexity measure. *IEEE Transactions on Software Engineering*, 2(4), pp. 308–320.

[38] S. Black. 2008. Deriving an approximation algorithm for automatic computation of ripple effect measures. *Information and Software Technology*, 50, 723–736.

[39] N. Anquetil and T. Lethbridge. 1998. *Extracting Concepts from File Names: A New File Clustering Criterion*. Proceedings of the International Conference on Software Engineering (ICSE), April, 1998, Kyoto, Japan, IEEE Computer Society Press, Los Alamitos, CA, pp. 84–93.

[40] A. E. Hassan and R. C. Holt. 2006. Replaying development history to assess the effectiveness of change propagation tools. *Empirical Software Engineering*, 11(3), 335–367.

[41] S. Ibrahim, N. Idris, M. Munro, and A. Deraman. 2005. Implementing a document-based requirement traceability: A case study. IASTED International Conference on Software Engineering (SE 2006), February, 2005, Innsbruck, Austria, ACTA Press, Calgary, Canada, pp. 124–131.

[42] A. Bianchi, A. Fasolino, and G. Visaggio. 2000. *An Exploratory Case Study of the Maintenance Effectiveness of Traceability Models*. Proceedings of International Workshop on Program Comprehension, 2000, IEEE Computer Society Press, Los Alamitos, CA, pp. 149–158.

[43] Luqi. 1990. A graph model for software evolution. *IEEE Transactions of Software Engineering*, 18(8), 917–927.

[44] M. Lindvall and K. Sandahl. 1998. Traceability aspects of impact analysis in object-oriented systems. *Journal of Software Maintenance and Evolution: Research and Practice*, 10, 37–57.

[45] J. Zhao, H. Yang, L. Xiang, and B. Xu. 2002. Change impact analysis to support architectural evolution. *Journal of Software Maintenance and Evolution: Research and Practice*, 14, 317–333.

[46] K. V. Berg, J. M. Conejero, and Juan Hernández. 2007. Analysis of crosscutting in early development phases base on traceability. In: *transactions on aspect-oriented software development* (Eds A. Rashid and M. Aksit), LNCS, Vol. 4620, November, pp. 73–104. Springer, Berlin.

[47] M. O. Elish and D. Rine. 2003. *Investigation of Metrics for Object-oriented Design Logical Stability*. Proceedings of Seventh European Conference on Software Maintenance and Reengineering (CSMR), 2003, IEEE Computer Society Press, Los Alamitos, CA, pp. 193–200.

[48] M. A. Chauman, H. Kabaili, R. K. Keller, and F. Lustman. 1999. *A Change Impact Model for Changeability Assessment in Object-oriented Software Systems*. Proceedings of Third European Conference on Software Maintenance and Reengineering (CSMR), 1999, IEEE Computer Society Press, Los Alamitos, CA, pp. 130–138.

[49] L. Li and A. J. Offut. 1996. *Algorithm Analysis of the Impacts of Changes to Object-oriented Software*. Proceedings of the International Conference on Software Maintenance (ICSM), Phoenix, Arizona, IEEE Computer Society Press, Los Alamitos, CA, pp. 171–184.

[50] H. Kabaili, R. K. Keller, and F. Lustman. 2005. Assessing object oriented software changeability with design metrics. IASTED International Conference on Software Engineering (SE 2006), February, 2005, Innsbruck, Austria, ACTA Press, Calgary, Canada, pp. 61–66.

EXERCISES

1. Which of the following relationships between SLOs indicate a potential dependency between the objects such that a change to the second may require a change to the first?

    (a) <Test case T> is derived from <requirement R>.

    (b) <Object code O> is compiled from <source code C>.

    (c) <Requirement spec S> was produced according to <plan P>.

    (d) <Module M1> was written by the same person as <module M2>.

    (e) <Requirement R> is tested with <test case T>.

    (f) <Program P1> is an earlier version of <program P2>.

2. Explain the adequacy and effectiveness aspects of impact analysis.

3. Determine the set of potentially impacted procedures due to the change in procedure **A** for the execution traces **M B G r G r r A C E r r r x** and **M A C E r D r r r x** using the call graph given in Figure 6.7.

4. Consider the execution trace **M B r A C D r E r r r r x M B G r r r x M B C F r r r r x** and the call graph given in Figure 6.7. For the above trace, determine the set of potentially impacted procedures due to changes in procedures: (a) **G**; and (b) **C**.

5. Discuss the differences between static and dynamic program slicing.

6. Consider the program given in Figure 6.15. Obtain the dynamic slice using the simple approach discussed in the book for the input value of 1 for N and variable Z at the end of execution. Explain your observation. Suggest a new approach that avoids the problem you observed.

begin

$S1$:	$read(N)$
$S2$:	$Z = 0$;
$S3$:	$Y = 0$;
$S4$:	$I = 1$;
$S5$:	$while(I <= N)$;
	do
$S6$:	$Z = f_1(Z,Y)$;
$S7$:	$Y = f_2(Y)$;
$S8$:	$I = I + 1$;
	end_white;
$S9$:	$while(Z)$;
	end.

FIGURE 6.15   Program

7. In a data dependency graph, what can you tell from the number of edges that enter a node corresponding to a statement S?

    (a) This is the number of variables appearing in the statement S.

(b) This is the number of statements which use the values of variables set by the statement S.

(c) This is the number of statements which assign values to variables, where those values may be used in the execution of statement S.

(d) This is the number of variables whose values are used in the execution of statement S.

8. What is the major difference between stability analysis and impact analysis?

9. Derive the average *recall* and average *precision* over time for M multiple change sets.

10. Given *predicted* = {B, X, Y, Z, W, D } and *occurred* = {B, C, D, E}, calculate the value of *recall* and *precision*.

11. Calculate the value of *recall* for the change set {{A,B}, {H, G, L}, {P, Q, S, T }}, where {A, B}, {H, G, L}, and {P, Q, S, T} are three connected components.

12. Which of the following characteristics of data-intensive systems make it difficult to use traditional impact analysis techniques?

(a) There are a large number of different users of the data.

(b) There is a large volume of data.

(c) The applications which access the data are mission critical.

(d) There is a lack of knowledge of what data is stored, and how and why it is used.

(e) The data is often of very poor quality.

7

REFACTORING

He who rejects change is the architect of decay. The only human institution which rejects progress is the cemetery.

—Harold Wilson

7.1 GENERAL IDEA

Developers continuously modify, enhance, and adapt software to new requirements and execution environments. The software evolves with time, and, most likely, it deviates from its intended design. As the software further evolves and strays too far away from its original design, three important things happen to the software:

- *Decreased understandability:* It becomes increasingly difficult to understand the software and it becomes less maintainable.
- *Decreased reliability:* The reliability of the software decreases. As the software deviates from its original design and as documentations become out-of-date, faults are inadvertently introduced into the software during maintenance.
- *Increased maintenance cost:* The cost of maintaining the software rises in the absence of preventive measures.

Software Evolution and Maintenance: A Practitioner's Approach, First Edition.
Priyadarshi Tripathy and Kshirasagar Naik.
© 2015 John Wiley & Sons, Inc. Published 2015 by John Wiley & Sons, Inc.

The difficulty in understanding the software is due to the:

- increased complexity of the code during the maintenance phase;
- out-of-date documentation;
- code not conforming to standards.

Therefore, there is a need to decrease the complexity of software by improving its internal quality. The internal quality of software is improved by means of *restructuring* the software. If restructuring is performed on an object-oriented software, then it is called *refactoring* [1]. Software should be continually restructured during and between other maintenance activities so that programmers find it easier and easier to work with it. If programmers find it easy to work with the software, new functions and features can be easily added to the system, and bugs can be easily fixed.

Restructuring means reorganizing software to give it a different look, or structure. Source code is restructured to improve some of its *non-functional* requirements, without modifying its *functional* requirements. For example, one may restructure source code to improve its *readability*, *extensibility*, *maintainability*, and *modularity*. Though restructuring does not modify the system's functional requirements, it can take place while adding new features, that is, functional requirements, to the system. Software restructuring is informally stated as the modifications of software in order to make it [2]:

- easier to understand;
- easier to change;
- easier to update its internal and external documentations; and
- less susceptible to faults when changes are made in the future.

The term *software* in *software restructuring* is used in a broad sense to refer to both code and documentations—both internal and external. A higher level goal of software restructuring is to increase the *software value* [2] as explained in the following:

- *External software value:* This is the value of the software as perceived by the customers. For example, a software with faults may fail to satisfy the business needs of the customers. Such software may be seen by the customers to have less value.
- *Internal software value:* This represents the cost saving due to three factors: (i) maintenance cost saving due to a good structure of the software; (ii) cost saving due to potential reuse of components of a software with good structure; and (iii) cost saving due to extended use of a software.

Software restructuring activities should be seen as increasing the value of the software under consideration. While choosing a software restructuring approach it is important to define goals so that achievement of those goals should produce better software value. The cost of restructuring should be justified in terms of the expected gain in software value. Ideally, the expected gain is desired to be quantified. However, in the absence of widely available quantified data about the effectiveness of structuring approaches, one could use qualitative data. Some simple restructuring activities are as follows:

- *Pretty printing:* Align code statements so that code becomes easier to understand as logical units.
- *Meaningful names for variables:* Variable names are chosen to give an indication of programming plans.
- *One statement per line:* Write one code statement in one line, as opposed to many statements in one line.

Developers and managers should be aware of software restructuring for the following reasons [2]:

- *Better understanding:* By reorganizing software with easily traceable structures, it becomes easier for programmers to understand it. Ease of understanding leads to easier documentation, easier testing, potentially greater programmer productivity, and reduced dependence of the maintenance group on a small number of programmers who alone understand the code.
- *Keep pace with new structures:* As time passes, new generations of programmers are taught new software structures. Therefore, transforming existing software into new software with structures that are close to what is taught to new programmers is beneficial because it will enhance the understandability of the software. This in turn will reduce the time that maintenance programmers take to become familiar with the software.
- *Better reliability:* It is easier to locate and fix bugs in well-structured, well-understood software than in poorly understood software. While fixing bugs in a poorly understood software, one may introduce more bugs due to side effects of code modification.
- *Longer lifetime:* The lifetimes of software can be increased by making them maintainable by means of improving their structures.
- *Automated analysis:* Programs with good structures are more amenable to automatic analysis than unstructured programs. For example, a test generation tool is likely to be more successful in generating an effective set of tests for a program with a good structure than for a program with complex dependencies among modules.

Before we move on to the next section, we summarize the characteristics of restructuring and refactoring as follows:

- The objective of restructuring and refactoring is to improve the internal and external values of software.

- When a subject program is transformed into a new program, the original program's external behavior is preserved by the new program. In other words, the two programs are functionally identical from the viewpoint of users.
- Restructuring does not normally involve code transformation to implement new requirements. Rather, restructuring can be performed without adding new requirements to the existing system.
- When a subject program is transformed into a new program, the relative level of abstraction is preserved. For example, a program in C is transformed into another C program, rather than a program in an assembly language. However, the concept of program restructuring can be applied to transform legacy code into a more structured form or migrate it to a different programming language. That is, restructuring and refactoring can be used in reengineering a system.

7.2 ACTIVITIES IN A REFACTORING PROCESS

To restructure a software system, programmers follow a process with well defined activities. Those activities are as follows:

- Identify what to refactor.
- Determine which refactorings should be applied.
- Ensure that refactoring preserves the software's behavior.
- Apply the refactorings to the chosen entities.
- Evaluate the impacts of the refactorings.
- Maintain consistency.

Next, we explain the above items one by one.

7.2.1 Identify What to Refactor

In this step, the programmer identifies what to refactor from a set of software artifacts. Some examples of software artifacts that the programmer can consider are source code, design documents, and requirements documents. Having identified the top level artifact, the programmer can focus on specific portions of the chosen artifact for refactoring. Specific modules, functions, classes, methods, and data structures can be identified from the source code for refactoring. For programs written in non-object-oriented languages, restructuring is generally limited to the level of a function or a block of code. For programs written in object-oriented languages, the richness of the languages, namely, interfaces, dynamic binding, subtyping, overriding, and polymorphism, make restructuring difficult.

The broad concept of *code smell* is applied to source code to detect where refactorings should be applied. A *code smell* is any symptom in the source code of a software that possibly indicates a deeper problem. Existence of code smells in source code do not imply the existence of problems in source code, such as, faults, low level of performance, and low level of reliability. On the other hand, what code smells do imply is that if the problems are not resolved sooner, then it is likely that future changes may introduce more faults and future changes may be more expensive to execute. Some examples of code smells are as follows.

- *Duplicate Code:* This smell occurs when segments of source code are repeated in many places in the program. If there is a need to change the duplicate code, it must be ensured that all segments are changed. If some segment is missed, which is likely to occur, then faults will be introduced. The solutions lie in the nature of code duplications. For example, if duplications occur in different methods of the same class, then duplicates can be extracted into a new method. On the other hand, if duplicate methods occur in subclasses, then the duplicate codes can be moved to the subclass. In simple cases, code duplication can be eliminated by introducing a new function and by inserting function calls. In complex cases, an intermediate subclass can be inserted to factor out the common code [3].

- *Long Parameter List:* When a method has too many formal parameters, say, more than four, programmers may make errors while designing calls to the method. A common error is to reorder the list of actual parameters. A solution may be found in designing a parameter object, thereby passing a single parameter instead of a long list of parameters.

- *Long Methods:* This occurs if a method has a long sequence of statements, say, hundreds of lines of code. A solution lies in extracting methods from long fragments of code.

- *Large Classes:* A smell is said to occur if a class has too many methods, say, more than 8, and too many variables, say, more than 15. A solution lies in splitting the class into component classes and creating superclasses.

- *Message Chain:* A message chain occurs when one calls several methods successively. An example of a message chain is: `student.getID().getRecord()` `.getGrade(course)`. Such a chain can be simplified by means of a helper function that performs part of the computation of another function. Thus, the above message chain can be rewritten as: `student.getGrade(course)`.

At the design level, the entities that can be considered for refactoring are software architecture, global control flow, and database schemas. Class diagrams, statechart diagrams, and activity diagrams are extensively used to describe various aspects of software design. Therefore, refactoring of software design involves manipulating those diagrams. To describe program structures at a very high level, designers apply design patterns. Therefore, refactoring of design can involve restructuring or replacing occurrences of poor design patterns in a legacy system with good design patterns [4]. To refactor a software architecture, Philipps and Rumpe [5] have proposed an approach where refactoring rules are based on the graphical representation of a system architecture.

7.2.2 Determine Which Refactorings Should be Applied

In this step, the programmer identifies which refactorings to apply to the portions of the software identified in the aforementioned first step. For ease of understanding, in

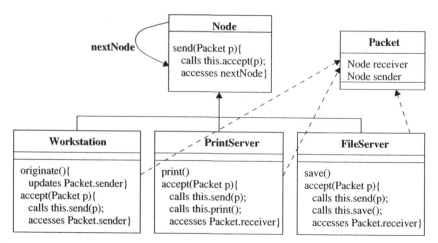

FIGURE 7.1 Class diagram of a local area network (LAN) simulator. From Reference 6.
© 2007 Springer

the following we give some examples of refactorings in the context of a class diagram shown in Figure 7.1 [6]. The intention is to show what refactorings look like. The class diagram is about a local area network (LAN) simulator.

- *R1:* Rename method *print* to *process* in class *PrintServer*. Perform this refactoring together with *R2*.

- *R2:* Rename method *print* to *process* in class *FileServer*. Perform this refactoring together with *R1*. In *R1* and *R2*, the new names of *print* are the same, because *process* prepares for the application of refactoring *R4*.

- *R3:* Create a superclass called *Server* from *PrintServer* and *FileServer*, because their behaviors are very similar.

- *R4:* Pull up method *accept* from classes *PrintServer* and *FileServer* to the superclass *Server* created with *R3*. Applications of *R1* and *R2* essentially makes the two original versions of *accept* in *PrintServer* and *FileServer* identical.

- *R5:* Move method *accept* from class *PrintServer* to class *Packet*, because method *accept* directly accesses the field *receiver* in class *Packet*. An advantage of moving *accept* from *PrintServer* to class *Packet* is that data packets themselves will decide what actions to take.

- *R6:* Move method *accept* from class *FileServer* to class *Packet* for the same reason given for *R5*.

- *R7:* Encapsulate field *receiver* in class *Packet*, so that another class cannot directly access this field. The advantages are: (i) there is increased modularity of the system; and (ii) internal representation of data packets can be modified without modifying the classes that use data packets.

- *R8:* Add parameter *p* of type *Packet* to method *print* in class *PrintServer* so that the contents of a packet can be printed.

- *R9:* Add parameter *p* of type *Packet* to method *save* in class *FileServer* so that the contents of a packet can be saved.

From the class diagram shown in Figure 7.1 and the nine refactorings *R1 – R9* it is apparent that one can design a large number of refactorings even for a small system. A subset of the entire set of refactorings must be carefully chosen, because of the following reasons.

- *Some refactorings must be applied together.* For example, refactorings *R1* and *R2* are applied together. It is of no use to apply only one of them. If both of them are not applied together, then *R4* cannot be applied, because applying just one of them or not applying them at all will not make method *accept* identical in both classes *FileServer* and *PrintServer*.

- *Some refactorings must be applied in certain orders.* For example, refactorings *R1* and *R2* must precede *R3*. One can apply *R3* only after applying *R1* and *R2*, because applications of *R1* and *R2* make the methods *accept* in classes *FileServer* and *PrintServer* identical. In other words, *R3* cannot be applied if *R1* and *R2* have not yet been applied.

- *Some refactorings can be individually applied, but they must follow an order if applied together.* For example, refactorings *R1* and *R8* can be applied in isolation. However, if a programmer chooses to apply both, then *R1* must occur before *R8*.

- *Some refactorings are mutually exclusive.* For example, refactorings *R4* and *R6* are mutually exclusive. Refactoring *R4* pulls up methods *accept* from classes *FileServer* and *PrintServer* into the superclass *Server*, whereas *R6* moves the method *accept* to class *Packet*. It is clear that one cannot apply both the refactorings together.

For large sets of refactorings, tool support is needed to identify a feasible subset of refactorings. The following two techniques can be used to analyze a set of refactorings to select a feasible subset.

- *Critical pair analysis:* Here the idea is to identify pairs of mutually exclusive refactorings. Given a set of refactorings, analyze each pair of refactorings for conflicts. A pair of refactorings is said to be conflicting if both of them cannot be applied together. For example, *R4* and *R6* constitute a conflicting set, which means that one cannot be applied after applying the other.

- *Sequential dependency analysis:* Sequential dependency of refactorings means that: (i) in order to apply a refactoring, one or more refactorings must have been applied before; and (ii) if one refactoring has already been applied, a mutually exclusive refactoring cannot be applied anymore. For example, after applying *R1*, *R2*, and *R3*, refactoring *R4* becomes applicable. On the contrary, if *R4* is applied, then *R6* is not applicable anymore.

7.2.3   Ensure that Refactoring Preserves the Behavior of the Software

Ideally, the behavior of a program after refactoring should be the same as the behavior before refactoring. In the original definition of behavior preservation proposed by Opdyke [1], program behavior simply referred to input–output behavior. In other words, for the same set of input values, the programs before refactoring and after refactoring were desired to produce the same output values. However, in many applications preservation of input–output behavior alone is not enough, because preservation of temporal constraints and non-functional requirements of the program may be key to the success of refactoring. A non-exclusive list of such non-functional requirements is as follows:

- *Temporal constraints:* A temporal constraint over a sequence of operations is that the operations occur in a desired order. For real-time applications, refactoring should preserve temporal constraints.

- *Resource constraints:* Memory, energy, and communication bandwidth are some examples of critical resources on some computers. Therefore, it is important that the software after refactoring does not demand more of those resources than what the software before refactoring demanded.

- *Safety constraints:* It is important that a software does not lose its safety properties after it is refactored.

Therefore showing that a refactored program behaves the same ways as the program before refactoring is a difficult task. Two pragmatic ways of showing that a refactored program behaves the same way as the original program are as follows:

- *Testing:* By means of extensive testing, observe the behavior of the program before and after refactoring to determine whether or not there is behavior preservation. However, it may be noted that refactoring may invalidate some tests that were designed based on the structure of the program.

- *Verification of preservation of call sequence:* The concept of *call preservation* means that all method calls are preserved in the refactored program. This is a slightly more formal, but still weak, way of showing that refactoring preserves behavior. In a further limited way, the type correctness of a sequence of calls can be preserved by using type constraints to verify the preconditions of refactorings and determining what source code to modify [7].

For programs written in languages with a simple and formally defined semantics, such as *Prolog*, one can prove for some kinds of refactorings that program semantics are preserved. On the other hand, for Java and C++ programs, much restrictions have to be put on language constructs and refactorings to show that program behavior is preserved.

7.2.4   Apply the Refactorings to the Chosen Entities

This means executing the steps of the refactorings chosen before. The class diagram of Figure 7.2a has been obtained from Figure 7.1 by focusing on the classes *FileServer*, *PrintServer*, and *Packet*, and applying refactorings *R1*, *R2*, and R3. Next, the class diagram of Figure 7.2b has been obtained by applying *R4* to the class diagram of Figure 7.2a. Similarly, the class diagram of Figure 7.2c has been obtained by applying *R6* to the class diagram of Figure 7.2a.

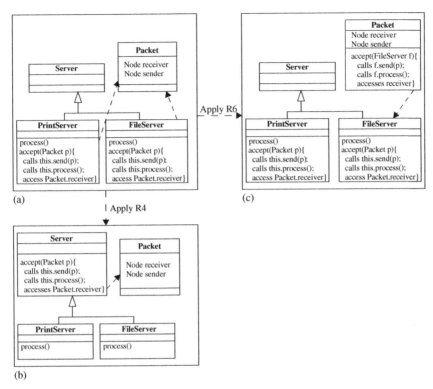

FIGURE 7.2   Applications of two refactorings. From Reference 6. © 2007 Springer

7.2.5   Evaluate the Impacts of the Refactorings on Quality

Both *internal* qualities and *external* qualities are impacted by refactorings. Some examples of internal qualities are *size, complexity, coupling, cohesion*, and *testability*. Similarly, some examples of external qualities are *performance, reusability, maintainability, extensibility, robustness*, and *scalability*. In general, refactoring techniques are highly specialized, which means that one technique is intended to improve a small number—generally one—of quality attributes of the program. For example, some refactorings eliminate code duplications, some raise reusability, some improve performance, and some improve maintainability. It is important to note that, refactorings directly impact internal qualities. Therefore, by measuring the impact of refactorings on internal qualities, their impacts on external qualities can be estimated.

Some examples of software metrics are *coupling, cohesion*, and *size*. Decreased coupling, increased cohesion, and decreased size are likely to make a software system more maintainable. Therefore, to assess the impact of a refactoring technique for better maintainability, one can evaluate the metrics before refactoring and after refactoring, and compare them. Kataoka et al. [8] have further investigated the idea of the coupling metrics by introducing three finer levels of coupling: *return value* coupling, *parameter* coupling, and *shared variable* coupling. Those couplings are explained as follows. If method *A* uses a return value from method *B*, there exists a return value coupling between the two methods. If method *B* receives *n* parameters from method *A*, there exists an *n* parameter coupling between the two methods. Similarly, if method *A* uses *n* class variables in common with method *B*, there exists *n* shared variable coupling between the two methods. The three kinds of coupling metrics can be combined to produce a single composite coupling metrics by taking their weighted sum.

Rather than evaluate the impacts *after* applying refactorings, one can select refactoring steps such that the program after refactoring possesses better quality attributes. Tahvildari and Kontogiannis [9] have used the concept of *soft-goal graph*— introduced in detail in the book by Chung, Nixon, Yu and Mylopoulos [10]—to help guide the application of refactorings. Intuitively, a soft-goal graph for a quality attribute, for example, maintainability, is a hierarchical graph rooted at the desired change in the attribute, for example, high maintainability. The internal nodes represent successive refinements of the attribute and are basically the soft goals. Finally, the leaf nodes represent refactoring transformations which fulfill or contribute positively/negatively to soft goals which appear above them in the hierarchy. A partial example of a soft-goal graph with one leaf node, namely, Move, has been illustrated in Figure 7.3. The dotted lines between the leaf node Move and three soft goals—High Modularity, High Module Reuse, and Low Control Flow Coupling imply that the Move transformation impacts those three soft goals.

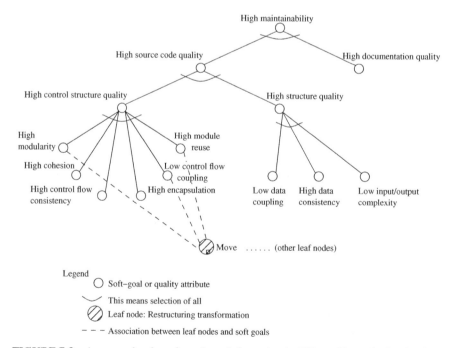

FIGURE 7.3 An example of a soft-goal graph for maintainability, with one leaf node. From Reference 11. © 2002 IEEE

7.2.6   Maintain Consistency of Software Artifacts

A software system is described by many artifacts at different levels of abstractions. Those artifacts include requirements documents, design documents, source code, and test suites. If one kind of artifact is changed, then it is important to change some or all of the other artifacts so that consistency is maintained across the artifacts. For example, changes in source code may require changes in the design documents and the test suites. Therefore, the concept of *change propagation* is used to cope with inconsistencies across different software artifacts. The concept of change propagation has been explained in Chapter 6.

7.3   FORMALISMS FOR REFACTORING

In this section, we explain three key formalisms for refactoring: assertions, graph transformation, and metrics. Assertions are useful in verifying the assumptions made by programmers. The concept of graph transformation is useful in viewing refactorings as applications of transformation rules. The concept of metrics is useful in quantifying to what extent the internal and external properties of software entities have changed as a result of applying refactorings.

7.3.1   Assertions

Programmers make assumptions about the behavior of programs at specific points of their interests, and those assumptions can be tested by means of assertions. Thus, an *assertion* is specified as a Boolean expression which evaluates to *true* or *false*. When an assertion is put at a certain point of execution in a program, the programmer thinks that the assertion always evaluates to true at that point. That is, a programmer can use an assertion to test their assumptions about the program at the point where the assertion occurs. If the assertion evaluates to true, normal execution of the program continues. On the other hand, if the assertion evaluates to false, then it is an indication of something gone wrong in the computation process. Different execution semantics can be associated with assertions, when they evaluate to false. For example, when the assertion fails, program execution is halted and a detailed message can be displayed.

There are three kinds of commonly understood assertions, namely, *invariants*, *preconditions*, and *postconditions*. An invariant is a Boolean expression that the programmer always expects to evaluate to true. In other words, an invariant evaluates to true wherever in the program it is invoked. The concept of a *class invariant* is a special case of the general concept of invariant. A class invariant is a condition that all instances of that class must satisfy. A precondition is a condition that must be satisfied *before* a computation, whereas a postcondition is a condition that must be satisfied *after* a computation.

Behavior preservation is a key requirement of refactoring and restructuring techniques. That is, the input–output behavior of a program must remain unchanged even after changes in a program's structure due to the applications of refactoring or restructuring techniques. Invariants, preconditions, and postconditions have been suggested by researchers to address the problem of behavior preservation. In the context of object-oriented database schemas, which have much similarities with UML class diagrams, Banerjee et al. [12] have shown that behavior preserving transformations can be applied to database schemas by using invariants. An example of invariant in the schema context is: *All instance variables of a class, whether defined or inherited, have distinct names. Similarly, all methods of a class, whether defined or inherited, must have distinct names.* An obvious problem with the use of assertions in testing the behavior preserving property of refactoring and restructuring techniques is the computationally expensive static checking of preconditions, postconditions, and invariants.

7.3.2 Graph Transformation

Programs and design diagrams, namely, class diagrams and statecharts, can be viewed as *graphs*, and refactorings can be viewed as graph production rules. Therefore, applying refactorings to software can be viewed as applying graph transformations. Software entities, namely, classes (C), method signatures (M), block structures (B), variables (V), parameters (P), and expressions (E) are represented by *typed nodes* in a graph. The possible relationships among the nodes are: method lookup (1), inheritance (i), membership (m), (sub)type (t), expression (e), actual parameter (ap), formal parameter (fp), cascaded expression (•), call (c), variable access (a), and update (u).

An example of a program graph has been shown in Figure 7.4. In a program graph, method bodies are represented as simplified trees with a root at a B-node, connected with E-nodes, where an E-nodes represent assignments, accessed variables, parameters, and function calls. A B-node with two E-nodes has been shown within the dotted box in Figure 7.4. The body of the `originate` method is contained in the Node superclass.

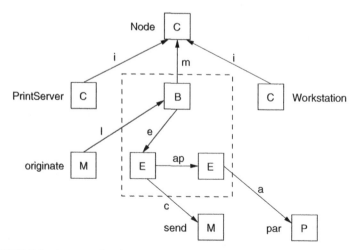

FIGURE 7.4 An example of a program graph. From Reference 13. © 2006 Elsevier

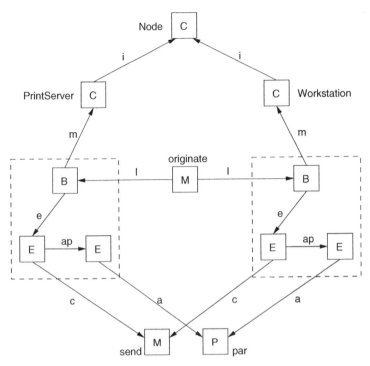

FIGURE 7.5   Program graph obtained after applying *push-down method* refactoring to the program graph of Figure 7.4. From Reference 13. © 2006 Elsevier

The *push-down method* refactoring is explained as follows. Assume that there is a superclass A and two subclasses X and Y designed to inherit A. Also assume that there is a method m defined in A. If m is not further redefined in X and Y, then method m is available in both X and Y. Note that if there is no need to use method m in subclass Y, there is no need to push it down to Y. Another way of accessing m in X and Y is to push m down to X and Y. The push-down method refactoring has been is applied to the method originate in the graph of Figure 7.4 to obtain a new graph shown in Figure 7.5.

7.3.3 Software Metrics

Software metrics can be used to quantitatively represent the internal and external qualities of software. In this subsection, we present the details of calculating two kinds of metrics, namely, cohesion and coupling. In general, a module consists of several components, with each component providing a defined functionality used by components within the same module and components within other modules. Therefore, it is useful to measure the strength of togetherness of components within a module so that one can decide whether or not some components should stay in the same module. The aforementioned concept of the strength of togetherness of components in the same module is expressed by means of cohesion metrics. On the other hand, the strength of dependency between modules is expressed by means of coupling metrics.

Cohesion Metrics   Simon et al. [14] have introduced the concept of a *distance-based* metric to express design cohesion, where cohesion refers to the degree to which module components belong together. The distance-based metric is explained in what follows. Let B be a set of considered properties for a special *similarity viewpoint*. Also, let x and y denote two entities (e.g., methods and attributes) of a "module" (e.g., a class) for which we are interested in finding its cohesion. Then, the *distance* between x and y with respect to the considered property set B, denoted by $dist_B(x, y)$ is computed as follows:

$$dist_B(x, y) = 1 - \frac{|p(x) \cap p(y)|}{|p(x) \cup p(y)|} \tag{7.1}$$

where $p(x) = \{p_i \in B | x \text{ possesses property } p_i\}$.

For a method f, the set of its properties, denoted by B_f, is given as follows:

$$B_f = \{f \cup \text{all methods directly used by} f \cup \text{all attributes used by } f\}. \tag{7.2}$$

Similarly, for an attribute g, the set of its properties, denoted by B_g, is given as follows:

$$B_g = \{g \cup \text{all methods using } g\}. \tag{7.3}$$

For the calculation of distance between two entities, the needed B is given by the union of the two corresponding sets of attributes. For example, if we are interested in calculating the distance between two methods f_1 and f_2, we have $B = B_{f_1} \cup B_{f_2}$. Similarly, if we are interested in the distance between a method f and an attribute g, then we have $B = B_f \cup B_g$.

Now, given a class C, let $M = \{m_1, \ldots, m_k\}$ be the set of methods and $A = \{a_1, \ldots, m_n\}$ be the set of attributes of C. Using the distance-based metric of Eq. 7.1, one can calculate the distance between all pairs of entities in the set $M \cup A$, and plot C in a graphical manner such that each attribute is represented by a square and each method by a circle such that the Euclidean distance between two entities is equal to their distance calculated using Eq. 7.1. Such a notation to represent a class is called a Virtual Reality Modeling Language [14]. In Figure 7.6, we show the VRML diagram of two classes C1 and C2. Though method m1 is a part of class C1, it is closer to the methods and attributes of class C2 than to the methods and attributes of class C1. Therefore, the *Move*-method refactoring can be applied to method m1 so that it becomes a part of class C2. The idea of *Move*-method refactoring has been explained by means of refactoring *R5* in Section 7.2.2.

Coupling Metrics   The idea of coupling presented here was introduced by Kataoka, Imai, Andou, and Fukaya [15]. First, three basic kinds of couplings are explained:

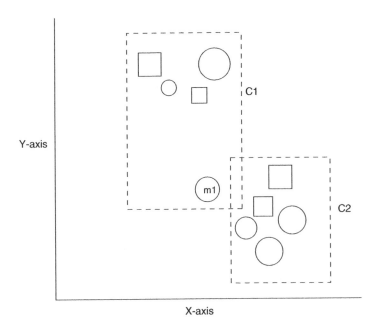

FIGURE 7.6 An example of a VRML diagram of two classes C1 and C2. Circles denote methods and squares denote attributes

return value coupling, parameter coupling, and *shared variable coupling*. Next, the three kinds of couplings are combined to obtain an overall, composite coupling metric.

- *Return value coupling:* Let there be two methods A and B. There exists a return value coupling between A and B if A *calls B* and B *returns* a value to A. Similarly, if B calls A and A provides a return value to B, then there also exists return value coupling between A and B. The quantity of return value coupling of a method A, denoted by $C_{rv}(A)$, with all the methods it calls and all the methods it is called from is computed as follows.

$$C_{rv}(A) = \sum_{m_\rho \in \rho(A)} K_{rv}(m_\rho) + \sum_{m_\sigma \in \sigma(A)} K_{rv}(m_\sigma), \qquad (7.4)$$

where,

$\rho(A)$ is the set of methods which provide return values to A.

$\sigma(A)$ is the set of methods that use the return values provided by A.

$K_{rv}(m)$ is the return value coupling inter-class coefficient. $K_{rv}(m) = 1$ if both methods m and A belong to the same class. On the other hand, if m and A are in different classes, then $K_{rv}(m) = \kappa_{rv}$, where $\kappa_{rv} > 1$.

The idea behind $K_{rv}(m)$ is to consider the likelihood that inter-class coupling by means of value passing can lead to higher maintenance cost than intra-class coupling.

- *Parameter coupling:* Parameter coupling is about the number of parameters passed when a method calls another method. Method A has n *parameter coupling* with method B if method A receives n parameters from B. Similarly, if A passes n parameters to method C, then there exists n *parameter coupling* with C. The quantity of parameter coupling of a method A, denoted by $C_{pp}(A)$, with all the methods it calls and all the methods it is called from is computed as follows.

$$C_{pp}(A) = \sum_{m_\zeta \in \zeta(A)} K_{pp}(m_\zeta)p_{m_\zeta} + \sum_{m_\xi \in \xi(A)} K_{pp}(m_\xi)p_{m_\xi}, \qquad (7.5)$$

where,

   $\zeta(A)$ is the set of methods that call A.

   $\xi(A)$ is the set of methods that are called by A.

   $K_{pp}(m)$ is the parameter coupling inter-class coefficient. $K_{pp}(m) = 1$ if both methods m and A are in the same class. On the other hand, if m and A are in different classes, then $K_{pp}(m) = \kappa_{pp}$, where $\kappa_{pp} > 1$.

   p_{m_ζ} is the number of parameters received by method m_ζ when m_ζ is called by another method.

   p_{m_ξ} is the number of parameters passed by method m_ξ when m_ξ calls another method.

The idea behind $K_{pp}(m)$ is to consider the likelihood that inter-class coupling by means of parameter passing can lead to higher maintenance cost than intra-class coupling.

- *Shared variable coupling:* Two methods A and B belonging in the same class are said to have n *shared variable coupling* if they use n class or instance variables. The quantity of shared variable coupling of method A, denoted by $C_{sv}(A)$, with all the methods in the same class is computed as follows.

$$C_{sv}(A) = \sum_{m_\chi \in \chi(A)} K_{sv}(m_\chi)v_{m_\chi}, \qquad (7.6)$$

where,

   $\chi(A)$ is the set of methods that use class or instance variables in common with A.

   v_m is the number of class or instance variables that are used both in m and A.

   $K_{sv}(m)$ is the shared variable inter-class coefficient. $K_{sv}(m) = 1$ if both methods m and A are in the same class. On the other hand, if m and A are in different classes, then $K_{sv}(m) = \kappa_{sv}$, where $\kappa_{sv} > 1$.

The motivation for introducing $K_{sv}(m)$ is similar to the motivation for introducing $K_{rv}(m)$.

Making decisions about the maintainability of a program from three different coupling perspectives is a difficult task. Therefore, it is useful to combine the three coupling metrics to obtain a single, composite coupling metric. While combining the three coupling metrics, it is useful to note that all the three metrics are not equally significant. For example, from the standpoint of maintainability of a program, the influence of accessing an instance variable from another class is arguably more severe than the influence of receiving a parameter from a method within the same class [15]. The concept of *weighted sum* is a simple strategy to combine the three coupling metrics. Three weighting factors, namely, W_{rv}, W_{pp}, and W_{sv} are introduced to represent the relative importance of $C_{rv}(A)$, $C_{pp}(A)$, and $C_{sv}(A)$, respectively, such that the following constraints, denoted by Eqs. 7.7 and 7.8, hold:

$$W_{rv} + W_{pp} + W_{sv} = 1. \tag{7.7}$$

$$0 < W_{rv} \leq W_{pp} \leq W_{sv}. \tag{7.8}$$

Now, the total coupling represented by a single metric can be given by Eq. 7.9:

$$C_T(A) = W_{rv}C_{rv}(A) + W_{pp}C_{pp}(A) + W_{sv}C_{sv}(A). \tag{7.9}$$

In their experiments, Kataoka et al. [15] have used the following values of the different parameters and weighting factors:

$$\kappa_{rv} = 1.5, \kappa_{pp} = 2.0, \kappa_{sv} = 3.0$$
$$W_{rv} = 0.2, W_{pp} = 0.2, W_{sv} = 0.6.$$

It is important to note that applications of good refactorings should lead to the reduction in the value of $C_T(A)$.

7.4 MORE EXAMPLES OF REFACTORINGS

In Section 7.2.2, we explained some examples of refactoring by applying them to class diagrams. In this section, we intuitively explain additional examples of refactorings, without code or class diagrams.

- *Substitute Algorithm:* A programmer may decide to replace an existing algorithm X in the code with a new algorithm Y for various reasons: (i) implementation of algorithm Y is clearer (i.e., it takes less time to understand) than the implementation of algorithm X; (ii) algorithm Y performs better than algorithm X; and (iii) standardization bodies have recommended to replace algorithm X with algorithm Y. Algorithm substitution can be easily applied if both the algorithms have the same input–output behaviors.

- *Replace Parameter with Method:* Consider the following code segment, where the method `bodyMassIndex` has two formal parameters.

```
int   person;
:
// person is initialized here;
:
int   bodyMass = getMass(person);
int   height   = getHeight(person);
int   BMI = bodyMassIndex(bodyMass, height);
:
```

The above code segment can be rewritten such that the new `bodyMassIndex` method accepts one formal parameter, namely, `person`, and internally computes the values of `bodyMass` and `height`. The refactored code segment has been shown in the following:

```
int   person;
:
// person is initialized here;
:
int   BMI = bodyMassIndex(person);
:
```

The advantage of this refactoring is that it reduces the number of parameters passed to methods. Such reduction is important because one can easily make errors while passing long parameter lists.

- *Push-down Method:* Assume that `Executive` and `Clerk` are two subclasses of the superclass `Employee` as shown in Figure 7.7a. Method `overTimePay` has been defined in class `Employee`. However, if the `overTimePay` method is used in the `Clerk` class, but not in the `Executive` class, then the programmer can push down the `overTimePay` method to the `Clerk` class as illustrated in Figure 7.7b.

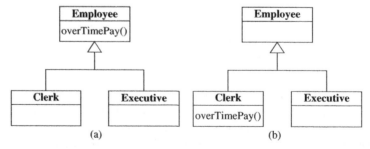

(a)   (b)

FIGURE 7.7   Illustration of the push-down method refactoring: (a) the class diagram before refactoring; (b) the class diagram after refactoring

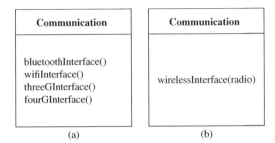

FIGURE 7.8 An example of parameterizing a method. There are four methods in (a), whereas there is one method in (b) with one parameter

- *Parameterize Methods:* Sometimes programmers may find multiple methods performing the same computations on different input data sets. Those methods can be replaced with a new method with additional formal parameters, as illustrated in Figure 7.8. In Figure 7.8a, we have the `Communication` class with four methods: `bluetoothInterface`, `wifiInterface`, `threeGInterface`, and `fourGInterface`. In Figure 7.8b, we have the `Communication` class with just one method, namely, `wirelessInterface` with one parameter, namely, `radio`. The method `wirelessInterface` can be invoked with different values of `radio` so that the `wirelessInterface` method can in turn invoke different radio interfaces.

7.5   INITIAL WORK ON SOFTWARE RESTRUCTURING

The concept of software restructuring dates back to the mid 1960s, almost as soon as programs were written in Fortran. In this section, we explain the factors that influence software structure, classification of early restructuring approaches, and some widely studied early restructuring techniques.

7.5.1   Factors Influencing Software Structure

Before we discuss restructuring approaches, it is useful to have a broad understanding of *software structure*. Software structure is a set of attributes of the software such that the programmer gets a good understanding of software. Therefore, any *factor* that can influence the state of software or the programmer's perception might influence software structure. One view of the factors that influence software structure has been shown in Figure 7.9. In the following, we explain the factors one by one.

- *Code:* Undoubtedly, the source code has the biggest influence on software structure. Code quality and style at all levels of details, namely, variables, constants, statement, level, function, and module, play key roles in understanding code.

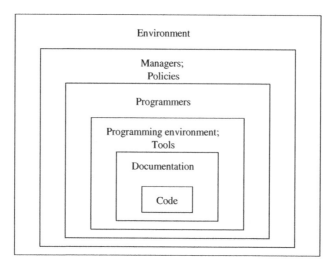

FIGURE 7.9   Factors which can influence software structure. From Reference 2. © 1989 IEEE

For example, adherence to coding standards significantly increases the readability of code. Similarly, adoption of common architectural styles enhances code understanding.

- *Documentation:* There are two kinds of documentations associated with source code: (i) in-line documentation of source code; and (ii) external documentations, namely, requirements documents, design documents, user manuals, and test cases. Often the in-line documentations determine the programmer's perception of code structure. Programmers' perception of software structure is influenced by clearly written, easily referenced, complete, accurate, and up-to-date documentations.

- *Tools—Programming environment:* Development tools can help programmers better understand source code. Tools can assist programmers trace through the source code to understand dynamic behavior, animation can help in understanding the dynamic strategy used in an algorithm, and cross-referencing of global variables reveal the interactions among modules. In addition, tools can reformat code for better readability via pretty printing, highlight keywords, and take advantage of color coding of source code. For example, comments can be displayed in one color and executable code in a different color.

- *Programmers:* Qualities of programmers influence their perception of software structure. Examples of programmer qualities are individual capabilities, education, experience, training, and aptitude. Happenings in their personal lives too can influence their perception of software structure.

- *Managers and policies:* Management can play an influencing role in having a good initial structure and sustain, or even improve, the initial structure by means of designing policies and allocating resources. Management can design general policies about means, such as adhering to standards, of achieving software qualities. Similarly, managers can influence the practice of achieving good software structures by tying the annual performance review of programmers with their adherence to those standards.

- *Environment:* This factor refers to the general working environment of programmers, including the physical facilities and availability of resources when needed.

All the factors shown in Figure 7.9 influence software structure, to varying degrees. For example, source code has more influence on restructuring than working environment of programmers. Consequently, approaches that influence any factor in Figure 7.9 can be applied to software restructuring. In the following section, we present some well-known structuring approaches found in the literature.

7.5.2 Classification of Restructuring Approaches

A broad classification of software restructuring approaches has been shown in Figure 7.10, and explained in the following.

- *Approaches not involving code changes:* There are several software restructuring approaches that do not involve making changes to the existing software. These approaches are as follows:
  - Train programmers: Programmers may be trained in structured programming and software engineering, including software architectural styles and modularization techniques.
  - Upgrade documentation: In-line comments in source code can be made more accurate and readable. Cryptic comments can be expanded to explain the rationale behind decisions, and what alternatives had been explored. Comments can be updated to reflect changes in the code. Similarly, external documentations can be updated to make them consistent with the code, accurate, and complete. Incomplete and inconsistent documentations constantly frustrate programmers.

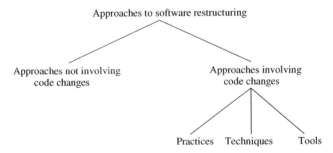

FIGURE 7.10 Broad classification of approaches to software structuring

- *Approaches involving code changes:* A large majority of the approaches involve making changes to source code in the form of writing new code, making changes to existing code, deleting code, reformatting code, and moving code chunks within and between modules. These approaches can be further divided into three major categories as follows:
  - Practices: Some examples of software restructuring practices are: (i) restructuring code with preprocessors; (ii) making code understandable by means of inspection and walkthroughs; (iii) formatting code by means of adhering to programming standards and style guidelines; and (iv) restructuring code for reusability.
  - Techniques: Some software restructuring approaches are based on defined techniques. Some examples of software restructuring techniques are: (i) incremental restructuring; (ii) goto-less approach; (iii) case-statement approach; (iv) Boolean flag approach; and (v) clustering approach.
  - Tools: Many tools have been designed for software restructuring since the late 70s. Some example tools are *Eclipse IDE* (Integrated Development Environment), *IntelliJ IDEA*, *jFactor*, *Refactorit*, and *Clone Doctor*. Some early day restructuring tools were *Refactoring Browser* for *Smalltalk*, *Moose Refactoring Engine*, *CStructure* for the *C* language, a prototype tool for *Oberon*, and Griswold's tool for *Scheme*.

7.5.3 Restructuring Techniques

In this section, we explain several restructuring techniques developed in the mid-1970s, before the time of object-oriented programming. The techniques are applied at different levels of abstractions: reorganization and rewriting of source code to eliminate goto statements, application of the concept of information hiding to C programs, wrapping of a highly unstructured system with newly written front ends and back ends, and remodularization of software with clustering.

A. Elimination-of-goto Approach   An important feature of structured programming is that it puts emphasis on the following control constructs: *for*, *while*, *until*, and *if-then-else*. It is easy to understand code with such constructs, because those constructs make occurrences of loop and branching of control clear. Before the onset of structured programming in the 70s, much source code had been written with *goto* statements. A *goto* statement is an unconditional jump statement that can be found in several high level programming languages, namely, Fortran, Cobol, and C. It is difficult to understand the control flow in programs with many *goto* statements in them. Ashcroft and Manna [16] have shown that every flowchart program with *goto* statements can be transformed into a functionally equivalent *goto*-less program by using *while* statements. They introduce new Boolean variables to keep track of information about the sequence of the computation. The resulting program has the same order of efficiency as the original program. Though it is easy to understand a flowchart program, it is implemented with *goto* statements to represent the unconditional jumps in the flowchart.

Baker [17] has given an algorithm to transform a flowgraph into a program with *repeat (do-forever)*, *if-then-else*, *break*, and *next* statements. The *break* statement causes a jump out of the enclosing *repeat* statement, whereas the *next* statement causes a jump to the next iteration of an enclosing *repeat*. The goal of this algorithm is to produce understandable programs, rather than completely eliminate the use of *goto* statements. The design of the algorithm is based on the idea of *properly nested* programs, where *repeat* statements reflect iteration in the program and *if-then-else* statements reflect branching and merging of control flow. The restructured program contains *goto* statements if no other available control construct describes the flow of control. The algorithm is central to the implementation of a tool called *STRUCT*, which translates Fortran programs into programs in *RATFOR*. *RATFOR* is an extended Fortran language that includes *while*, *if-then-else*, *break*, and *next*. The programs produced by *RATFOR* are more readable than the original Fortran programs.

B. Localization and Information Hiding Approach   *Localization* and *information hiding* are well-known software engineering principles that can be applied to design good quality software. As the name suggests, localization is the process of collecting the logically related computational resources in one physical module. Functions, procedures, operations, and data types are examples of computational resources in an imperative programming language, such as C. As a result of localizing computational resources into separate modules, programmers can restructure a program into a loosely coupled system of sufficiently independent modules. In the C and Fortran language, localization is difficult to achieve for the following reasons.

- A variable of a function may be referred by the *extern* and *include* statements and imported and exported to other program modules.
- Data sharing and relations among functions are not explicitly represented in source code.

By means of information hiding, one can suppress (i.e., hide) the details of implementations of computational resources, thereby enabling programmers to focus on high level concepts, which make it easier to understand programs. For example, a queue is a high level concept, which can be implemented by means of a variety of low level data structures, namely, singly linked list, doubly linked list, and even arrays. Therefore, a programmer can design a function by using `enqueue` and `dequeue` calls without any concern for their actual implementations. In other words, a programmer can design a program by using abstract data types without waiting for their actual implementations. In the C and Fortran languages, there are no constructs that support the principle of information hiding. Chu and Patel [18] developed a tool to localize variables and functions and support information hiding as follows.

- Localization of variables: Organize global variables and functions which refer to those global variables into package-like groups. This is achieved by applying the concept of *closure* of functions to a set of global variables. This step leads to groups of functions and the global variables referred to by those functions.

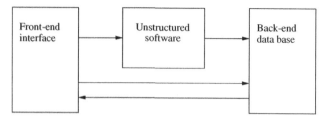

FIGURE 7.11   System sandwich approach to software restructuring. The arrows represent the flow of data and/or commands

- Localization of functions: Group locally called functions and the calling function in the same group.
- Information hiding and hierarchical structuring: Organize groups of functions into hierarchical package structures based on the visibility of functions within groups. Those functions and variables which are only externally referable and visible to other packages constitute the package specification, whereas the functions and variables in a package body are hidden from other packages and only visible to functions in the same package.

The restructuring steps explained above offer a framework for translating a program in imperative languages, such as C and Fortran, into other languages that support modularity and hierarchical structure.

C. System Sandwich Approach   For badly structured programs that need to be retained for their output and which cannot be restructured with any hope, a sandwich approach can be applied, as illustrated in Figure 7.11. The idea is to write a new front-end interface and a new back-end data base so that it is easy to interface with the program and the program's outputs are recorded in a more structured way. The front-end and the back-end communicate for report generation purpose. The old system is used just for producing outputs.

D. Clustering Approach   Software modularization is an important design step in which a larger system is partitioned into smaller-sized cohesive chunks, called modules. During maintenance, a program can be remodularized in two broad ways as follows:

- System level remodularization: A program is remodularized at the system level by partitioning the program into smaller modules. This is a top-down approach to remodularize a program. The concept of system level remodularization has been illustrated in Figure 7.12.
- Entity level remodularization: At this level, a program is remodularized by grouping the entities to form larger modules. This is a bottom-up approach to remodularizing a program. The concept of entity level remodularization has been illustrated in Figure 7.13.

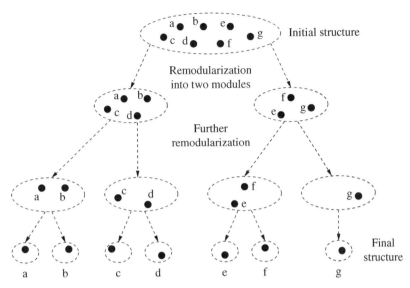

FIGURE 7.12 Illustration of system level remodularization. Bullets represent low level entities. Dotted shapes represent modules. Arrows represent progression from one level to the next

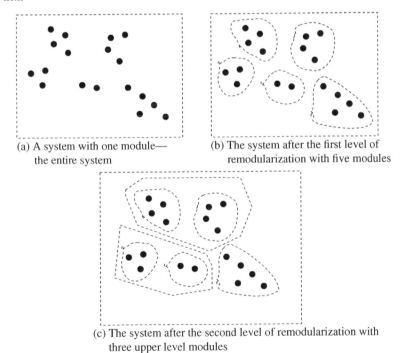

(a) A system with one module—
the entire system

(b) The system after the first level of
remodularization with five modules

(c) The system after the second level of remodularization with
three upper level modules

FIGURE 7.13 Illustration of entity level remodularization. Bullets represent low level entities. Dotted shapes represent modules

The concept of *clustering* plays a key role in modularization. Modularization is defined as the clustering of large amounts of entities in groups in such a way that the entities in one group are more closely related, based on some *similarity* metrics, than entities in different groups. Such groups are called clusters. A broad definition of clusters can be found in [19]: Clusters are defined as continuous regions of space containing a relatively high density of points, separated from other such regions by regions containing a relatively low density of points. Such a broad definition can be easily applied to software systems, as illustrated in the VRML diagram of Figure 7.6.

While applying the idea of clustering to a set of entities, two basic questions need to be answered.

- *Similarity metrics:* Clustering algorithms group similar entities together. There-fore, there is a need for a metric to capture the idea of similarity. For example, in a software system, entity a is more similar to b than to c. A similarity metric always yields a value between 0 and 1, where 1 means highly similar. A number of metrics to measure similarity are found in the literature: *distance measure, association coefficients, correlation coefficients*, and *probabilistic measures* [20]. In the following, we explain the first two measures.

  - Distance measure: The most common distance measures are the squared Euclidean distance and the Manhattan distance.

  - Association coefficients: This measure is also known as the *simple matching coefficient*. The association coefficient for two entities x and y are expressed in terms of the number of features which are present for both the entities. Let a be the number of features present for both x and y, b be the number of features present for x but not for y, c be the number of features present for y but not x, and d be the features *not* present for both x and y. The *simple matching coefficient* is defined as $simple(x, y) = (a + d)/(a + b + c + d)$. The *Jaccard coefficient* is defined as $Jaccard(x, y) = a/(a + b + c)$.

- *Selection of clustering algorithms:* Clustering algorithms have been developed in diverse application areas, namely, image processing, pattern recognition, biology, software testing, information retrieval, graph theory, and information architecture. The techniques used in those algorithms can broadly be grouped into the following four categories.

  - Graph theoretical algorithms: These algorithms work on graph representa-tions of systems to be clustered. The nodes of those graphs represent entities, and edges represent relationships between nodes. The graph algorithms try to find subgraphs where each subgraph is a cluster. Many graph theoretical clustering algorithms use the concepts of minimum-spanning trees, graph reduction, aggregate node, and k-components.

  - Construction algorithms: Clustering algorithms in this group assign the enti-ties to clusters in one pass. The resulting clusters are either predetermined or identified by the algorithms. Many algorithms in this category use the follow-ing common techniques: *geographic technique* and *density search technique*. In the algorithms which are based on geographic techniques, entities are represented on a two-dimensional plane; the algorithm divides the plane into two halves; and the entities lying on the same side of the dividing line are said to belong to the same cluster. The algorithms based on density search work as follows: (i) find regions containing a relatively high density of entities; each of those regions is a member of the set of initial clusters; (ii) merge clusters to find lager clusters; members of clusters may be moved to neighboring clusters while merging them.

- Optimization algorithms: Optimization algorithms are also called improvement algorithms or iterative algorithms. The basic structure of those algorithms has been illustrated in the following:

```
1. Find an initial partition of k clusters.

2. REPEAT
      Determine the seed point of each cluster.
      Move each entity to the cluster with the seed point
      having the highest level of similarity with the entity.
   UNTIL no entities can be moved from one cluster to another.
```

The *centroid* of a cluster is taken as the cluster's seed point. The centroid of a cluster is interpreted to be the "average" of the cluster. Selection of the initial set of k clusters can have an impact on the final clustering.

- Hierarchical algorithms: Hierarchical algorithms build a hierarchy of clustering. There are two broad kinds of hierarchical algorithms: *agglomerative algorithms* and *divisive algorithms*. The working of an agglomerative algorithm has been illustrated in Figure 7.13, whereas Figure 7.12 illustrates the working of a divisive algorithm. The clustering of a hierarchical algorithm can be visualized in a *dendogram*. The dendogram representation of the hierarchy in Figure 7.12 has been shown in Figure 7.14.

The general structure of an agglomerative algorithm is as follows:

```
1.  IF there are N entities, begin with N clusters such that
    each cluster contains a unique entity.
    Compute the similarities between the clusters.

2.  WHILE there is more than a cluster
    DO
       Find the most similar pair of clusters and merge them
       into a single cluster.
       Recompute the similarities between the clusters.
    END
```

Divisive clustering algorithms work in a top-down manner as follows. (i) in the beginning, all the N entities belong to one cluster; and (ii) in each step, a cluster is partitioned into two clusters. Finally, after N steps, there are N clusters with one entity in each cluster.

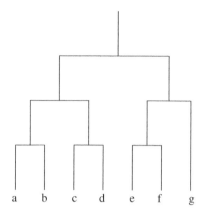

FIGURE 7.14 Dendogram representation of Figure 7.12

E. Program Slicing Approach The concept of program slicing, including forward program slicing and backward program slicing, has been explained in Chapter 4. Informally, the set of statements that can affect the value of a variable at some point of interest in a program is called a backward program slice. Similarly, the set of statements that are likely to be affected by the value of a variable at some point of interest in a program is called a forward program slice. The key idea in program slicing is to identify and extract a cohesive subset of statements from a program. Therefore, if a module supports multiple functionalities, a portion of the code can be extracted to form a new module. For example, let us consider a module A supporting functionalities $\{f_1, f_2, f_3, f_4\}$. If subsets $A' = \{f_1, f_2\}$ and $A'' = \{f_3, f_4\}$ are more cohesive, while the degree of cohesion between members of the two subsets is weak, then module A can be split up into two modules A' and A'' by applying the idea of program slicing [21].

In addition, large functions can be decomposed into smaller functions by means of program slicing to restructure programs [22] and reuse code segments [23]. The idea of program slicing can be applied to object-oriented programs as well [24].

7.6 SUMMARY

Software refactoring and restructuring are topics of continued research for more than three decades. Several books have been written on the topic of software refactoring. Therefore, this chapter opened with an introduction to the idea of software refactoring and restructuring. We explained the negative impacts of software straying away from its original design: decreased understandability, decreased reliability, and increased maintenance cost. Therefore, a higher level goal of software refactoring is to increase the external software value and internal software value. In the second section, we explained the activities in a refactoring process: identifying what to refactor, determine which refactorings to apply, ensure that refactorings preserve the behavior of the software, apply the refactorings to the chosen entities, evaluate the impacts of the refactorings, and maintain consistency. We explained the concept of code smell by means of many examples, and showed what many refactorings look like. The ideas of critical pair analysis and sequential dependency analysis were explained toward finding a feasible subset of refactorings from a given set. In order to ensure that refactoring preserves the program's behavior, we explained two pragmatic ways: testing and verification of preservation of call sequence. We argued that preservation of input–output behavior of programs is not enough, and identified three other important behaviors that must be preserved: temporal constraints, resource constraints, and safety constraints. Applications of a few common refactorings were explained with class diagrams.

In the third section, we explained formalisms and techniques for refactoring: assertions, graph transformation, and software metrics. We explained two kinds of software metrics: cohesion and three kinds of coupling. The three kinds of coupling are: return value coupling, parameter coupling, and shared variable coupling. In the fourth section, we gave more examples of refactorings.

In the fifth section, we discussed the initial work on software restructuring: factors influencing software structure, classification of restructuring approaches, and restructuring techniques. The factors affecting software structures are code, documentation, tools, programmers, managers and policies, and environment. The two broad categories of approaches to restructuring are approaches not involving code changes and approaches involving code changes. The restructuring techniques that we explained are elimination-of-goto, system sandwich, localization and information hiding, and clustering approaches.

LITERATURE REVIEW

Many researchers have contributed to various facets of software restructuring and software refactoring for more than three decades, with hundreds of research publications and numerous tools. In addition, excellent books have been written and edited on the topic.

The main research results in software restructuring until the mid 1980s have been succinctly compiled in the form of an edited book by Arnold [25]: *Tutorial on Software Restructuring*. The book has been organized into eight parts. After a very good introduction in Part I, perspectives on software structure are provided in five research articles in Part II. In Part III, origins and effects of poor software structure are discussed in five articles. Strategies and tools for recognizing software structure are discussed in Part IV. Code level approaches and system level approaches to infusing software with structure are discussed in Part V and Part VI, respectively. Finally, restructuring criteria and rule-based restructuring are presented in Parts VII and VIII, respectively.

Seventy-two refactorings have been explained with class diagrams and code by Fowler in his book *Refactoring: Improving the Design of Existing Code* [26]. In the chapter *Refactoring Tools* by Roberts and Brant, they explain the technical criteria and the practical criteria for a refactoring tool. The technical criteria are as follows.

- Program database: For a tool to be useful, it is important that search and meaningful operations (e.g., substitution) on program entities can be performed, without the need for program testing.
- Parse trees: Parse trees are an important representation of programs, because a large number of refactorings operate at the method level and below.
- Accuracy: Accuracy means to what extent the program behavior has been preserved by the refactorings.

On the other hand, the practical criteria are as follows.

- Speed: It may be noted that tools in software development are created to support programmers. If tools do not fit the way programmers carry out their tasks, then tools will not be adopted. Therefore, speed of refactoring is important to programmers. If some refactorings take too long to achieve accuracy, then tool designers may not support those refactorings.
- Undo: An undo operation comes very handy in exploring the consequences of refactorings. If a programmer does not like the results of refactorings, an undo operation allows him to revert to the original program, without having to explicitly keep a copy of the program.
- Integration with tools: For refactoring tools to be widely used, it is important that such tools are made a part of integrated development environments (IDE).

In the book entitled *Refactoring, Reuse, and Reality* [26], the author has identified some reasons why programmers did not refactor their code.

- Since the benefits of refactorings are long term, a programmer may not be motivated to do it now.
- Since refactoring is an overhead, it does not contribute to day-to-day productivity.
- There is no guarantee that implementations of some refactorings do not introduce faults.

The chapter also discussed how to reduce the overhead of refactoring and the idea of refactoring safely. Intuitively, safe refactoring means refactoring a program without introducing faults into the program.

Ping and Kontogiannis [27] have proposed an approach to refactor web sites to the controller-centric architecture. Their approach is twofold: (i) a domain model is defined to represent dependencies among web pages in order to understand the structure of the current web site; and (ii) a system architecture is designed as a reference model for restructuring the existing web site into a controller-centric architecture based on the well-known concept of odel view controller (MVC). A link between two web pages is said to exist if one page contains a link to the other. For dependency analysis, links are grouped into two broad categories: reference link and conditional link. They consider four kinds of reference links as follows.

- Inner link: This means a web page has a link to itself.
- Handover link: This means that a link leads to a different page.
- Include link: This means that the target page is included in the source page when the link is activated.
- Invocation link: This represents a communication link between a source page and a target page.

The book *Refactoring HTML: Improving the Design of Existing Web Applications* by Harold [28] is solely about refactorings of HTML code. The book has a full chapter about smells of bad HTML code. Some example smells are:

- Illegible code: This code is difficult to understand.
- Slow page rendering: Though communication networks, databases, and servers can contribute to delay in page display, there is said to be a problem if page rendering from a locally saved file takes a long time.
- Pages look significantly different in different browsers: A problem is said to be present if the pages are illegible when browsed with common browsers, namely, Internet Explorer and Firefox.

Next, the book explains six broad categories of refactorings for HTML code as follows.

- Well-Formedness: Add End-Tag is an example of this category of refactorings.
- Validity: Remove All Non-Existent Tags is an example of the validity category.
- Layout: Add an ID Attribute is an example of layout refactorings.
- Accessibility: Introduce Skip Navigation is an example of accessibility.
- Web Applications: Prevent Caching is an example of web application refactorings.
- Content: Correct Spelling is an example of content refactorings.

In their book *Refactoring in Large Software Projects* [29], Lippert and Roock explain architecture smells, best practices for large refactorings, refactoring relational databases, refactoring application program interfaces (API), and tool-based detection and avoidance of architecture smells. Intuitively, large refactorings possess the following characteristics.

- Long time: Here, days and weeks mean long time.
- Significant change: This means changes to the more significant concepts, namely, software architecture, databases, and APIs.
- Large team: Almost all the people currently involved with the development and/or maintenance of the software are involved.

An excellent survey of software refactoring can be found in the article by Mens and Tourwe [30]. By means of a running example, they explain all the refactoring activities found in Section 7.2. Additional discussions of refactoring techniques and formalisms and types of software artifacts can be found in the article. Finally, the article presents insightful discussions of tool support for automation of refactoring activities. The desirable features of a tool for refactoring are reliability, configurability, coverage, scalability, and language independence.

REFERENCES

[1] W. F. Opdyke. 1992. Refactoring: A program restructuring aid in designing object-oriented application framework. PhD thesis, University of Illinois at Urbana-Champaign.

[2] R. S. Arnold. 1989. Software restructuring. *Proceedings of the IEEE*, 77(4), 607–616.

[3] S. Ducasse, M. Rieger, and S. Demeyer. 1999. *A Language Independent Approach for Detecting Duplicated Code*. Proceedings of the International Conference on Software Maintenance, 1999, IEEE Computer Society Press, Los Alamitos, CA, pp. 109–118.

[4] J. H. Jahnke and A. Zundorf. 1997. *Rewriting Poor Design Patterns by Good Design Patterns*. Proceedings of the ESE/FSE Workshop on Object-Oriented Reengineering, 1997, ACM, New York.

[5] J. Philipps and B. Rumpe. *Refinement of Information Flow Architecture*. Proceedings of the International Conference on Formal Engineering Methods, 1997, IEEE Computer Society Press, Los Alamitos, CA.

[6] T. Mens, G. Taentzer, and O. Runge, 2007. Analyzing refactoring dependencies using graph transformation. *Software and Systems Modeling*, 63, 269–285.

[7] F. Tip, A. Kiezun, and D. Baumer. 2003. *Refactoring for Generalization Using Type Constraints*. Proceedings of SIGPLAN Conference on Object-Oriented Programming, 2003, Systems, Languages, and Applications, ACM, New York, pp. 13–26.

[8] Y. Kataoka, M. D. Ernst, W. G. Griswold, and D. Notkin. 2001. *Automated Support for Program Refactoring using Invariants*. Proceedings of the International Conference on Software Maintenance, 2001, IEEE Computer Society Press, Los Alamitos, CA, pp. 736–743.

[9] L. Tahvildari and K. Kontogiannis. 2002. *A methodology for Developing Transformations Using the Maintainability Soft-goal Graph*. Proceedings of Working Conference on Reverse Engineering, 2002, IEEE Computer Society Press, Los Alamitos, CA, pp. 77–86.

[10] L. K. Chung, B. A. Nixon, E. Yu, and J. Mylopoulos. 2000. *Non-Functional Requirements in Software Engineering*. Kluwer Publishing.

[11] L. Tahvildari and K. Kontogiannis. 2002. *A Software Transformation Framework for Quality-driven Object-oriented Re-engineering*. Proceedings of the International Conference on Software Maintenance, 2002, IEEE Computer Society Press, Los Alamitos, CA, pp. 596–605.

[12] J. Banerjee, H. Kim W. Kim, and H. F. Korth. 1987. *Semantics and Implementation of Schema Evolution in Object-oriented Databases*. Proceedings of the ACM SIGMOD Conference, 1987, ACM, New York, pp. 311–322.

[13] B. Hoffmann, D. Janssens, and N. V. Eetvelde. 2006. Cloning and expanding graph transformation rules for refactoring. *Electronic Notes in Theoretical Computer Science*, 152, 53–67.

[14] F. Simon, F. Steinbruckner, and C. Lewerentz. 2001. *Metrics Based Refactoring*. Proceedings of the European Conference on Software Maintenance and Reengineering, 2001, IEEE Computer Society Press, Los Alamitos, CA, pp. 30–38.

[15] Y. Kataoka, T. Imai, H. Andou, and T. Fukaya. 2002. *A Quantitative Evaluation of Maintainability Enhancement by Refactoring*. Proceedings of the International Conference on Software Maintenance, 2002, IEEE Computer Society Press, Los Alamitos, CA, pp. 576–585.

[16] E. Ashcroft and Z. Manna. 1971. *The Translation of 'goto' Programs to 'while' Programs*. Proceedings of the 1971 IFIP Congress, 1971, pp. 250–260.

[17] B. S. Baker. 1977. An algorithm for structuring flowgraphs. *Journal of the ACM*, 24(1), 98–120.

[18] W. C. Chu and S. Patel. 1992. *Software Restructuring by Enforcing Localization and Information Hiding*. Proceedings of the Conference on Software Maintenance, 1992, IEEE Computer Society Press, Los Alamitos, CA, pp. 165–172.

[19] B. Everitt. 1974. *Cluster Analysis*. Heineman Educational Books, London.

[20] T. A. Wiggerts. 1997. *Using Clustering Algorithms in Legacy Systems Remodularization*. Proceedings of the Working Conference on Reverse Engineering, 1997, IEEE Computer Society Press, Los Alamitos, CA, pp. 33–43.

[21] H. S. Kim, Y. R. Kwon, and I. S. Chung. 1994. Restructuring programs through program slicing. *International Journal of Software Engineering and Knowledge Engineering*, 4(3), 349–368.

[22] A. Lakhotia and J.-C. Deprez. 1998. Restructuring programs by tucking statements into functions. *Information and Software Technology*, 40, 677–689.

[23] F. Lanubile and G. Ducasse. 1997. Extracting reusable functions by flow graph-based program slicing. *IEEE Transactions on Software Engineering*, 23(4), 246–258.

[24] L. Larsen and M. J. Harrold. 1996. *Slicing Object-oriented Software*. Proceedings of the International Conference on Software Engineering, 1996, IEEE Computer Society Press, Los Alamitos, CA, pp. 495–505.

[25] R. S. Arnold. 1986. *Tutorial on Software Restructuring*. IEEE Computer Society Press, Los Alamitos, CA.

[26] M. Fowler. 1999. *Refactoring: Improving the Design of Existing Programs*. Addison-Wesley.

[27] Y. Ping and K. Kontogiannis. 2004. *Refactoring Web Sites to the Controller-centric Architecture*. Proceedings of the 8th European Conference on Software Maintenance and Reengineering, 2004, IEEE Computer Society Press, Los Alamitos, CA, pp. 204–213.

[28] E. R. Harold. 2008. *Refactoring HTML: Improving the Design of Existing Web Applications*. Addison Wesley.

[29] M. Lippert and S. Roock. 2006. *Refactoring in Large Software Projects: Performing Complex Restructurings Successfully*. John Wiley.

[30] T. Mens and T. Tourwe. 2004. A survey of software refactoring. *IEEE Transactions on Software Engineering*, 30(2), 126–139.

EXERCISES

1. Briefly explain the need for restructuring software.
2. List the key activities in a software refactoring process.
3. How do programmers identify what to refactor?
4. How do you identify what refactorings to apply?
5. How do you select a feasible subset from a given set of refactorings?
6. Briefly explain the concept of preserving the software's behavior while refactoring.
7. Identify four key formalisms and techniques for refactoring.
8. Briefly explain the concept of assertions by means of examples.

8

PROGRAM COMPREHENSION

The most incomprehensible thing about the world is that it is comprehensible.

— Albert Einstein

8.1 GENERAL IDEA

It is important to comprehend the details of any complex artifact to be able to maintain it, because maintenance requires modifications to portions of the systems—and maintaining a software system is no different. Inaccurate and incomplete understanding of a software system before performing a modification on it is likely to severely degrade its performance and reliability. Therefore, good program comprehension plays an important role in providing effective software maintenance and enabling successful evolution of software systems. In order to get a handle on the role of program comprehension, we look at the five types of tasks commonly associated with software maintenance and evolution and the types of activities involving those tasks. As listed in Table 8.1, the five kinds of maintenance and evolution tasks are *adaptive*, *perfective*, and *corrective* maintenance; *reuse*; and *code leverage*. The detailed activities associated with each of the five tasks have been listed in the second column of Table 8.1. Table 8.1 indicates that understanding the system or problem is common to all maintenance and evolution tasks. It may be noted that understanding of a system is a cognitive issue, and to study the cognitive processes behind the tasks in Table 8.1, a number of cognition models have been developed, as listed in Table 8.2.

Software Evolution and Maintenance: A Practitioner's Approach, First Edition.
Priyadarshi Tripathy and Kshirasagar Naik.
© 2015 John Wiley & Sons, Inc. Published 2015 by John Wiley & Sons, Inc.

TABLE 8.1   Tasks and Activities Requiring Code Understanding

Maintenance Tasks	Activities
Adaptive	Understand system
	Define adaptation requirements
	Develop preliminary and detailed adaptation design
	Code changes
	Debug
	Regression tests
Perfective	Understand system
	Diagnosis and requirements definition for improvements
	Develop preliminary and detailed perfective design
	Code changes/additions
	Debug
	Regression tests
Corrective	Understand system
	Generate/evaluate hypotheses concerning problem
	Repair code
	Regression tests
Reuse	Understand problem
	Find solution based on close fit with reusable components
	Locate components
	Integrate components
Code leverage	Understand problem
	Find solution based on predefined components
	Reconfigure solution to increase likelihood of using predefined components
	Obtain and modify predefined components
	Integrate modified components

Source: From Reference 1. © 1995 IEEE.

TABLE 8.2   Code Cognition Models

Model	Maintenance Activity	Authors
Control flow	Understand	Pennington
Functional	Understand	Pennington
Top-down	Understand	Soloway, Adelson, and Ehrlich
Integrated	Understand, Corrective, Adaptive, and Perfective	Von Mayrhauser and Vans
Other	Enhancement	Letovsky
	Understand	Brooks
		Shneiderman and Mayer

Source: From Reference 1. © 1995 IEEE.

8.2   BASIC TERMS

Some researchers use the term *maintainer* to refer to the person who is maintaining a software system. They want to differentiate a maintainer from a programmer. In order to understand the cognition models of Table 8.2, we discuss the following set of terms in the following subsections:

- Goal of code cognition
- Knowledge
- Mental model

8.2.1   Goal of Code Cognition

A maintainer sets out to understand a program with a specific goal in her mind. An example of specific goal is debugging the program to detect a fault, that is, the cause of a known failure. Another example is adding a new function to the existing system. Identifying the goals can help in defining the scope of program comprehension, where scope refers to complete or partial understanding of code.

A program comprehension process is a sequence of activities that use existing knowledge about a system to acquire new knowledge that ultimately meets the goals of a code comprehension task. In other words, program comprehension is a process of knowledge acquisition about the program. The different kinds of knowledge associated with program comprehension are explained below.

8.2.2   Knowledge

As software specialists, programmers possess two kinds of knowledge:

- General knowledge: This covers a broad range of topics in computer systems and software development. A non-exhaustive list of topics is: algorithms and data structures, operating systems, programming principles, programming languages, programming environment, software architectures and design techniques, testing and debugging techniques, different solution approaches, and computer networks. More general knowledge enable a programmer to gain more software-specific knowledge.
- Software-specific knowledge: This represents an understanding of the details of the software to be comprehended. The details of a software system include the application domain, the problem being solved by the software, and the solution strategy adopted in the software system.

While gaining software-specific knowledge during the process of program comprehension, programmers may find the need to have more general knowledge about computer systems and, therefore, acquire the relevant general knowledge by referring to other sources. For example, in order to comprehend the performance aspect of a wireless Internet-based application, a programmer may want to know some details of the medium access control (MAC) protocols for wireless local area networks

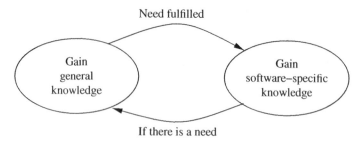

FIGURE 8.1   Gaining general knowledge and software-specific knowledge

(WLAN). The general knowledge may involve the concept of maximum data packet size, for example. The programmer may also want to learn how the transmission control protocol's (TCP) congestion control mechanism affects data delivery performance. Therefore, there is a need for a programmer to go back and forth between acquiring general knowledge and software-specific knowledge, as illustrated in Figure 8.1. Some examples of software-specific knowledge are as follows:

- The software system implements public-key cryptography for data encryption.
- The software system has been structured as a three-tier client–server architecture.
- Module x implements a location server.
- A certain *for* loop in method y may execute for a random number of times.
- Variable *mcount* keeps track of the number of times module z is invoked.

In the process of gaining new knowledge about a software system, a programmer essentially learns the details concerning the following aspects:

- Functionality: This includes an understanding of the functional and non-functional requirements of the software system.
- Software architecture: Knowledge about a system's software architecture leads to further inquisitions about the system. For example, if a programmer knows that the system has been designed with a three-tier client/server architecture, then he will try to know more about distribution of functionalities, assignment of resources to services, and so on.
- Control flow and data flow: Understanding the control flow in a system helps comprehend the execution sequences of the modules. The programmer gets to know the sequences in which data are accessed and updated.
- Exception handling: The programmer needs to know what actions the software system takes in response to exceptions, such as timeout, unavailability of run-time resources, and execution errors, to name a few.
- Stable storage: This refers to the means for storing intermediate results in non-volatile memory so that program execution can be resumed at a point where failure occurred.

- Implementation details: The programmer may want to know what algorithms have been chosen and how those have been implemented. Moreover, the programmer may want to know the functionality and data scope of objects and their implementation details.

8.2.3 Mental Model

The concept of *mental model* [2] is frequently used in the discussion of program comprehension. A mental model describes a programmer's mental representation of the program to be comprehended. Consequently, a mental model of a program is not unique. Rather, different programmers may have different mental models depending upon their own knowledge and interpretation about the same program. A programmer develops a mental model of a software by identifying both *static* and *dynamic* elements of the software system. For example, a *for* loop is an element of a program. A system call to open a TCP connection is a program element. Similarly, the overall control flow is a program element. A programmer must have a good understanding of the individual program elements as well as how some of them interact.

*A. **Static Elements of the Mental Model***   The static elements of a program are as follows:

- Text-structures
- Chunks
- Schemas
- Plans
- Hypotheses

Text-structure: Code text and its structure are known as text-structure. Text-structure knowledge is useful in gaining control flow knowledge for program understanding. A programmer can easily identify the following kinds of text-structures: (i) *loop* constructs, namely, *for*, *while*, and *until*; (ii) *sequences*; (iii) *conditional* constructs, namely, *if-then-else*; (iv) *variable* definitions and initializations; (v) *calling* hierarchies within and among modules; and (vi) definitions of module parameters. A programmer can examine text-structure at the statement level and for their dependencies. Understanding text-structure is the beginning of program comprehension.

Chunk: The concept of program chunks enables programmers to create higher level abstractions from lower level abstractions. A program chunk is a block of related code segments. For example, a code block initializing a module's parameters is a useful chunk that tells the programmer about the nature of the parameters and their value ranges. A *for* loop is another example of code chunk, whose understanding will create an abstraction of the loop as an internal functional step performed by the program.

Schema: Research on text comprehension has produced an important concept called *schema.* Schemas are *generic knowledge structures* that guide the comprehender's interpretations, inferences, expectations, and attention when passages are comprehended [3]. The concept of programming plans, to be explained in this chapter, corresponds to the above notion of schemas [4].

Plans: Plans are broad kinds of *knowledge elements* used by programmers in order to comprehend programs. A knowledge element is anything that is useful in understanding a program. For example, if the name of a function gives an indication of the activity performed by the function, then the function identifier is a knowledge element. A second example of knowledge element is a block of comments describing a for() loop. In addition, a for() loop itself is a knowledge element, because a programmer can read the chunk of code representing the loop and get a good idea about what the code does. A third example of knowledge element is the description of the problem domain of the program. Plans easily attract the attention of programmers while they are reading a program and its documentations. A doublylinked list and a heap data structure are examples of plans. The designer has planned to implement certain concepts with those data structures. A plan is a kind of schema with two parts: *slot type* and *slot filler.* Slot types describe generic objects, whereas slot fillers are customized to hold elements of particular types. For example, a tree data structure is a generic slot type, whereas a code segment, such as a for() loop's code, is an example of a slot filler. The programmer links the slot-type and slot-filler structures by means of the widely used modeling relationships, namely, *kind-of* and *is-a.*

There are two broad kinds of plans as follows:

- *Domain plans:* These include knowledge about the real-world problem, including its environment, that the software system is solving. For example, if a software system is for numerical analysis application, plans to develop a software package will include schemas for different aspects of linear algebra, such as matrix multiplication and matrix inversion. As another example, if a software system is for voice-over-IP (Internet Protocol) applications, plans to develop the package will include schemas for locating destinations and setting up a call. Domain plans help programmers understand the code. For example, without a basic understanding of how destination users are located before setting up a call, code comprehension will not be accurate.

- *Programming plans:* Programming plans are *program fragments* representing action sequences that programmers repeatedly apply while coding. A repeated action sequence is also known as a stereotypic action sequence. A programmer may design a for() loop to search an item in a data set and repeatedly use the loop in many places in the program. Such a for() loop is an example of a programming plan to implement the system. Programming plans differ in their granularities to support low level or high level tasks.

Hypotheses: As programmers read code and the related documents, they start developing an understanding of the program to varying degrees. The qualities of their understanding can be characterized in terms of depth, breadth, and degree of accuracy.

Programmers can test the results of their understanding as *conjectures*, which are also called *hypotheses* by Letovsky [5]. The three kinds of conjectures are as follows:

- **Why:** *Why* conjectures hypothesize the *purpose* of a program element. A program element can be a function, a procedure, a design choice, or even a conditional statement at the lowest level of code. Verification of a *why* conjecture allows the programmer to have a good understanding of the purpose of the program element.
- **How:** *How* conjectures hypothesize the *method* for realizing a program goal. Given a program goal, say, as a deliverable functionality, the programmer needs to understand how that goal has been accomplished in the program.
- **What:** *What* conjectures enable programmers to classify program elements. For example, when a programmer finds an identifier, she should be able to classify it according to known, high level types, such as, constants, variables, and functions. Further classification of identifiers can be done in terms of their functions. For example, a variable called *TCPcon1* may hold a TCP connection identifier, and another variable called *RetransTimer* may hold a timer for packet retransmission.

A conjecture may not be completely correct because of the incomplete understanding of code by the programmer. Therefore, it is useful to talk about the degree of certainty of conjectures. At the beginning of the comprehension process, a programmer might make uncertain guesses, whereas she may be able to make almost certain conclusions after having a good comprehension of the program. Hypotheses are a way for a programmer to understand code in an incremental manner. After some understanding of the code, the programmer forms a hypothesis and verifies it by reading code. Verification of a hypothesis results in either accepting the hypothesis or rejecting it. By continuously formulating new hypotheses and verifying them, the programmer understands more and more code and in increasing details.

B. Dynamic Elements of the Mental Model   The dynamic elements of a program are as follows:

- Chunking
- Cross-referencing
- Strategies

Chunking: Recall that lowest level chunks are code fragments representing low level functionalities. In order to understand a program in terms of its higher level functionalities, a programmer creates higher level abstraction structures by combining lower level chunks. This process of creating higher level chunks is called chunking. Note that chunking is not a one-step process. Rather, the concept of chunking can be repeatedly applied to create increasingly higher levels of abstractions. When a block of code is recognized, it is replaced by the programmer with a *label* representing the functionality of the code block. Similarly, a block of lower level labels can be replaced with one higher level label representing a higher level functionality.

Cross-referencing: Cross-referencing means being able to link elements of different abstraction levels. This helps in building a mental model of the program under study. For example, control flow and data flow can be program elements at a lower level, whereas functionalities are higher level program elements—and there is a need for being able to make links between control flow and data flow elements and program functionalities.

Strategies: Intuitively, a strategy is a planned sequence of actions to reach a specific goal. A strategy is formulated by identifying actions to achieve a goal. For example, if the goal is to understand the code representing a function, one can define a strategy as follows. Understand the overall computational functionality of the function, that is, what the function is expected to compute, by reading its specification, if it exists; understand all the input parameters to the function; read all code line-by-line; identify chunks of related code; and create a higher level model of the function in terms of the chunks. Creating a higher level model from lower level models requires cross-referencing, as explained before. In other words, strategies guide the two dynamic elements, namely, chunking and cross-referencing, to produce higher level abstraction structures.

8.2.4   Understanding Code

The two key factors influencing code understanding are: (i) acquiring knowledge from code; and (ii) the level of expertise of the code reader. Code is a rich source of information to understand it, while the level of expertise determines how quickly the code is understood. Experienced programmers can manipulate the information available in code more easily and quickly than novice programmers to construct more accurate mental models. These two factors are explained in detail in the following.

A. Acquiring Knowledge from Code   Several concepts can be applied while reading code in order to gain a high level understanding of programs. In the absence of those concepts, code comprehension can be a difficult task. In what follows, we explain those concepts.

- *Beacons:* A beacon is code text that gives us a cue to the computation being performed in a code block. For example, meaningful procedure names, such as swap(), sort(), select(), startTimer(), and openTCPconnection give us a high level understanding of code blocks. Code with good quality beacons are easier to understand. By good quality beacons we mean whether or not the beacons precisely reflect the code functionalities. For example the beacon *sendTCPpackets* is more useful than the beacon *sendpackets*, because the former indicates that data packets are sent over a TCP connection.

- *Rules of programming discourse:* Rules of programming discourse specify the conventions, also called "rules," that programmers follow while writing code.

The rules are increasingly followed as programmers become more experienced. Some examples of those rules are the following:

– *Function name:* The function name agrees with what the function does. For example, function names `sort()`, `delete()`, `startTimer()`, and `openTCPconnection()` are clearly understood, and those functions should perform tasks implied by their names. Moreover, a function should return the kind of arguments implied by its name. For example, `sort()` should return a sorted data structure, `delete()` should return OK status, `startTimer()` should return a timer object, and `openTCPconnection()` should return an opened TCP connection identifier.

– *Variable name:* Choose meaningful names for variables and constants. By looking at the name of a variable, one should be reasonably clear about the purpose of the variable. For example, the variable `count` indicates that the programmer is counting something. Similarly, the integer constant `MAX_USERS` gives an indication that the maximum number of users supported by the system is given by the constant `MAX_USERS`.

Essentially, the rules set up expectations in the minds of a reader about what should be in the program. In addition, it is assumed that programs are composed from programming plans governed by rules of programming discourse. Otherwise, a correct program from the viewpoint of solving the problem can be difficult for a programmer to write and difficult for a reader to comprehend.

B. Levels of Expertise of Code Readers   Programmer experience and domain knowledge have a positive impact on code comprehension. Expert programmers tend to possess the following characteristics [6, 7]:

- *Organization of knowledge by functional characteristics:* A novice programmer is likely to organize program knowledge in terms of the program syntax, whereas experts organize knowledge in terms of algorithms and program functionalities. Consequently, the constructs used by experts are succinct and more informative than the program syntax used by novice programmers. In other words, expert programmers create a complementing view of the program, rather than what is plainly seen as a result of using program syntax.

- *Comprehension with flexibility:* Experts tend to generate a breadth-first view of the program, and keep adding useful details as more information is available during the understanding process. This is due to their better understanding of the program and their ability to more quickly discard invalid hypotheses and assumptions than novice programmers.

- *Development of specialized design schemas:* A schema is a higher order knowledge structure for describing program behavior in a specific domain of activity [8]. The knowledge structure specifies principal elements in a domain and includes mechanisms which facilitate the comprehension and generation processes. It is used to organize complex entities or concepts into constituents. An example of a specialized design schema is the *divide-and-conquer* schema

[7]. Using the divide-and-conquer schema, a programmer can divide a system into subsystems, and a problem into subproblems. Design schemas can vary in complexity and granularity, and, even some schemas can be simple rules: if the caller and the callee are independent processes, let them communicate by passing messages.

8.3 COGNITION MODELS FOR PROGRAM UNDERSTANDING

Research literature on software engineering is replete with cognition models. In this section, we explain the commonly referenced models one-by-one:

- Letovsky model
- Shneiderman and Mayer model
- Brooks model
- Soloway, Adelson, and Ehrlich model (top-down model)
- Pennington model (bottom-up model)
- Integrated metamodel

8.3.1 Letovsky Model

Letovsky's program comprehension model has been shown in Figure 8.2 [5]. The model consists of five main components: a knowledge base, a mental model, an assimilation process, some external representations about the software system, and, possibly, a dangling purpose unit. In the following we explain the above five components one by one.

1. **Knowledge base:** A programmer needs to assimilate a large body of knowledge to create a mental model of the software system under consideration. A

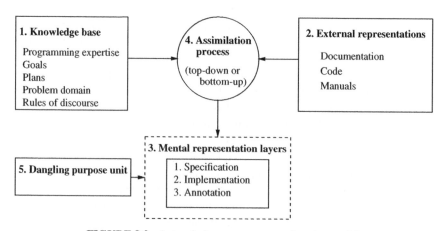

FIGURE 8.2 Letovsky's program comprehension model

knowledge base is a body of information about the program, and it includes the following:

- *Programming expertise:* Programming expertise is useful in asking probing *questions*, making *conjectures* to create abstractions from low level details by connecting observed code details with known program goals, and *searching* for specific information in the code. Conjectures are also called *hypotheses* [1]. The questions are grouped into five categories: *why, how, what, whether,* and *discrepancy. Why* questions are designed to know about the purpose of actions and design choices. *How* questions assist the programmer to learn about the way some goal of the code is accomplished. *What* questions are used to find out what a variable or code fragment is. *Whether* questions are asked to know if the code behaves in a certain way. *Discrepancy* questions are meant for resolving confusions and apparent inconsistencies in the code. Some example questions are: *Why is the variable being reset to zero?, What is being done to the memory block after the data is transmitted?,* and *Why (confusion) is the memory block being deleted in two places?* After asking questions, programmers often conjecture answers to their own questions based on their current understanding of the program. Similar to the classification of questions, programmers design *why, how,* and *what* conjectures. A *why* conjecture is made to assert an understanding of the purpose of an action or a design choice. A *how* conjecture is constructed to show an understanding of the way some goal of the program is accomplished. A *what* conjecture is formulated to demonstrate an understanding of what a variable or code segment does. Some conjectures could be pure guesses, because insufficient information may be available to make a conjecture with a higher degree of certainty.

- *Goals:* A programmer may find recurring computational code blocks, such as sort, search, delete, connect (to servers), start timers, transmit, and receive. It is useful to know the meaning of those recurring computational goals in the program, especially, why those computations are being performed, to be able to create a higher level of abstraction.

- *Problem domain:* Programmers need to have a broad understanding of the application domain of the code. A good understanding of the application domain serves as a backdrop for clearly and quickly understanding code segments in order to identify their goals and creating abstractions. For example, a programmer with a background in computer networks and distributed computing will find it easier to understand code for web-based applications than understanding the MATLAB libraries.

- *Plans:* Programmers have their own ways (also called plans) of finding solutions to problems that they need to solve. In addition, they use widely used solutions to some common problems, such as running-total loop, converging-iteration loop, handling a received message, and handling an event. Programmers' own plans and widely used plans by others are helpful in recognizing code patterns.

- *Rules of discourse:* Programmers have knowledge of *stylistic* conventions in writing code, which assist them in recognizing the goals of procedures and interpreting variables. For example, if a constant is called MAX_RECORDS and is used in a record processing loop, the programmer quickly recognizes that the loop is going to iterate for a maximum count of MAX_RECORDS. Similarly, if a method in Java is called OpenTCPConnection(), then the programmer recognizes that the program will most likely open a TCP connection with a remote computer. It takes much effort to understand variable names, such as i, with no clear meaning. One may guess that the variable is being used as a loop counter, an array index, and so on.

2. **External Representations:** The external representations of a program include its source code, documentation in the form of some comments, and manuals. The comments may appear in varying degrees of details, accuracies, and consistencies. The manuals are useful in understanding the high level goals of the code, whereas the inline comments are useful in understanding the low level details.

3. **Mental Representation:** By reading code and the accompanying documents, if there are any, ideally, a programmer may strive to create the following:

- *Specification of the program:* Here specification means a complete and unambiguous description of the goals of the programs. The goals of the program can be specified by identifying the user-level functions (i.e., the functional requirements), attributes of the functions (i.e., the non-functional requirements), and constraints. Understanding the complete non-functional requirements and program constraints is more difficult than understanding the functional requirements.

- *High level implementation of the program:* This means producing a complete and unambiguous description of the actions and data structures of the program. The actions can be identified at many levels of abstractions, such as individual statements, individual function calls, and sequences of calls. Similarly, the data structures can be identified at many levels of abstractions, such as individual variables, fields of structures (or, records), complete structures, and files. It is important to choose the right level of abstractions, because there are large numbers of individual statements and sequences of calls. Therefore, function calls appear to be the right kind of abstraction to describe actions.

- *Annotation of the program:* Having understood the *goals* of the programs and identified the program's *actions* and *data structures*, it is important to make a two-way association between the goals and the *actions* and *data structures*. The two-way association is made by annotating the program in the following ways: (i) How each goal in the specification is accomplished and by which actions and data structures; and (ii) what goals use the services of a given action or a data structure. In other words, a programmer establishes a kind of traceability matrix between program goals and actions and data structures. If one views the development process of the program as a layered system where the top layer is the set of program goals and the bottom layer is source code, then the annotation can be viewed as the abstraction of the middle layer connecting the top and the bottom layers. Basically, a program annotation is used to bridge the abstraction gap between the top and the bottom layers.

A programmer may not be able to create the final mental model, that is correct and complete, in one pass. The initial mental model may be incomplete and inconsistent. For example, many goals might be missing from the initial mental model. Similarly, the programmer might make mistakes in annotating the goals and the actions. Ambiguity may arise by identifying multiple goals with the same action (i.e., code segment).

4. **Assimilation Process:** Programmers combine their knowledge base and the external representations (i.e., documentation, code, and manuals) to create their mental models. Such a task is performed with a process called the *assimilation process*. The assimilation process guides the programmer to look at certain pieces of information, such as a code segment or a comment, and move forward/backward while reading the code. The assimilation process can work in three ways: *top-down*, *bottom-up*, and *opportunistic*. In the top-down approach, a programmer first identifies the goals of the program, followed by possible implementations of those goals such that the implementations match against the code. In the bottom-up approach, a programmer first identifies program plans from source code, makes annotations, and moves up to the top, goal layer. In reality, programmers rarely follow such pure top-down or bottom-up approaches. Rather, programmers combine the two approaches to take best advantage of whatever opportunity is available to make best progress in terms of knowledge gain at any given time. For example, one may start the assimilation process by reading code and identifying some goals. Next, the programmer may consider those goals and further understand the program in a top-down manner to gain a more complete knowledge about the identified goals and their implementations.

5. **Dangling Purpose Unit:** It may be recalled that the annotation layer serves as a *link* between the high level goal layer and the low level implementation layer, thereby showing what actions implement what goals and what goals have been implemented by what actions. Sometimes, it may be difficult to achieve a complete understanding of the relationship between the specification layer (i.e., the goals) and the low level actions. Therefore, the *dangling purpose* unit captures those goals whose implementations have not been clearly understood.

8.3.2   Shneiderman and Mayer Model

Shneiderman–Mayer's program comprehension model [9] has been depicted in Figure 8.3. The model consists of three key components: *short-term memory* of the programmer, the programmer's *knowledge* (both semantic knowledge and syntactic

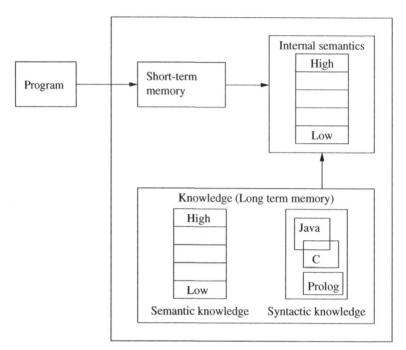

FIGURE 8.3   Shneiderman and Mayer program comprehension model

knowledge) to understand the code, and *internal semantics* of the code as understood by the programmer. In the following, we explain those three items in detail:

- *Internal semantics:* A programmer can read the code of a software system and develop an understanding of the code at different levels of abstractions. At the highest level of abstraction, the programmer develops an understanding of *what* the program does. In other words, develop an understanding of the functionalities of the program. The *what* aspect of a program gives us an idea about the *purpose* of the program. Some examples are as follows: a program inverts a matrix, a program encrypts a file with the triple data encryption standard (3DES), and a program sorts input records. One may understand the purpose of the program before understanding the statement-level details. At the lowest level of abstraction, the programmer understands the purpose of code segments and algorithms used to realize the program goals. In between the two extreme levels, programmers develop an internal semantic structure to represent the program details. An example of intermediate-level abstraction is the concept of *call graphs*—what modules are called by a given module and what modules use the services of the given module.
- *Knowledge:* Here knowledge refers to the application domain knowledge and programming knowledge, which are stored in the long-term memory of the programmer. Programming knowledge includes both semantic knowledge and

syntactic knowledge. On the one hand, semantic knowledge means programming concepts and techniques at different levels of abstractions. For example, (i) at a lower level, the programmer understands the meaning of individual program statements; (ii) at the intermediate level, the programmer understands how the values of two variables are swapped; (iii) at a high level, the programmer knows how to perform sorting and binary searching; and, (iv) at a further high level, a programmer with domain knowledge in computer networking knows how to route IP packets. Semantic knowledge is better gained and stored by means of abstractions, away from the details of programming languages. On the other hand, syntactic knowledge concerns individual programming languages and it is more specific, detailed, and generally arbitrary. For example, the concept of *value assignment* is represented by means of at least two notations in computer programming: "=" and ":=". Syntactic knowledge is quickly gained and quickly forgotten, whereas it takes more time to gain semantic knowledge and it stays longer in the long-term memory of programmers. Often languages share syntactic representations (Java and C languages share some syntactic structures.) The "knowledge" that we refer to in this section exists in the memory of the programmers.

- *Short-term memory:* While a programmer is reading code, *information* about the code enters the short-term memory of the programmer. The capacity of the short-term memory is very limited, and, therefore, the programmer must be able to quickly identify chunks, create their abstractions, and represent those abstractions in some internal form explained before. The programmer processes its short-term memory by using the semantic and syntactic knowledge of the code.

In the Shneiderman and Mayer model, program comprehension involves utilizing one's knowledge in identifying chunks of source code and creating an internal representation of the code in the form of a hierarchy of abstractions. One may have to create the hierarchy in several iterations, because it may not be possible to completely understand code in one pass of reading.

8.3.3 Brooks Model

There are three key elements in the program comprehension model of Brooks [10], illustrated in Figure 8.4 and explained in the following:

- *Code viewed as performing mappings from a problem domain to the programming domain:* Developing a software system can be seen as performing a series of mappings from one domain to the next, starting from the problem domain and finishing in the programming domain (i.e., solution domain). The results of the mappings are documented with varying degree of details, whereas the thought processes that perform the mappings are generally missing from the documentations. Let us consider the problem of routing data packets by a router on the Internet.

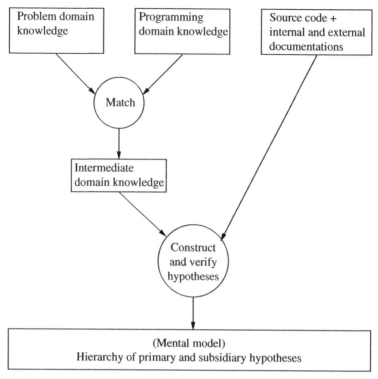

FIGURE 8.4   An overview of Brooks comprehension model

- *Step 1:* The input to a router is an IP data packet.
- *Step 2:* The *destination address* of the packet is *extracted* from the packet *header*.
- *Step 3:* A local *routing table* is *looked up* to find the *output port* on the router.
- *Step 4:* The IP packet is *transmitted* on that output port to reach the *next router* on the path to the *destination address*.

In Step 2, a standard data structure is used to extract the *destination address* value. In Step 3, a *prefix matching* algorithm is used for table look-up to find the *output port* to reach the destination. In Step 4, the IP packet is handed over to the lower protocol layer, namely, *data link* layer, with a request to transmit the packet on the given *output port*. Thus, the concept of packet routing has created a new level of domain knowledge, namely, standard data structure to access the fields of IP packets, prefix matching algorithm, and interfacing with data link layer. Next, the standard data structure for IP packets, prefix matching algorithm, and interfacing with data link layer are implemented in the programming language. Finally, when the router executes the code, an IP packet on a given input port appears on a certain output port of the router. This example illustrates the presence of three domains of knowledge: modeling of IP packets, modeling of table look-up, and modeling of the interface with the lower layer protocol. One may note that there is domain-specific information in each domain and there is information about relationships between entities belonging to nearby domains. An example of relationship between entities in nearby domains is as follows: the model of an IP packet contains information about the destination address and the model of table look-up uses the destination address to find out the output port to reach the destination. For correct and complete understanding of the program, it is important to understand the mappings and their relationships, which is realized by means of constructing hypotheses and validating them.

- *Understanding the mappings in terms of hypotheses:* Programmers read all available documentations—requirements documents, source code, users manuals, maintenance manuals, and all other available information about the system— and try to reconstruct the mappings as much as they can. They are said to have truly comprehended the program if all the mappings are exactly reconstructed. However, for complex systems, such a task is far from complete and may be incorrect. Programmers try to understand the program by formulating hypotheses in terms of what they find from the available documentations, their expectations, their current level of understanding of the program, and their knowledge of the problem domain and programming in general. Hypothesis construction begins with the generation of a *primary* hypothesis concerning the global structure of the program in terms of inputs, outputs, major data structures, and the processing sequences. A programmer familiar with the program's application domain can form the primary hypothesis by looking at the name of the program and reading its brief description. The primary hypothesis must be general enough to cover the breadth of the program and specific enough to guide the construction of subsequent hypotheses. Hypotheses can be organized in a hierarchical manner to represent both the breadth and depth of comprehending the program. A large fraction of the hypotheses constructed by experienced programmers is likely to be valid, whereas novice programmers generally take more time in constructing valid hypotheses.

- *Verification and refinement of hypotheses:* A hypothesis represents a programmer's understanding of a certain aspect of the program— and that understanding may be correct, incorrect, or partially correct. Therefore, a hypothesis must be verified or refined by means of further understanding of the program. Programmers verify a hypothesis by searching the program text and related documentations for beacons that confirm the hypothesis. While reading code to find beacons, programmers try to develop a broad understanding of the program by having an open mind about the system, rather than stay focused only on the hypothesis under consideration. Therefore, strong beacons for any structure are very likely to be noticed, even if the structure is not related to the present hypothesis. Noticing strong beacons for structures, whether or not they are used in the verification of the current hypothesis, is useful for the following reasons:
  - The structure can be readily used in a later hypothesis, thereby speeding up program comprehension.

– By discovering new structures in the code, a programmer can design new hypotheses. A new hypothesis can increase the breadth or depth of comprehension.

A programmer can continue constructing and validating hypothesis, thereby creating a hierarchical structure of hypotheses, where the top one is the primary hypothesis and the others are subsidiary hypotheses, and code segments are bound to specific hypothesis. Ideally, all program segments are unambiguously bound to the hypothesis structure, thereby indicating complete comprehension of the program. However, programmers may encounter a number of problems while verifying hypotheses.

- The programmer fails to find code to bind to a subsidiary hypothesis.
- The same code is bound to multiple subsidiary hypotheses.
- The programmer fails to bind a code segment to any hypothesis.

The above problems can be resolved by adopting new hypotheses, refining the existing hypotheses, and altering and adding to the bindings of code segments to hypotheses. Therefore, programmers need to iterate the process of hypothesis construction and verification. Brooks has identified a number of factors having an impact on program comprehension, as explained in the following:

- *Programs differ in comprehensibility:* We can identify two broad aspects of programs that affect their comprehensibility, namely, characteristics of the executable portion of the source code and the quality of documentation. In the following, we explain the above two items in detail:
  - *Characteristics of source code:* The number of identifiers, the number of statements, and the amount of branching affect program comprehension. If a programmer finds a large number of identifiers and conditional statements in a program, they need to keep a lot of information in their short-term memory and will ask many "why" questions while reading code. However, the constructs that have a higher level of impact on program understanding are the *control* constructs. For example, a program with many `for` and `while` loops make understanding difficult. Concurrency and synchronization also make program understanding very difficult. Finally, process synchronization techniques, such as synchronization via global variables, make program understanding very difficult.
  - *Quality of documentation:* Documentation of programs can be classified into two groups: *internal* and *external*. Internal documentation is closely intertwined with the program text, whereas external documentation are found in entities separated from source code. The programmers can find internal documentations in the following *indicator* forms:
    * prologue comments, including data and variable dictionaries;
    * variable, structure, procedure and label names;

* declarations;
* comments associated with statements and code segments;
* code indentation; and
* input/output formats and header.

On the other hand, external documentation includes the following *indicator* forms:

* user's manual;
* program logic manuals;
* flowcharts;
* cross-reference listing;
* published descriptions of algorithms; and
* published standards referenced by the program.

The usefulness of a certain documentation is a function of the beacon it describes and the importance of the beacon for the specific hypothesis under consideration. Different documentations are useful in different stages of hypothesis construction. For example, in the initial stages of hypothesis verification, the hypotheses tend to be very broad and focus on the global properties of the system. Therefore, documentations with a focus on the overall functionality of the system, such as user's manual and flowcharts, are more effective in comprehending the program. It is important to note that more documentation may not necessarily lead to better accuracy in program comprehension. If a program concept has been described by means of many different indicators, it is likely that the programmer will easily notice one form and use it. For instance, a functionality of a program can be considered as a program concept, and the concept may be described in different ways in different places: requirements specification, user's manual, and inline comments. As a concrete example, "draw a line" is a functionality of a graphics program, and this functionality can be described in many ways in many places. Different indicators mean different ways of describing a program concept. For example, the "draw a line" functionality is generally described in different ways in requirements specification, user's manual, and inline comments. On the other hand, if a large number of indicators redundantly present the same information, then they may obscure or overwhelm other indicators that contain unique information. In other words, over documentation may be counter-productive to program comprehension. In addition, a programmer needs to be aware of the possibility of contradicting indicators, that is, the user's manual says one thing and the inline comments say something contradicting.

* *Task differences affect comprehension:* Programmers may comprehend the same program from different viewpoints, depending upon the *tasks* they want to perform after comprehending the program. Some examples of tasks that programmers may perform on the program are: fixing bugs, modifying the contents and format details of output, and increasing the readability of code. A programmer

who needs to fix bugs in a program needs to be more concerned with the control structure of the program, whereas a programmer who is trying to reformat the output will be more focused on the output statements. Therefore, a programmer's perspective of the source code affects how they start their comprehension process.

- *Programmers differ in their ability to comprehend programs:* Programmers possess different abilities to comprehend programs. Their individual abilities to construct effective hypotheses and verify them depend on the programmer's following abilities:
    - Domain knowledge: A programmer's knowledge about the problem domain plays an important role in understanding the top level goals of the program and the mappings from layer to layer. For example, a programmer with deep mathematics background is better positioned to understand code for numerical analysis than a programmer without much mathematics background. Similarly, a programmer with background in aeronautics is likely to be more capable of quickly understanding code for airplane wing design.
    - Programming knowledge: It is needless to say that programmers must have a thorough knowledge of the programming language to understand the code details.
    - Comprehension strategies: Comprehension strategies include a large number of fine decisions: where to start, how to proceed, how to construct hypothesis, how to verify hypothesis, how to refine hypothesis, how quickly to reject hypothesis, when to postpone the verification of a hypothesis, when to reconsider a hypothesis whose verification had been postponed before, and how to read code and documentations. An experienced programmer may move between program text and documentations quickly, whereas a novice programmer may read everything line-by-line.

In summary, the comprehension model of Brooks puts emphasis on constructing a hierarchy of verified hypothesis and associating code segments with lower level, subsidiary hypotheses. A programmer is said to have completely and correctly comprehended a program if each code segment has been assigned to some hypothesis, no code segment remains unassigned, and no code segment is assigned to multiple hypothesis. An overview of the Brooks model has been illustrated in Figure 8.4.

8.3.4 Soloway, Adelson, and Ehrlich Model

The top-down program comprehension model of Soloway, Adelson, and Ehrlich [4, 11], depicted in Figure 8.5, works in a top-down manner, and it applies when the code or type of code is familiar to the programmer. Two fundamental concepts in the model are *programming plans* (also called *schemas*) and *programming rules of discourse*, as explained in Section 8.2.3. Expert programmers have and use specific programming plans and rules of programming discourse to comprehend programs.

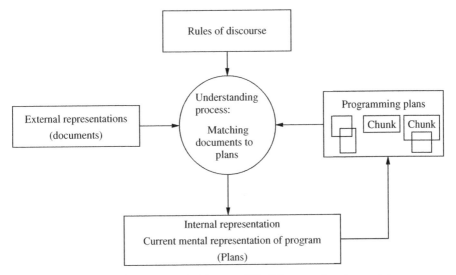

FIGURE 8.5   Soloway, Adelson, and Ehrlich comprehension model

Programs that do not follow the plans and violate the rules of discourse are harder to understand. Some concrete rules of programming discourse are as follows:

- The names of the variables reflect their purpose.
- Code that is not going to be executed is not included.
- A tested condition must have the potential of evaluating to *true*.
- A variable that is initialized by means of an assignment statement is subsequently updated with assignment statements.
- Use an `if` statement to execute a code segment once, whereas `for()` and `while()` loops are used to repeatedly execute code segments.

Expert programmers have strong expectations about what programs should look like. When those expectations are not fulfilled, their comprehension performance drops significantly, almost to the levels of novice programmers.

Similar to the other models, external representations, namely, documentations, play a key role in program understanding in this model. Examples of documentations are requirements documents, design documents, source code, user manuals, reference manuals, maintenance manuals, test case documents, test execution reports, and even field reports. As depicted in Figure 8.5, the understanding process matches programming plans found in source code with external documentations using rules of discourse. During the understanding process, the programmer creates a hierarchical knowledge structure representing their understanding of the code. Therefore, comprehension begins with a high level program goal, and finer, lower level subgoals are generated to realize the upper level goals. Programming comprehension is an iterative process, such that, in each iteration, the programmer expands their understanding of the code by refining the already identified subgoals and identifying new subgoals. The process is said to be complete when the programmer has associated all the programming plans with the goal hierarchy.

8.3.5   Pennington Model

The Pennington model [12, 13] has been depicted in Figure 8.6. The model applies two concepts, namely, *textbase* and *situation model*, developed by van Dijk and Kintsch [14]. It is important to pay attention to the loop {*Match – Mental representation – Text structure knowledge*} followed by the *textbase*. The programmer iterates through the loop, thereby incrementally creating the mental representation. Finally, when the programmer stops iterating through the loop, the final mental representation is known as the textbase. There is a similar relationship between the second *mental*

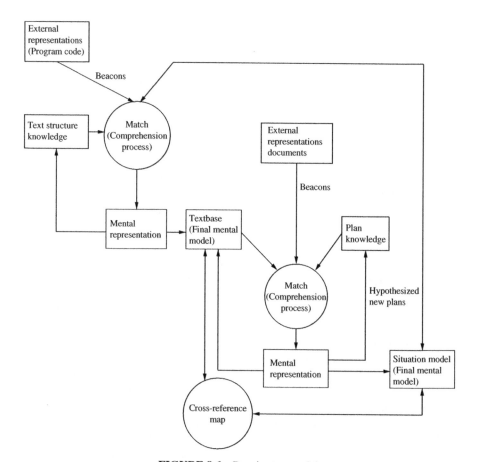

FIGURE 8.6   Pennington model

representation box and the *situation model.* The concepts of *textbase* and *situation model* are explained as follows.

- *Textbase (Program model):* Some people equate being able to recall portions of a text with comprehending the text. A textbase represents information that the reader of a text can recall from memory after reading the text. A textbase includes a hierarchy of representations comprising a surface-level knowledge of the text, a *microstructure* of relationships among text propositions, and a *macrostructure* organizing the text representation. One may note that a textbase does not necessarily contain the exact words or lines used in the text. Though a textbase represents the superficial understanding of a programmer, it is a useful abstraction of a program for many reasons, because major code segments are recognized more easily than minor segments. The textbase basically describes a *program model* in terms of the control flow of the program, because when programmers read new code they build a control flow abstraction of the code. This model is built in a bottom-up manner by:
  - identifying beacons for elementary code blocks;
  - chunking microstructures into macrostructures; and
  - cross-referencing the existing contents of the textbase with the situation model.
- *Situation model:* A situation model represents *what the text is about.* The model requires knowledge of the real-world domains and objects. Programmers mentally represent the code in terms of real-world objects by using plan knowledge. For example, the code line "status = delete(ProcessQueue, printJob1);" is mentally represented as "delete the printJob1 from the queue of processes." Also, lower level plan knowledge is chunked into higher level plan knowledge by using the concepts of operations, control flow, data flow, state, and functions. The situation models are built via cross-referencing and chunking. To build the situation model, the cross-referencing process takes information from the textbase and builds higher order plans by means of constructing hypotheses.

A high level description of the model is as follows:

- The programmer assimilates their understanding of the code, knowledge of the text structure, and the situation model to create a mental model in the form of a textbase.
- The programmer assimilates the external representations of the code, (i.e., documentations), plan knowledge (i.e., problem domain knowledge and intermediate-level programming concepts), and the textbase to create the situation model.
- The textbase and the situation model are cross-referenced to refine and update the two models.

Figure 8.6 indicates that the program model represented by the textbase can change after a programmer starts constructing the situation model. In addition, a new program model can impact the situation model. Cross-referencing between the program model and the situation model enables the programmer to maintain consistency between the two models.

While reading code, programmers gain knowledge about the following aspects of code to varying degree of details.

- *Operations:* At the level of source code, operations are *actions* that the program performs. Some examples are assigning a value to an integer variable, comparing the values of two integer variables, and swapping the values of two character variables. Therefore, operations can have varying levels of granularities. After reading code for a while, a programmer learns what operations the program is performing.

- *Control Flow:* Control flow refers to the ordering of operations (i.e., actions) in a program. By looking at sequences of actions, a programmer can identify *before* and *after* relationships between actions. For example, a programmer can ask: *Has a timer been started after transmitting a data packet?* and *What actions are taken after a timer expires?*

- *Data Flow:* Data flow refers to the sequences of transformations being performed on input data to produce program outputs. The concept of input data is very broad, including values of variables and file contents. Variables are defined (i.e., initialized), used, redefined, reused, and so on. The value of a variable can be used in two ways: (i) to perform a computation, known as c-use; and (ii) to construct a predicate, known as p-use. For example, a variable appearing in the condition portion of an if() statement is an example of predicate use of the variable. By understanding the data flow aspect of a program, one can ask: *What are the input variables that determine the values of output variable* LossCount?

- *State:* In general, the values of all variables of a program define the state of execution of the program. Programmers can ask useful questions relating to program states: *When an acknowledgement packet arrives, has the timer expired?*

- *Function:* Programs can be characterized by top level goals and subgoals. Also, programs can be characterized by hierarchies of functions performed by code blocks. Functional relations concern the goals and subgoals of the program and their associations with code segments. By understanding functional relations in a program, one can answer questions such as *Is this loop computing the average monthly credit of a customer?* and *Is this sequence of actions establishing a phone connection between two customers?*

8.3.6   Integrated Metamodel

When programmers read the code and documentations, they start understanding the code at all levels of abstractions simultaneously. As they read the code, they simultaneously understand the program's control flow (i.e., *how* the program works), the program's functions (i.e., *what* the program does), and the overall situation of the program (i.e., what the code *is about*). Moreover, programmers do not follow a

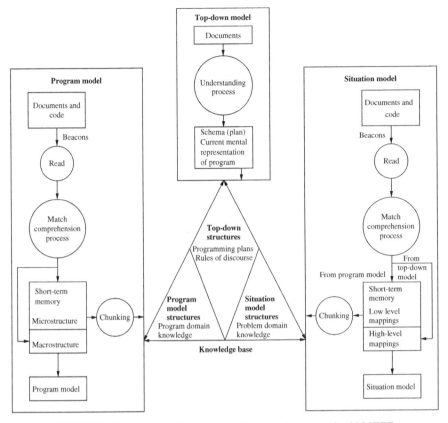

FIGURE 8.7   Integrated Metamodel. From Reference 1. © 1995 IEEE

purely top-down or bottom-up approach to comprehending code. Rather, they become opportunistic and their strategy combines both top-down and bottom-up approaches.

The integrated code comprehension metamodel proposed by Mayrhauser and Vans [1, 15] has been depicted in Figure 8.7. The four major components of the model are explained in the following.

- *Top-down model:* The top-down model, also known as *domain model*, represents domain knowledge about the program [11]. For example, domain knowledge about IP routing includes IP packet header format, IP table look-up, prefix matching, and packet transmission. Similarly, domain knowledge about operating systems includes process scheduling, memory management, and device management. Domain knowledge provides guidance to programmers while designing effective strategies to read and understand code. Construction of the top-down model is effective for familiar code or type of code, because it requires that the reader possess domain knowledge.

- *Program model:* When a programmer reads unfamiliar code, he tries to understand the *control flow* aspect of the code via his programming skills and standard programming constructs [12, 13]. If the programmer understands *what* the program is doing from the control flow aspect, then he has a *program model* of the code. However, the programmer has not developed a complete understanding of the functions of the program.

- *Situation model:* We have already explained the concept of a situation model while discussing Pennington's model in this section. After building a program model (or, at least a portion of the program model), a programmer builds a situation model by using control flow and data flow information in a bottom-up manner. Referring to the earlier example of IP routing (see the top-down model above), *packet forwarding* is an example of the situation model.

- *Knowledge base:* The knowledge base provides a medium for interactions among the above three models, namely, top-down model, program model, and situation model, and comprises the following three kinds of knowledge structures:

  - *Top-down structures:* The top-down structures include two key elements from the Soloway, Adelson, and Ehrlich model, namely, *programming plans* and *rules of discourse*. The programming plans are categorized into *strategic plans*, *tactical plans*, and *implementation plans*. Strategic plans describe language-independent, global strategies used in a program. An example of a strategic plan is the state model of packet discard policy used by an IP router. Tactical plans are local strategies for solving problems described by the higher level strategic plans. Therefore, strategic plans are further decomposed into language-independent tactical plans. For IP routing, tactical plans may include classification of packets based on the time elapsed so far since their creation, the average times needed to route them to their destinations, the service category of the packet (e.g., voice-over-IP). Algorithms for management of packet queues are also a part of tactical plans. Strategic plans are understood by means of fine-grained tactical plans. Finally, implementation plans are language dependent and are used to code tactical plans. A Java method used to implement a queue to reflect the order of arrivals of packets is an example of implementation plan. Such a queue can be implemented as a doubly linked list.

  - *Program model structures:* The program model structures include two kinds of knowledge, namely, *text-structure knowledge* and *plan knowledge*. Text-structure knowledge is described by means of control primes, and plan knowledge is described in terms of algorithms, control flow, data flow, and data structures.

  - *Situation model structures:* The situation model structures are described in terms of *problem domain knowledge* and *functional knowledge*. The problem domain knowledge is also known as *real-world knowledge*.

In the integrated metamodel, all the three models, namely, the top-down model, the program, and the situation model, are simultaneously built. Here, the meaning of simultaneity is that no model waits for another model to be completely built; rather, the programmer takes an opportunistic approach and simultaneously built all the three models by updating the knowledge base with the understanding of one model and applying the knowledge to further build another model. For example, the knowledge generated from the program model can be used to expand and/or refine the situation model, and vice versa. The programmer uses the knowledge base for guidance to make a transition from one model to another.

The knowledge base is also called *long-term memory*, and it is generally organized into *schemas* (or, *plans*) as explained before in this section. Schemas are knowledge structures with two parts: *slot types* and *slot fillers*. Knowledge structures are linked by means of the commonly used concepts of modeling associations, namely, *kind-of* and *is-a* relationships. As shown in Figure 8.7, the knowledge base is partitioned into three groups specifically related to the three comprehension models: *programming plans* and *rules of discourse* are related to the *top-down* model; *program domain knowledge* is related to the *program model*, and *problem domain knowledge* and *functional knowledge* are related to the *situation model*. However, structures built by any of the three models are available to the other models.

8.4   PROTOCOL ANALYSIS

Novice programmers can learn by observing how experienced programmers *behave* during program comprehension. Similarly, researchers can learn by observing how both novice and experienced programmers behave during program comprehension. Ideally, we want to observe all aspects of programmers' behavior while they are trying to understand the code, such as the following:

- What is the programmer studying?
- What is the programmer thinking when he sees something interesting?
- What does the programmer do after he finds something interesting?
- What is the rational thinking behind the programmer's action?

Answering the above questions is a cumbersome—if not impossible—task. An elaborate mechanism and much resources are required to be able to observe how programmers behave during program comprehension. *Protocol analysis*, studied in the field of psychological research, is a key concept used in finding answers to the above questions. It is a methodology for eliciting verbal reports from participants (programmers in our case) about their thought sequences as a valid source of data on thinking [16]. In the field of psychology, protocol analysis is used to study cognitive processes and behavior analysis. It has also been used in usability testing and educational psychology. Protocol analysis is composed of two sequential steps:

- *Concurrent verbalization of a comprehension task:* This step produces textual data representing the thought sequence of a programmer as he performs the comprehension task by reading the code. This text is known as *protocol data*.
- *Analysis of protocol data:* The protocol data is analyzed to understand the characteristics of the thinking performed by the programmer.

Concurrent verbalization of comprehension tasks: Programmers trying to understand a software are asked to verbalize their thoughts while working on a specific task, and the said verbalization is recorded on audio-visual systems. In other words, programmers are asked to "think aloud" while working: they say loudly everything that they think, evaluate, and (mentally) move. This is called *think-aloud protocol* (TAP). Thinking aloud reflects the knowledge currently active in the programmer's working memory. The verbal reports almost always indicate the programmer's goals, operators, and evaluative processes [17]. Some examples of concurrent verbalization is as follows:

- I want to read the external documentations. What? No external documentations! I wanted to speak with the developers who designed and implemented the system, but they are all gone! I mean they have left the company.
- Okay. I am reading the code prologue.
- Now I know that the system is for enabling customers to make seat reservations in a restaurant and placing orders.
- I find interesting keywords in the prologue: phone, cell phone, and laptops. I think one could make reservations by calling a restaurant or on the Web. I guess … customers might be able to place orders from their cell phones.
- Let me read the module called `MakeReservation`.
- …
- On line# 206, I see `MobileDeviceType` in a data structure to interpret received messages from clients. This verifies my guess that the system supports user interactions via smartphones.
- …

The above thinking-aloud action of the programmer can be recorded and transcribed. The transcribed verbal report is called *protocol data* (or, simply *protocol*) about the comprehension process. Protocol data is a list of statements, questions, and, sometimes, amazements, uttered by a programmer while reading code and documentations. Protocol data reflects not only the programmer's thought process, but also much interesting details noticed about the program. Different programmers with the same level of experience will most likely produce different protocol data for the same program, because they are likely to think differently. Protocol data produced by a novice programmer and an experienced programmer will be very different in their details, sources of those data, and reasoning.

Analysis of protocol data: There is no common, detailed procedure to analyze protocol data. Rather, a very general description of protocol analysis is as follows.

- Divide protocol data into several *segments*, say, *speech sentences.*
- Assign the segments to different *predefined categories.* Assignment of protocol segments to different categories is called *encoding.* Coding categories are generally selected with a model of the verbalization process in mind. For example, in the coding system of Ericsson and Simon [16], there are four types of

segments: *intentions*, *cognitions*, *planning*, and *evaluations*. Intentions are easily recognized by verbs of the type, "shall," "will," "must," and so on. The cognition category contains segments which put attention on *selected aspects* of the current situation, and those segments are recognized by constructions indicating *presence* and *immediacy*. Planning is easily recognized by conditional constructions, namely, "if A then B else C." Evaluations are recognized by indications of implicit and explicit comparisons of alternatives, namely, "yes," "no," "okay," and "fine."

- Analyze the categorized protocol data to build a comprehension model of the programmer. A comprehension model can be represented as a *transition net*, which resembles finite-state machines, where computations (represented with cognitions and intentions) are associated with states, and planning and evaluations are associated with transitions. Transition nets are easy to construct and understand, and those are simple tools to model thought processes, verbalized as a TAP, of programmers.

8.5   VISUALIZATION FOR COMPREHENSION

Software visualization is one of the techniques applied in reverse engineering, and it has been explained in detail in Section 4.6.6. In this section, we further explain the idea as it has been supported with various tools for program comprehension.

Cleveland [18] has described a tool, called Program UNderstanding Support environment (PUNS), developed at IBM to provide *multiple views* of a program to aid its understanding. The tool supports the program understanding task by organizing and presenting the different viewpoints of a program: a *call graph* for a set of procedures, a *control flow* graph for an individual procedure, a graph representing the relationship between a file and a procedure that uses the file, a *data flow* graph, and a *definition-use* chain for a variable. By performing static analysis of the code, the tool detects low level relationships and organizes them in a user-friendly environment so that the user can easily navigate through the graphs while switching between low level and high level objects. The two key components of the tool are as follows: (i) a repository and the associated routines—the routines load the repository and generate responses to queries from the user; and (ii) a user interface presents information about the program to the user and aids the user in navigating through the graphs.

Harandi and Ning [19] have presented a program analysis tool (PAT) to represent programming concepts with an object-oriented framework and a heuristic-based concept recognition mechanism to extract high level functional concepts from source code. The tool is based on the human expert's analysis model, and tries to aid programmers answer the following questions. (i) What high level concepts does the program implement? (ii) How are the high level concepts coded in terms of low level details? Two types of knowledge are explicitly represented by PAT: *program knowledge* and *analysis knowledge*. The former is represented by programming concepts found in the code, whereas the later is represented by information contained in program plans. The tool manages two databases to manipulate the two types of knowledge: (i) a database of coding heuristics, data structure definitions, and functional coding pattern; and (ii) a database of rules for program plans covering value accumulation, counting, sequential search of ordered and unordered structures, different kinds of searching, and sorting.

The positive impact of *software visualization*, by means of *control structure diagrams* (CSD), on program comprehension has been shown by Hendrix, Cross II, and Maghsoodloo [20]. Graphical notations are used to render source code in the CSD approach. The CSD is an algorithmic level diagram that clearly depicts control constructs, control paths, and the overall structure of each program unit, say, function or method. The CSD is a kind of extension to other diagrams, such as class diagrams and data flow diagrams. The authors performed experiments with two groups of students: one group was given the source code in plain text only, whereas the second group received the source code rendered with CSD. All the students were asked to respond to questions regarding the structure and execution of one source code module of a public domain graphics library. The response time and the correctness of the responses were recorded. Statistical analysis revealed that the CSD significantly enhanced the students' program comprehension capabilities.

The concept of *fisheye* view [21] is another visualization technique to support programmer's navigation and comprehension. A fisheye view displays those parts of the source code that have the highest degree of interest (DOI) related to the current focus of the programmer. Jakobsen and Hornbaek [22] have presented the design of a fisheye interface based on the Eclipse Java development environment. Both the proposed and Eclipse's interfaces use an *overview plus detail* approach: an overview of the entire document is displayed to the right of the detailed view window. The overview displays the source code reduced in size to fit the entire document within the space of the overview area. Because of size reduction, the text displayed in the overview area is unreadable, but one can discern some structural features of the code, such as method boundaries and blocks of comments. The portion of the code shown in the detail area is visually connected with its location in the overview. In addition, the fisheye interface of Jakobsen and Hornbaek possesses the following features.

- *Focus and context area:* The detailed view of the code divided into two areas: the focus area and the context area. The context area displays the code context of the code shown in the focus area. Moreover, the context area displays a distorted view of the context, because much code needs to be squeezed into a small area – and this is achieved by diminishing the font size of text.

- *Degree of Interest Function:* A DOI function is used to determine if and how much the text lines are diminished in size in the context area. The DOI function is based on an a priori interest defined by: (i) the type of code line for which the DOI is being calculated; and (ii) the line's distance from the focus point. The type of a code line is determined by deducing the abstract syntax tree node from the line. Code lines containing keywords `package`, `class`, `interface`, or `method` are assigned a higher a priori interest than other lines. Lines containing `if`, `for`, `switch`, `try`, `while`, `catch`, or `finally` are also assigned a higher a priori interest. The distance of a line from the focus point is calculated by using the concepts of *syntactic distance* and *semantic distance*. Syntactic distance is measured in terms of the "gap" in their indentation levels; that is, lines in the same indented block as the focus point are thought to be closer to the focus point than lines on other indentation levels and lines in other blocks, thus contributing to a higher DOI. Semantic distance is about the similarity of information contained between two lines; that is, lines containing declarations of classes, methods, and variables that are used in the focus point are considered to be closer to the focus point, thus contributing to a higher DOI. Lines with semantic closeness to the focus point are highlighted with an alternate background color to show their semantic relation to the lines in the focus point.

- *Magnification Function:* A magnification function assigns a priority to each line of code according to its DOI so that the font size of less interesting lines can be reduced. Lines with similar degrees of interest are assigned priorities according to their distance in lines from the focus area so that lines closest to the focus area are allocated space first. Such a strategy is useful in deciding how to effectively use the display space.

- *User Interaction:* The focus area offers the same functionalities for interactions with the code file as a standard text editor. As the user navigates through the focus area, the context area automatically changes. Conversely, clicking on a line in the context area highlights the focus area around that line.

The authors conducted an experiment with 16 participants to compare the usability of fisheye view with a common, linear presentation of code. The participants generally preferred the fisheye view interface and performed comprehension tasks significantly faster.

UML (Unified Modeling Language) class diagrams can aid programmers in code comprehension, and the spatial organization of those diagrams play a key role [23]. There are numerous algorithms for drawing UML class diagrams (see [23]). Based on *perceptual theory* [24], Sun and Wong [23] have classified criteria and guidelines for effective layout of UML class diagrams. Several theories of perception have been proposed: *Marr's theory*, *Gibson's theory*, *Gestalt's theory*, and *Theory of notation*. Two broad principles, namely, *perceptual organization* and *perceptual segregation* can be applied to organize UML class diagrams. The former indicates when entities are organized in near proximity, whereas the latter indicates when entities are separated in Gestalt's theory of figure–ground segregation. The following are some important principles of *perceptual organization*, most of which are from Gestalt's theory.

- *Good figure:* Generally, simpler figures with the right amount of details are considered to be good. Complex figures and figures with a lot of details do not increase our understanding of structures represented by those figures.

- *Similarity:* Similar entities appear to be grouped together. For example, entities with the same shape, say, a circle, appear to indicate the same concept, say, processing.

- *Proximity:* Entities that are close to each other are grouped together.

- *Familiarity (Meaningfulness):* If a group of elements appear to be familiar, it is more likely that they are grouped together.
- *Element Connectedness:* Entities that are physically connected are seen to be constituting a single unit.

On the other hand, the concept of perceptual segregation is explained as follows. When one looks at the environment, what is seen is a whole picture, not as separate parts. There are images in the environment that people are aware of in a particular moment—this would be the figure. The ground makes up the image if one does not focus on it or one is not aware of it. The following factors make an entity more like a figure that can be easily recognized.

- *Symmetry:* Symmetric areas are commonly seen as a figure.
- *Orientation:* Entities with horizontal and vertical orientations are more likely to be seen as figures than other orientations.
- *Contours:* Edges are useful in perceiving if something is a figure.

The above explained principles of perceptual organization and perceptual segregation are expressed in terms of "laws" for drawing UML class diagrams. Those laws are called:

- Law of good figure
- Law of similarity
- Law of continuation
- Law of proximity
- Law of familiarity
- Law of connectedness
- Law of symmetry
- Law of orientation
- Law of contour.

For example, the law of continuation is described as: *minimize edge crossings and bends*, because it is easy to follow a class diagram with minimum number of edge crossings and bends. They have evaluated the class diagrams produced by two tools, namely, *Borland Together* and *Rational Rose*, by applying the above laws.

Wettel and Lanza [25] have proposed a three-dimensional (3D) visualization of programs based on the *city metaphor*. With the city metaphor, classes are represented as buildings located in city districts which in turn represent packages. The concept of *habitability*, which makes a place livable, is at the core of the city metaphor, and the corresponding programming concept is *familiarity*. The more familiar a programmer is with the code, the easier it is to understand the code. Thus, intuitively, habituality is the characteristic of code that enables programmers coming to the code later in the software system's life to understand its intentions and constructions [26]. They also support the concept of *locality* by providing a navigable environment in which one can move. In summary, the programmer perceives code as a city with visual orientation points and freedom of movement and interaction.

8.6   SUMMARY

The chapter began with a general introduction to program comprehension. Next we explained the concepts of *knowledge* and *mental model*. The concept of mental model was explained by means of the static elements of mental models, dynamic elements of mental models, and acquiring knowledge from code. This was followed by a discussion of the characteristics of expert programmers. Static elements of mental models include: text-structures, code chunks, schemas, plans, and hypotheses. On the other hand, the dynamic elements of mental models are: chunking, cross-referencing, and strategies. Next, we explained the following comprehension models: Letovsky model, Shneiderman and Mayer model, Brooks model, Soloway, Adelson, and Ehrlich model, Pennington model, and Integrated metamodel. Studying programmers' behaviors and actions during their program comprehension processes are key to understanding the details of their thinking. Therefore, we explained the concept of *protocol analysis* that involves the *think-aloud protocol* in which programmers are asked to verbalize their thinking. Finally, we explained the idea of program understanding by means of software visualization.

LITERATURE REVIEW

A programmer is said to have understood a program when he is able to explain the program by means of human-oriented *concepts* different from the *tokens* used to construct the source code of the program. Examples of human-oriented concepts are the program's structure and behavior and the program's relationships to its application domain. The concept "Allow the customer to withdraw money" is a high-level concept, which is much different from the following C-program statement:

```
if (Balance > RequestedAmount && DailyLimitNotReached)
        then GrantWithdrawalRequest(RequestedAmount, Customer).
```

While reading code, it is important that programmers are able to associate high level concepts to code segments. Biggerstaff, Mitbander, and Webster [27, 28] have studied the *concept assignment problem*: discovering the human-oriented concepts and assigning them to their implementations as code segments. Human-oriented concept recognition requires plausible reasoning and relies on a priori knowledge from the specific application domains. Two general steps are applied when attempting to assign concepts to code: (i) identify which entities and relationships in a large program are important; (ii) assign those entities and relationships to known or discovered domain concepts and relations. Deep understanding of programs relies on an a priori knowledge of the expectations about the problem domain and commonly used software architectures. The authors have reported a *design recovery* tool, called DESIRE, developed at the Microelectronics and Computer Consortium. The tool uses informal knowledge, such as variable names and comments, a domain model, and traditional formal analysis to build a hierarchy of concepts to collectively describe a program.

Gold and Bennett [29] have proposed a hypothesis-based concept assignment method. The method assigns *descriptive terms* to their implementations in source code. The terms relate to computational intents and are nominated by the programmer. Informal information, such as identifier names and comments are used in assigning concepts. The method works in three phases: (i) generate an ordered list of hypotheses from code; (ii) group the hypotheses using their conceptual affiliation to produce a list of hypothesis segments; and (iii) evaluate the evidence in the segments and assign a concept to each segment. The overall output of the method is a list of concepts, associated with blocks of source code. The effectiveness of the method has been demonstrated by applying it to legacy code in COLBOL II.

Tonella [30] has proposed to represent a program as a *concept lattice of decomposition slices*, by combining the concepts of *decomposition slice graphs* and *concept lattice*. A decomposition slice graph is obtained by applying the idea of program slicing [31]. Visual inspection of this representation aids programmers in understanding the decomposition of the program into functionalities and subfunctionalities.

REFERENCES

[1] A. V. Mayrhauser and A. M. Vans. 1995. Program comprehension during software maintenance and evolution. *Computer*, 28(8), 44–55.

[2] P. N. Johnson-Laird. 1983. *Mental Models.* Harvard University Press, Cambridge, MA.

[3] A. C. Graesser. 1981. *Prose Comprehension Beyond the Word.* New York: Springer-Verlag.

[4] E. Soloway and K. Ehrlich. 1984. Empirical studies of programming knowledge. *IEEE Transactions on Software Engineering*, SE-10(5), 595–609.

[5] S. Letovsky, 1986. *Cognitive Processes in Program Comprehension.* Proceedings of the First Workshop in Empirical Studies of Programmers, 1986, Ablex, Norwood, NJ, pp. 58–79.

[6] I. Vessey. 1985. Expertise in debugging computer programs: A process analysis. *International Journal of Man-Machine Studies*, 23, 459–494.

[7] R. Guindon. 1990. Knowledge exploited by experts during software systems design. *International Journal of Man-Machine Studies*, 33, 279–282.

[8] R. Jeffries, A. A. Turner, P. Polson, and M. E. Atwood. 1981. The processes involved in designing software. In: *Cognitive Skills and Their Acquisition* (Ed. R. R. Anderson) , Erlbaum, Hillsdale, NJ.

[9] B. Shneiderman and R. Mayer. 1995. Syntactic and semantic interactions in programmer: A model and experimental results. *International Journal of Computer and Information Sciences*, 8(3), 219–238.

[10] R. Brooks. 1983. Towards a theory of the comprehension of computer programs. *International Journal of Man-Machine Studies*, 18, 543–554.

[11] E. Soloway, B. Adelson, and K. Ehrlich. 1988. Knowledge and Processes in the Comprehension of Computer Program (Eds M. Chi, R. Glaser, and M. Farr), pp. 129–152. A. Lawrence Erlbaum Associates, Hillsdale, NJ.

[12] N. Pennington. 1987. *Comprehension Strategies in Programming*. Proceedings of the 2nd Workshop on Empirical Studies of Programmers, 1987, Ablex, Norwood, NJ, pp. 100–112.

[13] N. Pennington. 1987. Stimulus structures and mental representations in expert comprehension of computer programs. *Cognitive Psychology*, 19, 295–341.

[14] T. A. van Dijk and W. Kintsch. 1983. *Strategies of Discourse Comprehension*. Academic Press, New York.

[15] A. V. Mayrhauser and A. M. Vans. 1994. *Comprehension Processes During Large-scale Maintenance*. Proceedings of the 16th International Conference on Software Engineering, 1994, IEEE Computer Society Press, Los Alamitos, CA, pp. 39–48.

[16] K. A. Ericsson and H. A. Simon. 1984. *Protocol Analysis: Verbal Reports as Data*. MIT Press, MA.

[17] C. Fisher. 1987. *Advancing the Study of Programming with Computer-aided Protocol Analysis*. Proceedings of the 2nd Workshop on Empirical Studies of Programmers, 1987, Ablex, Norwood, NJ, pp. 198–216.

[18] L. Cleveland. 1989. A program understanding support environment. *IBM Systems Journal*, 28(2), 324–344.

[19] M. T. Harandi and J. Q. Ning. 1990. Knowledge-based program analysis. *IEEE Software*, January, pp. 74–81.

[20] D. Hendrix, J. H. Cross II, and S. Maghsoodloo. 2002. The effectiveness of control structure diagrams in source code comprehension activities. *IEEE Transctions on Software Engineering*, 28(5), 463–477.

[21] G. W. Furnas. 1981. The fisheye view: A new look at structured files. In: *Readings in Information Visualization: Using Vision to Think* (Eds S. K. Card, J. D. Mackinlay, and B. Shneiderman), pp. 312–330, Morgan-Kaufmann.

[22] M. R. Jakobsen and K. Hornbaek. 2006. *Evaluating a Fisheye View of Source Code*. Proceedings of ACM CHI 2006 Conference on Human Factors in Computing Systems, 2006, ACM, New York.

[23] D. Sun and K. Wong. 2005. *On Evaluating the Layout of UML Class Diagrams for Program Understanding*. Proceedings of the 13th International Workshop on Program Comprehension (IWPC'05), 2005, IEEE Computer Society Press, Los Alamitos, CA.

[24] M. Petre, A. Blackwell, and T. Green. 1998. Cognitive questions in software visualization. In: *Software Visualization: Programming as a Multimedia Experience* (Eds J. Stasko, J. Domingue, M. Brown, and B. Price), pp. 453–480. MIT Press.

[25] R. Wettel and M. Lanza. 2007. *Program Comprehension Through Software Habitability*. Proceedings of the 15th International Conference on Program Comprehension (ICPC'07), 2007, IEEE Computer Society Press, Los Alamitos, CA.

[26] R. P. Gabriel. 1996. *Patterns of Software*. Oxford University Press, New York, NY.

[27] T. J. Biggerstaff, B. Mitbander, and D. Webster. 1993. *The Concept Assignment Problem in Program Understanding*. Proceedings of the 15th International Conference on Software Engineering, 1993, IEEE Computer Society Press, Los Alamitos, CA.

[28] T. J. Biggerstaff, B. Mitbander, and D. Webster. 1994. Program understanding and the concept assignment problem. *Communications of the ACM*, 37(5), 72–83.

[29] N. Gold and K. Bennett. 2002. Hypothesis-based concept assignment in software maintenance. *IEE Proceedings-Software*, 149(4), 103–110.

[30] P. Tonella. 2003. Using a concept lattice of decomposition slices for program understanding and impact analysis. *IEEE Transactions on Software Engineering*, 29(6), 495–509.

[31] M. Weiser. 1984. Program Slicing. *IEEE Transactions on Software Engineering*, 10(4), 352–357.

EXERCISES

1. What is meant by program comprehension?

2. Explain the two broad kinds of *knowledge* that programmers need to possess for program comprehension.

3. Explain the concept of *mental model* in program comprehension.

4. Identify and summarize the *static* elements of mental models.

5. Identify and summarize the *dynamic* elements of mental models.

6. Identify and summarize three *characteristics* of expert programmers from the standpoint of program comprehension.

7. Briefly explain the Letovsky model for program comprehension.

8. Briefly explain the Shneiderman and Mayer model for program comprehension.

9. Briefly explain the Brooks model for program comprehension.

10. Briefly explain the Soloway, Adelson, and Ehrlich model for program comprehension.

11. Briefly explain the Pennington model for program comprehension.

12. Briefly explain the Integrated metamodel for program comprehension.

9

REUSE AND DOMAIN ENGINEERING

Before software can be reusable it first has to be usable.

—Ralph Johnson

9.1 GENERAL IDEA

Software reuse continues to be practiced since the early days of programming. Separate compilation of Fortran II subroutines and increased use of Fortran subroutine libraries are examples of reuse practiced in the early days of programming [1]. Formal software reuse was first introduced by Dough McIlroy. He envisioned an industry for the development of reusable components and the industrialization of the production of application software from off-the-shelf components [2]. Other examples of early development of reuse include the concept of program families introduced by David Parnas [3] and the concepts of domain and domain analysis introduced by Jim Neighbors [4]. A set of programs with several common attributes and features is known as a program family. On the other hand, domain analysis means finding objects and operations of a set of similar software systems in a specific problem domain. A domain is a field of expertise or a specialized body of knowledge. The concept of program families is related to the concept of domain analysis [3, 5, 6]. In this context, software reuse involves two main activities: software development *with* reuse and software development *for* reuse.

Software Evolution and Maintenance: A Practitioner's Approach, First Edition.
Priyadarshi Tripathy and Kshirasagar Naik.
© 2015 John Wiley & Sons, Inc. Published 2015 by John Wiley & Sons, Inc.

Intuitively, software reuse means using existing assets in the development of a new system. Reusable assets can be both reusable artifacts and software knowledge. There are four types of reusable artifacts as follows [7]:

- *Data reuse:* It involves a standardization of data formats. A standard data interchange format is necessary to design reusable functions.
- *Architectural reuse:* This means developing: (i) a set of generic design styles about the logical structure of software; and (ii) a set of functional elements and reuse those elements in new systems.
- *Design reuse:* This deals with the reuse of abstract design. A selected abstract design is custom implemented to meet the application requirements.
- *Program reuse:* This means reusing executable code. For example, one may reuse a pattern-matching system, that was developed as part of a text processing tool, in a database management system.

The reusability property of a software asset indicates the degree to which the asset can be reused in another project. For a software component to be reusable, it needs to exhibit the following properties that directly encourage its use in similar situations.

1. *Environmental independence:* This means that a component performs a task, and it makes minimal interactions with other components. Dependencies arise from the referencing of global data and assumptions made about the operational usage. The components with the environmental independence characteristic can be reused irrespective of the environment from which they were originally captured.
2. *High cohesion:* A component is said to have high cohesion, if its subsystems cooperate with each other to achieve a single objective. Components with high cohesion allow easy interpretation of their functionality.
3. *Low coupling:* If two components either do not interact with each other at all or at best interact by passing no data or only a few primitive data items, there is said to be low coupling. Low coupling components are excellent candidates for reuse. If a component or function performs one specific task and has few or no dependencies, it will be much more reusable than if it performs multiple tasks, has many side effects, and needs other components.
4. *Adaptability:* Adaptability means being easily changed to run in a new environment.
5. *Understandability:* If a program component is easily comprehended, programmers can quickly make decisions about its reuse potential.
6. *Reliability:* It is the ability of a software system to consistently perform its intended function without degradation or failure.
7. *Portability:* It is the usability of the same software in different environment. Therefore, components that are portable are excellent candidates for reuse.

9.1.1 Benefits of Reuse

One benefits in several ways from software reuse. The most obvious advantage of reuse is economic benefit. Projects become more cost-effective if some existing assets are reused. Other tangible benefits of reuse are as follows [8, 9]:

1. *Increased reliability:* Reusable components tend to reveal more failures because of the extra efforts put in their design and their extensive usage.

2. *Reduced process risk:* Reusing components can reduce risks inherent in software projects, because a working, presumed fault-free component is being reused, thereby reducing much uncertainty.

3. *Increase productivity:* By reusing artifacts and processes, software engineers become more productive because their activities, namely, specification, design, implementation, and testing, consume less time and effort. For reuse to be justified, the time to find the reuse component and adapt it must be much less than the time needed to develop the component anew. A reuse library stores reuse assets and provides an interface to search the repository [10, 11].

4. *Compliance with standards:* Reusing code in a software system being developed can improve its compliance with standards, thereby raising its quality. For example, by reusing familiar user interfaces, the usability of a system is increased.

5. *Accelerated development:* Software development time can be reduced by reusing assets.

6. *Improved maintainability:* Reusable components generally possess some desired characteristics: modularity, compliance with standards, low coupling and high cohesion, and consistent programming style. Not surprisingly, these characteristics are very much sought in maintainable programs. Therefore, any attempt to raise the reusability of an asset will contribute to better maintainability.

7. *Less maintenance effort and time:* Reusable components are easy to understand and change during a software modification. A significant benefit is obtained while executing perfective maintenance for two reasons: (i) new components needed during perfective maintenance can be obtained from reuse libraries and (ii) almost 50% of maintenance cost is attributed to perfective maintenance [12].

9.1.2 Reuse Models

Development of assets with the potential to be reused requires additional capital investment. The organization can select one or more reuse models that best meet their business objectives, engineering realities, and management styles [13]. Reuse models are classified as *proactive*, *reactive*, and *extractive*.

- *Proactive approaches:* In proactive approaches to developing reusable components, the system is designed and implemented for all conceivable variations; this includes design of reusable assets. A proactive approach is to product lines what the Waterfall model is to conventional software. The term product line development, which is also known as domain engineering, refers to a "development-for-reuse" process to create reusable software assets (RSA). This approach might be adopted by organizations that can accurately estimate the long-term requirements for their product line. However, this approach faces an investment risk if the future product requirements are not aligned with the projected requirements.

- *Reactive approaches:* In this approach, while developing products, reusable assets are developed if a reuse opportunity arises [14]. This approach works, if (i) it is difficult to perform long-term predictions of requirements for product variations; or (ii) an organization needs to maintain an aggressive production schedule with not much resources to develop reusable assets. The cost to develop assets can be amortized over several products. However, in the absence of a common, solid product architecture in a domain, continuous reengineering of products can render this approach more expensive.

- *Extractive approaches:* The extractive approaches [15] fall in between the proactive approaches and the reactive ones. To make a domain engineering's initial baseline, an extractive approach reuses some operational software products. Therefore, this approach applies to organizations that have accumulated both artifacts and experiences in a domain, and want to rapidly move from traditional to domain engineering.

9.1.3   Factors Influencing Reuse

Reuse factors are the practices that can be applied to increase the reuse of artifacts. There are several factors that influence software reuse. Frakes and Gandel [16] identified four major factors for systematic software reuse: *managerial, legal, economic, and technical.*

- *Managerial:* Systematic reuse requires upper management support, because: (i) it may need years of investment before it pays off; and (ii) it involves changes in organization funding and management structure that can only be implemented with executive management support. The management activities that directly support a reuse program are creating and managing incentives, educating personnel, and effecting a change in culture [17].

- *Legal:* This factor is linked with cultural, social, and political factors, and it presents very difficult problems. Potential problems include proprietary and copyright issues, liabilities and responsibilities of reusable software, and contractual requirements involving reuse. Use of third-party software makes this issue more important [18].

- *Economic:* Software reuse will succeed only if it provides economic benefits. A study by Favaro [19] found that some artifacts need to be reused more than 13 times to recoup the extra cost of developing reusable components.

- *Technical:* This factor has received much attention from the researchers actively engaged in library development [11], object-oriented development paradigm

[20], and domain engineering [21]. A reuse library stores reusable assets and provides an interface to search the repository. One can collect library assets in a number of ways: (i) reengineer the existing system components; (ii) design and build new assets; and (iii) purchase assets from other sources. Next, those reusable components are put through a *certification* process, including testing and verification, to assure that the components have the desired attributes [22]. Finally, the components are put into various categories for effective searching.

9.1.4   Success Factors of Reuse

An organization that attempts to implement a reuse program needs to address a broad spectrum of technical and nontechnical problems. It is difficult and risky to execute a successful reuse program. There is no common solution that all organizations can follow. Rather, each organization must analyze its own requirements, implement a process to measure the effectiveness of reuse, define the expected benefits, discover and eliminate impediments, and manage risks. The following steps aid organizations in running a successful reuse program [20]:

- Develop software with the product line approach.
- Develop software architectures to standardize data formats and product interfaces.
- Develop generic software architectures for product lines.
- Incorporate off-the-shelf components.
- Perform domain modeling of reusable components.
- Follow a software reuse methodology and measurement process.
- Ensure that management understands reuse issues at technical and nontechnical levels.
- Support reuse by means of tools and methods.
- Support reuse by placing reuse advocates in senior management.
- Practice reusing requirements and design in addition to reusing code.

9.2   DOMAIN ENGINEERING

The term domain engineering refers to a "development-for-reuse" process to create RSA. It is also referred to as product line development. Domain engineering is the set of activities that are executed to create RSA to be used in specific software projects. For a software product family, the requirements of the family are identified and a reusable, generic software structure is designed to develop members of the family. In the following, we explain analysis, design, and implementation activities of domain engineering.

- *Domain analysis* comprises three main steps: (i) identify the family of products to be constructed; (ii) determine the variable and common features in the family of products; and (iii) develop the specifications of the product family.

The feature-oriented domain analysis (FODA) method developed at the Software Engineering Institute [23] is a well-known method for domain analysis. The FODA method describes a process for domain analysis to discover, analyze, and document commonality and differences within a domain.

- *Domain design* comprises two main steps. (i) Develop a generic software architecture for the family of products under consideration; and (ii) develop a plan to create individual systems based on reusable assets. The design activity emphasizes a common architecture of related systems. The common architecture becomes the basis for system construction and incremental growth. The design activities are supported by architecture description languages (ADLs), namely, Acme [24], and interface definition languages (IDLs) [25], such as Facebook's Thrift.

- *Domain implementation* involves the following broad activities: (i) identify reusable components based on the outcome of domain analysis; (ii) acquire and create reusable assets by applying the domain knowledge acquired in the process of domain analysis and the generic software architecture constructed in the domain design phase; (iii) catalogue the reusable assets into a component library. Development, management, and maintenance of a repository of reusable assets make up the core of domain implementation.

Application engineering (a.k.a. product development) is complementary to *domain engineering*. It refers to a "development-with-reuse" process to create specific systems by using the fabricated assets defined in domain engineering [26]. Application engineering composes specific application systems by: (i) reusing existing assets; (ii) developing any new components that are needed; (iii) reengineering some existent software; and (iv) testing the overall system. Similar to the standard practices in software engineering [27], it begins by eliciting requirements, analyzing the requirements, and writing a specification. However, the requirements are specified in incremental chunks, called delta, from a set of generic system requirements developed during domain engineering.

Both domain and application engineering processes feed on each other, as illustrated in Figure 9.1. Application engineering is fed with reusable assets from domain engineering, whereas domain engineering is fed with new requirements from application engineering. A closed loop occurs between the two engineering processes because application engineers may discover that the present reusable assets do not cover some requirements. Therefore, some application-specific development and/or

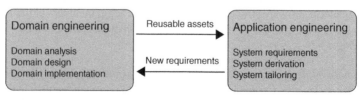

FIGURE 9.1   Feedback between domain and application engineering

tailoring is required [28]. To make the reusable assets consistent with the needs of the product, the new requirements are fed back into domain engineering.

In the following sections, we briefly discuss *nine* domain engineering approaches reported in the literature [13, 29, 30]: Draco, domain analysis and reuse environment (DARE), family-oriented abstraction, specification, and tTransportation (FAST), feature-oriented reuse method (FORM), "Komponentbasierte Anwendungsentwicklung" (KobrA), product line UML-based software engineering (PLUS), product line software engineering (PuLSE), Koala, and reuse-driven software engineering business (RSEB).

9.2.1 Draco

Based on transformation technology, Draco is the first prototype of the domain engineering approach proposed by Neighbors [5]. Neighbor's work provided an important contribution in domain engineering in the form of generative programming and transformation systems. However, it is very complex to apply in production environment.

9.2.2 DARE

A method and a toolset for performing domain engineering constitute DARE [31]. To make domain models, the DARE process utilizes three information sources: code, documents, and expert knowledge. The generic architectures, feature tables, and facet tables, and all models and information are stored in a domain book. Successful industry applications of DARE include building of database at Oracle [32].

9.2.3 FAST

The former Lucent Technologies (now Alcatel-Lucent) introduced the FAST method in 1999 [33] to develop telecommunication infrastructure. Applied in product line engineering, FAST defines a pattern of engineering processes. Three sub-processes constitute FAST: domain qualification (DQ), domain engineering (DE), and application engineering (AE). A product line that is worthy of investment is identified with domain qualification. Domain engineering enables the development of product line environments and assets. By using product line assets, application engineering develops products rapidly.

9.2.4 FORM

FORM, developed at Pohang University of Science and Technology [34, 35], is basically an extension of the FODA method [23]. FORM finds commonalities and differences in a product line in terms of features, and uses those findings to develop architectures and components for product lines. A feature model captures the commonalities and variabilities to support: (i) development of assets for reusable product lines; and (ii) development of products using the reusable assets. Therefore, two processes are key to FORM: asset development and product development.

9.2.5   KobrA

KobrA is a method for component-based application development [30]. The two main activities in KobrA are: *framework engineering* and *application engineering*. By means of framework engineering, one makes a common framework that manifests all variations in products making up the family. A set of components are organized in the form of a tree in a framework, and each component is described at the specification level and realization level. The specification level of abstraction described the components externally visible properties and behavior. The realization level of abstraction describes how the component satisfies the contracts with other components. Next, application engineering is applied on the framework to build specific applications.

9.2.6   PLUS

The UML-based modeling method to develop single systems has been extended in PLUS to support product lines [36]. In PLUS, (i) for requirements analysis activities, use-case modeling and feature modeling are provided; (ii) there are mechanisms to model the static aspects, dynamic interactions, state machines, and class dependency for product lines; and (iii) component-based software design and software architecture patterns are supported for product line design activity.

9.2.7   PuLSE

Product line software engineering (PuLSE) methodology was developed to enable the conceptualization and deployment of software product lines for large enterprises [37]. The PuLSE methodology comprises three key elements: (i) the deployment phases; (ii) the technical components; and (iii) the support components. The deployment phases describe activities for initialization, construction of infrastructure, usage of infrastructure, and management and evolution of product lines. The technical components describe how to operationalize the development of the product line. The support components are guidelines enabling better evolution, adaptation, and deployment of the product line.

9.2.8   Koala

Koala is a language to describe architectures for product lines for embedded software to be used in home appliances [38]. It was originally developed at Philips Corporation. To support product variations, diversity interfaces and switches are provided in Koala. Internal diversity of components are handled by means of diversity interfaces and the switches are used to route connections between interfaces. The extra functions of a component are treated as optional interfaces.

9.2.9   RSEB

RSEB is a use-case-driven reuse method based on UML [39]. It was designed to facilitate both asset reuse and the development of reusable software. RSEB supports both domain engineering and application engineering. The former comprises two processes: application family engineering and component system engineering. The former is used to develop and maintain the overall layered system architecture. On the other hand, the latter is used to develop component systems.

9.3   REUSE CAPABILITY

Reuse capability concerns gaining a comprehensive understanding of the development process of an organization with respect to reusing assets and establishing priorities for improving the extent of reuse. It is defined by Ted Davis [40] as "the range of expected results in reuse proficiency, efficiency, and effectiveness that can be achieved by an organizations process" (p. 128). The concept of reuse *opportunities* is used as a basis to define reuse *efficiency* and reuse *proficiency*. An asset provides a reuse opportunity when the asset—to be developed or existing—satisfies an anticipated or current need. There are two broad kinds of reuse opportunities: *targeted* and *potential*. Targeted reuse opportunities are those reuse opportunities on which the organization explicitly spends much efforts. On the other hand, potential reuse opportunities are those reuse opportunities which will turn into actual reuse, if exploited. Not always a targeted opportunity turns into a potential opportunity.

Now we define reuse *proficiency* and reuse *efficiency* by means of

$$R_A, R_P, \text{ and } R_T,$$

where:

R_A counts the actual reuse opportunities exploited;
R_P counts the potential opportunities for reuse; and
R_T counts the targeted opportunities for reuse.

Reuse proficiency is the ratio R_A/R_P, and reuse efficiency is the ratio R_A/R_T. The benefits and costs of reusing assets in a project are succinctly captured by the concept of reuse *effectiveness*, which is represented as:

$$N(C_{NR} - C_R)/C_D,$$

where:

N = number of products, systems, or versions developed with the reusable assets;
C_{NR} = cost of developing new assets without using reusable assets;
C_R = cost of utilizing, that is, identifying, assessing, and adapting reusable assets;
C_D = cost of domain engineering, that is, developing assets for reuse and building a reuse infrastructure.

The concepts of reuse efficiency and reuse proficiency are used to measure the impacts of reuse capability. The linkage between the two concepts and reuse capability has been illustrated in Figure 9.2. The ovals denote the sets of potential, target, and actual reuse opportunities. For simplicity, assume that the areas of the ovals denote the counts of the assets corresponding to those opportunities. Now, in terms of the elements of the figure, reuse efficiency is calculated by dividing the area of the actual reuse oval by the area of the target oval. Similarly, reuse proficiency is calculated by

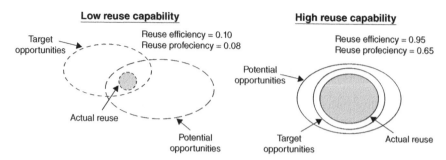

FIGURE 9.2   Reuse capability. From Reference 40. © 1993 IEEE

dividing the area of the actual reuse oval by the area of the oval representing potential reuse.

Two possible scenarios of low reuse capability and high reuse concerning the extent of reuse capability can be found in Figure 9.2. An informal approach to reuse results in low reuse, because potential opportunities—shown as dashes—are overlooked. In Figure 9.2, potential opportunities may exclude target opportunities, because: (i) the potential opportunities are unknown; and (ii) target opportunities may not be planned explicitly. Therefore, with many target opportunities falling outside the potential opportunities, the resulting reuse efficiency and proficiency become low. In addition, with resources being spent on many opportunities not resulting in actual reuse, reuse effectiveness becomes low.

9.4   MATURITY MODELS

A reuse maturity model (RMM) is an aid for performing planning and self-assessment to improve an organization's capability to reuse existing software artifacts. Such a model helps the organization's understanding of their existing and future goals for reuse activities. In other words, such a model can be used in planning systematic reuse. Organizations developing and maintaining multiple products, software systems, and versions are the primary stakeholders of the maturity models. In this section we discuss briefly three maturity models: reuse maturity model [41], reuse capability model [40], and RiSE maturity model [42].

9.4.1   Reuse Maturity Model

In circa 1991, Koltun and Hudson [41] presented the first RMM. The model provides a concise form of obtaining information on reuse practices in organizations. The model comprises 5 levels and 10 dimensions of reuse maturity as shown in Table 9.1. The columns of the table indicate the different levels of reuse maturity. Maturity improves on a scale from 1 to 5, where level 1 corresponds to Initial/Chaotic state and level 5 corresponds to the Ingrained state. Much automated tool support and measurement of reuse to track progress are the hallmarks of level 5. The rows of the table correspond to different dimensions of reuse maturity, namely, Planning to reuse

TABLE 9.1 Reuse Maturity Model

			Reuse Maturity Levels		
Dimension of Reuse	1. Initial/Chaotic	2. Monitored	3. Coordinated	4. Planned	5. Ingrained
Motivation/Culture	Reuse discouraged	Reuse encouraged	Reuse incentivized reinforced rewarded	Reuse indoctrinated	Reuse in the way we do business
Planning to reuse	None	Grassroots activity	Targets of opportunity	Business imperative	Part of strategic plan
Breadth of reuse	Individual	Work group	Department	Division	Enterprise wide
Responsible for making reuse happen	Individual initiative	Shared initiative	Dedicated individual	Dedicated group	Corporate group with division liaisons
Process by which reuse is leveraged	Reuse process chaotic; unclear how reuse comes in	Reuse questions raised at design reviews (after the fact)	Design emphasis placed on off-the-shelf parts	Focus on developing families of products	All software products are genericized for future reuse
Reuse assets	Salvage yard (no apparent structure to collection)	Catalog identifies language- and platform-specific parts	Catalog organized along application specific lines	Catalog includes generic data processing functions	Planned activity to acquire or develop missing pieces in catalog
Classification activity	Informal, individualized	Multiple independent schemes for classifying parts	Single scheme catalog published periodically	Some domain analyses done to determine categories	Formal, complete consistent timely classification
Technology support	Personal tools, if any	Many tools, but not specialized for reuse	Classification aids and synthesis aids	Electronic library separate from development environment	Automated support integrated with development environment
Metrics	No metrics on reuse level, payoff, or costs	Number of lines of code used in cost models	Maturity tracking of reuse occurrences of catalog parts	Analyses done to identify expected payoffs from developing reusable parts	All system utilities, software tools and accounting mechanisms instrumented to track reuse
Legal, contractual accounting considerations	Inhibition to getting started	Internal accounting scheme for sharing costs and allocating benefits	Data rights and compensation issues resolved with customer	Royalty scheme for all suppliers and customers	Software treated as key capital asset

Source: From Reference 43. © 1996 ACM.

and Motivation/Culture. For each row, the amount of organizational commitment increases as the organization moves from level 1 to level 5.

To benefit from this model, an organization evaluates its current maturity level before embarking on a reuse improvement program. Essentially, the organization identifies its placement on each of the 10 dimensions. Next, activities are performed to raise the level of reuse maturity. Upon reaching the highest level of reuse maturity, reuse activities become part of the business practice. The main obstacles to reaching the highest level of reuse are: technical, cultural, financial, institutional, and legal. This model was not applied in real case studies, but are considered as the key insights for the reuse capability model developed by Ted Davis [40].

9.4.2 Reuse Capability Model

The reuse capability model (RCM) [40] is used together with the reuse adoption process defined by the Software Production Consortium (SPC) [44]. The adoption process for reuse is a solution to implement a program for reuse, and it is based on the implementation model defined by Rubén Prieto-Diaz [14]. RCM comprises two models, namely, an assessment model and an implementation model. An organization can use the assessment model to: (i) understand its current capability to reuse artifacts; and (ii) discover opportunities to improve its reuse capability. A set of critical success factors are at the core of the assessment model. The success factors are described as goals that an organization uses to evaluate the present state of their reuse practice. The organization will get to know its strengths and learn opportunities for improvement. On the other hand, the organization can apply the implementation model in prioritizing the critical factor goals by grouping them into stages.

Assessment model: The success factors in the assessment model are grouped into four categories: application development, asset development, management, and process and technology. The critical success factors have been listed in Table 9.2. The various groups of critical success factors reflect the different views of reuse in an organization.

Now we briefly explain the four groups of factors one-by-one.

- Application Development Factors: The application development factors concern issues which are critical to the successful reuse of assets in the development of products. These factors relate to all the activities in the processes followed by the organization to develop software products.
- Asset Development Factors: The asset development factors concern issues which are critical to the successful development or acquisition of assets for reuse. These factors relate to all types of reusable assets, namely, requirements, architectures, design, source code, and test cases.
- Management Factors: The management factors concern issues which are critical to management's role in enabling reuse. These factors are quite broad, relating to such diverse aspects as products, business of the organization, finance, marketing, and product management.
- Process and Technology Factors: This group of factors concern general process issues across asset development, application development, and the management.

TABLE 9.2   Critical Success Factors

Application Development Factors	Asset Development Factors	Management Factors	Process and Technology Factors
Asset awareness and accessibility	Needs identification	Organizational commitment	Process definition and integration
Asset identification	Asset interface and architecture definition	Planning and direction	Measurement
Asset evaluation and verification	Needs and solution relationships	Cost and pricing	Continuous process improvement
Application integrability	Commonality and variability definition	Legal and contractual constraints	Training
	Asset value determination		Tool support
	Asset reusability		Technology innovation
	Asset quality		

Each critical success factor is defined in terms of one or more goals. The critical success factors and the corresponding goals have been described in the guidebook for adopting reuse [44]. The goals describe *what* is to be achieved—and not *how* those goals can be realized. Therefore, there is much flexibility in achieving those goals. As an example, the *needs identification* factor has the following goals:

- Identify the current needs for solutions of the developer.
- Identify the anticipated needs for solutions of the developer.
- Identify the current needs for solutions of the customer.
- Identify the anticipated needs for solutions of the customer.
- Use the identified needs as a reference to develop or acquire reusable assets to meet the specified needs.

Implementation model: Establishing goals and making strategies to achieve those goals are complex tasks. The goals are divided into four stages, namely, opportunistic, integrated, leveraged, and anticipating. In this section, brief descriptions of the four stages will be provided by focusing on the key characteristics of the stages. Specifically, each characteristic relates to a goal in the implementation model. More details of the implementation model can be found in the reuse adoption guidebook [44].

- **Opportunistic**: A common reuse strategy does not fit all projects so each project develops its own strategy to reuse artifacts. The strategy includes: (i) defining reuse activities in the project plan; (ii) using tools to support the reuse activities; (iii) identifying the needs of the developers and developing or acquiring reusable artifacts; and (iv) identifying reusable artifacts throughout the life cycle of the project.

- **Integrated**: The organization defines a reuse process and integrates it with its development process. It is important for the organization to support the reuse process by means of policies, procedures, resource allocation, and organizational structure.

- **Leveraged**: To extract the maximum benefits from reuse in groups of related products, a strategy for reuse in product lines is developed.

- **Anticipating**: Reusable assets are acquired or developed based on anticipated customer needs.

9.4.3 RiSE Maturity Model

The RiSE maturity model [42] was developed during the RiSE project through discussions with industry partners [45]. The model structure intends to be flexible, modular, and adaptable to the needs of the organization that will use them. Thus, the model was based on two principles: modularity and responsibility. The term modularity is used in the sense of processes with less coupling and maximum cohesion, and the term responsibility is used in the sense of the possibility to establish one or more team responsible for each process, or activity. The RiSE maturity model includes: (i) reuse practices grouped by perspectives and in organized levels representing different degrees of software reuse achieved; and (ii) reuse elements describing fundamental parts of reuse technology, such as assets, documentation, tools, and environments. Reuse elements and reuse assets are synonymous.

Maturity levels, as listed below, indicate the: (i) reuse elements that are expected to be used in the organization; and (ii) the reuse practices that are expected to be implemented and followed in the organization. The activities at level n and higher are based on the reuse elements implemented and practices followed at level $n - 1$, such that $1 < n \leq 5$. The five maturity levels are as follows:

1. **Level 1:** Ad hoc Reuse
2. **Level 2:** Basic Reuse
3. **Level 3:** Initial Reuse
4. **Level 4:** Organized Reuse
5. **Level 5:** Systematic Reuse

Associated with each level of maturity are a list of reuse practices and a list of reuse elements. Each maturity level is characterized by its own goals to be achieved. The maturity levels are discussed next.

Level 1: Ad hoc Reuse At Level 1: (i) software is developed in a traditional way, without reusing assets; (ii) management does not support reuse; and (iii) reuse practices might be performed as an individual initiative by developers. By default, all organizations making no reuse efforts fall in Level 1.

Level 2: Basic Reuse   At Level 2, simple tools are used to develop reusable technical assets, namely, documents, software design, and code. Those technical assets consider all the requirements of the system without making any distinction between domain-specific aspects and business aspects. Developers manually modify the reusable assets to complete an implementation. Organizations benefit by acquiring experience in system design and software reuse. The following goals are defined for Level 2.

- Goal 1: Best practices in reuse are adopted in the design and implementation of the software product.
- Goal 2: Use the technical assets, namely, code and documentation, to build software.

Level 3: Initial Reuse   At Level 3, organizations make a distinction between business assets and domain-related assets, because it is useful to maintain the business issues independent from the implementation issues. The advantage of the aforementioned decoupling is that the same implementation asset can be reused in different projects having slightly different business requirements. Separating business assets from domain-related assets is important for system families. Next, reuse practices are institutionalized. Moreover, to automate the engineering process, efforts are made. An asset manager, which is basically a reuse repository, stores the engineering process knowledge [41]. To evaluate the effectiveness of reuse activities and practices, metrics are defined. For example, a count of the times a certain module is reused is a measure of the reuse of that module. At Level 3, the following goals are defined:

- Goal 1: Separate business-specific aspects from domain-related aspects.
- Goal 2: Use defined process.

Level 4: Organized Reuse   Level 4 is characterized by a better integration of all reuse abstraction levels. Reuse is introduced at the highest abstraction level. Staff members know the reuse vocabulary and have reuse expertise. Reuse occurs across all functional areas. At Level 4, domain engineering is performed. Reuse-based processes are in place to support and encourage reuse, and the organization has a focus on developing families of products. The organization has all the data needed to decide which assets to build or what to acquire, because it has a reuse inventory organized along application-specific lines. The reuse practices within the projects start to be quantitatively managed, and quality metrics are collected and analyzed. All costs associated with assets development and all savings from its reuse are reported and shared. Projects are statistically controlled through standardized metrics that lead to a better control of the objectives of the project. For Level 4, the goals and practices are as follows:

- Goal 1: Enhance the organization's competitive advantage.
- Goal 2: Integrate reuse activities in the whole software development process.
- Goal 3: Ensure efficient reuse performance.

Level 5: Systematic Reuse   At Level 5, the organization's knowledge base is planned, organized, stored, and maintained in a reuse inventory (a.k.a. asset manager) and is used with focus on the software development process. By the time an organization reaches this level, all major obstacles to reuse have been removed. All definitions, guidelines, and standards are in place enterprise wide. Domain engineering practices are put in place. Knowledge and reusable assets are regularly validated to make strategic assets reusable. For future reuse, all software products are generalized. Domain analysis is performed across all product lines. All system utilities, tools, and accounting mechanisms are instrumented to track reuse. From the reuse inventory perspective, the development process supports a planned activity to acquire or develop missing pieces in the catalog. From the technological perspective, the organization has automated reuse support integrated with their development process. From the business perspective, the organization benefits from having implemented a software reuse approach. The organization expresses its system development capability in the form of reusable assets. The capability to reuse assets accelerates the time to market. All costs are associated to a product line or a particular asset and all savings from its reuse are reported and shared. At Level 5, the goals and practices are as follows.

- Goal 1: Reuse is "the way we do business."
- Goal 2: Establish and maintain complete reuse-centric development.

Perspective and Factors   In the RiSE maturity model, 15 factors were considered, and those are divided into 4 perspectives: organizational, business, technological, and processes. The organizational perspective concerns activities that are closely related to management decisions required to organize and manage a reuse project. Table 9.3 shows the factors related to the organizational perspective and their distribution across the RiSE maturity model levels. The business perspective addresses issues related to the business domain and market decisions for the organization. Table 9.4 shows the factors related to the business perspective. The technological perspective covers development activities in the software reuse engineering discipline and factors related to the infrastructure and technological environment. Table 9.5 shows the factors related to the technological perspective. Finally, the processes perspective includes only those activities which support the implementation of the engineering and the project management practices. Table 9.6 shows the factors related to the processes perspective.

9.5 ECONOMIC MODELS OF SOFTWARE REUSE

Project managers and financial managers can use the general economics model of software reuse in their planning for investments in software reuse. The project manager needs to estimate the costs and potential payoffs to justify systematic reuse. Increased productivity is an example of payoff of reuse. In the following section, we discuss cost model of Gaffney and Durek [46], application system cost model of Gaffney and Cruickshank [47], and business model of Poulin and Caruso [48].

TABLE 9.3 RiSE Maturity Model Levels: Organizational Factors [42]

				Levels	
Factors of Influence	1. Ad hoc	2. Basic	3. Initial	4. Organized	5. Systematic
Planning for reuse	– Non-existent	– Grassroot activity – Reuse is viewed as single-point opportunities – Individual achievements are rewarded	– Targets of opportunity – Organization responsible for reuse – A key business strategy	– Business imperative – Reuse occurs across all functional areas	– Part of a strategic plan – Discriminator in business success
Software reuse education	– Lack of expertise by staff members – Frequent resistance to reuse	– Basic definitions of reuse are agreed upon	– The staff has the expertise and know-how to obtain benefits with reuse	– The staff members know the reuse vocabulary and have reuse expertise	– All definitions, guidelines, and standards are in place, enterprise wide
Legal, contractual, accounting considerations	– Inhibition to getting started	– Internal accounting scheme for sharing costs allocating benefits	– Data rights and compensation issues resolved with customer	– Royalty scheme for all suppliers and customers	– Software treated as key capital asset

(continued)

TABLE 9.3 (continued)

Factors of Influence		Levels			
	1. Ad hoc	2. Basic	3. Initial	4. Organized	5. Systematic
Funding, costs, and financial features	– Costs of reuse are unknown	– Costs of reuse are "feared"	– Payoff of reuse is "known" and understand for a given domain – Investments made in reuse, payoffs expected – Costs of reuse are "known"	– All costs associated with an asset's development and all savings from its reuse are reported and shared	– All costs associated to a product line or a particular asset and all saving from its reuse are reported and shared
Rewards and incentives	– Reuse is discouraged by management	– Reuse is encouraged	– Reuse is motivated reinforced, rewarded	– Reuse is indoctrinated	– Reuse is "the way we do business"
Independent reusable asset development team	– Individual initiative (personal goal as time allows)	– Shared initiative	– Dedicated individual	– Dedicated group	– Corporate group (for visibility not control) with division liaisons

TABLE 9.4 RiSE Maturity Model Levels: Business Factors [42]

Factors of Influence	Levels				
	1. Ad hoc	2. Basic	3. Initial	4. Organized	5. Systematic
Product family approach	– Isolated products – No family product approach	– Common features and requirements across the products – Commonalities and reuse possibilities were identified	– Product line domain analyses performed	– Focus on developing families of products – Domain engineering performed	– Domain analysis performed across all product lines – Product family approach
Software reuse education	– Chaotic development process unclear where reuse comes in	– Reuse questions raised at design reviews (after the fact) – Development process defined (some reuse activity indications)	– Design emphasis placed on reuse of off-the-shelf parts – Product line domain analyses performed – Shared understanding of all the activities needed to support reuse	– Focus on developing families of products – Reuse-based processes are in place to support and encourage reuse – Domain engineering performed	– All software products generated for future reuse – Domain analyses performed across all product lines – Product family approach

TABLE 9.5 RiSE Maturity Model Levels: Technological Factors [42]

Factors of Influence		Levels			
	1. Ad hoc	2. Basic	3. Initial	4. Organized	5. Systematic
Repository systems usage	– Salvage yard (No apparent structure to collection)	– Catalog identifies language-and platform-specific parts – Simple structure like concurrent versions systems – Considered mainly source code	– Catalog includes generic data processing functions – Considered software components, reports and document models	– Catalog organized along application specifications – Have all data needed decide which assets to build/acquire – Considered screen generators database elements and test cases	– Planned activity to acquire or develop missing pieces in catalog – Considered all artifacts of software development life cycle
Technology support	– Personal tools, if any	– A collection of tools, e.g., CM, but not specialized to reuse – General-purpose analyzers combined to assess reuse levels	– Classification aids and synthesis aids – Standardization on components and architecture – Tools customized to support reuse	– Digital library separate from development environment	– Automated support integrated with development system – Fully integrated with development and reporting systems

TABLE 9.6   RiSE Maturity Model Levels: Processes Factors [42]

Factors of Influence	Levels				
	1. Ad hoc	2. Basic	3. Initial	4. Organized	5. Systematic
Quality models usage	– No quality model adoption	– Some quality activities were incorporated in the software development process	– Software development process guided by a quality model	– High quality model usage in the engineering department	– Quality model completely adopted in the organization activities
Software reuse measurement	– No metrics on level of reuse, payoff, or cost of reuse	– Number of lines of reused code factored into cost models	– Manual tracking of reuse occurrences of catalog parts	– Analyses performed to identify expected payoffs from developing reusable parts	– All system utilities, software tools, and accounting mechanisms instrumented to track reuse
Systematic reuse process	– No reused-based process	– Some reuse activities were adopted in the development process – Planning to adapt the software development process of the organization for a reuse-based process	– Development process of the organization is adapted to reuse concepts	– Reuse benefits and concepts are clear for the engineering team – Development process is reused based	– Systematic reuse process is enterprise wide
Origin of the reused assets	– No reuse assets	– Build from scratch, sometimes indirectly	– Build from existent products; adapting existing products	– Build from existing products; extracted through a reengineering process	– Planning the design and building of reusable assets according to product family
Previous development of reusable assets	– No development of reusable assets	– Parallel with development	– Before development	– Before development	– Before development

9.5.1 Cost Model of Gaffney and Durek

The two cost and productivity models proposed by Gaffney and Durek [46] for software reuse are: *first order reuse cost model* and *higher order cost model*. The cost of reusing software components has been modeled in the *first order reuse cost model*, whereas the *higher order cost model* considers the cost of developing reusable assets.

First Order Reuse Cost Model In this model, we assume the following conditions [49].

1. The reused software satisfies the black-box requirements in the sense that it is stable and reliable. If the behavior of the component becomes unreliable, unstable, or inconsiderably different than the project's needs, the component becomes a white box because it needs to be fixed.
2. Users of the reusable components have adequate expertise in the context of reuse.
3. There is adequate documentation of the components to be reused.
4. The cost of reusing the components is negligible.

As explained in what follows, three broad categories of program code are used in a project.

- S_n: It represents the new code added to the system.
- S_o: It represents the original source code from the preexisting system. S_o includes both *lifted* code and modified code. *Lifted* code means unchanged, original code taken from past releases of a product. The source code from modified (partial) parts are not considered as reused code.
- S_r: It represents the reuse source code that are not developed or maintained by the organization. The reuse code is obtained from completely unmodified components normally located in a reuse library.

The *effective size*, denoted by S_e, is an adjusted combination of the modified source code and the new source code, as given in the following equation.

$$S_e = S_n + S_o(A_d \times F_d + A_i \times F_i + A_t \times F_t)$$

where:

A_d = is a normalized measure of design activity,
A_i = is a normalized measure of integration activity,
A_t = is a normalized measure of testing activity, and
$A_d + A_i + A_t = 1$.

The expression within the parentheses, namely, $(A_d \times F_d + A_i \times F_i + A_t \times F_t)$, is a weighted sum of relative efforts from design, implementation, and test; F_d, F_i, and F_t represent relative efforts from design, implementation, and test, respectively.

One or more reusable components comprise the rest of the system. Reusable components are assumed to be black boxes so their sizes are assumed to be not available. Therefore, the relative sizes of reusable components can be obtained by estimating the size of the reusable components with the assumption that those are built from the scratch. Letting S_r denote the estimated size of reusable components, the relative sizes of reusable components is given by R, where R is expressed as follows:

$$R = \frac{S_r}{S_e + S_r}.$$

Let C be the cost of software development for a given product relative to that for all new code (for which $C = 1$). Let R be the proportion of reused code in the product as defined earlier ($R \leq 1$). Let b be the cost, relative to that for all new code, of incorporating the reused code into the new product. Note that $b = 1$ for all new code. The relative cost for software development is:

[(relative cost of all new code) $*$ (proportion of new code)]
+
[(relative cost of reused software) $*$ (proportion of reused software)].

Therefore:

$$C = (1)(1 - R) + (b)(R) = (b - 1)R + 1$$

and the associated relative productivity is:

$$P = \frac{1}{C} = \frac{1}{(b - 1)R + 1}.$$

b must be <1 for reuse to be cost-effective. The size of b depends on the life cycle phase—requirements, design, implementation, or testing—of the reusable components. As an example, let us consider the relative cost of the development activities as shown in Table 9.7. Table 9.8 shows example relative activity costs to calculate the relative component reuse cost b. For instance, if we want to reuse a requirements component, then the accompanying costs are in the form of design, implementation, and test activities, which are 0.37, 0.22, and 0.33, respectively. Therefore, the relative cost to reuse requirements is $b = (0.37 + 0.22 + 0.33) = 0.92$. On the other hand, if code is reused, then the additional tasks will involve requirements and testing. Therefore, the relative cost to reuse code is $b = (0.08 + 0.33) = 0.41$.

TABLE 9.7   Relative Costs of Development Activities

Activity	Activity Code	Activity Cost
Requirements	Req	0.08
Design	Des	0.37
Implementation	Imp	0.22
Test	Test	0.33

TABLE 9.8   Relative Reuse Cost (b)

Component Type	Activities to be Completed	Relative Reuse Cost (b)
Requirements	Des, Imp, Test	0.92
Design	Req, Imp, Test	0.63
Code	Req, Test	0.41
Requirements, Design, Code,	Test	0.33

Higher Order Reuse Cost Model   Estimating the cost of developing reusable components is key to formulating a reuse cost model. By combining the development cost of the reusable components into the economic model, we have

$$C = (1 - R) \times 1 + \left(b + \frac{a}{n} \right) R,$$

where a is the cost of developing reusable components relative to the cost of building new non-reusable components from the scratch, and n is the number of uses over which the cost of reusable components is amortized. Now, the model can be rewritten as

$$C = \left(b + \frac{a}{n} - 1 \right) R + 1.$$

9.5.2   Application System Cost Model of Gaffney and Cruickshank

An application system cost model based on domain engineering and application engineering was proposed by Gaffney and Cruickshank. The cost of an application system is expressed as the sum of two component costs: (i) the investment in domain engineering apportioned over N application systems; and (ii) the cost of application engineering to develop a specific system. Therefore, the cost of an application system, C_s, is equal to the prorated cost of domain engineering plus the cost of application engineering. In addition, let the cost of application engineering be the cost of the new code plus the cost of the reused code in the new application system, and let R denote the fraction of code that is reused code.

Now, we have

$$C_s = C_{dp} + C_a$$
$$C_s = C_d/N + C_n + C_r,$$

where:

$C_{dp} = C_d/N$ and $C_a = C_n + C_r$;
C_s = the total cost of the application system;
C_d = the total cost of domain engineering;

C_{dp} = the prorated portion of C_d shared by each of the N application systems;
C_a = the cost of an application system;
C_n = the cost of the new code in the application system;
C_r = the cost of the reused code in the application system.

Each of the costs, C_d, C_n, and C_r, is taken to be the product of a unit cost (LM/KSLOC) and an amount of code (KSLOC), where LM/KSLOC stands for labor months/1000 source lines of code (LOC). Hence,

$$C_d = C_{de} * S_t, C_n = C_{vn} * S_n,$$

and

$$C_r = C_{vr} * S_r.$$

The equation for reuse cost is

$$C_s = C_{us}S_s = \frac{C_{de}S_t}{N} + C_{vn}S_n + C_{vr}S_r,$$

where:

C_{us} = unit cost of the application system;
C_{de} = unit cost of domain engineering;
C_{vn} = unit cost of new code developed for this application system;
C_{vr} = unit cost of reusing code in this application system;
S_t = expected value of the unduplicated size of the reuse library, measured in source statements;
S_n = amount of new code in terms of source statements developed for this application system;
S_r = amount of reused code incorporated into this application system in source statement;
S_s = total size of the application system in source statement.

Let $S_n/S_s = 1 - R$ and $S_r/S_s = R$, where R is the proportion of reuse. The reuse cost equation can be rewritten as

$$C_{us} = \frac{C_{de}}{N}\frac{S_t}{S_s} + C_{vn}(1 - R) + C_{vr}R.$$

Now let $S_t/S_s = K$, the library relative capacity. Thus, the basic reuse cost equation is

$$C_{us} = \frac{C_{de}}{N}K + C_{vn} - (C_{vn} - C_{vr})R.$$

The basic reuse cost equation assumes a single reuse of S_r units (SLOC, KSLOC) in each of the "N application" systems. Thus, this expression is applicable to systematic reuse of units of code relatively dense in functionality.

9.5.3   Business Model of Poulin and Caruso

Poulin and Caruso [48] developed a model at IBM to improve measurement and reporting software reuse. The authors present a measure for reuse level, the financial and the productivity benefit of reuse. They consider potential benefits of reuse against the cost of resources expended to identify and integrate reusable assets into a system. Their results are based on a set of data points as follows:

- *Shipped source instruction* (SSI): SSI is the total count of executable code lines in the source files of a product. Calling a reused part is counted as one SSI.
- *Changed source instruction* (CSI): CSI is the total count of executable code lines that are new, added, or modified in a new release of a product. Note that CSI does not include RSI and unchanged instructions from past releases of the system. Calling a reused part is counted as one CSI.
- *Reused source instruction* (RSI): RSI is the total source instructions shipped but not developed or maintained by the reporting organization. RSI does not include base instructions from past releases of a product. In addition, RSI does not include source instructions from partly changed components. Independent of the number of times the component is called or expanded, source instructions from a reused component are counted just once.
- *Source instruction reused by others* (SIRBO): SIRBO is the total lines of source instructions of an organization reused by others. SIRBO is a measure of the contributions of an organization to reuse, and it is calculated as follows:

$$SIRBO = \text{(Source instructions per part)}$$
$$\times \text{(The number of organizations using the part)}.$$

- *Software development cost* (Cost per LOC): This metric concerns the development of new software, and it is calculated in two steps. (i) Let S denote the total cost of the organization, including overhead; and (ii) divide S by the total outputs of the organization in number of LOC. It may be noted that one needs to know the cost of developing the software without reuse so as to understand the financial benefit of reuse.
- *Software development error rate* (Error rate): It is a historical average number of errors uncovered in the products. To estimate the cost of avoiding maintenance, a historical average value is used.
- *Cost per error:* To quantify the advantage of better quality reusable assets, the historical mean cost of maintaining components with traditional development methods is used as a base line. Now, the cost per error metric is calculated in two steps: (i) let S denote the sum of *all* costs; and (ii) divide S by the number of errors repaired.

The aforementioned metrics are combined to form three derived metrics: reuse percent, reuse cost avoidance, and reuse value added. The reuse percent and reuse cost avoidance metrics give indications of an organization's reuse activities. The reuse value added metric includes recognition for writing reusable code.

1. *Reuse Percent* (RP): It reflects the extent of reuse in a product. *RP* is analogous to *R* in the model of Gaffney and Durek. Poulin and Caruso make a distinction between the reuse percent of a product release and the reuse percent of a product:

$$Reuse\ percent\ of\ a\ product = \frac{RSI}{RSI + SSI} \times 100\%.$$

$$Reuse\ percent\ of\ a\ product\ release = \frac{RSI}{RSI + CSI} \times 100\%.$$

2. *Reuse cost avoidance* (RCA): The purpose of this metric is to measure reduced total product costs as a result of reuse. One must retrieve and evaluate the reusable assets to choose the appropriate ones to be integrated into the system being developed. According to studies performed by Poulin et al. [50], there are significant financial benefits due to reusing assets. For example, the cost of integrating a reusable software element is 20% of the cost of developing the same element anew. The financial benefit due to adopting reuse in the development phase of a project is calculated as follows:

$$Development\ cost\ avoidance = RSI \times (1 - 0.2) \times (new\ code\ cost).$$

In addition, saving in maintenance cost attributed to reuse is much more than those during software development, because of the fewer defects in reused components [51]. The saving is

$$Service\ cost\ avoidance = RSI \times (error\ rate) \times (cost\ per\ error).$$

The total reuse cost avoidance is calculated as the sum of cost avoidance in the development and maintenance activities, which is

$$Reuse\ cost\ avoidance = Development\ cost\ avoidance \\ + Service\ cost\ avoidance.$$

3. *Reuse value added* (RVA): The main idea behind RVA is to provide a metric to reward an organization that reuses software components and help other organizations by developing reusable components. RVA is derived from SSI, RSI, and SIRBO:

$$Reuse\ value\ added = \frac{(SSI + RSI) + SIRBO}{SSI}.$$

Organizations with no involvement in reuse have an RVA $= 1$. An RVA $= 2$ indicates that the organization is twice as effective as it would be without reuse. In this case the organization was able to double its productivity either directly by reusing it or indirectly by maintaining software that other organizations are using.

9.6 SUMMARY

We explained the concepts of reuse including program families and domain analysis. In addition, we discussed four major factors that influence software reuse: managerial, legal, economic, and technical.

Next we examined two concepts: domain engineering and application engineering. Domain engineering is also known as product line development, while application engineering being known as product development. Domain engineering is a set of activities that produce RSA to be used in several software projects. It includes analysis, design, and implementation activities. On the other hand, application engineering refers to a "development-with-reuse" process to create specific systems. Then we introduced nine domain engineering approaches reported in the literature: Darco, DARE, FAST, FORM, KobrA, PLUS, PuLSE, Koala, and RSEB.

Next, we discussed three maturity models: RMM, RCM, and RiSE maturity model. We concluded the chapter with a discussion of economic model of software reuse to justify. Finally, we discussed three models: the cost model of Gaffney and Durek, the application system cost model of Gaffney and Cruickshank, and the business model of Poulin and Caruso.

LITERATURE REVIEW

Numerous books and articles have been written about reuse. There are two good reuse research articles by Frakes and Kang [13] and Mili et al. [52]. A two-part book about reuse has been authored by Stanislaw Jarzabek (*Effective Software Maintenance and Evolution: A Reuse-Based Approach*, Auerbach Publications, Boca Raton, FL, 2007). The first part focuses on traditional methods for software maintenance. The second part describes a novel approach called "mixed strategy." In mixed-strategy program representation, code contains information about program design and modifications occurring over the lifetime of the system. A good discussion of integration reuse with an object-oriented development process can be found in *"Software Reuse: Architecture, Process and Organization for Business Success"* (I. Jacobson, M. Griss and P. Jonsson, Addison-Wesley, 1997).

A thorough treatment of a framework for practicing reuse within the software life cycle can be found in IEEE Std 1517-1999, "IEEE Standard for Information Technology – Software Life Cycle Processes – Reuse Processes." The standard provides a framework to extend the software life cycle processes to include software reuse. Moreover, the reuse adoption process [44], defined by the Software Productivity Consortium (SPC), provides a solution to implement a reuse program, and it is based on the implementation of the model proposed by Prieto-Diaz [14]. RCM [40] is used together with the reuse adoption process defined by SPC.

The article by Parastoo Mohagheghi and Reidar Conradi, "An empirical investigation of software reuse benefits in a large telecom roduct." *ACM Transactions on Software Engineering and Methodology*, 17(3), 2008, pp. 13:1–31, based on an empirical study, describes the benefits of software reuse in a large telecommunication product. The key observation was that lower fault density and less modified code occurred between successive releases of the reused components.

Software product lines enjoy increasingly wide adoption in the software industry. The Software Engineering Institute defines basic concepts, activities, and practices that ensure success. In the article "SEI's software product line tenets," *IEEE Software*, July/August, 2002, pp. 32–40, the author Linda M. Northrop described the success stories and lessons learned while defining and applying this approach. Readers who are interested in relationships between software evolution and software product line process are recommended to study the following two articles.

Samuel A. Ajila and Ali B. Koba, Evolution support mechanisms for software product lines process. *Journal of Systems and Software*, 81(10), 2008, pp.1784–1801.

Stephen R. Schach and Amir Tomer, Development/maintenance/reuse: Software evolution in product lines. *Proceedings of the first Conference on Software Product Lines: Experience and Research Directions*, Denver, Colorado, Kluwer Academic, Norwell, MA, 2000, pp. 437–450.

The first article describes mechanisms to support evolution of software product lines. In the second article, the authors extend the *evolution tree model* and *propagation graph model* to describe the evolution of a software product line.

Readers interested in product-line development may read the article by Capretz, Ahmed, Al-Maati, and Al Aghbari (COTS-based software product line development. International Journal of Web Information Systems, Emerald Group Publishing, 4(2), 2008, pp. 165–180). The authors discussed COTS-based software product line development methodology based on Y-model [53]. The methodology integrates the concept of software product line with COTS.

REFERENCES

[1] J. Backus. 1998. The history of fortran i, ii, iii. *IEEE Annals of the History of Computing*, 20(4), 68–78.

[2] M. D. McIlroy. 1969. *Mass Produced Software Components*. Proceedings of Software Engineering Concepts and Techniques, 1968 NATO Conference on Software Engineering (Eds P. Naur, B. Randell, J. N.), pp. 138–155, Available through Petrocelli-Charter, New York.

[3] D. L. Parnas. 1976. On the design and development of program families. *IEEE Transactions of Software Engineering*, 2(1), 1–9.

[4] J. M. Neighbor. 1980. Software construction using components. Technical Report 160, Department of Information and Computer Sciences, University of California, Irvine, CA.

[5] J. M. Neighbors. 1984. The draco approach to constructing from software reusable components. *IEEE Transactions of Software Engineering*, 10(5), 564–574.

[6] R. Prieto-Diaz. 1990. A domain analysis: An introduction. *ACM Software Engineering Notes*, 15(2), 47–54.

[7] T. C. Jones. 1984. Reusability in programming: A survey of the state of the art. *IEEE Transactions of Software Engineering*, 10(5), 488–494.

[8] P. Grubb and A. Takang. 2003. *Software Maintenance Concepts and Practice*, 2nd edition. World Scientific, Singapore.

[9] I Sommervilles. 2001. *Software Engineering*, 6th edition. Pearson Education Limited, Harlow, England.

[10] R. Prieto-Diaz. 1991. Implementing faceted classification for software reuse. *Communications of the ACM*, 34(5), 88–97.

[11] A. Mili, R. Mili, and R. T. Mittermeir. 1998. A survey of software reuse libraries. *Annals of Software Engineering*, 5, 349–414.

[12] B. P. Lientz and E. B. Swanson. 1980. *Software Maintenance Management*. Addison-Wesley, Reading, MA.

[13] W. Frakes and Kyo Kang. 2005. Software reuse research: Status and future. *IEEE Transactions of Software Engineering*, 31(7), 529–536.

[14] R. Prieto-Diaz. 1991. Making software reuse work: An implementation model. *ACM Software Engineering Notes*, 16(3), 61–68.

[15] C. Krueger. 2002. Eliminating the adoption barrier. *IEEE Software*, 19(4), 29–31.

[16] W. Frakes and P. Gandel. 1990. Representing reusable software. *Information and Software Technology*, 32(10), Butterworth-Heinemann Ltd, 1990, pp. 653–664.

[17] W. Frakes and S. Isoda. 1994. Success factors of systematic reuse. *IEEE Software*, 11(5), 14–19.

[18] M. L. Griss. 1993. Software reuse: From library to factory. *IBM Systems Journal*, 32(4), 548–564.

[19] J. Favaro. 1991. What price reusability? a case study. *Ada Letter*, 11(3), 115–124.

[20] D. C. Rine. 1993. Supporting reuse with object technology. *IEEE Software*, 30(10), 43–45.

[21] J. L. Diaz-Herrera. 2001. Domain engineering. In: *Handbook of Software Engineering and Knowledge Engineering* (Ed. S. K. Change), Vol. 1, pp. 305–328. World Scientific Publishing Co., Singapore.

[22] S. Beydeda and V. Gruhn (Eds.). 2005. *Testing Commerical-off-the-Shelf Components and Systems*. Springer, Berlin, Germany.

[23] K. C. Kang, S. G. Cohen, J. A. Hess, W. E. Novak, and S. A. Peterson. 1990. Feature-oriented domain analysis (foda) feasibility study. CMU/SEI-90-TR-21, ADA 235785, Pittsburgh, PA, Software Engineering Institute, Carnegie Mellon University.

[24] B. Schmerl and D. Garlan. 2004. *Acmestudio: Supporting Style-centered Architecture Development (Research Demonstration)*. Proceedings of the 26th International Conference on Software Engineering, May, 2004, IEEE Computer Society Press, Los Alamitos, CA, pp. 23–28.

[25] J. Nester, J. M. Newcomer, P. Giannini, and D. Stone. 1990. *IDL: The Language and its Implementation*. Prentice-Hall, Upper Saddle River, NJ.

[26] L. M. Northrop. 2002. SEI's software product line tenets. *IEEE Software*, 19(4), 32–40.

[27] R. H. Thayer. 2002. Software system engineering: A tutorial. *IEEE Computer*, 2002, pp. 68–73.

[28] R. R. Macala, L. D. Stuckey, and D. C. Gross. 1996. Managing domain-specific product-line development. *IEEE Software*, 13(3), 57–67.

[29] E. S. Almeida, A. Alvaro, D. Lucrédio, V. C. Garcia, and S. R. L. Meira. 2005. A survey on software reuse processes. IEEE International Conference on Information Reuse and Integration (IRI), August, 2005, Las Vegas, Nevada, IEEE Computer Society Press, Los Alamitos, CA, pp. 66–71.

[30] C. Atkinson, J. Bayer, C. Bunse, E. Kamsties, O. Laintenberger, R. Laqua, D. Muthiq, B. Paech, J. Wust, and J. Zettel. 2002. *Component-based Product Line Engineering with UML*. Addison-Wesley, Reading, MA.

[31] W. Frakes, R. Prieto-Diaz, and C. Fox. 1998. Dare: Domain analysis and reuse environment. *Annals of Software Engineering*, 5, 125–141.

[32] O. Alonso. 2003. Generating text search application for databases. *IEEE Software*, 20(3), 98–105.

[33] D. M. Wiess and C. T. R. Lai. 1999. *Software-line Engineering: A Family-based Software Development Process*. Addison-Wesley, Reading, MA.

[34] K. C. Kang, J. Lee, and P. Donohoe. 2002. Feature-oriented product line engineering. *IEEE Software*, 19(4), 58–65.

[35] K. C. Kang, S. Kim, J. Lee, K. Kim, E. Shin, and M. Huh. 1998. Form: A feature-oriented reuse method and domain-specific reference architecture. *Annals of Software Engineering*, 5, 143–168.

[36] H. Gomaa. 2004. *Designing Software Product Lines with UML: From Use Case to Pattern-Based Software Architectures*. Addison-Wesley, Reading, MA.

[37] J. Bayer, O. Flege, P. Knauber, R. Laqua, D. Muthig, K. Schmid, T. Widen, and J-M. Debaud. 1999. *Pulse: A Methodology to Develop Software Product Lines*. Proceedings of the 1999 Symposium on Software Reusability, May, 1999, Los Angeles, CA, ACM Press, New York, pp. 122–131.

[38] R Ommering, F. Linden, J. Kramer, and J. Magee. 2000. The koala component model for consumer electronics software. *IEEE Software*, 78–85. doi: 10.1109/2.825699

[39] I. Jacobson, M. L. Gries, and P. Jonsson, 1997. *Reuse-driven Software Engineering Business (RSEB)*. Addison-Wesley, Reading, MA.

[40] T. Davis. 1993. *The Reuse Capability Model: A Basis for Improving an Organization's Reuse Capability*. Proceedings of 2nd IEEEACM International Workshop on Software Reusability, 1993, Herndon, VA, IEEE Computer Society Press/ACM Press, Los Alamitos, CA, pp. 126–133.

[41] P. Koltun and A. Hudson. 1991. A reuse maturity model. In 4th Annual Workshop on Software Reuse, Herndon, VA, IEEE Computer Society Press/ACM Press, Los Alamitos, CA.

[42] V. C. Garcia, D. Lucrédio, A. Alvaro, E. S. Almeida, R. P. M. Fortes, and S. R. L. Meira. 2007. Towards maturity model for a reuse incremental adoption. Brazilian Symposium on Software Component, Architectures and Reuse (SBCARS), August, 2007, Campinas, São Paulo, Brazil, pp. 61–73.

[43] W. Frakes and C. Terry. 1996. Software reuse: Metrics and models. *ACM Computing Surveys*, 28(2), 415–435.

[44] SPC. 1993. Reuse adoption guidebook. Version 02.00.05., Technical Report SPC-92051-CMC, Software Productivity Consortium, 279.

[45] E. S. Almeida, A. Alvaro, D. Lucrédio, V. C. Garcia, and S. R. L. Meira. 2004. *Rise Project: Towards a Robust Framework for Software Reuse.* IEEE International Conference on Information Reuse and Integration (IRI), August, 2004, Las Vegas, Nevada, IEEE Computer Society Press, Los Alamitos, CA, pp. 48–53.

[46] J. E. Gaffney and T. A. Durek. 1989. Software reuse - key to enhanced productivity: Some quantitative models. *Information and Software Technology,* 31(5), 258–267.

[47] Jr. J. E. Gaffney and R. D. Cruickshank. 1992. *A General Economics Model of Software Reuse.* Proceedings of the 14th International Conference on Software Engineering (ICSE), May, 1992, Melbourne, Australia, ACM Press, New York, pp. 327–337.

[48] J. S. Poulin and J. M. Caruso. 1993. *A Reuse Measurement and Return on Investment Model.* Second International Workshop on Software Reusability, March, 1993, Lucca, Italy, IEEE Computer Society Press, Los Alamitos, CA, pp. 152–166.

[49] R. W. Jensen. 2004. An economic analysis of software reuse. *CrossTalk A Journal of Defense Software Engineering,* 4–8.

[50] J. S. Paulin, J. M. Caruso, and D. R. Hancock. 1993. The business case for software reuse. *IBM Systems Journal,* 32(4), 567–594.

[51] S. R. Schach. 1994. The economic impact of software reuse on maintenance. *Journal of Software Maintenance and Evolution: Research and Practice,* 6(4), 185–196.

[52] H. Mili, F. Mili, and A. Mili. 1995. Reusing software: Issues and research directions. *IEEE Transactions of Software Engineering,* 21(6), 528–562.

[53] L. F. Capretz. 2005. Y: A new component-based software life cycle model. *Journal of Computer Science,* 1(1), 76–82.

EXERCISES

1. Explain the terms reuse and reusability with respect to software development and maintenance.

2. Explain why it is important to reuse software instead of writing it from the scratch.

3. Explain the difference between reverse engineering and reuse engineering. What is software reclamation with regard to reuse engineering?

4. Compare and contrast the different approaches to reuse: proactive, reactive, and extractive.

5. Explain the differences between: (i) vertical and horizontal reuse; and (ii) generative and compositional reuse.

6. Explain the concepts of "development-for-reuse" and "development-with-reuse."

7. Briefly explain the five maturity levels in the RiSE maturity model.

8. Briefly explain the two components (assessment and implementation) of reuse capability model.

9. A programming team develops and maintains 80K SSI and the team additionally uses 20K RSI from a reuse library. Calculate the reuse percentage for the team.

10. An organization has a historical new code development cost of $200 per line, an error rate of 1.5/KLOC, and cost of $43K to fix an error. Calculate the value of RCA for integrating 20K RSI into the product.

11. A programming team maintains 80KLOC and uses 20KLOC from a reuse library. In addition, five other departments reuse a 10KLOC module the programming team contributed to the organizational reuse library. What is the value of RVA of the programming team?

12. Suppose that you joined a new company that has no reuse program. The first task for you is to implement the reuse program.
    (a) What is the first step that you would take?
    (b) Outline the technical, managerial, economical, organizational and legal steps that you would go through.
    (c) What difficulties do you anticipate and how would you mitigate them?

GLOSSARY

A man is born alone and dies alone; and he experiences the good and bad consequences
of his karma alone; and he goes alone to hell or the supreme abode.

—Chanakya

Abstract syntax tree (AST) An abstract syntax tree is a tree representation of the
syntax of some source code that has been written in a programming language.
Each node of the tree denotes a construct occurring in the source code. The tree
is abstract in the sense that it may not represent some constructs that appear in
the original source. An AST is often built by a parser as part of the processing of
compiling source code.

Accidental reuse This informal practice, in which components are selected from
general libraries, is usually called opportunistic reuse or accidental reuse.

Activity An action of one of the following types: an investigation activity, a modification activity, a management activity, or a quality assurance activity. An activity
may be made up of a number of sub-activities. Usually, it takes as input one or
more existing artifacts and outputs zero, one, or many new or modified artifacts.

Actual impacted set (AIS) The set of components actually modified as the results
of performing a change request.

Adaptive maintenance The process that modifies the software to properly interface with a changing or changed environment. Adaptive maintenance includes

Software Evolution and Maintenance: A Practitioner's Approach, First Edition.
Priyadarshi Tripathy and Kshirasagar Naik.
© 2015 John Wiley & Sons, Inc. Published 2015 by John Wiley & Sons, Inc.

system changes, additions, deletions, modifications, extensions, and enhancements to meet the evolving needs of the environment in which the system must operate.

Adequacy It is the capability of an impact analysis approach to produce a set of potentially affected elements that includes all the objects to be modified.

Adherence It is the ability of the approach to produce a CIS which is as adherent as possible to the AIS. The smaller the difference between these two sets, the smaller the number of candidate objects that will fail to be included in the actual modification, and the smaller the effort required to specify the change. Adherence is expressed by means of the following ratio called *S-Ratio*:

$$S\text{-}Ratio = \frac{|\,AIS\,|}{|\,CIS\,|}.$$

If the approach is adequate, AIS is included in CIS, so that $|\,AIS\,| \leq |\,CIS\,|$ and *S-Ratio* varies in the range from 0 to 1.

Agile software development It is an iterative and incremental (revolutionary) approach to software development which is performed in a highly collaborative manner with "just enough" ceremony that produces high quality software. Agile methods refer to a collection of "lightweight" software development methodologies that are basically aimed at minimizing risk and achieving customer satisfaction through a short feedback loop.

Annotation of the program If one views the development process of the program as a layered system where the top layer is the set of program goals and the bottom layer is source code, then the annotation can be viewed as the abstraction of the middle layer connecting the top and the bottom layers. Basically, a program annotation is used to bridge the abstraction gap between the top and the bottom layers.

Antiregression work A term introduced by Lehman and Belady to describe the work done to decrease the complexity of a program without altering the functionality of the system as perceived by the users. Anti-regressive work includes activities such as code rewriting, refactoring, reengineering, restructuring, and redocumenting.

Application engineering The process of constructing or refining application systems by reusing assets.

Application gateway An *application gateway* is used for a semidecomposable LIS. This gateway is positioned between separable user and system interfaces and the legacy application.

Artifact Artifacts that together correspond to a software product can be of the following types: document that can be subdivided into textual and graphical documents, component off-the-shelf products, and object code components. Textual documents include source code listings, plans, design, and requirements specifications.

Aspect A modular unit designed to implement a (crosscutting) concern. In other words, an aspect provides a solution for abstracting code that would otherwise be spread throughout, that is, crosscut the entire program.

Aspect-oriented software development An approach to software development that addresses limitation inherent in other approaches, including object-oriented programming. The approach aims to address crosscutting concerns by providing means for systematic identification, separation, representation, and composition. Crosscutting concerns are encapsulated in separate modules, known as aspects, so that localization can be promoted. This results in better support for modularization, thereby reducing development, maintenance, and evolution costs.

Assembler Refers to a computer program to translate between lower level representations of computer programs. The original sequence is usually called the assembly language and the output called object code.

Assertion An assertion is a Boolean statement which should never be false or can be false only if an error has occurred. In other words, an assertion is a check on a condition which is assumed to be true, but it can cause a problem if it is not true.

Asset An item, such as design, specifications, source code, documentation, test suites, manual procedures, that has been designed for use in multiple contexts.

Backward wrappers Backward wrappers emulate the legacy technology on top of the new database.

Bad smell A bad smell is a structure in the code that suggests— and sometimes even scream for—opportunities for refactoring.

Baseline Specification or product that has been formally reviewed and agreed upon that thereafter serves as the basis for further development, and can be changed only through a change control procedure.

Beacon A beacon is a code text that gives a clue to the computation being performed in a code block.

Big bang It is a reengineering approach to replace an entire system at one. It is also known as Cold turkey strategy.

Black-box testing It is a method of software testing that examines the functionality of an application without peering into its internal structures or workings.

Butterfly A methodology to migrate a mission-critical LIS to a target system in a simple, fast, and safe way. The methodology eliminates, during the migration, the need of simultaneously accessing both the legacy and target systems, and, therefore, avoids the complexity of maintaining the consistency between these two information systems.

Call graph It is a directed graph in which nodes represent functions (components or methods) and an edge from node A to node B means that A may call B.

Candidate impact set (CIS) The set of components estimated to be affected according to a particular impact analysis approach. It is also known as estimated impacted set.

Change control   Change control is the process responsible for evaluating the results of maintenance event investigations and deciding whether or not to approve a product modification.

Change coupling   It is the implicit dependency between two or more software entities that have been observed to frequently change together during the evolution of a system. This co-change information can either be present in the versioning system, or must be inferred by analysis.

Change management   The process of making changes to software and controlling their effects during the entire life cycle of the software.

Change propagation activity   It ensures that a change made in one component is propagated properly throughout the entire system.

Chicken little   This migration methodology is a refinement of the composite database migration approach.

Chunk   A chunk is a block of related code segment. The concept of program chunks enable programmers to create higher levels of abstractions from the lower level of abstractions.

Chunking   A programmer creates higher level abstraction structures by combining lower level chunks. The process of creating higher level of chunks is called chunking.

Cliché   A cliché is a pattern that appears frequently in programs (e.g., algorithms, data structures, domain-specific patterns).

Closed source software (CSS)   Closed source software is developed by a single person or company. Only executable code is made available, while the all important source code is kept secret. The software is normally copyrighted or patented and is legally protected as intellectual property. The owner of the software distributes the software directly or via vendors to the end user.

Cold turkey   It is a migration strategy that rewrites LIS from scratch using modern architecture, tools, and databases, running on a new platform.

Code decay   Code decay is antithesis of evolution. While the evolution process involves progressive changes, the changes are degenerative in the case of decay.

Code churn   It is the amount of code change taking place within a software unit over time.

Code smell   A code smell is a symptom in the source code of a software that possibly indicates a deeper problem.

Commercial off-the-shelf (COTS) components   Software components produced by third-party vendor organizations, that can be reused in a system, are known as commercial off-the-shelf components. Often, these types of components are delivered without their source code.

Compilation   It refers to the translation of source code into object code by a compiler. A compiler is a computer program that translates text written in one computer language (the source language) into another computer language (the target language). The original sequence is usually called the source code and the output is called object code.

Composite database It is a migration methodology in which the LIS and its target IS operated in parallel throughout the migration project. The target applications are gradually rebuilt on the target platform using software tools and technology.

Concepts Concepts are units of human knowledge that can be processed by the human mind in one instance.

Conceptual schema A conceptual schema of a database is an abstract, computer-independent description of the information that the data implement. A conceptual schema expressed into the entity-relationship model comprises entity types, relationship types, attributes and various properties and constraints that translate the concepts and structures of the application domain.

Configuration A configuration is a set of related items (a.k.a. configuration items) satisfying three criteria: (i) the configuration is uniquely identifiable; (ii) the items are consistent, that is, the items work with one another in a way that is well understood; and (iii) the set of items is recreatable as a unit.

Configuration item It is an elementary part (usually a file) of the configuration that must be: (i) identified or versioned; (ii) tracked; and (iii) controlled.

Configuration management The set of activities that is developed to manage changes to the software's documentation and code throughout the software life cycle.

Construction The process of writing, assembling, or generating assets.

Control flow analysis It refers to the order in which the individual statements, instructions, or function calls of an imperative or functional program are executed or evaluated.

Corrective maintenance A process that includes isolation and correction of defects in the software. The correction repairs the software product to satisfy requirements.

Crosscutting concerns Concerns that do not fit within the dominant decomposition of a given software system, and as such have an implementation that cuts across that decomposition. Aspect-oriented programming is intended to be a solution to modularize such crosscutting concerns.

Cross-referencing It means being able to link elements of different abstraction levels. This helps in building a mental model of the program under study.

Customer The person or persons for whom the product is intended, and usually, but not necessarily, who decides the requirements.

Cut over It is the last step in the migration process from the LIS to the target system.

Data administration Data administration or data resource management is an organizational function working in the areas of information systems that plans, organizes, describes, and controls data resources.

Data conversion Data conversion is the migration of the data instance from the old database to the new one.

Database gateway Both the *forward gateway* and *reverse gateway* are also known as *database gateways*, since it encapsulates the entire database service and database from the perspective of application modules.

Database reverse engineering It is a software engineering process through which one tries to understand and redocument the files and/or the database of an application. In the process, conceptual schema is recovered from the application.

Data flow analysis Data flow analysis is a technique for gathering information about the possible set of values calculated at various points in a computer program. A program's control flow graph (CFG) is used to determine those parts of a program to which a particular value assigned to a variable might propagate. The information gathered is often used by compilers when optimizing a program.

Data reverse engineering (DRE) The use of structured techniques to reconstitute the data assets of an existing system. The two vital aspects of the DRE process are to: (i) recover *data assets* that are useful or valuable; and (ii) *reconstitute* the recovered data assets to make them more useful. Thus, DRE can be regarded as adding value to the existing data assets, making it easier for organizations to conduct business efficiently and effectively.

Decompilation It is a tool by which a high level source code of an executable program is discovered. A decompiler is the name given to a computer program that performs the reverse operation to that of a compiler.

Design recovery It aims at recreating design abstractions from the source code, existing documentation, experts' knowledge, and any other source of information. In design recovery the domain knowledge, external information, and deduction or fuzzy reasoning are added to the observations of the subject system to identify meaningful higher level abstractions beyond those obtained directly by examining the system itself.

Decay Decay is the antithesis of evolution. While the evolution process involves progressive changes, the changes are degenerative in the case of decay.

Development model A framework used to guide the set of activities performed to translate user needs into software product.

Development process One of the primary processes of the ISO/IEC life cycle model. It provides guidance for the development of software.

Development technology The technology used when the product and its constituent artifacts were originally constructed. The original development technology constraints the possible maintenance procedures.

Disassembler A disassembler is a computer program that translates machine language into assembly language—the inverse operation to that of an assembler. Disassembly, the output of a disassembler, is often formatted for human readability rather than suitability for input to an assembler, making it principally a reverse engineering tool.

Discovered impact set (DIS) New impact components that are discovered during the implementation of the change request which are not included in the candidate impact set (CIS).

Domain A problem space. A sphere of activity, concern, or function.

Domain analysis Domain analysis is the process of analyzing related software systems in a domain to find their common and variable parts. Domain analysis is the first phase of domain engineering. It is a key method for realizing systematic software reuse.

Domain design It covers the development of a common architecture for all the members of the system family and a plan of how individual systems will be created based on the reusable assets.

Domain engineering A reuse-based approach to defining the scope, specifying the structure, and building the assets for a class of systems, subsystems, or applications. Domain engineering may include the following activities: domain definition, domain analysis, domain design, and domain implementation.

Domain implementation a.k.a. product line The process of creating adaptable assets that can be reused in the development of software systems within a domain. Domain implementation may also include the specification of a software development process that describes how software systems in the domain are developed through reuse of assets.

Domain model A product of domain analysis that provides a representation of the requirements of the domain. The domain model identifies and describes the structure of data, flow of information, functions, constraints, and controls within the domain that are included in software systems in the domain. The domain model describes the commonalities and variabilities among requirements for software systems in the domain.

Domain-specific language A problem- or task-oriented modeling language used to simplify the process of assembling, customizing, generating, or configuring a system or component.

Effectiveness It is the ability of the impact analysis approach to produce results that actually benefit the maintainer's work. The abstract definition of *effectiveness* is refined by means of three characteristics: *Ripple-sensitivity*, *Sharpness*, and *Adherence*.

Equivalence tests The equivalence test aims to ensure that the behavior of the software system after a maintenance activity of one or more of its components is exactly the same as before the change.

E-type program The distinctive properties of E-type programs are: (i) the problem that they address cannot be formally and completely specified; (ii) the program has an imperfect model of the operational domain embedded in it; (iii) the program reflects an unbounded number of assumptions about the real world; (iv) the installation of the program changes the operation domain; and (v) the process of developing and evolving E-type software is driven by feedback.

Event management Event management is the process responsible for handling the stream of events received by the maintenance organization.

Evolution process A software process model that explicitly takes into account the iterative and incremental nature of the software development.

External reuse (a.k.a. public reuse) The portion of a product which was constructed externally.

Extreme programming (XP) This is a software development methodology which is self-adaptive and people oriented. It is a specific instance of agile software development that aims to simplify and expedite the development of new software in a volatile environment of rapidly changing requirements. XP begins with five values: communication, feedback, simplicity, courage, and respect. It then builds up 12 rules/recommendations, which XP projects should follow.

False positive impact set (FPIS) The set of components in the candidate impact set (CIS) that are not impacted by the implementation of a change request.

Feedback In engineering, feedback refers to the case when at least some part of the output(s) of the system are fed back to the input, normally for control purposes. In systems thinking and related disciplines, that is system dynamics, feedback describes a property of many complex systems in which the outputs determine the inputs.

Forward engineering Forward engineering is the traditional process of moving from high level abstractions and logical, implementation-independent designs to the physical implementation of a system.

Forward gateway The forward gateway translates and redirects LIS application calls to the new database service. The LIS interoperates with its target system through a *forward gateway* while legacy applications and interfaces are being reengineered.

Forward migration It is a type of migration methodology which involves the initial migration of database including the data to a modern DBMS then gradually migrating the legacy application program and interfaces. It is also known as database first approach.

Forward wrappers The forward wrappers translate data and queries from the legacy data model and interface to those expected by the new components.

Framework A set of cooperating classes or frames that makes up a reusable design for a specific class of software.

Free and open source software (FOSS) Software of which the source code is available for users and third parties to be inspected and used. It is made available to the general public with either relaxed or non-existent intellectual property restrictions. It is generally used as a synonym of free software even though the two terms have different connotations. *Free* emphasizes the freedom to modify and redistribute under the terms of the original license while open emphasizes the accessibility to the source code.

Fully decomposable information system A fully decomposable information system is one where applications, interfaces and databases are considered to be distinct components with clearly defined interfaces. Applications must be independent of each other and interact only with the database service.

Gateway A software module introduced between operational software components to mediate between them.

Glue A glue is a piece of code that one builds to combine different components.

Graph exchange language (GXL) It is an XML-based standard exchange format for sharing data between tools. Formally, GXL represents typed, attributed, directed, ordered graphs which are extended to represent hypergraphs and hierarchical graphs. The GXL has been ratified by reengineering and graph transformation research communities and is being considered for adoption by other communities.

Graph transformation (a.k.a. graph rewriting) A theory and a set of associated tools that allows to modify graph-based structures by means of transformation rules, and to reason about the formal properties of these rules.

Hazard State of a system or a physical situation which, when combined with certain environmental conditions, could lead to an accident or mishap. A hazard is a prerequisite for an accident.

Horizontal reuse A type of reuse where assets are used across domains.

Horizontal (a.k.a. external) traceability It refers to the ability to trace artifacts between different models.

Horseshoe It is a visual metaphor to describe a three-step architectural reengineering process. The first step—represented on the left side of the horseshoe—aims at extracting the architecture from the source code (abstraction principle). The second part of the process—represented in the upper part of the horseshoe—is related to architecture transformation toward the target architecture (alteration principle). The last part—on the right side of the horseshoe—represents the instantiation of the new architecture (refinement).

Hypothesis Programmers test the results of their program understanding as a conjecture.

Impact analysis (IA) Task of identifying potential consequences of a change, or estimating what needs to be modified to accomplish the change.

Incremental development It is a staging and scheduling strategy in which the various parts of the system are developed at different times or rates, and integrated as they are completed.

Information system (IS) It is often used to designate large-scale business applications.

Information system gateway It is a kind of gateway for nondecomposable systems which are positioned between end-user and other information systems and LIS. An information system gateway encapsulates the whole functionality of the legacy system. It is a primary means for dealing with the migration of user interface.

Internal reuse (a.k.a. private) The extent to which modules within a product are reused within the same product.

Investigation activity An activity that assesses the impact of undertaking a modification arising from a change request.

Iterative development It is a rework scheduling strategy in which time is set aside to revise and improve parts of the system.

Knowledge base A knowledge base is a body of information about the program.

Knowledge elements A knowledge element is anything that is useful in understanding a program.

Knowledge structure It specifies principal elements in a domain and includes mechanisms which facilitate the comprehension and generation process. It is used to organize complex entities or concepts into constituents.

Legacy system a.k.a. Legacy information system (LIS) A legacy system is any system that significantly resists modifications and change. It may have been developed using an outdated programming language or an obsolete development method. Most likely it has changed hands several times and shows signs of many modifications and adaptations.

Lexical analysis It is the process of converting a sequence of characters into a sequence of tokens. Programs performing lexical analysis are called lexical analyzers.

Logical schema The description of the data structures as they are implemented by the data manager, and they are seen by the application programmer. For example, the logical schema of a relational database describes its tables, columns, and primary and foreign keys as well as all the explicit and implicit constraints to which the data are submitted.

Maintainer An organization or a personal who performs maintenance activities.

Maintenance event A problem report or change request originating from a customer or user of the maintained product or a member of the maintenance organization.

Maintenance management The process used to manage the maintenance service as opposed to the procedure used to manage individual maintenance requests. The organization process is established and maintained by senior maintenance managers. It is responsible for defining the structure of the maintenance organization such that it can fulfill its service level agreement. Maintenance management has three main concerns other than the normal concerns of quality assurance and project management: event management, configuration control, and change control.

Maintenance model A framework used to guide the set of activities to perform maintenance.

Maintenance organization structure The roles undertaken by maintenance human resources in a maintenance organization in order to perform the required administrative procedures.

Maintenance process One of the primary processes of the ISO/IEC life cycle model. It provides guidance for the maintenance of software.

Management activity An activity related to the management of the maintenance process or to the configuration control of the maintained product.

Mental model It describes a programmer's mental representation of the program to be comprehended.

Method A systematic procedure defining steps and heuristics to permit the accomplishment of one or more activities.

Metric A metric is a quantitative measure of the degree to which a system, component, or process possesses a given attribute.

Migration A variant of reengineering in which the transformation is driven by a major technology change is called *migration*.

Migration of information legacy system LIS migration basically moves an existing, operational system to a new platform, retaining the legacy system's functionality and causing minimal disruption to the existing operational business environment.

Mishap Also called an accident, an unintended event that results in death, injury, illness, damage or loss of property, or harm to the environment.

Model A model is a simplified representation of a system on a higher level of abstraction. It is an abstract view on the actual system emphasizing those aspects that are of interest to someone. Depending on the system under consideration, we talk about, for example, *software models* (for software systems) and *database model* (for database systems).

Model-driven engineering A software engineering approach that promotes the use of models and transformations as primary artifacts throughout the software development process. Its goal is to tackle the problem of developing, maintaining and evolving complex software systems by raising the level of abstraction from source code to models. As such, model-driven engineering promises reuse at the domain level, increasing the overall software quality.

Modification activity An activity that takes one or more input artifacts and produces one or more output artifacts that, when incorporated into an existing system, change its behavior or implementation.

Modification request The means by which problems are reported and enhancements are requested. It is also known as change request.

Nondecomposable information system A nondecomposable information system is one in which no functional components are separable.

Non-functional requirements Non-functional requirements are requirements which specify criteria to be used to judge the operation of a system, rather than specific behavior. Non-functional requirements are often called qualities of a system.

Normalization A normalization reduces a program to another program in a sublanguage, with the purpose of decreasing its syntactic complexity. Elimination of GOTO and module flattening in a program are examples of program normalization.

Open source software (OSS) Software of which the source code is available for users and third parties to be inspected and used. It is made available to the general public with either relaxed or non-existent intellectual property restrictions. It is generally used as a synonym of free software even though the two terms have different connotations. *Open* emphasizes the accessibility to the source code, while *free* emphasizes the freedom to modify and redistribute under the terms of original license.

Obfuscation   It is a transformation that makes a program harder to understand. Programs known as obfuscators operate on source code, object code, or both, mainly for the purpose of deterring reverse engineering, disassembly, or decompilation.

Optimization   An optimization is a transformation that improves the run-time and/or space performance of a program.

Paradigm   The philosophy adopted during the original construction of the maintained product, for example, the object-oriented paradigm or procedural paradigm. The original paradigm constrains the possible maintenance procedures.

Perfective maintenance   The process that improves the software in terms of performance, processing efficiency, or maintainability. These activities may include restructuring the code, creating and updating documentations, or tuning the system to improve performance.

Physical schema   A physical schema of a database is the implementation of its logical schema. It is the technical descriptions of a database where all the physical constructs, such as indices, and parameters, such as page size or buffer management policy, are specified.

Plan   A plan is an abstract representation of a cliché.

Portfolio analysis   The portfolio analysis establishes measures of technical quality and business value for a set of software systems and evaluate this against the measure on a chi-square chart.

Precision   In data mining or information retrieval, precision is defined as the proportion of retrieved and relevant data or documents to all the data or documents retrieved:

$$precision = \frac{|\ \{relevant\ documents\} \cap \{retrieved\ documents\}\ |}{|\ \{retrieved\ documents\}\ |}$$

Precision is a measure of how well the technique performs in not returning non-relevant items. Precision is 100% when every document returned to the user is relevant to the query. Being very precise usually comes at the risk of missing documents that are relevant, hence precision should be combined with recall.

Preventive maintenance   Software maintenance performed for the purpose of preventing problems before they occur. It is an activity during which one attempts to prevent an unnecessary change in the future.

Principle of abstraction   The gradual increase in the abstraction level of a system representation is created by the successive replacement of existing detailed information with information that is more abstract. Abstraction produces a representation that emphasizes certain system characteristics by suppressing information about others.

Principle of alteration   Alteration is the making of one or more changes to a system representation without changing the degree of abstraction, including addition, deletion, and modification of information.

Principle of refinement The gradual decrease in the abstraction level of a system representation is caused by the successive replacement of existing systems with more detailed information.

Procedure The conduct followed to perform an activity. A procedure may be classified as a method, technique, or script. A procedure may be adopted to perform a specific activity from a set of possible procedures.

Process A process is a collection of related activities to accomplish some task. A process can be described by creating a process model.

Process model A process can be described by creating a process model. A process model represents key relationships among a variety of objects, such as activities, data objects, tools, and human roles within a process. In other words, it is a framework to identify, define, and organize data, strategies, rules, and processes needed to support the way an organization wants to do business. Process models are important vehicles for understanding, evaluating, reasoning, and improving process.

Product A product is a software application, product, or package that is undergoing modification. A product is a conglomerate of a number of different artifacts.

Product upgrade A change to the baseline product that implements or documents a maintenance activity. An upgrade may be a new version of the product, an object code patch, or a restriction notice.

Program analysis Program analysis reduces a program to one aspect, such as its control flow or data flow. Analysis can thus be considered a transformation to a sublanguage or an aspect language.

Program comprehension (a.k.a. program understanding) It is a process of knowledge acquisition about the program. It is the task of building mental models of an underlying software system at various abstraction levels, ranging from models of the code itself to ones of the underlying application domain, for software maintenance, evolution, and reengineering purposes.

Program dependency graph (PDG) The program dependency graph (PDG) of a program has one node for each simple statement and one node for each control predicate expression. It has two types of directed edges—data dependency edges and control dependency edges. A data dependency edge from vertex v_i to vertex v_j implies that the computation performed at vertex v_i directly depends on the value computed at vertex v_j. A control dependency edge from v_i to v_j means that node v_i may or may not be executed depending on the Boolean outcome of the predicate expression at node v_j.

Program families A set of programs whose common properties are so extensive that it becomes advantageous to study the common properties of these programs before analyzing individual differences.

Program migration In migration, a program is transformed to another language at the same level of abstraction. This can be a translation between dialects, or a translation from one language to another.

Program rephrasing Program rephrasing is source-code-level changes. Rephrasings are transformations that transform a program into a different program in the same language.

Program slicing Program slicing is a method used by experienced computer programmers for abstracting from programs. Starting from a subset of a program's behavior, slicing reduces that program to a minimal form which still produces that behavior. The reduced program, called a "slice," is an independent program guaranteed to faithfully represent the original program within the domain of the specified subset of behavior.

Program translation Program translation is a source-code-level change. In program translation a program is transformed from a source language into a program in a different target language.

Protocol analysis It is a methodology for eliciting verbal reports from participants about their thought sequences as a valid source of data on thinking.

Protocol data The thinking-aloud action of the programmer can be recorded and transcribed. The transcribed verbal report is called protocol data.

P-type program It is based on a practical abstraction of the problem rather than on a completely defined specification. Even though the exact solution may exist, the solution produced by a P-type program is tempered by the environment in which it must be produced. The solution of a P-type program is acceptable if the results make sense to the stakeholder(s) in the world in which the problem is embedded.

Quality assurance activity An activity aimed at ensuring that a modification activity does not damage the integrity of the product being maintained. Quality assurance activities may be classified as testing.

Recall In data mining or information retrieval, recall is defined as the proportion of relevant data or documents retrieved, out of all relevant data or documents known or available:

$$precision = \frac{|\ \{relevant\ documents\} \cap \{retrieved\ documents\}\ |}{|\ \{relevant\ documents\}\ |}$$

Recall is 100% when every relevant item is retrieved. In theory, it is easy to achieve good recall: simply return every item in the collection, thus recall by itself is not a good measure and should be combined with precision.

Reclamation Reclamation is the process of reclaiming something from loss or from a less useful condition. Some technical articles use this term as a synonym of reengineering.

Re-code In the context of software engineering, re-code involves changing the implementation characteristics of the source code.

Re-design In the context of software engineering, re-design involves changing the design characteristics. Possible changes include restructuring a design architecture, altering a system's data model as incorporated in data structures or in a database, and improving an algorithm.

Redocumentation Redocumentation aims at producing/revising alternate views of a given artifact, at the same level of abstraction, for example, pretty printing source code or visualizing control flow graph. It is a weak form of *restructuring*.

Reengineering Software reengineering is an activity that: (1) improves one's understanding of software, or (2) prepares or improves the software itself, usually for increased maintainability, reusability, or evolvability.

Refactoring Refactoring is the object-oriented equivalent of restructuring. Refactoring is a change to the internal structure of software to make it easier to understand and cheaper to modify without changing its observable behavior.

Rehosting It means reengineering of source code without addition or reduction of features in the transformed targeted source code. It includes porting, migration, or conversion of the existing code and data from one computing platform to another, from one operating system to another, from one language to another, or all of the above, but no new features are added to the code.

Rejuvenation It is a periodic preemptive rollback of continuously running applications to prevent failures in the future. Rejuvenation may sometimes increase the downtime of the application, however it prevents the occurrence of more severe and costly failures.

Release A release is a version of a software system that has been approved and distributed to users outside the development team.

Replace It is a type of software reengineering strategy that incorporates the principles of abstraction and refinement. To change an existing system characteristic, abstraction is used to reconstruct a system representation at a level of abstraction that contains no information about the characteristic. Refinement is then used to create a suitable target system representation at a lower level of abstraction.

Repository A kind of database, or file system in which the version history of a software system are stored. The repository may be used to store source code, executable code, documentation or any other type of software artifacts of which different versions may exist over time or even at the same time.

Resource Everything that is used to perform an activity. Resources may be hardware, software, and human resources.

Respecify In the context of software engineering, respecify involves changing the requirement characteristics. This type of changes can refer to changing only the form of existing requirements that is taking informal requirements expressed in English and generating a formal specification expressed in a formal language such as SDL or UML. This type of change can also refer to changing system requirements, such as the addition of new requirements, or the deletion or alteration of existing requirements.

Restructuring Restructuring is the transformation from one representation form to another at the same relative abstraction level, while preserving the system's external behavior.

Rethink In the context of software engineering, rethink involves changing the conceptual characteristics. This type of change can result in drastic changes to a system. Rethinking a system means manipulating the concepts embodied in an existing system to create a system that operates in a different problem domain.

Reusability The degree to which an asset can be used in more than one software system, or in building other assets.

Reuse The use of an asset in the solution of a different problem.

Reuse capability The range of expected results in reuse proficiency, efficiency, and effectiveness that can be achieved by an organization's process.

Reuse effectiveness It is the ratio of the reuse benefit to the reuse cost.

Reuse efficiency It is the ratio of the actual reuse opportunities exploited to the organizations targeted reuse opportunity.

Reuse maturity model It is a self-assessment and planning aid for improving an organization's reuse capability. A reuse maturity model is at the core of planned reuse, helping organizations understand their past, current, and future goals for reuse activities.

Reuse opportunity It is an occasion where an asset (existing or to be developed for reuse) may satisfy a need (current or anticipated). Within the set of reuse opportunities there are potential reuse opportunities and targeted reuse opportunities. Potential reuse opportunities are the set of reuse opportunities that will result in actual reuse when exploited. Targeted reuse opportunities are the set of reuse opportunities toward which an organization directs its effort implicitly and explicitly. A targeted reuse opportunity may not always be a potential reuse opportunity.

Reuse proficiency It is the ratio of the value of actual reuse opportunities exploited to the value of potential reuse opportunities.

Reuse library A classified collection of assets that allows searching, browsing, and extracting.

Reverse engineering In the context of software, reverse engineering is defined as the process of analyzing a subject system to: (i) identify the system's components and their interrelationships; and (ii) create representations of the system in another form or at a higher level of abstraction.

Reverse gateway A *reverse gateway* enables target applications to access the LIS database. It is employed to convert calls from the newly created applications and redirect them to the legacy database service.

Reverse migration It is a type of migration methodology in which the LIS applications are gradually migrated to the target platform while the legacy database remains on the original platform. The LIS database migration is the final step of the migration process. It is also known as database last approach.

Rework This is a type of software reengineering strategy that incorporates the principles of abstraction, alteration, and refinement. To change an existing system's characteristics, abstraction is used to reconstruct a system representation at the appropriate abstraction level. Alteration is then used to transform the reconstructed system representation into the target system representation at the same level of abstraction. Finally, refinement is used to create a suitable target system representation at a lower level of abstraction.

Rewrite It is a type of software reengineering strategy that incorporates only the principle of alteration. To change an existing system, alteration is used to transform the existing system, represented at some level of abstraction, into the target system, represented at the same abstraction level.

Ripple effect The effect caused by making a small change to a system which affects many other systems.

Ripple-sensitivity It is the property of the approach to produce results that are affected by the *ripple effect*. From the point of view of an impact analysis approach, an indicator of the ripple effect may be the cardinality of the set of objects that are indirectly impacted by the change (IIS) (a.k.a. secondary impacted set), given the set of objects that are directly affected by the change (DIS) (a.k.a. primary impacted set). The software maintenance engineer expects the cardinality of IIS to be not very far from the cardinality of the direct impact set; in other words,

$$Amplification = \frac{\mid IIS \mid}{\mid DIS \mid} \longrightarrow 1$$

where $\mid IIS \mid$ is the cardinality of the indirectly impact set and $\mid DIS \mid$ is the cardinality of the direct impact set. Ripple-sensitivity is expressed by the *Amplification* ratio. If *Amplification* is much greater than 1, this means that the approach produces a much larger indirect impact set than the direct impact set.

Rules of programming discourse It specifies the conventions, also called "rules," that programmers follow while writing code.

Scattering and tangling Occur when the code needed to implement a given concern is spread out (scattered) over and clutters (is tangled with) the code needed to satisfy one or more other concern. Scattering or tangling are typically the results of a program's inability to handle what is called a crosscutting concern.

Schema It is a knowledge structure for describing program behavior in a specific domain of activity.

Script A guideline for constructing and amending a specific type of document.

Screen scrapping It is a wrapping technique that replaces old, text-based interfaces with new graphical interfaces.

Semidecomposable information system A semidecomposable information system is one where only the user and the system interfaces are separate components, but applications and database service are not separable.

Service-level agreement (SLA) An agreement between the providers of a maintenance service and the customers of a maintenance service that specifies the performance targets for the maintenance service.

Service-oriented Architecture (SOA) In software engineering, an SOA is a set of principles and methodologies for designing and developing software in the form of interoperable services. These services are well-defined business functionalities that are built as software components that can be reused for different purposes.

Sharpness It is the property of the impact analysis approach to avoid including all the objects or components belonging to the software system in the candidate impact set, unless they really should be included. Sharpness is expressed by means of the following ratio called *Change Rate*:

$$Change\ Rate = \frac{|\ CIS\ |}{|\ System\ |}$$

where | *System* | is the cardinality of the set of the software system objects; | *CIS* | is the cardinality of the candidate impact set. CIS is of course included in "System," so that | CIS | ≤ | System | and *Change Rate* falls in the range from 0 to 1.

Side effect It is an error or other undesirable behavior that occurs as a result of a modification.

Soft-goal graph A soft-goal graph for a quality attribute is a hierarchical graph rooted at the desired change in the attribute. Internal nodes represent successive refinements of the attribute and are the soft goals. The leaf nodes represent refactoring transformations which fulfill or contribute positively/negatively to soft goals which appear above them in the hierarchy.

Software aging Software product aging is degradation in software code and documentation quality by frequent maintenance, whereas software process execution aging manifests as degradation in performance or transient failures in a continuously running software system.

Software clone Copying code fragments and then reuse by pasting with or without modifications is called software cloning and pasted code fragment (with or without modifications) is called a clone of the original.

Software clone detection The activity of locating duplicates or fragments of code with a high degree of similarity and redundancy.

Software configuration management (SCM) It is configuration management applied to software systems.

Software entropy The combination of defect repairs and enhancements tends to gradually degrade the structure and increase the complexity of the software application. The increase in software complexity (e.g., Cyclomatic complexity) over time is called software *entropy*.

Software evolution It is defined as "the applications of software maintenance activities and processes that generate a new operational software version with a changed customer-experienced functionality or properties from a prior operational version, where the time period between versions may last from less than a minute to decades, together with the associated quality assurance activities and processes, and with the management of the activities and processes."

Software life cycle objects (SLOs) SLOs are work products representing documents of one kind or another containing varied levels of software engineering information.

Software maintenance The totality of activities required to provide cost-effective support to a software system. Activities are performed during pre-delivery stage as well as the post-delivery stage. Note that pre-delivery activities include planning for post-delivery operations, supportability, and logistics determination. Post-delivery activities include software modification, training, and operating help desk.

Software migration An activity of the ISO/IEC 14764 maintenance process. It includes the activity of moving an old system to a new operational environment.

Software reclamation A technique to convert the existing software into standard building blocks (objects) to form new programs.

Software retirement An activity of the ISO/IEC 14764 maintenance process. It involves removing a product from service in an orderly manner once it has outlived its usefulness.

Stability measures The resistance to the potential ripple effect that a program would have when it is modified.

Stakeholder Person or organization that influences a system's behavior or is impacted by the system.

Starting impact set (SIS) The initial set of components thought to be affected by a software change request.

Strategy A strategy is a planned sequence of actions to reach a specific goal. A strategy is formulated by identifying actions to achieve a goal.

S-type program It implements solution to the problems that can be completely and unambiguously specified, for which, in theory at least, a program implementation can be proven to be correct with respect to the specification. The definition of the S-type requires that the program is correct in the full mathematical sense relative to the specification.

Syntactic analysis It is the process of analyzing a sequence of tokens to determine their grammatical structure with respect to a given (more or less) formal grammar.

Systematic reuse The practice of reuse according to a well-defined repeatable process.

Tailoring Tailoring is a piece of code to enhance the functionality of a component. Tailoring is done by adding some elements to a component to enrich it with a new functionality not provided by the original component.

Technique A procedure used to accomplish an activity that is less rigorously defined than a method.

Text-structure Code text and its structure are known as text-structure. Understanding text-structure is the beginning of program comprehension.

Thinking aloud It reflects the knowledge currently active in the programmer's working memory.

Usability A measure of an executable software unit's or system's functionality, case of use, and efficiency.

User The person or persons operating or interacting directly with the system. The user often states requirements to the customer, supplier, or maintainer.

Version A version is a snapshot of a certain software system at a certain point in time. Whenever a change is made to the software system, a new version is created. The version history is the collection of all versions and their relationships.

Version control It is a software tool to retrace and restore programming past, proceed along two or more development lines in a single project, and coordinate the work with other people in the same project.

Vertical reuse A type of reuse in which assets are reused within an application domain.

Vertical (a.k.a. internal) traceability It refers to the ability to trace dependent artifacts within a model.

Wrapping It is a black-box modernization technique– surrounds the LIS with a software layer that hides the unwanted complexity of the existing data, individual programs, application systems and interfaces with the new interfaces. Essentially, this gives old components new operation or a "modern and improved" look.

White-box reuse Reuse of a component by applying major changes to the component.

White-box testing It is a method of testing software that tests internal structures or workings of an application, as opposed to its functionality that is black-box testing.

INDEX

One of the great defects of English books printed in the last century is the want of an index.

—Lafcadio Hearn a.k.a Koizumi Yakumo

Abstract syntax tree (AST), 157, 318, 358
Abstraction, 135–136, 142, 149
Accelerated development, 327
Acceptance
    test, 98–99
    testing, 153
Accidental reuse, 358
Accounting, 116
Activity, 40, 358
Activity definition, 95
Activity-based classification, 28
Actual impact set (AIS), 225–226, 358
Ad hoc reuse, 338
Ada SDA (System Dependency Analyzer),
    171
Adaptability, 16, 326
Adaptive, 1, 30–31, 289
Adaptive maintenance, 27, 358
Adequacy, 227, 359

Adherence, 227–228, 274, 359
Age, 39
Agglomerative algorithms, 281
Agile
    programming, 58
    software development, 359
    software methodology, 13
Aging, 53, 375
Aiken, Peter, 11
Albrecht, A. J., 162
Alteration, 10, 137–138, 140
Amplification, 227
Analysis
    knowledge, 317
    and planning, 150–151
    of protocol data, 315–316
    state, 123
Annotation, 164, 300
Annotation of the program, 359

Software Evolution and Maintenance: A Practitioner's Approach, First Edition.
Priyadarshi Tripathy and Kshirasagar Naik.
© 2015 John Wiley & Sons, Inc. Published 2015 by John Wiley & Sons, Inc.

Anomaly, 60
Antiregression, 35, 58, 359
Antithesis, 54
Application
  domain, 39
  engineering (AE), 330–331, 348, 359
  gateway, 206, 359
  program interface (API), 189
  wrappers, 191
Approval, 104
Approval task steps, 106
Architectural reuse, 15, 326
Architecture description languages (ADLs),
  330
Architecture extraction, 135
Arnold, Robert S., 176
Arthur, Jay Lowell, 2, 45
Artifacts, 12, 38, 42, 133, 258, 359
Aspect, 360
Aspect-oriented software development, 155,
  360
Assembler, 165, 360
Assertion, 164, 265, 360
Assessment model, 336
Asset, 360
Assimilation process, 15, 301
Association coefficient, 280
Assumptions management, 56
Audit, 116
Auditing, 116, 118
Automated analysis, 257
Available support community, 68

Backus–Naur Form (BNF), 157
Backward
  search, 235
  slice, 159
  wrappers (b-wrappers), 189, 191, 360
Bad smell, 360
Baseline, 37, 118, 360
Basic conceptualization, 170
Basic reuse, 338–339
Bazaar, 58
Beacon, 296, 360
Behavior preserving transformation, 266
Belady, Laszlo, 1
Bennett, Keith H., 45
Behavioral dependencies, 69
Big bang, 360

Big Bang approach, 144, 202
Black-box
  components, 5
  reengineering, 11, 189
  requirements, 346
  testing, 360
Bottom-up, 301
Branch, 114
Brooks model, 303
Build process, 70
Building, 115
Business model of Poulin and Caruso,
  350
Business
  process reengineering (BPR), 199
  rules, 159
Butterfly, 12, 360
Butterfly methodology, 208
Byrne, Eric J., 138

Call graph, 13, 158, 234–235, 317, 360
Call graph-based analysis, 13, 224
Call preservation, 262
Call, use and define (CUD), 245
Candidate impact set (CIS), 225–226, 231,
  360
Canning R. G., 1, 25
Capability Maturity Model (CMM), 64
Carry on maintenance, 11, 188
Cathedral, 58
Causation, 149
Centroid, 281
Certification, 149, 329
Change
  control, 42, 361
  coupling, 361
  management, 115, 361
  mini-cycle model, 7, 91
  propagation, 13, 245, 265
  propagation activity, 94, 225, 361
  propagation heuristics, 243, 247
  propagation model, 242–243
  rate, 228
  request (CR), 26, 43, 92, 116, 119, 215,
    223, 225, 243
  request schema, 121
  set, 243–244
  source instruction (CSI), 350
  system, 42

Chapin, Ned, 28–29, 45
Chicken little, 12, 361
Chicken little
   migration, 207
   strategy, 206
Chidamber and Kemerer (CK) metrics, 162,
   164
Chikofsky and Cross II, 153–154
Chrysaliser, 208, 210–212
Chunk, 293, 361
Chunking, 15, 295, 361
City metaphor, 320
CK metric suite, 162
Class diagram, 260, 262, 265–266
Cleansing, 195
Clearcase, 115, 118
Cliché, 171, 361
Client organization, 43
Clone, 61, 164, 177, 375
Closed source software (CSS), 3, 49, 58, 87,
   361
Closed state, 125
Closedown, 88–89
Clustering, 278, 280
Clusters
   business rules, 29, 31, 36
   documentation, 29, 31, 34
   software properties, 29, 31, 35
   support interface, 29, 31, 34
COCOMO model, 199
Code
   changes, 275–276
   churn, 361
   cognition, 291
   decay, 53–54, 361
   layout (FIL), 246
   leverage, 289
   readers, 297
   smell, 258, 361
CodeCrawler, 171
Cognitions, 317
Cohesion, 263
Cohesion metric, 267–268
Cold turkey, 12, 201, 361
Commercial off-the-shelf (COTS), 5–6, 36,
   62, 361
Commit state, 123
Common goals, 44
Compilation, 141, 152, 165, 361

Complex refactoring, 14
Complexity, 263
Complexity metrics, 162
Compliance, 327
Component
   collaboration, 68
   reconfiguration, 65
   reuse, 167
   selection, 67
Component-based software (CBS), 5–6,
   62
Composite database, 12, 362
Composite database approach, 205
Comprehension strategies, 308
Computationally redundant data, 213
Computer-aided software engineering
   (CASE), 40
Concept assignment problem, 228
Concepts, 93, 228, 362
Conceptual
   data, 213
   level, 136
   normalization, 170
   phase, 168
   schema, 167, 195, 362
Concurrent version system (CVS), 118
Configuration, 362
   baseline, 117
   control board (CCB), 118
   item, 362
   management (CM), 9, 42, 66–67, 103,
     111, 148, 362
Conformance, 150
Conjectures, 14, 295, 299
Connectivity matrix, 232
Conservation of familiarity, 3, 39, 50, 52,
   60, 242
Conservation of organizational stability, 3,
   50, 52, 60, 242
Construction, 362
Construction algorithms, 280
Constructive Cost Model II (COCOMO II),
   202
Consultive, 30–31
Context area, 318
Continuing change, 3, 50–51, 134, 242
Continuing growth, 3, 50, 52, 134, 242
Contours, 320
Contracting, 12

Control
  data, 213
  dependency edges, 236
  flow, 292, 312
Control flow
  analysis (CFA), 10, 362
  graph (CFG), 142, 158, 317
Control structure diagram (CSD), 318
Controlled interfaces, 69
Controlling, 118
Corrections, 28
Corrective, 1, 30–31, 289
Corrective maintenance, 26, 362
Correlation coefficients, 280
Cost estimation, 12
Cost model of Gaffney and Durek, 340
Cost per error, 350
Cost-benefit analysis, 12, 200
Coupling, 54, 263
Coupling between object class (CBO), 163
Coupling metrics, 268
Critical pair analysis, 261
Crosscutting concerns, 362
Cross-referencing, 15, 295–296, 362
Customer, 362
Cut over, 196, 362
Cut-and-run, 196
Cyclomatic complexity, 162–163, 197–198, 241

Dangling purpose, 301
Data
  access-allocator (DAA), 208, 210–212
  administration, 166, 362
  analysis, 169
  archival, 109, 111
  assets, 166
  banker, 214
  cleaning, 195
  conversion, 167, 195, 362
  dependency edges, 235–236
  description language (DDL), 168
  flow, 292, 312
  flow analysis (DFA), 10, 158, 363
  flow graph (DFG), 317
  forward engineering, 166
  locator, 214
  management system (DMS), 168
  reduction, 148

reengineering, 152
representation, 148
reuse, 15, 326
reverse engineering (DRE), 11, 166, 363
structure conceptualization, 168
structure extraction, 168
Database, 166
Database
  first, 12, 189, 203
  gateway, 206, 362
  last, 12, 204
  management system (DBMS), 167–168
  reverse engineering (DBRE), 167, 195, 363
  wrappers, 189
Data-oriented application, 165–167
Data-Transformer, 208, 212
Davis, Ted, 336
Decay, 363
Decision tree, 32
Decision tree-based criteria, 31
Declining quality, 3, 50, 53, 134, 242
Decompilation, 135, 141, 165, 363
Decompiler, 152, 164
Definition-use, 317
Degree of interest (DOI), 318
Delivery, 99
Density search technique, 280–281
Dependency analysis, 12
Dependency graph, 13, 229, 234
Dependency graph-based analysis, 13, 234
Depth of inheritance tree (DIT), 163
Design, 96
Design
  level, 136
  recovery, 154, 363
  reuse, 16, 326
  clones, 164
Developer, 2
Developer information (DEV), 246
Development
  cost avoidance, 351
  model, 363
  process, 111, 363
  replay (DR), 246
  for reuse, 325, 328, 329
  with reuse, 325, 330
  staff, 44
  technology, 41, 363

Device-drivers, 61
Direct impact, 231
Disassembler, 164, 363
Discard and redevelop, 11, 188
Discovered impact set (DIS), 225–226, 363
Distance measure, 280
Distance-based, 268
Distance-based approach, 233
Distinctive appearance, 160
Divide-and-conquer schema, 297–298
Divisive algorithms, 281
DMS (Design Maintenance System), 171
DMS–DDL text analysis, 169
Documentation, 104, 146, 166, 274
    change, 94
    task steps, 105
Documenting, 118
Domain, 325, 363
    analysis, 15, 325, 329, 36
    design, 330, 364
    engineering (DE), 328–329, 331, 348, 364
    implementation, 330, 364
    knowledge, 303, 304, 308, 314
    model, 313, 331, 364
    plans, 294
    qualification (DQ), 331
    specific languages (DSLs), 364
Domain analysis and reuse environment (DARE), 331
Draco, 331
Duplicate code, 259
Dynamic
    call graph, 158
    elements, 295
    growth, 44
    program slice, 225, 237–238

Economic, 328
Effective size, 346
Effective visual metaphors, 162
Effectiveness, 227, 363
Eighth law, 50, 53
Element connectedness, 320
Elimination-of-goto, 276
Embedded knowledge, 53
Empirical studies, 54, 60

Encapsulation, 146–148
Encoding, 316
Engineering change (EC), 112, 124
Engineering view point, 46
Enhancements, 28
Enhancive, 30–31
Enterprise JavaBeans (EJB), 201
Entity-relationship (ER), 167
Entropy, 53, 375
Environment, 275
Environmental independence, 326
Equivalence tests, 217, 364
Error flow analysis, 238
Establishing baseline, 118
Estimated impact set (EIS), 93
E-type program, 48, 51, 134, 364
E-type software, 56
E-type systems, 3
Euclidean distance, 268
Evaluation, 317
Evaluative, 30–31
Event management, 42, 364
Evidence-based classification, 28
Evolution, 1, 7, 44–45, 87–88
Evolution
    of E-type software, 49
    management, 57
    process, 49, 51, 53, 89, 364
    of software, 44
Evolutionary
    approach, 146
    model, 92
    trajectory, 51
Evolves, 2
Exception handling, 292
Execution history, 237
Explanatory (what/why), 45
Extensibility, 256, 263
External
    documentation, 307
    interface, 192
    representation, 300
    reuse (a.k.a. public reuse), 364
    software value, 256
External traceability, see Horizontal traceability
Extract, transform, and load (ETL), 195
Extractive, 327–328
Extreme programming (XP), 13, 365

Facebook, 330
Failure handling, 70
False positive, 233
False positive impact set (FPIS), 225–226, 365
Familiarity, 320
Fan-in, 162–163
Fan-out, 162–163
Family-oriented abstraction, specification, and translation (FAST), 331
Feature location, 229
Feature-oriented domain analysis (FODA), 330
Feature-oriented reuse method (FORM), 331
Features, 228
Feedback, 365
Feedback system, 3, 49, 50, 53, 242
Feedback, evolution, and software technology (FEAST), 54
FermaT, 172
Fifth law, 50, 52
First law, 50–51
First order reuse cost model, 346
Fisheye view, 318
Focus area, 318
Forward
    engineering, 10, 135, 139, 154, 365
    gateway, 203, 205–206, 365
    migration, 203, 365
    searching, 235
    slicing, 159, 225
    software engineering principles, 210
    wrappers (f-wrappers), 189, 365
FOSS evolution, 60
Fourth law, 50, 52
Framework, 365
Free and Open Source Software (FOSS), 4, 58, 365
Free software, 4, 58
Free software, 58
Free/Libre/Open Source Software (FLOSS), 58, 90
Freeze, 11, 188
Frequency, 246
Friendly user interface, 162
Frozen, 209
Frozen functionality, 63
Full reuse model, 85, 87

Fully decomposable, 204–205, 365
Function, 146, 312
Function
    name, 297
    point (FP), 162, 163
    wrappers, 191
Functional
    knowledge, 314–315
    requirements, 256
    enhancement, 134
Functionality, 292
Functionalization, 149

Gate keepers, 59
Gateway, 203, 365
Gateway co-ordinators, 208
General knowledge, 291
Generation of
    code, 149
    design, 149
Generic knowledge structure, 294
Geographic technique, 280–281
Gestalt's theory, 319
Gibson's theory, 319
Global
    factors, 60
    variable (GV), 163
Glue, 62–63, 365
Goals, 155, 164, 291, 299
Goals/models/tools, 10, 155
Good figure, 319
Good use of interactions, 162
Goto-less, 276
Granularity, 191
Graph exchange language (GXL), 172, 366
Graph rewriting, *see* Graph transformation
Graph theoretical algorithm, 280
Graph transformation, 265–266, 366
Graphical user interface (GUI), 194
Grep, 228
Groomative, 30–31
Groups, 29
Guru, 243

Habitability, 320
Halpern, Mark I., 1, 44
Halstead complexity (HC), 163
Halstead, Maurice, 164
Hardware maintenance, 2

Hazard, 28, 366
Hex-Rays Decompiler, 172
Hierarchical algorithms, 281
High cohesion, 16, 326
High information content, 160–161
High level of visibility, 70
Higher order reuse cost model, 346, 348
Historical co-change (HIS), 245
Horizontal reuse, 366
Horizontal traceability, 224, 229–230, 366
Horseshoe, 366
Horseshoe model, 138
human resource, 43
Hypertext markup language (HTML), 194
Hypotheses, 14, 293–295, 299, 305, 308,
    366
Hypotheses strategies, 14

I/O-emulator, 194
Iceberg, 1, 92
IDA Pro Disassembler and Debugger, 172
Identification, 113
IEEE 1042, 9
IEEE/EIA 1219, 8, 94, 99
Imagix 4D, 172
Immediacy, 317
Impact analysis (IA), 12, 93, 223, 225, 366
Implement
    change, 94
    parallel operations and training, 110
    state, 123
Implementation, 97
    details, 293
    level, 136
    model, 337
Improvement algorithm, 281
Improving maintainability, 134
Improving quality, 134
Incompatibility of upgrades, 63
Increasing complexity, 3, 50–51, 134, 242
Incremental
    approach, 145, 233
    development, 86, 366
Indirect impact, 231
Individuality, 160
Information system (IS), 187, 366
Information system gateway, 206–207, 366
Information-flow metric, 164
Initial development, 7, 87–88

Initial entity, 244
Initial reuse, 338, 339
Input, 95
Inspection, 276
Integrated, 338
Integrated metamodel, 312, 314
Integration, 166
Intention-based classification, 26
Intentions, 317
Inter-class coupling, 269
Interface converter, 193
Interface description languages (IDLs),
    330
Intermodule change propagation, 240
Internal
    documentation, 306
    interface, 193
    reuse, 366
    semantic, 302
    software value, 256
    traceability, *see* Vertical traceability
Internet Protocol (IP), 39
Interpretation, 149
Interprocedural analysis, 158
Intra-class coupling, 269
Intramodule change propagation, 238
Intraprocedural analysis, 158
Invariants, 265
Inverse square law, 54–56
Investigation activity, 40, 366
Investigation report, 42
IRAP (Input–Output Reengineering and
    Program Crafting), 172
is-a, 294, 315
ISO/IEC 12207, 8, 107
ISO/IEC 14764, 8, 25–26, 99
Isolation, 115, 148
Iterative, 12
    algorithm, 281
    approach, 145
    development, 86, 366
    enhancement model, 85–86
    method, 212
    models, 7
    process, 99

JAD (JAva Decompiler), 173
Java 2 Enterprise Edition (J2EE), 201
Jazayeri, Mehdi, 2

Kaizen, 86
kind-of, 294, 315
Kitchenham, A, 28
Knowledge, 291, 301–302
    acquisition, 166, 291
    base, 15, 298, 314, 366
    elements, 294, 367
    structure, 297, 309, 315, 367
Koala, 332
KobrA, 332

Lack of cohesion in methods (LCOM), 163
Law of
    connectedness, 320
    continuation, 320
    contour, 320
    evolution, 3
    familiarity, 320
    good figure, 320
    orientation, 320
    proximity, 320
    similarity, 320
    software evolution, 49
    symmetry, 320
Legacy, 187
Legacy
    DB, 214
    DB manager, 214
    information systems (LIS), 140, 188,
        367
    SampleData, 208
    software, 11
    state, 213
    system, 11, 89, 187–188, 192, 195, 203,
        367
Legal, 328
Lehman, Meir M., 1, 3, 44
Lehman's law, 3, 51, 212
Letovsky model, 298
Leveraged, 338
Lexical analysis, 10, 157, 367
Library, 118
License agreements, 165
Lines of code (LOC), 163
Linus's law, 59
Linux, 4, 59–60
LIS migration, 195–196
Local area network (LAN) simulator, 260
Locality, 321

Logical
    phase, 168
    schema, 167–168, 195, 367
Long-term memory a.k.a. knowledge base,
        315
Low coupling, 16, 326
Low visual complexity, 160–161

Macrostructure, 311
Magnification function, 319
Maintainability, 256, 263, 327
Maintained
    product, 37–38
    product dimension, 37
Maintainer, 2, 291, 367
Maintenance, 1, 4, 25, 45
    activities, 26
    activities-based classification, 4
    adaptive, 4
    corrective, 4
    cost, 327
    of COTS-based systems, 5–6
    engineer, 2
    event, 42, 367
    evidence-based classification, 5
    factors, 37
    iceberg, 1, 25
    intention-based classification, 4
    management, 42, 367
    model, 84, 367
    organization, 41–43
    organization structure, 42, 367
    perfective, 4
    plan, 99, 101–102
    preventive, 4
    process, 37–38, 95, 100, 367
    request, *see* Change request (CR)
    review, 100, 105
    staff, 44
Make, 112, 115
Management activity, 40, 367
Managerial, 328
Managers and policies, 274
ManSART, 173
Marr's theory, 319
McCabe IQ, 173
McIlroy, Dough, 15
Mean time to maintenance request
        (MTMR), 215

Mediator, 68
Medium access control (MAC), 291
Mental model, 14, 291, 293, 367
Mental representation, 300
Merging, 114
Message
    chain, 259
    handler, 193
    oriented middleware (MOM), 201
Metadata, 214–215, 217
Method, 41, 367
Metric, 95, 265, 267, 368
Metrication, 146
Microstructure, 311
Middleware, 64–65
Migrate, 12, 188
Migrate data, 216
Migrating to a new technology, 134
Migration, 12, 100, 106, 140–141, 368
    of legacy information system, 140, 368
    of LIS, 195
    plan, 107
    plan task steps, 108
    planning, 196
    process, 215
    projects, 12
    standard, 107
    build, 70
Minimal component coupling, 70
Mishap, 28, 368
Mission-critical
    legacy system, 201
    project, 196
Model, 156, 368
Model-driven engineering, 140, 368
Modification activity, 40, 368
Modification
    implementation, 100, 105
    of specification, 149
    request (MR), 95, 102, 119, 368
Modification request
    analysis, 103
    task steps, 104
Modularity, 256
Module
    connection analysis, 238
    level, 192
    wrapper, 194
Monolithic systems, 4

Multi-agent, 53
Multi-level, 53
Multi-loop, 53

Neighbors, Jim, 15, 325
New DB, 214
New DB manager, 214
New state, 213
Nondecomposable, 205–206
Nondecomposable information system, 204, 368
Non-functional requirements, 256, 368
Normalization, 141, 148, 368
Notification
    of completion, 108, 110
    intent, 107
    of intent, 110
Number of children (NOC), 163

Obfuscation, 369
Object
    identification, 149
    interpretation, 149
Objectives, 134
Observable behavior, 13
Occurred set, 244
Off-the-shelf component, 329
Onion model, 58–59
Open source community (OSC), 58
Open source software (OSS), 368
Openness of components, 67
Operations, 312
Opportunistic, 301, 337
Optimization, 141, 369
Optimization algorithm, 281
Option task steps, 104
Options, 104
Organized reuse, 338–339
Orientation, 320
Original equipment manufacturer (OEM), 67
OS/360 operating system, 54
Output, 95
Outsource, 11, 188
Overloading, 195

Paradigm, 41, 369
Parallel operation, 196, 108
Parameter coupling, 263–264, 269–270

Parameterize methods, 273
Paranas, David, 15, 325
Parse tree, 157
Parsing, 148
Partial approach, 145
Partially persistence, 166
Path-based dynamic impact analysis, 235
PBS (Portable Bookshelf), 173
Pennington model, 310
Peopleware, 43
Perceptual
    organization, 319
    segregation, 319
    theory, 319
Perfective, 1, 289, 327
Perfective
    maintenance, 27, 49, 369
    modification, 45
Performance, 30, 31, 263
Permanent files, 166
Persistent data structure, 166
Phase model, 150
Phased interoperability, 196
Phaseout, 8, 88–89, 187
Physical phase, 168
Physical schema, 168, 195, 369
Plan, 171, 369
Plan
    change, 93
    recognition, 171
Planning, 117, 317
Plans, 164, 293–294, 299, 315
PLUS, 332
Pollution, 53
Poor lexicon, 54
Portability, 15, 326
Portfolio analysis, 12, 197, 369
Postconditions, 265
Post-delivery activities, 26
Post-operation review, 109
Practices, 276
Precision, 226–227, 243–244, 246–247, 369
Preconditions, 265
Pre-delivery activities, 26
Predicted set, 244
Presence, 317
Pretty printing, 257
Preventive, 30–31
Preventive maintenance, 27, 51, 137, 369

Primary data, 212
Primitive refactoring, 14
Principle of
    abstraction, 135, 369
    alteration, 137, 142, 369
    refinement, 135, 370
Priority, 122
Proactive, 327
Probabilistic measures, 280
Problem
    domain, 299
    domain knowledge, 311, 314
    identification, 95
Procedural
    granularity, 148
    level, 192
Procedure, 41, 370
Procedure wrapper, 194
Process, 59, 144, 370
Process
    implementation, 100
    improvement (how), 45
    information, 246
    level, 191
    metrics, 230
    model, 92, 144, 370
Product, 37, 370
    component, 39
    development, 330
    line development, 328–329
    line, *see* Domain implementation
    metrics, 230
    quality, 40
    reconfiguration, 68
    upgrade, 37, 370
Productivity, 327
Program
    analysis, 169, 370
    analysis tool (PAT), 317
    comprehension, 14, 93, 165, 291,
        309–310, 370
    conversion, 196
    dependency, 224
    dependency graph (PDG), 235, 370
    documentation, 94
    domain knowledge, 315
    families, 15, 325, 370
    fragments, 294
    graph, 266

knowledge, 317
level, 192
metrics, 162
migration, 152, 165, 370
model, 311, 313–314, 315
model structure, 314
plans, 171
reading, 149
rephrasing, *see* Rephrasing
restructuring, *see* Restructuring
reuse, 16, 326
slices, 10
slicing, 158, 282, 371
translation, 141, 371
understanding, *see* Program
    comprehension
wrapper, 194
Programmers, 274
Programming
environment, 274
knowledge, 302, 308
plans, 294, 308, 315
rules of discourse, 308
Project justification, 12
Prolog, 262
Properly nested programs, 277
Proprietary software, 49
Protocol
analysis, 315, 371
data, 315–316, 371
Proximity, 319
Pruning, 246
P-type program, 47, 371
PuLSE, 332
Push down method, 267, 272

Quality assessment, 167
Quality assurance activity, 40, 371
Query the tool first, 245
Quick fix model, 85

Random, 246
Rationalization of control flow, 148
Raymond, Eric S., 58–59
Reachability
graphs, 232
matrix, 233
Reactive, 327–328
Read coupling, 163

Readability, 256
Real-world knowledge, *see* Domain
    knowledge
RE-Analyzer, 173
Recall, 226–227, 243–244, 246–247, 371
Recency, 246
Reclamation, 371
Recode, 140, 143, 152, 371
Reconstitute, 166
Redesign, 141, 143, 371
Redocumentation, 152–153, 372
Redocumentation of artifacts, 154
Reductive, 30–31
Redundant structural data, 213
Reengineered components, 214
Reengineered state, 213
Reengineering, 9–10, 133, 138–139, 154,
    372
Reengineering
assistant (RA), 174
process, 144
Refactor, 258
Refactoring, 13, 94, 141, 256, 259, 372
Refinement, 135–136, 142
Reflexive property, 240
Reformative, 30–31
Regeneration, 149
Regression testing, 13, 94
Rehosting, 140, 372
Rejuvenation, 27, 372
Release management, 57
Releases, 60, 372
Reliability, 16, 255, 257, 326–327
Remote procedure calls (RPCs), 189
Renovation, 141, 150–151
Rephrasing, 140, 371
Replace, 141, 143, 372
Replace parameter with method, 272
Replace strategy, 142
Replacement strategies, 152
Repository, 118, 372
Repository database, 146
Representation, 160
Requirements level, 136
Residual
data, 213
DB, 214
DB manager, 214
Resilience to change, 161

Resource, 372
    constraints, 262
    dependencies, 69
Respecify, 141, 143, 372
Response for a class (RFC), 163
Restored components, 214
Restored state, 213
Restructuring, 13–14, 94, 137, 256–258,
    372
Restructuring algorithm, 142
Rethink, 141, 143, 373
Retirement, 100, 109, 376
Retirement plan, 110
Return value coupling, 263–264, 269
Reusability, 16, 263, 373
Reusable
    artifacts, 326
    assets, 15, 330
    components, 347–348
    software assets (RSA), 328–329
Reuse, 289, 373
    assets, 346
    capability, 333–334, 373
    capability model (RCM), 334–336
    cost avoidance (RCA), 351
    effectiveness, 333–334, 373
    efficiency, 333, 373
    library, 327, 329, 346, 349, 373
    maturity model (RMM), 334, 373
    opportunity, 333, 373
    oriented model, 84
    percent (RP), 351
    proficiency, 333, 373
    program, 329
    value added (RVA), 351
Reused source instruction (RSI), 350
Reverse
    engineering, 10, 135, 139, 153–154,
        156, 164, 373
    gateway, 204–206, 373
    migration, 204, 373
Review state, 122
Review task steps, 106
Revision control system (RCS), 112
Rework, 141, 143, 373
Rework strategy, 142
Rewrite, 141, 143, 373
Rewrite strategy, 142
Rigi, 174

Ripple effect, 13, 39, 93, 238, 374
    analysis, 13, 225
    for a program (REP), 242
    and stability tool (REST), 242
Ripple effects measurement, 242
Ripple-sensitivity, 227, 374
RiSE maturity model, 334, 338
Risk, 327
Risky, 57
Robustness, 263
Roll over, 212
Royce, Winston, 6, 86
RSEB, 332
Rules of
    discourse, 300, 315
    programming discourse, 296, 374

Safe, 57
Safety constraints, 262
Sample DataStore, 208–210
Sandbox, 115
Scalability, 263
Scalability of visual complexity, 161
Scattering and tangling, 374
Schema(s), 293–294, 308, 315, 374
    analysis, 166
    conversion, 195
    de-optimization, 170
    integration, 169
    translation and redesign, 166
    untranslation, 170
Scientific view point, 46
Screen scrapping, 194, 374
Script, 41, 374
Scrubbing, 195
Second law, 50–51
SEELA, 174
Self-regulation, 3, 50–51, 60, 242
Semantic
    distance, 319
    knowledge, 301, 303
Semantically redundant data, 213
Semidecomposable, 204–205
Semidecomposable information system,
    204, 374
Sequential dependency analysis, 261
Service cost avoidance, 351
Service-level agreement (SLA), 42–43,
    374

Service-oriented architecture (SOA), 42, 375

Servicing, 8, 88–89

Seventh law, 50, 53

Severity, 122

Shared variable coupling, 263–264, 269–270

Sharpness, 227–228, 375

Shipped source instruction (SSI), 350

Shneiderman and Mayer Model, 301

Short-term memory, 301, 303

Side effect, 93, 154, 236, 375

Similarity, 319

Similarity metrics, 280

Simple navigation, 161

Single entity suggestions, 245

Situation model, 310–311, 314–315

Situation model structures, 314

Sixth law, 50, 52

Size, 38, 44, 263

Slot-filler, 294

Slot-type, 294

Slot fillers, 315

Slot types, 315

Sneed, Harry M., 12

Sockets, 189

Soft-goal graph, 264, 375

Software

  agents, 53

  aging, *see* Aging

  architecture, 292

  artifacts, 258

  assessment, 167

  asset, 326

  certification laboratories (SCL), 64

  clone, *see* Clone

  configuration management (SCM), 9, 84, 111, 375

  crises, 15

  development, 26

  development cost, 350

  development error rate, 350

  development life cycle (SDLC), 83–84

  entropy, *see* Entropy

  evolution, 375

  geriatrics, 39

  lifecycle objects (SLOs), 231–232, 376

  maintainability, 26

  maintenance, 2–3, 6, 25–26, 83–84, 376

  maintenance life cycle (SMLC), 7

  maintenance standards, 8

  metric, *see* Metric

  migration, 376

  production consortium (SPC), 336

  quality, 53

  reclamation, 376

  reconnaissance, 228

  reengineering, 9–10

  rejuvenation, 27

  restructuring, 256, 275–276

  retirement, *see* Retirement

  reuse, 15, 325–326

  specific knowledge, 291

  structure, 273

  value, 256

  visualization, 135, 360, 317

Soloway, Adelson, and Ehrlich model, 308

Source code

  control system (SCCS), 112

  reengineering reference model (SCORE/RM), 146

Source instruction reused by others (SIRBO), 350

Source-to-source translation, 152

SPE taxonomy, 46

Specification

  of actions, 149

  of constraints, 149

Speech sentences, 316

S-Ratio, 228

Stability

  analysis, 238

  measure, 238, 376

Stable storage, 292

Staged model, 7, 87, 187

Staged model

  for CSS, 87–88

  for FLOSS, 90

Stakeholders, 117, 198–199, 376

Starting impact set (SIS), 93, 225, 228–231, 376

State, 312

Statecharts, 266

Static

  call graph, 158

  elements, 293

  program slice, 236

Static (*continued*)
   program slicing, 224
   slice, 237
Strategy, 295–296, 376
Structural data, 213
S-type program, 46, 376
Submit state, 120
Substitute algorithm, 271
Suitability for automation, 161–162
Support levels, 43
Swanson, E. Burton, 1, 4
Swanson's classification, 4
Symmetric suggestions, 244
Symmetry, 320
Syntactic
   analysis, 10, 157, 376
   dependencies, 69
   distance, 319
   knowledge, 301–303
System
   monitoring, 66, 69
   sandwich approach, 278
   service wrappers, 191
   test, 98
   transition, 153
Systematic reuse, 338, 340, 376

Tailorability of components, 68
Tailoring, 62, 376
Target SampleData, 208
Target system, 133–134, 142, 144, 208
Target system testing, 150, 152
Team structure, 58
Technical, 328
Technical dimension, 113
Technique, 41, 276, 376
Temporal constraints, 262
TempStore (TS), 208–210, 212
Termination-condition, 208–209, 212
Test generation, 148–149
Test Maturity Model (TMM), 64
Test Process Improvement (TPI) model, 64
Test verdict, 124
Testability, 263
Testing, 196, 262
Testing and debugging, 66
Textbase model, 310–311
Text-structure, 293, 376
Textual information, 246

Theory of notation, 319
Think aloud protocol (TAP), 316
Thinking-aloud, 316, 376
Third law, 50–51
Threshold value, 208–209, 212
Tools, 156, 274, 276
Top-down, 301
Top-down model, 313, 315
Top-down structure, 314
Torvals, Linus Benedict, 59
Traceability, 224, 229
Traceability analysis, 12
Training, 30–31
Training task steps, 108
Transaction level, 192
Transaction wrapper, 194
Transformation, 148
Transition net, 317
Transitive, 240
Transitive closure, 234
Transmission control protocol (TCP), 292
Trojan horse, 64
Trouble shooting, 68
Trunk, 114
Tuval Software Industries, 174
Two-phase commit protocol, 205
Type decision question, 33

Understandability, 16, 326
Unix operating system, 115
Unreliable COTS components, 64
Unsafe, 57
Updative, 30–31
Usability, 377
User, 377
   interaction, 319
   interface, 214, 216
   manual, 94
   request, 45

Validation and verification, 149
Variability, 44
Variable name, 297
Varying levels of detail, 161
Verification, 103, 262
Verification of hypothesis, 14
Verification state, 124
Version, 377
Version control (VC), 113, 377

Versioned staged model, 89–90
Vertical reuse, 377
Vertical traceability, 224, 230, 377
Virtual Reality Modeling Language
    (VRML), 268
Visualization, 160

Walkthrough, 276
Waterfall model, 6–7, 86
Weighted methods per class (WMC), 162
Weighted sum, 271
Weiser, Mark, 158
White-box reuse, 377
White-box testing, 377

Whole path profiling, 235
Wide Spectrum Language (WSL), 172
Wireless local area networks (WLAN), 292
Workspace control, 115
Wrap, 11, 188
Wrapper, 11, 64–65, 189, 192
Wrapping, 62, 195, 377
Wrapping legacy systems, 12
Write coupling, 163

YACC, 157

Zero–one (0–1) matrix, 239
Zipf distribution, 246

Printed and bound by CPI Group (UK) Ltd, Croydon, CR0 4YY

27/10/2024

14580252-0004